AF707599

THE COLLECTED COURSES OF THE ACADEMY OF EUROPEAN LAW

Series Editors

PROFESSOR LOÏC AZOULAI,

PROFESSOR MARISE CREMONA,

PROFESSOR FRANCESCO FRANCIONI

European University Institute, Florence

Assistant Editor

ANNY BREMNER

European University Institute, Florence

VOLUME XXII/2

Constitutionalization of European Private Law

THE COLLECTED COURSES OF THE ACADEMY OF EUROPEAN LAW

Edited by

Professor Loïc Azoulai,
Professor Marise Cremona, and Professor Francesco Francioni

Assistant Editor
Anny Bremner

Each year the Academy of European Law in Florence, Italy, invites a group of outstanding lecturers to teach at its summer courses on Human Rights law and European Union law.

A 'general course' is given in each of the two fields by a distinguished scholar or practitioner, who examines the field as a whole through a particular thematic, conceptual, or philosophical lens, or looks at a theme in the context of the overall body of law. In addition, a series of 'specialized courses' brings together a group of highly qualified scholars to explore and analyse a specific theme in relation to Human Rights law and EU law.

The Academy's mission, to produce scholarly analyses which are at the cutting edge of these two fields, is achieved through the publication of this series, the Collected Courses of the Academy of European Law.

Constitutionalization of European Private Law

Edited by

HANS-W. MICKLITZ

OXFORD
UNIVERSITY PRESS

OXFORD
UNIVERSITY PRESS

Great Clarendon Street, Oxford, OX2 6DP,
United Kingdom

Oxford University Press is a department of the University of Oxford. It furthers the University's objective of excellence in research, scholarship, and education by publishing worldwide. Oxford is a registered trade mark of Oxford University Press in the UK and in certain other countries

© The several contributors 2014

The moral rights of the authors have been asserted

First Edition published in 2014

All rights reserved. No part of this publication may be reproduced, stored in a retrieval system, or transmitted, in any form or by any means, without the prior permission in writing of Oxford University Press, or as expressly permitted by law, by licence or under terms agreed with the appropriate reprographics rights organization. Enquiries concerning reproduction outside the scope of the above should be sent to the Rights Department, Oxford University Press, at the address above

You must not circulate this work in any other form and you must impose this same condition on any acquirer

Crown copyright material is reproduced under Class Licence Number C01P0000148 with the permission of OPSI and the Queen's Printer for Scotland

Published in the United States of America by Oxford University Press
198 Madison Avenue, New York, NY 10016, United States of America

British Library Cataloguing in Publication Data
Data available

Library of Congress Control Number: 2013953615

ISBN 978–0–19–871210–7

Links to third party websites are provided by Oxford in good faith and for information only. Oxford disclaims any responsibility for the materials contained in any third party website referenced in this work.

Contents

Table of Cases

Table of Legislation

BRAZILIAN LEGISLATION

CHINESE LEGISLATION

FRENCH LEGISLATION

GERMAN LEGISLATION

IRISH LEGISLATION

ITALIAN LEGISLATION

NETHERLANDS LEGISLATION

POLISH LEGISLATION

PORTUGUESE LEGISLATION

SPANISH LEGISLATION

SWEDISH LEGISLATION

UNITED KINGDOM LEGISLATION

UNITED STATES LEGISLATION

EU LEGISLATION

INTERNATIONAL LEGISLATION

List of Abbreviations

ACLU	American Civil Liberties Union
ADR	alternative dispute resolution
BGH	German Supreme Court (*Bundesgerichtshof*)
BverfG	German Constitutional Court (*Bundesverfassungsgericht*)
CAFC	US Court of Appeals for the Federal Circuit
CCEPL	Common Core of European Private Law
CESL	Common European Sales Law
CJEU	Court of Justice of the European Union
CMLRev	*Common Market Law Review*
CMR	Convention on the Contract for the International Carriage of Goods by Road
CRD	Consumer Rights Directive
DCFR	Draft Common Frame of Reference
EBA	Enlarged Board of Appeal
EC	
ECCHR	European Center for Constitutional and Human Rights
ECHR	European Convention on Human Rights
ECtHR	European Court of Human Rights
EEC	
EJIL	*European Journal of International Law*
ELJ	*European Law Journal*
ELRev	*European Law Review*
EPC	European Patent Convention
EPO	European Patent Office
ERCL	*European Review of Contract Law*
EUCFR	European Charter of Fundamental Rights
GCC	German Constitutional Court
GRUR	*Gewerblicher Rechtsschutz und Urheberrecht*
GRURInt	*Gewerblicher Rechtsschutz und Urheberrecht-Internationaler Teil*
HESC	human embryonic stem cells
HRA	Human Rights Act 1998
ICCPR	International Covenant on Civil and Political Rights
ICESCR	International Covenant on Economic, Social and Cultural Rights
ICLQ	*International and Comparative Law Quarterly*
IIC	*International Review of Intellectual Property and Competition Law*
ILJ	*Industrial Law Journal*
ILO	International Labour Organization
IP	intellectual property
IPRs	intellectual property rights
ISP	internet service provider
JZ	*Juristen Zeitung*
LQR	*Law Quarterly Review*
MiFID I	Directive 2004/39 on the markets in financial instruments
MLR	*Modern Law Review*
NJW	*Neue Juristische Wochenschrift*
OHIM	Office for Harmonization in the Internal Market
PRIPs	packaged retail investment products
QPC	'*la question prioritaire de constitutionnalité*'

TEC	
TEU	Treaty on European Union
TFEU	Treaty on the Functioning of the European Union
UDHR	Universal Declaration of Human Rights
UPOV	International Union for the Protection of New Varieties of Plants

Notes on Contributors

Mark Bell is Head of the School of Law at the University of Leicester. He conducts research in the areas of national and European anti-discrimination law and employment law. He is the author of *Racism and Equality in the European Union* (2008) and *Anti-Discrimination Law and the European Union* (2002). He is an active participant in the European Working Group on Labour Law and he was a member of the European Commission's Network of Legal Experts in the Non-Discrimination Field (2004–2010). He has collaborated with many national and European NGOs working on equality law as well as with the ILO.

Olha O. Cherednychenko is Associate Professor at the University of Groningen, where she holds the Chair in European Private Law and Comparative Law. She studied law at Kiev National Taras Shevchenko University in Ukraine and at Utrecht University where she obtained her PhD. Her thesis was published as *Fundamental Rights, Contract Law and the Protection of the Weaker Party: A Comparative Analysis of the Constitutionalisation of Contract Law, with Emphasis on Risky Financial Transactions* (2007). Prof. Cherednychenko worked as a Senior Lecturer in Private Law at the VU University of Amsterdam, where she received a three-year research grant for talented researchers. She has been a visiting scholar at the Institute of Advanced Legal Studies in London, the London School of Economics and Political Science and the European University Institute in Florence. She is currently a research fellow at the Amsterdam Centre for Insurance Studies (ACIS). Olha Cherednychenko's research focuses on the interaction between European private law, in particular European contract law and financial services law, European public law and national legal orders.

Aurelia Colombi Ciacchi has held the Endowed Chair in Law and Governance at Groningen University since October 2010. She is one of two Academic Directors of the Groningen Centre for Law and Governance, and one of four Directors of the Netherlands Institute for Law and Governance. She received her first PhD in comparative law in Italy and her second PhD in Germany at the Bucerius Law School in Hamburg. She has held positions as a research fellow at the Universities of Kiel and Bremen and as a Marie Curie Fellow at the University of Oxford. Prior to joining the faculty at Groningen University, Professor Ciacchi taught comparative law and European and international private law at the University of Bremen and the Hanse Law School. Many of her publications deal with the application of fundamental rights in the adjudication of private litigations. She has written two monographs on comparative law and has co-edited eight books.

Hugh Collins is the Vinerian Professor of English Law, All Souls College, Oxford. He studied law at Oxford and Harvard. He was previously a Fellow in Law of Brasenose College, Oxford, and Professor of English Law at the London School of Economics. He serves on the editorial committee of the *Modern Law Review* and the *European Review of Contract Law*. Recent publications include: *The European Civil Code: The Way Forward* (2008); *Employment Law* 2nd ed. (2010); *Teubner's Networks as Connected Contracts*, edited with an introduction (2011).

Giovanni Comandé teaches Comparative Law and EU Law at the Scuola Superiore S. Anna, Pisa, where he is full professor and director of the Interdisciplinary Research Lab LIDER-Lab. He is the author of four monographs and numerous articles, and is the editor or co-editor of many collective works. He has led research projects funded by national, international, public, and private entities on various topics of private law and European law. He is a member of the American Law Institute; the European Law Institute; the European Centre of Tort and Insurance Law; and the European Tort Law Group. He has been a visiting professor at several universities, including Fordham Law School, Université Paris II, Hofstra School of Law, Wake Forrest University School of Law, the Hebrew University (Jerusalem), and the University of South Carolina School of Law. He held the Jean Monnet Chair researching 'Human Rights and Remedies for Personal Injuries in European Community Law' (1994–2001). His principal research interests revolve around comparative and European private law, including contract, torts, insurance, information society law, and citizenship.

Christine Godt holds the Jean Monnet Chair for European and International Economic Law at the Carl von Ossietzky-University in Oldenburg, where she is also Director of the Hanse Law School. She teaches in the areas of intellectual property, comparative property law, and private environmental law. Professor Godt obtained her PhD in 1995, which was published as *Haftung für Ökologische Schäden* (1997) and her 'Habilitation' in 2005, published as *Eigentum an Information* (2007). Her current research focuses on genetic resources, technology transfer, and property regimes.

Chantal Mak is an Associate Professor of European Private Law at the Centre for the Study of European Contract Law (CSECL) and deputy director of the Amsterdam Research Institute for Legal Studies (ARILS) of the University of Amsterdam in the Netherlands. Her research focuses on the effects of fundamental rights in European contract law, with special attention for the role of the judiciary.

Hans-W. Micklitz joined the European University Institute in 2007 as Professor for Economic Law, where he has also been Head of Department since 2012. He is on leave from his position as Jean Monnet Chair of Private Law and European Economic Law at the University of Bamberg, Germany. Professor Micklitz is the holder of a European Research Council Grant 2011–2016 on European Regulatory Private Law. His main fields of research include European law, European private and consumer law, legal theory.

1

Introduction

Hans-W. Micklitz

I will first place the debate on constitutionalization of private law in the overall context of the increased role of fundamental rights and human rights not only in private law but in the overall interpretation of legal rules at the member states level. Constitutionalization suggests the process which is inherent in the transformation of private law; constitutionalization instead of constituent power, *demos* and the magical constitutional moment. In a second step I will introduce the seven contributions, link them to the broader framework of constitutionalization of European private law via human and fundamental rights, before I return in a third step to identifiable common denominators and under-discussed issues which deserve closer inspection.

1. Framing the Debate on European Human and Fundamental Rights in European Private Law

In the last five to ten years the impact of human rights and fundamental rights on private law has gained increasing prominence and has led to a whole series of in-depth studies.[1] 'Constitutionalization of private law' is the flag under which this literature sails. Most of the research undertaken so far focuses on the increasing impact of national constitutional rights on national private legal orders. That is where the constitutionalization rhetoric comes from. It means that national private legal orders cannot be conceived of (any longer) as self-standing legal orders but are rather embedded in a higher legal order, the national constitution, against which the values underpinning private law can be measured. There is an undercurrent in the debate. Submitting private law to a constitutional test is tied to the idea that new values have to be integrated into private law in order to make it more 'just'.[2] Constitutionalization of private law presupposes the existence of a constitution, which is not the case in the United Kingdom, at least not in the meaning given to the term in light of the French and the American Constitutions. However, the differences between the continental legal order and UK common law has lost importance

[1] This is the list of major monographs and edited selections to which H. Collins refers: D. Oliver and J. Fedtke (eds), *Human Rights and the Private Sphere: A Comparative Study* (2007); C. Mak, *Fundamental Rights in European Contract Law: A Comparison of the Impact of Fundamental Rights on Contractual Relationships in Germany, the Netherlands, Italy and England* (2008); S. Grundmann (ed), *Constitutional Values and European Contract Law* (2008); G. Brüggemeier, A. Colombi Ciacchi, and G. Comandé (eds), *Fundamental Rights and Private Law in the European Union. Volume 1: A Comparative Overview* (2010); O. O. Cherednychenko, *Fundamental Rights, Contract Law and the Protection of the Weaker Party* (2007); D. Hoffman (ed), *The Impact of the UK Human Rights Act on Private Law* (2011); C. Busch and H. Schulte-Nölke (eds), *Fundamental Rights and Private Law* (2011).

[2] Collins, 'The Constitutionalisation of Private Law: a Path to Social Justice', in H.-W. Micklitz (ed), *The Many Faces of Social Justice in Private Law* (2011) 133.

since the UK Parliament adopted the Human Rights Act which grants standing to UK citizens to invoke the European Convention on Human Rights before UK courts. Since 2000, the date of the coming into force of the Human Rights Act, the common law has had to face the same challenges as the member states on the continent.

What has been the subject of much less research is the link between European human rights and the European Charter of Fundamental Rights (EUCFR) and European private law. The European Union has no constitution, leaving aside the question whether the long discussed and failed European Constitution, even in its most ambitious form, could meet the standards of a 'constitution'. However, the Lisbon Treaty gave the Charter of Fundamental Rights the same legal standing as the Treaty and paved the way for the European Union to join the European Convention on Human Rights (ECHR). This process is still pending and its outcome is hard to predict. The key question in our context is the following: will the ECHR be given a higher standing than the Treaty and the Charter of Fundamental Rights or will the two legal orders, the ECHR and the EU legal order (the Treaties and the Charter of Fundamental Rights), be put on a par?[3] Before the integration of the Charter of Fundamental Rights into the European legal order, the Court of Justice (CJEU) had different options to initiate constitutionalization through (a) reference to the 'constitutional traditions common to the Member States'—in reaction to the *Solange* judgment of the German Constitutional Court;[4] (b) reference, or perhaps better, integration of the ECHR into the common principles; and (c) reference to the Charter of Fundamental Rights after its declaration but before its formal integration into the EU legal system. The reasons why the CJEU uses one option or the other are not always clear in its judgments. This might be why we do not find a clear distinction between human rights (the European Convention on Human Rights), the common constitutional principles, and the Charter of Fundamental Rights in the discussion around the constitutionalization of private law. Membership of the EU in the ECHR will not necessarily contribute to a clear distinction between the two areas: not in institutional terms—the CJEU tends to refer here and there to the ECHR, nor in substantive terms—there is an overlap between the two sets of rules. For the purpose of this contribution the distinction is of limited importance. That is why I speak of European Human and Fundamental Rights, in order to make clear that I am looking at substance.[5]

In the meantime, the European Court of Justice is entitled to and makes ever stronger use of the Charter of Fundamental Rights. Whether human rights/fundamental rights and the EU legal order should be understood as two separate legal orders underpins the discourse initiated by this book. The hopes and expectations of human and fundamental rights activists mirror the development of constitutionalization at the member states level. They argue that human rights and fundamental rights shall contribute to 'improving' the European legal order, which is regarded as biased towards and driven by a liberal market ideology. It is not so much the lack of the 'political'[6] but the contended

[3] For a strong view on a monist legal system, where the ECHR and the ECtHR would rank on top, see Zucca, 'Monism and Fundamental Rights', in J. Dickson and P. Eleftheriadis (eds), *Philosophical Foundations of European Union Law* (2012) 331 arguing a possible membership of the EU would decide the question who has the last word—the ECtHR; but see for the opposite position—nobody has the last word because there is no last word to give on moral values—Letsas, 'Harmonic Law: the Case Against Pluralism', in J. Dickson and P. Eleftheriadis (eds), *The Philosophical Foundations of European Union Law* (2012) 91.

[4] ECJ Case C-44/79, *Hauer* [1979] ECR I-3727, at 15 and GCC, *Solange I*, BVerfGE 37, 271.

[5] The next step is to analyse the impact of the ECtHR on private law and the relationship between the case law of the two courts.

[6] Dehousse, 'Constitutional Reform in the EC', in J. Hayward (ed), *The Crisis of Representation in Europe* (1995) 124.

'social deficit' which lies at the forefront of concern of human and fundamental rights activists. According to this view, Human Rights and Fundamental Rights shall serve as a substitute for the non-(never?) existent European 'Social' Constitution.[7] The European Court of Justice in Luxembourg together with the European Court of Human Rights in Strasbourg shall compensate for the unwillingness or the incapacity of the EU member states to take political decisions, which balance the market bias through giving shape to 'the Social'.[8] Whilst the various Treaty amendments have strengthened 'the Social' in the EU and have even led to a certain detachment of the 'the Social' from the 'market',[9] it is clear that the Lisbon Treaty has not established a European variant of a welfare state. It should be reiterated, however, that the European Constitution project did not go much further with regard to 'the Social' than the Treaty of Lisbon.

In light of the extant political and social constitutional deficit in the EU Treaties, the two transnational courts are expected to 'take over'. They should turn into the social engineers of the EU. The consequence could/would be an ever stronger juristocracy[10] at the expense of democratic politics. Courts would become the forum for fighting out controversies over conflicting values. Keleman identifies an already emerging 'eurolegalism'.[11] In a way, the various contributions in this book provide evidence for such an argument. Most of the litigation at stake bears a strong social outlook. Reference to the CJEU is seen as a measure of last resort to invoke European human and fundamental rights, in order to remedy suggested social deficits in the national private law systems. So there is this element of 'making our world better through human and fundamental rights'. The risk of euro-juristocracy and eurolegalism not only lies in the shift in the institutional forum, from parliaments to courts, but also in the strong individualization which goes hand in hand with the rise of fundamental and human rights.[12] The public good inherent in the fight over social values which govern a national or an emerging European society is compartmentalized, broken down into fragments, and put into the hands of 'elite' individuals who have the resources to improve not necessarily the public good but at least their personal situation. Durkheim's observation of the 'cult of the individual'[13] finds confirmation in the twentieth and even the twenty-first century.

However, a considerable number of the cases that come under scrutiny bear a collective dimension. The individual at the European courts often represents a conflict which reaches far beyond his or her individual concerns. Digging deeper into the facts of the cases brought to the European courts via the preliminary reference procedure reveals what I would term, in line with Joel Handler,[14] 'public interest litigation'. Contrary to class action in the United States, the European variant of public interest litigation cannot extend res judicata.[15] Decisions of the CJEU aim to interpret EU law, not to

[7] K. Tuori and S. Sankari (eds), *The Many Constitutions of Europe* (2010).

[8] Kennedy, 'Three Globalizations of Law and Legal Thought: 1850–2000', in D. Trubek and A. Santos (eds), *The New Law and Economic Development: A Critical Appraisal* (2006) 19.

[9] Damjanovic and De Witte, 'Welfare Integration through EU Law: The Overall Picture in the Light of the Lisbon Treaty', in U. Neergaard, R. Nielsen, and L. M. Roseberry (eds), *Integrating Welfare Functions into EU-Law? From Rome to Lisbon* (2009) 53.

[10] R. Hirschl, *Towards Juristocracy: The Origins and Consequences of the New Constitutionalism* (2007).

[11] D. Keleman, *Eurolegalism: The Transformation of Law and Regulation in the European Union* (2011).

[12] A. Somek, *Individualism: An Essay on the Authority of the European Union* (2008).

[13] See Marske, 'Durkheim's "Cult of the Individual" and the Moral Reconstitution of Society', 5 *Sociological Theory* (1987) 1.

[14] J. Handler, *Social Movements and the Legal System: A Theory of Law Reform and Social Change* (1978).

[15] With the exception of Directive 93/13/EEC, OJ 1993 L 95/29, on unfair terms in consumer contracts, see ECJ Case C-472/10, *Invitel*, judgment of 26 April 2012, not yet published.

decide conflicts between parties. So far the final result of strategic litigation before European courts aimed at improving private law, prior to the adoption of the Charter of Fundamental Rights, is rather mixed. It suffices to recall the attempts of the UK Equal Opportunities Commission to increase the social dimension during the Thatcher era,[16] or of the German consumers and their organizations to use the CJEU as a forum of last resort to grant remedies against failed investments, which the German Supreme Court denied.[17] Whether or not Spanish consumers succeed in using the CJEU with reference to the Charter in their fight against unjustified evictions due to the unaffordable rise of mortgage interest rates after the Eurocrisis, remains to be seen.[18]

We can, however, easily identify the potential of human and fundamental rights litigation to improve 'the Social' not only to the benefit of certain individuals, but, within limits, to establish a genuine 'European public good'. This may be said safely at least with regard to the equality and anti-discrimination principle, which was developed by the CJEU but then clarified into a series of secondary community legislative acts and later even Treaty amendments.[19] At the other end are the risks that eurolegalism, euro-juristocracy, and European public interest litigation entail for the national and European political institutions and for the building of a transnational democratic order. Put this way, judicial activism, as positive as it might be for the development of the European Union's social dimension, forms an integral part of the 'political problem'. Courts might be pushed into action by the litigation and might feel legitimated by political inaction. Politically speaking, they are part of the problem.[20] The contributions in this volume move between the two poles—promoting judicial activism via human and fundamental rights and sounding warnings against the political institutional implications.

Where is the solution, is there a solution and what can private law do to overcome the tension? Can it do anything at all? Before I try to give some tentative answers, I have to go back to the specificities of private law. The human and fundamental rights rhetoric implies the assumption that private legal orders suffer from the same social deficit. They are presumed to show the same market bias as the European legal order, translated into private law language, promoting freedom of contract and private autonomy at the expense of social justice. The entire 20th century could be read as an attempt by the European nation states to remedy social deficits through legislative intervention in the fields of labour law, tenant law, and consumer law. All three fields are at the forefront of the contributions in this book. Collins[21] goes as far as to argue that employment law in the UK has lost its origin in freedom of contract and has turned into social regulation.

[16] Kilpatrick, 'Gender Equality: A Fundamental Dialogue', in S. Sciarra (ed), *Labour Law in the Courts: National Judges and the ECJ* (2001) 31; H.-W. Micklitz, *The Politics of Judicial Co-operation in the EU: Sunday Trading, Equal Treatment and Good Faith* (2005).

[17] The story of the *Schrottimmobilien*: pulled into mortgage credit financed investments via direct selling at the doorsteps, consumers lost their property as they could not find a tenant who was able and willing to pay a rent that would have allowed to cover the costs of the mortgage. This conflict led to more than five references to the CJEU. Only a few were compensated.

[18] This is the story behind ECJ Case C-415/11, *Aziz*, judgment of 14 March 2013, not yet published, but discussed by O. Cherednychenko and C. Mak in this volume.

[19] For the role and function of the equality principle in the building of a European society, R. Münch, *European Governmentality: The Liberal Drift of Multi-Level Governance* (2010).

[20] Weiler, 'Deciphering the Political and Legal DNA of European Integration: An Exploratory Essay', in J. Dickson and P. Eleftheriadis (eds), *Philosophical Foundations of European Union Law* (2012) 137.

[21] Collins, 'Justifications and Techniques of Legal Regulation of the Employment Relation', in H. Collins, P. Davies, and R. Rideout (eds), *Legal Regulation of the Employment Relation* (2000) 6.

A similar assessment could certainly be made in relation to tenancy[22] and consumer law.[23] The concern expressed by private lawyers is not so much directed against the integration of social values or even social justice into private law.[24] The concern results from the fear that private law is being swallowed not by democratic social regulation, but by a 'higher legal order'. Human rights and fundamental rights understood as constitutional rights might tend to absorb genuine private law values such as freedom of contract. Private law would lose its character as a self-standing legal order, separate and distinct from any form of a higher legal order.

What are the stakes in the conflicting arguments? In essence, the claim is that there is something special about private law, which justifies its separation from the regime of a national constitution and from a regime of universal human rights or the European Charter of Fundamental Rights. There are different strands of discussions to be distinguished. The origins of private law are older than constitutions and human/fundamental rights. Continental and common law find its roots in the *ius commune* of the old Roman law.[25] This is the historical argument. The counterarguments are that even the older private law embodied many of the values now found in human and fundamental rights.[26] Ordo-liberalism promotes an economic constitution which is based on two pillars, the so-called *Privatrechtsgesellschaft* (the liberal element—private autonomy) and competition law (the 'ordo' element), eliminating private power via competition. The European economic constitution is said to have been based exactly on this premise, but the Single European Act and the Maastricht Treaty amended the European economic constitution at the expense of the *Privatrechtsgesellschaft*.[27] The third strand of arguments points to the differences between the role and function that human and fundamental rights fulfil in state–citizen or in citizen–citizen relations. This last argument dominates the discourse on the impact of human and fundamental rights, enshrined in the distinction between vertical/horizontal and direct/indirect effect. This is certainly not the place to go deeper into the added value of the third series of arguments. Elsewhere I have argued that this distinction does not take the changing role of the state into account and that the public/private divide is gradually fading away.[28] None of the different strands provides satisfactory answers to the question of the particular character of private law. I will leave this for another contribution.[29]

[22] See <http://ec.europa.eu/research/social-sciences/projects/522_en.html>, responsible C. Schmidt, ZERP, University of Bremen.

[23] S. Weatherill, *European Consumer Law and Policy* (2nd ed.; 2014, forthcoming); H.-W. Micklitz et al., *Understanding EU Consumer Law* (2nd ed.; 2013).

[24] There are differences, but setting 'hard core' law and economics aside, there is agreement that private law cannot be built on private autonomy or freedom of contract alone.

[25] R. Zimmermann, *The Law of Obligations: Roman Foundations of the Civilian Tradition* (1996).

[26] Collins in this volume refers to Barak, 'Constitutional Human Rights and Private Law', in D. Friedmann and D. Barak-Erez (eds), *Human Rights in Private Law* (2001) 13, at 21–22; Smits, 'Private Law and Fundamental Rights: A Sceptical View', in T. Barkhuysen and S. Lindenbergh (eds), *Constitutionalisation of Private Law* (2006) 9; R. Stevens, *Torts and Rights* (2007).

[27] Joerges, 'A Renaissance of the European Economic Constitution?', in U. Neergaard, R. Nielsen, and L. M. Roseberry (eds), *Integrating Welfare Functions into EU Law: From Rome to Lisbon* (2009) 29.

[28] Micklitz, 'Rethinking the public/private divide', in M. Maduro, K. Tuori, and S. Sankari (eds), *Transnational Law: Rethinking European Law and Legal Thinking* (forthcoming).

[29] I would like to thank my colleague Loïc Azoulai for drawing attention to the question whether and to what extent private law can be regarded as different from constitutional and public law. This yields the need to go even deeper into system theory (Luhmann) and discourse theory (Habermas), which both promote the existence of 'private autonomy' enshrined in society distinct from the state order. See Renner, 'Grand Theories of Private Law', in S Grundmann, H.-W. Micklitz, and M. Renner (forthcoming).

Both H. Collins and G. Comandé explicitly address the relationship between private law and human/fundamental rights in this volume, though in very different ways. Collins uses the metaphor of a semi-detached house to catch the relationship between private law and a higher legal order. Translated into constitutional language, he identifies potential for the improvement of private law via human and fundamental rights,[30] but he wants to keep basic value decisions in the hands of democratic institutions. The way to keep the two systems separated is through the instrument of indirect effect, which is due to the difference between vertical citizen-state and the horizontal citizen-citizen relations. In such a perspective the impact of human and fundamental rights on the development of a genuine European social model and on compensating for the deficiencies in the Treaty via judicial activism remains limited. His vision of European private law, which enshrines social justice, is not a European top-down codification, not even through a fully democratized European Union, but is a bottom-up process through the economic and social actors as well as their organizations.[31] This goes along quite well with the common law case-law tradition. It also stresses the role and function of civil society and the separateness of private law from public/constitutional law at whatever level, national or European.

Comandé, on the contrary, understands private law as a tool to build a European society, a European identity, if not a European democracy. His contribution is therefore not so much linked to the social dimension, although this plays a role, but to the 'political' dimension of private law. Contrary to the critiques raised against juristocracy and the problematic shift from parliament to the judiciary, he understands courts and the cases they have to decide in the triangle of citizenship—the fifth European Union freedom—, economic freedoms/fundamental rights, and private law, as the appropriate addressees to contribute to the building of a European society, even a European identity, and beyond to a European democracy. The preliminary reference procedure then appears as a means of European democracy building.[32] The key is the link between private law and citizenship. His argument is that the seemingly neutral character of private law allows for the transport of (social) values, which allow for the building of a shadow citizenship different from the European Union citizenship. In fact, in Comandé's argument, the deeper political character of the private legal order comes to the fore. The connection to Collins and his bottom-up approach is evident, although Comandé understands private law and public law (fundamental rights, economic freedoms, citizenship) not as semi-detached houses, but as one house, perhaps not with two storeys, but at least as one single house.

So far, I have assumed that there is a common easily agreeable understanding of what might and should be understood by private law generally, and more particularly what European private law stands for. For a number of years, I have argued that there is a difference between nation state private legal orders, be they codified or not, and European private law. This has to do with my rejection of an understanding of the EU as a federal state in the making. Instead I put emphasis on the transformation of the nation state, thereby comprehending the European Union as the prototype of an emerging market state, following Bobbitt[33] and Patterson and Afilalo.[34] The European Union understood

[30] With regard to what the House of Lords could and should do: Collins, 'Lord Hoffmann and the Common Law of Contract', 5 *European Review of Contract Law (ERCL)* (2009) 474.

[31] H. Collins, *The European Civil Code: The Way Forward* (2008).

[32] Micklitz, *supra* note 16, at 165.

[33] P. Bobbitt, *The Shield of Achilles: War, Peace and the Course of History* (2002).

[34] D. Patterson and A. Afilalo, *The New Global Trading Order: The Evolving State and the Future of Trade* (2010).

as a market state does not allow for a connection between European state-building via a European Constitution and a parallel plan for the development of a European Civil Code. If this argument is correct, European private law must look different, as its task is to serve the completion of the Internal Market which allows for realizing (some) social values in a pick and pack procedure.

European private law is regulatory in nature. It serves the opening of markets by establishing opportunities for the market participants and the embedding of market opportunities in a tight legal framework. From a more traditional private law perspective, the strongest links to national private laws can be found in the Brussels Regulation, the Rome I and II Regulations, in international private law, regulating jurisdiction, the applicable law, and execution of judgments. National private law systems remain unaffected as the EU limits itself to harmonizing the legal mechanisms which tie the different legal orders of the member states together. The more intrusive impact of European private law-making results from the comprehensive set of rulings on consumer contract law. In the so-called Acquis Group, which was mandated by the European Commission to identify and formulate the European private law acquis, consumer law directives and their interpretation through the CJEU play a crucial role. What has been neglected here as well as in the overall project on a European Civil Code is the regulatory dimension of European private law rules that do not fit into traditional categories of contract and tort and that do not start from the premise of freedom of contract, private autonomy or *liberté de la volonté*.[35] It is this rather messy field of opening and closing, of granting and restricting party autonomy, which I call regulatory private law, which forms the core of European private law. Consumer law and anti-discrimination is simply the most visible sign of the change, but the two areas in no way exhaust the reach of regulatory private law.

Over the last decades, the European Union has developed a dense net of rules, covering a broad field of economic activities, which deeply affect private law, although quite often the potential effect is only discovered on a second and closer look. The following summary account is taken from earlier writings. I have updated the content without adding references.[36]

(1) Anti-discrimination. The European Community modernized and extended anti-discrimination law by way of a whole series of Directives (2000/43/EC, 2000/78/EC, 2002/73/EC, 2004/113/EC and 2006/54/EC) to private law, i.e. beyond labour law. Anti-discrimination law introduces new values into the private law system—these values are not bound to particular areas of the visible law, they govern private law relations per se.

(2) Regulated markets. The privatization (liberalization) of former state monopolies in the sector of telecommunication, energy and transport has raised the importance of contract law. The regulatory role of contract law as a device between the regulated markets to serve the overall purpose of liberalization and privatization is largely neglected. The network law develops within the boundaries of universal services whose reach have to be tested with regard to its potential for being generalized beyond the narrow subject matter.

[35] Each of the three has a different meaning resulting from the different socio-economic and cultural context.

[36] Micklitz, 'The Visible Hand of European Private Law', 28 *Yearbook of European Law* (2009) 3. In Italian, in G. Alpa and R. Mazzei (eds), *Studi storici e guiridici* (2010) 125; in Finnish, 3 *Lakimies* (2010) 330; in Japanese, 12 *Hokkaido Journal of New Global Law and Policy* (2011); in French, *Revue Internationale de Droit Economique* (2013, forthcoming).

Insurance law (which is usually regarded as a subject of its own) and capital market law (investor protection law). EC Directive 2004/39/EC on Markets in Financial Instruments—the so-called MIFID—lays down a broad framework within level 1 of the Lamfalussy approach, completed by two level 2 pieces, Directive 2006/73/EC on organizational requirements and operating conditions for investment firms and the implementing Regulation 2006/1287/EC. They establish a dense network of rules which contain strong links to the contractual relations in which a professional or a private investor engages with his or her investment firm.

(3) Commercial practices. The most important elements are Directive 2005/29/EC on unfair commercial practices dealing with b2c relations, and Directive 2006/114/EC on misleading and comparative advertising in b2b relations. The e-commerce Directive 2000/31/EC has to be taken into account as well. Directive 99/44/EC on consumer sales links contract law and advertising in that third party advertising may affect contractual duties. EC commercial practices law affects the modalities under which a contract is concluded.

Intellectual property rights. EC policy is intended to extend existing intellectual property rights law and give it a European outlook coupled with appropriate legal redress mechanisms to sanction violations of property rights (Directive 2004/48/EC). The significant expansion of intellectual property rights at the same time restricts users' rights. These restrictions are often found in standard terms which form part of the licence contract that the consumer concludes, often via the internet.

(4) Private competition law (*Kartellprivatrecht*). The diverse regulations on exclusive and selective distribution, the umbrella Regulation 330/2010, Regulation 461/2010 on the car sector, and Regulation 772/2004 on technology transfer (under revision), intervene indirectly in contract making. The content of the rights and duties in vertical agreements is determined to a large extent by block exemptions. The parties will often literally copy the articles in the block exemptions into their contracts to avoid discrepancies between the EC rules and contractual rights.

The new economic approach to state aid has led to the adoption of the *de minimis* Regulation 1998/2006. European state aid law may be divided into a substantive and a procedural part. Illegal state aid, that is to say, the question of repayment of unlawful state aid and the possible remedies of third parties, are key questions in private law. Similar effects can be reported from Directive 2009/81/EC amending Directive 2004/17/EC dealing with procurement procedures for entities operating in the water, energy, transport and postal services, and Directive 2004/18/EC on the coordination for the procurement procedure on public works contracts, public supply contracts and public services contracts. Whilst the purpose of these directives is to enhance competition and strengthen the market freedoms, at the same time they shape contractual relations. This is particularly true with regard to appropriate remedies.

(5) Product safety and food safety law. In Directive 2001/95/EC on product safety there are new devices that enhance the role of contract law as a means to shape contractual relations. Liability rules may be found in the Feed Hygiene Regulation 183/2005, the Food Hygiene Regulation 852/2004; the Regulation on Official Feed and Food Controls 882/2004 and Regulation 178/2002 on Food Law.

The so-called Services Directive 2006/123/EC enhances the elaboration of 'technical standards' by the European standard bodies, CEN/CENELEC, as well as by National Standards Bodies that come near to some sort of standard contract conditions which might be subject to control under Directive 93/13/EEC on unfair contract terms.

The conception of the Law of the European Union summer school of the Academy of European Law held in 2011, which underlies this book and the design of the different subject-related contributions, reflects this understanding of European private law. To be sure, the contributions do not cover the full range of the regulatory private law, but they deal with representative parts of it. The contributions analyse European private law and national law in tandem, partly because of a lack of case law at the European level, and in a deeper sense because national and European private law are viewed as one integrated field of research. They do not draw a distinction between different concepts of national and private law. In a way, the ideology is that private law remains private law in a deeper sense, no matter what is behind it, no codification, a codification, or fragmented regulations.

2. The Contributions

The present book does not explore the constitutional values of the Draft Common Frame of Reference, the Common Frame of Reference, or the Optional Code. Hesselink has discussed the guiding constitutional principles and its changing outlook.[37] This book focuses on European private law in action. Colombi Ciacchi looks into European contract law rules, mainly in consumer law. Her contribution can be read as a horizontal analysis of constitutionalized private law across the relevant fields. Bell focuses on employment law, where constitutionalization via human and fundamental rights is by far the most advanced. Cherednychenko has chosen, out of the range of regulated markets, financial services. In consumer surveys, finance always ranks at the top of consumer concern.[38] Her interest lies in the search for the impact of fundamental and human rights on consumer law in financial services. Godt stretches the boundaries towards the relationship between IP rights, human, and fundamental rights, and their radiating impact on private law. In the future this field, now being discussed under the concept of 'digital contracts', might be of great significance.[39] Last but not least, Mak stresses the impact of the principle of judicial protection in Article 47 EUCFR on substance, procedure, and remedies in private law across the different fields, testing the importance of the stand-alone article disconnected from substance.

A. Human Rights/Fundamental Rights vs Private Law—a Semi-Detached House? (H. Collins)

In his contribution 'On the (In)compatibility of Human Rights Discourse and Private law', Collins sharpens his concept of the structural relationship between constitutional law and private law. He advocates the model of a semi-detached house: independent homes, but joined by a common wall against the concept of constitutional laws or at least the basic constitutional principles such as fundamental rights, which provide the common foundations for what is ultimately a single structure. This is a distinction which goes very deep and claims in essence that private law cannot be reconstructed in constitutional terms alone, as argued by M. Kumm.[40] It implies that private law exists or existed

[37] Hesselink, 'If you don't like our principles we have others: on core values and underlying principles in European private law. A critical discussion of the new "Principles" section in the draft Common Frame of Reference', in R. Brownsword et al. (eds), *Foundations of European Private Law* (2011) 59.

[38] See the Consumer Scoreboard: <http://ec.europa.eu/consumers/consumer_research/editions/cms7_en.htm>.

[39] The most advanced proposal is to be found in the CESL, for a discussion: Micklitz and Reich in H.-W. Micklitz et al. (eds), *Understanding European Union Consumer Law* (2nd ed.; 2013, forthcoming).

[40] Kumm, 'Who is Afraid of the Total Constitution? Constitutional Rights as Principles and the Constitutionalization of Private Law', 7 *German Law Journal* (2006) 341.

prior to its public institution via nation state legal orders. Against this clarification, Collins refers to O. Gerstenberg,[41] who spelt out clearly the three reasons (though not accepting them) against an unreflecting opening of the floodgates to human rights and fundamental rights in order to reshape private law: (1) the threat to private law's libertarian core of private autonomy; (2) sweeping usurpation of legislative prerogatives in determining the boundaries of spheres of private autonomy; and (3) the shifting of authority to interpret private law's core concept from ordinary to constitutional and/or generalist courts. Collins' focus is directed towards what he calls the 'puzzle of horizontality'—the distinction between vertical and horizontal direct effect of human/constitutional rights. He uses case law of the European Court of Human Rights, mainly with an impact on private law, to demonstrate his concerns.

Whilst Collins admits that there is a thin line between the potential effects of indirect and direct horizontality, he insists on the different embeddedness of private versus public law. A simple transfer to public law values as enshrined in human rights could lead to severe distortions at all three levels. Collins' intention is not to discredit the potential impact of human rights on private law; he agrees that human rights may initiate a rethinking and an adjustment of private law concepts, provided courts stick to what he calls the 'double proportionality test'. Contrary to the proportionality test in a state–citizen relation, in private relations the court has to start from the presumptive (human/fundamental) parity of the parties' rights, which have to be balanced against each other.[42] The competition between the right to freedom of expression and the right to respect of privacy demonstrates the tension. Neither right has precedence over or trumps the other. The proportionality test must be applied in scope, reach and justifiability to both rights, similar to Mak's analysis.[43] There is a difference between a relationship of power and dependence between the citizen and state where the normal proportionality test applies and the weighing of autonomy and consent in relations between individuals. This distinction cannot be overcome by drawing parallels between public power (the state) and economic power (transnational companies). Private parties cannot become the direct addressees and bearers of human rights. Collins obviously rejects the idea of CJEU case law as a way not only to make private parties direct beneficiaries of fundamental freedoms, but also of fundamental rights,[44] or to apply the US Alien Tort Act to multinationals.[45]

Collins' conclusion is to strengthen a positive conception of liberty, where human rights and fundamental rights may have a radiating impact. Civil law remedies, if properly applied, suffice to tame a one-sided, unrestricted use of economic power.[46] This is very much in line with what the Bremen School of Law[47] called materialized private

[41] Gerstenberg, 'Private Law and the New European Constitutional Settlement', 10 *European Law Journal (ELJ)* (2004) 766, at 769.

[42] Referring to Sir Mark Potter in *A Local Authority v W* (2005) EWHC 1564 (Fam).

[43] C. Mak, *Fundamental Rights in European Contract Law: A Comparison of the Impact of Fundamental Rights on Contractual Relationships in Germany, the Netherlands, Italy and England* (2008), at 54. See also Chantal Mak in this volume.

[44] L. Azoulai, 'The Court of Justice and the Social Market Economy: The Emergence of an Ideal and the Conditions for its Realization', 45 *Common Market Law Review* (2008) 1335.

[45] See, in that context, C. Godt in this volume and the abundant literature on the *Kiobel* case (569 US).

[46] In very much the same direction, Douglas-Scott, 'The Problem of Justice in the European Union: Values, Pluralism and Critical Legal Justice', in J. Dickson and P. Eleftheriadis (eds), *Philosophical Foundations of European Union Law* (2012) 412, at 447.

[47] Most prominent are H. D. Assmann et al. (eds), *Wirtschaftsrecht als Kritik des Privatrechts; Beiträge zur Privat- und Wirtschaftsrechtstheorie* (1980); N. Reich, *Markt und Recht* (1976).

autonomy (*materialisierte Privatautonomie*), just like in the sense that the German Constitutional Court (GCC) did in the *Bürgschafts* judgment.

B. Building Shadow Citizenship via Private Law—the Political Dimension (G. Comandé)

In 'The Fifth Union Freedom: Aggregating Citizenship . . . around Private Law', Comandé formulates the hypothesis that European citizenship has to be understood as being composed of two different strains: the official language of citizenship in the Treaty on the Functioning of the European Union (TFEU) and what he calls 'shadow citizenship'. Shadow citizenship is said to technically operate as an economic freedom; it expands and redefines the scope of fundamental rights by aggregating new bundles of rights. The going together of economic freedoms and fundamental rights in an open process necessitates an interplay with all constituencies involved at the national and the European level. Private law is the tool to aggregate shadow citizenship in the everyday lives of EU citizens. The potential outcome is the building of a European polity and a European identity bottom up via the CJEU. This hypothesis shifts the perspective of the overall case law of the CJEU around economic freedoms, fundamental rights, and citizenship to its deeper connection to private law relations. Market participants appear as citizens who participate in the building of shadow citizenship. There is a connection to Collins' plea for building a European Civil Code bottom-up via the private actors and associations involved.[48] However, contrary to Collins, Comandé argues that such a process is already under way and that the CJEU is the key actor. Both are united in their resistance to any idea of using legislation for society and identity building.[49] Comandé's truly innovative argument is the connection between citizenship and private law, a link which seems to run counter to any conception of private law which does not distinguish between nationals, at least not as long as they are operating under the same legal order.

Comandé develops his argument in four steps. He begins with the perceived role of human and fundamental rights in modern societies. The tension provoked by the insertion of human and fundamental rights into private law allows for the building of new equilibria. Unstable ambiguity is claimed to offer a fertile ground upon which shadow citizenship can flourish. The shift from the universal claim of human rights to the EU language of fundamental rights is claimed to offer more room for the protection of individual dignity and a corresponding strengthening of the democracy. Shadow citizenship is more than mere constitutionalization through the integration of values. The path can only be successful—he stresses this argument with varying degrees of emphasis throughout the text—if it occurs in a 'disguised' form, using the economic freedoms as the vehicle. Human rights and fundamental rights are perceived as 'an opportunity of sharing' a common project—of European society and identity—rather than an actual sharing of rights. The next step then is the identity-shaping role of human rights within the boundaries of the multilevel structure of the EU. Differences and tensions between and over values are understood as opportunities for dialogue and political participation. The failure of the European Civil Code project can be explained by the open 'tampering' with the different values underpinning the various national private legal orders. The success of the EU depends on avoiding systematic solutions, thereby benefiting from the legitimizing role of seemingly 'neutral' private law regulation. Linking EU citizenship to

[48] Collins, *supra* note 31.

[49] This, however, happened in the 1990s in the new member states.

private law binds individuals to a political community protected by fundamental rights, beyond their function as mere factors of economic production.

'Aggregating European Citizenship from the Internal Market Building Process' operates along two strata: first it gives more weight to EU citizens' rights outside their own nation/member state, initially by way of economic freedoms and subsequently via citizenship; secondly the process attributes significance to citizens' rights in their own nation/member state by redefining the rights citizens enjoy in their own nation/member state. Comandé relies on the case law resulting from areas that are not necessarily considered as traditional fields of private law, mainly fundamental rights cases and citizenship cases with a private law background. In a last step, he defines the contours of shadow citizenship. He is aware that shadow citizenship driven by economic freedoms may be biased, in promoting individualism at the expense of solidarity. But he insists that the concept of shadow citizenship, of discussing and merging values from the bottom up, allows for a development of a European polity which is not based on economic freedom alone. Echoes of the fifth freedom in the case law, not only mirrored in civil status and family law but also in civil and commercial law, serve to drive his argument home. Building on Collins,[50] he argues that 'business associations, social networks, technical standards bodies and scientific associations, together with long term family relations and more transient transactions such as package holidays, are the building blocks of a transnational civil society in Europe'.

In his conclusion, Comandé goes as far as saying that a restrictive reading of Article 6 TFEU is more promising for the 'muffled rising of a citizenship coupled with private law, the principles of which are forming in the metaphorical cauldron with an eventual view to developing a sort of transnational civil society'. To be sure, his argument raises questions on the deeper link between shadow citizenship and private law beyond family law, on society and democracy building via case law, on the prominent position of fundamental freedoms as a placeholder for social and fundamental rights, on the degree to which the case law of the CJEU, as referred to, underpins his argument.

C. Common Fact Patterns of Constitutionalized Contract and Tort Law (A. Colombi Ciacchi)

Whilst Collins and Comandé problematize the relationship between human rights/fundamental rights on the one hand, and private law on the other, the former in drawing a dividing line between the two, the latter in using the transformation of private law via human and fundamental rights through the CJEU as a trigger for building a European society and a European identity, Colombi Ciacchi digs deeper into the intricacies of the horizontal/vertical, direct/indirect relationship between public and private law in order to structure the discourse around 'fact patterns' in 'general contract and tort law' to be identified in the national and European litigation.

Her conceptual starting point is the distinction between direct/indirect horizontal and vertical direct effect, which she takes for granted, highlighting typical classical constellations in the relationship between the private and the public and the private towards another private party.[51] This fits well with Collins, who equally insists that a basic difference

[50] Collins, *supra* note 31, at 7.

[51] See for a thorough analysis of the horizontal vs the vertical in the case law of the CJEU: Van Leeuwen, 'An Illusion of Protection and an Assumption of Responsibility: The Possibility of Swedish State Liability after *Laval*', 14 *Cambridge Yearbook of European Legal Studies* (2011–2012) 453.

between the vertical and horizontal remains. Throughout her contribution, Colombi Ciacchi distinguishes between the national and the European level in the application of human rights, fundamental rights, and constitutional rights. This approach allows her to fine-tune the differences between the national and the European transformation processes. There are remarkable differences in the degree to which member state courts use either national fundamental rights as a yardstick or European human rights, or the Charter of Fundamental Rights or international conventions. These may result from *institutional* deviations, but also from whether the European and international conventions on human rights are self-executing within the respective national system or not.

The *substantive* dimension aims at developing common fact patterns of horizontal direct/indirect application at the national and the European level within more traditional fields of (consumer) contract law, tenant law and to some extent tort law. At the member state level, these amount to nine different situations around which the case law is grouped together: (1) freedom of speech, freedom of information, and privacy rights; (2) unauthorized publication of photographs; (3) the landlord's obligation to cease emissions constituting intolerable nuisance; (4) the landlord's obligation to tolerate the installation of a satellite; (5) the protection of tenants from termination of tenancy contracts; (6) adjustment of imbalanced contracts through general principles; (7) invalidity of employment or agency contracts; (8) protection of freedom of religion in employment contracts; and (9) equal treatment of men and women. At the EU level, there are not yet enough cases, which would allow for an equally sophisticated fact pattern. However, she claims that 'liberty rights' prevail in number and concern over 'social-economic rights' in the case law of the CJEU. Colombi Ciacchi looks into what she calls 'the double horizontal effect' of EU fundamental rights. Rights and duties of the parties to a private relationship are shaped by EU fundamental rights through two different layers, first through the CJEU, later through the interpretation of national courts. Links to the double proportionality test as promoted by Collins and Mak can easily be made.

National and European courts, in Colombi Ciacchi's argument, are engaged in judicial governance.[52] The identifiable policy patterns are said to correlate to the existing case law. National courts manage the protection of the weaker party in contract law, the reduction of discrimination, the economic upgrade of the interests of the individual and social equality in tort law, the control of media power, exercise of political rights in privately managed spaces, and environmental protection. The CJEU is involved in the reduction of discrimination on the ground of gender or age, reduction of discrimination on the ground of nationality, protection of freedom of establishment and freedom to provide services, protection of privacy, freedom of information, and freedom to conduct business. Courts thereby use a normative individualistic understanding of human rights and fundamental rights in the meaning of von der Pforten,[53] which allows for giving voice to underprivileged and less powerful private parties towards their counterpart. In so doing, courts re-establish private autonomy. The dark side is the strong individualization of public goods through a process of decollectivization.[54]

This latter statement runs counter to Comandé, who understands shadow citizenship as a way to build not only 'public goods' but a European society and a European identity.

[52] S. Frerichs, *Judicial Governance in der europäischen Rechtsgemeinschaft: Integration durch Recht jenseits des Staates* [Judicial Governance in the European Community of Law: Integration Through Law Beyond the State] (2006).

[53] Von der Pforten, 'Normativer Individualismus und das Recht', *Juristen Zeitung* (*JZ*) (2005) 1069.

[54] Somek, 'Das Europäische Sozialmodell und Diskriminierungsschutz', *Juridikum* 2 (2008) 118.

However, the case law he uses is taken mainly from citizenship and family law. Colombi Ciacchi's 'fact patterns' are much nearer to a traditional understanding of private law, where she underpins the overall hypothesis that the intrusion of human rights and fundamental rights contribute to making the contracts more 'just'. Judicial governance would then lead to social engineering via courts. Constitutionalization increases individual justice at the expense of justice for all. Comandé includes in private law what I would call 'access rights'[55] to shadow citizenship. The 'marketization' of citizenship would go along with fundamental freedoms carrying the cargo of citizen and family rights. Contrary to Colombi Ciacchi, it builds on individual rights as a 'tool' to achieve at least access justice.[56]

D. Constitutionalized Equality and a Fundamental Right to be Treated as a Worker (M. Bell)

The first concrete field of private law to be examined is 'Constitutionalization and EU Employment Law'. Bell starts from the idea that constitutionalization means attributing 'higher status' to certain legal norms. This implies a distinction between ordinary norms where regulatory standards apply and norms which are shielded against legislative amendments and against private misconduct that might affect these higher rights. Although employment belongs in essence to contract law, to the idea of mutual freedom of contract for both parties, labour law regulation long served to establish what could be called, with Sinzheimer and Kahn-Freund, 'industrial constitution' (*Arbeitsverfassung*). The industrial constitutions set a frame for collective actions of both employers and employees, allowing them to freely define the substantive outcome in terms of pay and working conditions. National legislators and later the EU regulator have ever more densely intruded into the direct shaping of contractual relations, without meeting too much resistance from the addressees. The constitutionalization of employment law through 'rights' is then just a further step towards restricting freedom of contract. However, there is a difference. Constitutionalization via rights empowers workers to seek the enforcement of their rights before courts. They take over the societal role of collective organizations, a process which the EU has considerably augmented despite its rhetoric on dialogue in industrial relations. In line with Colombi Ciacchi's observations, courts are turning into societal engineers, outbalancing the effects of the transformation of the industrial constitution.

Constitutionalization takes two forms, first via courts through the use of the general principles of equal treatment and respect for human rights, and secondly via the codification of labour and social rights through charters and treaties. Bell uses equality law and the personal scope of employment rights to assess the impact of constitutionalization; the former because it is here that constitutionalization is most visible, the latter because the shaping of the personal scope is much more difficult to catch via constitutionalization. The CJEU had developed a number of key characteristics: the uncoupling of equality legislation from market regulation objectives, the trend towards direct applicability of the general principle of equality in private relations, thereby

[55] Micklitz, 'Do Consumers and Business Need a New Architecture for Consumer Law? A Thought Provoking Impulse', *Yearbook of European Law* (2013/2014, forthcoming) German version: Micklitz, 'Brauchen Konsumenten und Unternehmen eine neue Architektur des Verbraucherrechts?' *Gutachten A zum 69. Juristentag* (2012).

[56] H.-W. Micklitz (ed), *The Many Faces of Social Justice in Private Law* (2011).

relegating secondary Union law to a 'residual role'. These phenomena, however, cannot be condensed in a general rule. Bell underlines that the Court invokes the Charter and or the general principles *on occasion* only, being 'cognizant of the polemical debate that surrounds such cases'.

The growing outsourcing of working relations leads to quadrilateral relations yielding the need to define the scope and reach of the different pieces of EU law. Bell's investigation into 'whether there is any fundamental right to be treated as a worker' resembles Comandé's attempt to reconceptualize marketized citizenship.[57] Bell identifies a gap between Equality Law and Working Time Law (though to a lesser extent) on the one hand and the Acquired Rights Directive on the other. The 'worker' enjoys a certain constitutionalization whenever there is a connection to (particular) fundamental rights in EU and international law, a link which is easier to identify in Equality Law and Working Time Law. It seems difficult to make sense out of this difference. I tend to argue that in the former category the protective outlook gains supremacy over the market-based deconstruction of the worker; the opposite is true for mergers and takeovers. Here the worker cannot maintain her status, she keeps her job but has to accept the competition pressure on her working conditions.

Bell claims that the expansion of fundamental social rights 'risks swallowing up the whole of employment law'. Contract law in employment relations would then be more or less substituted by a body of fundamental rights which shapes the content of the working relations. Drawing together the bits and pieces of the CJEU case law, and maybe national case law on fundamental rights, the emergence of a 'constitutionalized' employment contract law could be imagined. The question remains, however, whether a constitutionalized employment law would dilute the meaning and significance of what 'a fundament right' entails, as Bell puts it.

E. Gateways to the Constitutionalization of Access, Substance, and Procedure of Financial Services (O. Cherednychenko)

In her contribution on 'Fundamental Rights, European Private Law, and Financial Services', Cherednychenko deals with European and national private law rules. Her focus on the legal position of the consumer in financial transactions goes along with the assumption inherent in the contribution of Colombi Ciacchi that the consumer is the weaker party in financial transactions and that consumer financial services are (or might be?) a prominent field for constitutionalization.

Cherednychenko starts by defining four 'gateways to constitutionalization of European private law': (1) requirements of conformity in rule-making, broadly understood legislators, and public authorities; (2) requirements on the interpretation and application by legislators and public authorities; (3) requirements on implementing EU fundamental rights in private law relations by taking positive action—in contrast to negative action, by not interfering with such rights; and (4) the distinction between horizontal and vertical direct effect of fundamental rights. The shift in focus from the analysis of the case law to the analysis of the impact on human rights and fundamental rights on rule drafting and administrative decisions might be due to two reasons: first, case law is scarce and, secondly, the existing law on financial services lacks the fundamental rights dimension.

[57] The so-called citizen-consumer. See M. Everson and Ch. Joerges, 'Consumer Citizenship in Postnational Constellations' (2006). Available on SSRN: <http://papers.ssrn.com/sol3/papers.cfm?abstract_id=964187>; See also J. Davies, *The European Consumer Citizen in Law and Policy* (2011).

With regard to gateway (1), Cherednychenko finds no consistency in the degree to which the relevant directives refer to fundamental rights or not in the recitals. Why do the Markets in Financial Instruments Directive and the Consumer Credit Directive have such a reference, but not the Directive on Payment Services?[58] Interpretation and application, gateway (2), lies mainly in the hands of the national courts. There are only a few decisions in which the CJEU explicitly refers to fundamental rights, but they do not originate from financial services. Whether or not the EU and the member states are under a positive obligation, gateway (3), to protect fundamental rights by taking positive action through legislative or administrative measures, is subject to controversy.[59] The German Constitutional Court and the European Court of Human Rights (ECtHR) are said to be at the forefront of the development of imposing a positive duty to legislate, although *Commission v France*[60] and *Promusicae*[61] demonstrate a certain preparedness of the CJEU to follow suit. (4) With some sympathy, the author refers to Advocate General Trstenjak, who does not exclude 'the direct application of fundamental rights in the form of general principles in relationships between private individuals'.[62] As is well known, the CJEU has referred in a series of judgments to 'general principles of civil law'. In *Messner*[63] the CJEU found that 'good faith and unjust enrichment' can be added to the 'principles', a conclusion which was not welcomed in the common law countries, where good faith as a general standard for fairness does not exist.[64]

Whereas the first part of Cherednychenko's contribution applies to all fields of (private) law, the second part analyses the potential impact of the gateways on financial services. She discusses the actual (*de lege lata*) and the potential (*de lege ferenda*) impact of fundamental rights in relation to three major issues: consumer access to financial services, substantive consumer protection in financial services, and procedural consumer protection in financial services. First, Cherednychenko explains the consumer problem behind the three issues, she then looks at the negative (confiscatory) side of fundamental rights as contrasted with a potential positive obligation to legislate, and last but not least she examines horizontal direct effect. Fictitious examples are introduced to illustrate the potential impact of fundamental rights in reshaping European financial services law. *Mohamed Aziz*[65] is one of the few cases which demonstrates a potential for a fundamental rights analysis both at the substantive and the procedural level. However, neither the Advocate General nor the CJEU refer to fundamental rights, even though the fundamental rights dimension is all too obvious. This judgment correlates perfectly well with Comandé's concept of 'shadow citizenship', in that the political dimension of the judgment through reference to fundamental rights remains obscure.

[58] See for a deeper discussion on the policy of the European Commission, V. Kosta, 'Fundamental Rights in Internal Market Legislation' (PhD thesis on file at the EUI, Florence 2013).

[59] Zucca, 'Monism and Fundamental Rights', in J. Dickson and P. Eleftheriadis (eds), *Philosophical Foundations of European Union Law* (2012) 331.

[60] ECJ Case C-265/95, *Commission v France* [1997] ECR I-6959, Recs 30–32.

[61] ECJ Case C-275/06, *Promusicae* [2008] ECR I-271, Rec. 70.

[62] But see AG Trstenjak in Case C-282/10, *Dominguez*, at para. 71.

[63] ECJ Case C-89/07, *Messner* [2009] ECR I-7315; Opinion of AG Trstenjak, at 91 and 108, and Rec. 29 of the judgment.

[64] Weatherill, 'The principles of civil law as a basis for interpreting the legislative acquis', 6 *ERCL* (2010) 74.

[65] ECJ Case C-415/11, *Mohamed Aziz*, judgment of 14 March, not yet published. Comment by Micklitz, 'Unfair Contract Terms—Public Interest Litigation before European Courts—Case C-415/11 Mohamed Aziz', in E. Terryn, G. Straetmans, and V. Colaert (eds), *Landmark Cases of EU Consumer Law: in Honour of Jules Stuyck* (2013) 615.

In her conclusion, Cherednychenko expresses support for integrating fundamental rights in the making and application of European private law. However, she equally warns against an unbridled constitutionalization, which moves sensitive political and socio-economic issues away from the legislative process. I am rather sceptical of the hope that the EU legislator will establish deeper consumer rights in financial services. None of the EU directives dealing with financial services for consumers has established effective EU rights and remedies. *Mohamed Aziz* was decided under Directive 93/13/EEC on unfair terms. The majority of references to the CJEU—normally without a visible fundamental rights dimension—is based on directives with a broad scope of application.[66]

F. The Impact of Constitutionalization of IP Controversies on the Substance, the Remedies, and the Procedure of Private Law (C. Godt)

Godt's topic is the constitutionalization of intellectual property (IP) rights. The link to private law is not immediately visible. Already, the relationship between IP rights and fundamental rights is a difficult one and not yet widely discussed, at least not in the European context.[67] Integrating the private law dimension into the discourse looks like an opening for a new book. It takes Godt two steps to build the bridge, first via the growing but to a large extent potential impact of the Charter of Fundamental Rights on the way in which conflicts around IP rights are shaped and debated—the reconstruction in 'a democratic and deliberative debate on modern European IP conflicts which arise from the societal transformation towards information societies embedded in global markets'; and secondly, by transferring these findings to private law relations.

Constitutionalization of IP rights, this is Godt's credo, means first and foremost a readjustment of the deeper foundations of property rights, from the idea that restrictions to IP rights are the exception to the rule to the modern approach promoted but not yet really cemented in *Promusicae*,[68] *Scarlet*,[69] and *Oracle*[70]—where the CJEU grants the exceptions fundamental rights status and puts them on a par with IP rights. However, there is said to be a notable difference between IP rights and the pillars of private law, private autonomy, and contractual freedom. She writes: 'IP is in essence regulatory. The right only comes into existence when regulatory requirements are met.' This suggests that freedom of contract and private autonomy are not constituted through regulation, at least a debatable consequence, as Collins made clear.[71]

With reference to Van Overwalle, Godt asks: 'do IP and Human Rights "collide" or do they co-exist and further each other'? This question is the subject of discussion at the international level, but not yet at the European level. The difference between the international and the European discourse on human rights results from the Charter of Fundamental Rights, which is meant to constitute individually enforceable rights, independent from state action, either directly or indirectly, if the diverse principles are concretized via secondary community law so as to make them enforceable.

[66] Kas and Micklitz, 'Rechtsprechungsübersicht zum Europäischen Vertrags- und Deliktsrecht (2008–2013)', *Europäisches wirtschafts und steuerrecht* (*EWS*) (2013) issues 9 and 10.

[67] See the contributions in F. W. Grosheide (ed), *Intellectual Property and Human Rights: a Paradox* (2010).

[68] ECJ Case C-275/06, *Promusicae* [2008] ECR I-271.

[69] ECJ Case C-70/10, *Scarlet*, judgment of 24 November 2011, not yet published.

[70] ECJ Case C-128/11, *UsedSoft v Oracle*, judgment of 3 July 2012, not yet published.

[71] In a similar vein, H. Collins in this volume.

Seven factual IP controversies stand out because of their relevance: (1) Articles 16, 11, and 8 EUCFR and enforcement measures against providers—the trilateral balance of copyright, freedom to operate business, data protection, freedom of information in *Scarlet* and *Netlog*;[72] (2) Article 1 and 2 EUCFR and embryonic stem cells—the human embryo cannot be less protected in research than in a commercial setting, which implies recognition of the German definition of life as beginning with the merging of the germ cells;[73] (3) Article 3(2) EUCFR and diagnostics—the *Myriad* case, access of patients and public hospitals to a test kit which indicates a statistical predetermination for breast cancer; (4) Article 3(2) EUCFR and tissue banks—the question of whether the donating individual has the power to veto the filing of patents based on her material; (5) Article 35 EUCFR and compulsory licensing—access to drugs against AIDS; (6) food security/food quality—the right to choose between genetically modified and unmodified products, the right to security; and (7) cultural autonomy and community rights to their medicinal and plant knowledge, their drawings, and their music.

In each of the seven factual controversies, Godt demonstrates how the reconstruction of the conflicts in fundamental rights language opens the discourse from a bilateral conflict between the holder and the user to a societal and public conflict about competing legal positions and values. In line with G. Resta, she observes a bipolar regime: 'intangible aspects of identity are increasingly protected against commercialization of property rules, whereas the corporate elements are protected through liability rules'.[74] It is worth noting the difference between Colombi Ciacchi's fact patterns and Godt's groups' factual controversies. Colombi Ciacchi identifies a critical mass of cases, which allows for a tentative structuring, whilst Godt has just a set of concrete problems at hand.

In her concluding remarks on the interplay between IP rights and fundamental rights, Godt focuses on the novel public/private interface via 'the access challenge' (access to information or technology which lies in the hands of the property rights holder) and preceding entitlements (e.g. homeowners hold a right to their home's façade and pictures thereof which are to be respected by Google Street View). This could be understood as a first attempt to move from controversies to fact patterns, at least in the relationship between IP rights and human rights/fundamental rights.

In a second step, Godt transfers her findings on reconceptualized and fundamental rights loaded IP rights to European private law. Constitutionalization of IP rights, this is the message, might serve as just another example to conceive of European private law not as modelled by freedom of contract but as a body of law embedded in regulatory policies. The seven factual controversies can be associated with what I have termed elsewhere as 'European regulatory private law'.[75] They all bear a particular regulatory dimension and they all show that there is a link between IP rights and private law, a link which is all too often forgotten and which has not yet gained much attention in the analysis of the relationship between EU law and private law.[76]

Godt distinguishes four different layers of constitutionalization: (1) the impact on *substantive* private law via scope, patentability, exceptions, and limitations—examples 2, 3, 7; (2) the emergence of new *remedies*—example 1; and (3) new forms

[72] ECJ Case C-360/10, *Netlog*, judgment of, 16 February 2012, not yet published.

[73] ECJ Case C-34/10, *Brüstle*, judgment of 18 October 2011, not yet published.

[74] Resta, 'The New Frontiers of Personality Rights and the Problem of Commodification: European and Comparative Perspectives', 26 *Tulane European and Civil Law Forum* (2011) 33, at 54.

[75] H.-W. Micklitz and Y. Svetiev (eds), *A Self-Sufficient European Private Law—A Viable Concept*, EUI Working Paper Law 2012/31.

[76] E. Steindorff, *EG-Vertrag und Privatrecht* (1996).

of *standing*—examples 2, 3, 5; (4) a new institutional design of how and by whom upcoming conflicts are decided, by the CJEU and/or by a Unitary Patent Court—example 7. The Charter, she notes, will 'presumably become the central reference for IP conflicts'.

The links to more traditional forms of constitutionalized private law are easy to demonstrate. The scope of EU law decides over the applicability of the fundamental rights. When IP holders are made the addressees of fundamental rights, which happens when IP and fundamental rights are put on a par with each other, the distinction between the public and the private, on which Collins insists, becomes blurred. It equally shows that private power approved through the official recognition of the EU legislator might be balanced against fundamental rights. One might even wonder whether and to what extent a fundamental rights bound property rights holder forms an integral part of Comandé's shadow citizenship.

G. The Implications of Article 47 EUCFR as a Self-Standing Remedy (C. Mak)

Mak looks into 'Rights and Remedies: Article 47 EUCFR and Effective Judicial Protection in European Private Law Matters'. This contribution shifts the focus entirely to the enforcement side. Whereas rights, remedies, and procedures—to use the terminology coined by W. van Gerven[77]—are already discussed in connection with the substance of European private law, contract law, labour law, financial services, and IP law, Mak asks what is added by Article 47 EUCFR to the effective judicial protection of private law interests. Her assumption is that the hotly debated distinction between vertical and horizontal direct effect is of little value as Article 47 EUCFR is said to integrate the horizontal relationship into the vertical institutional framework. This consequence questions the positions taken by Collins, Colombi Ciacchi, Bell, and Cherednychenko.

Article 47 EUCFR may even impose a positive duty on courts, provided an appropriate methodology can be found which respects the reach of the *Schutzgebotsfunktion* (protective function) (Canaris).[78] Inspiration for the shaping of remedies and procedures under Article 47 EUCFR can be drawn from *Alassini*[79] and the *ex officio* case law in consumer contract law[80] as well as, and maybe even more so, from *Kadi*[81] (with regard to procedure) and *Fuss v Stadt Halle*[82] (with regard to remedies). *Kadi* and *Fuss v Stadt Halle* demonstrate the potential of cross-fertilization between different fields of EU law; transferring Article 47 EUCFR reasoning from the outside—*Kadi* and *Fuss v Stadt Halle*—into private law relations.

In the potential search for a judge-made 'European Law on Remedies',[83] Mak identifies six dimensions of Article 47 EUCFR where a clarification is needed: (1) its place

[77] Van Gerven, 'Of Rights, Remedies and Procedure', 37 *Common Market Law Review (CMLRev)* (2001) 501.

[78] Following Calliess, 'Die Leistungsfähigkeit des Untermaßverbotes als Kontrollmaßstab grundrechtlicher Schutzpflichten', in R. Grote et al. (eds), *Die Ordnung der Freiheit: Festschrift für Christian Starck zum siebzigsten Geburtstag* (2007) 204.

[79] ECJ Joined Cases C-317-320/08, *Alassini* [2010] ECR I-2213.

[80] See Kas and Micklitz, *supra* note 66.

[81] ECJ Joined Cases C-402/05 P and 415/05, *Kadi* [2008] ECR I-6351.

[82] ECJ Case C-243/09, *Fuss v Stadt Halle* [2005] ECR I-2579.

[83] Mak, 'The ECJ between the individual citizen and the Member States—A plea for a judge-made European law on remedies', in B. de Witte and H.-W. Micklitz (eds), *The ECJ and the Autonomy of the Member States* (2012) 349.

between the older means of effective judicial protection via the ECHR and the new remedies enshrined in the EUCFR; (2) its relation to the division of labour between national and EU institutions—EU remedies vs national remedies; (3) the procedure guaranteeing effective judicial protection itself—what happens if the CJEU does not offer effective judicial protection?; (4) the relationship between the CJEU and the ECtHR—whether EU citizens have standing before the ECtHR against judgments of the CJEU; (5) the constitutionalizing effects on European private law adjudication—who has the last say?—and (6) the relationship between the regimes of collective and individual rights.

Whilst Mak sees some potential for Article 47 to be used to shape effective judicial protection, she is equally concerned about the limits on the production of the public good through litigation and not through democratic opinion building.[84] *Viking* and *Mangold* stand out as controversial examples from the area of fundamental freedoms; *Alassini*, which was based on Article 47 EUCFR, raised the expectation that the Charter might provide access to justice not only via alternative dispute resolution (ADR).

3. Preliminary Considerations on the Future of Constitutionalized Private Law

The various contributions in this volume clearly demonstrate that a change has taken place, at the national and at the European level. Private law is no longer immune to the intrusion of fundamental and human rights—if it ever was. Whilst member states and the EU are driving the process by adopting ever more concrete and more comprehensive lists of human and fundamental rights, at the national, the European, and international level with overlapping content, the true and key players in this development are the national and European courts. This is why I will first paint a scenario of judicial activism versus judicial restraint. Where should a constitutionalized private law be located in the overall system of the European legal order? This is my second point of concern. Last but not least, I will try to outline—based on the seven contributions—five key elements around which a constitutionalized European private law seems to be built. These are preliminary considerations, which deserve further research and further development.

A. Private Law and Human/Fundamental Rights—Courts as Substitutes

Constitutionalization of private law at the EU level serves two purposes, a political function—identity/society building—and a social function—making the EU 'better', 'more just'. The ECHR and the Charter of Fundamental Rights bring the ECtHR and the CJEU to a prominent position. The effects will be redoubled once the EU has joined the ECHR. By now the focus is directed towards the role and function of the CJEU.

Again, it might well be that the CJEU could become the victim of its own success, again because the judicial activism in the building of the European legal order, even in the building of the European constitutional charter, cannot compensate for the

[84] Mak, 'Europe-Building through Private Law. Lessons from Constitutional Theory', 8 *ERCL* (2012) 326.

democratic deficit or, in more cautions terms, the lack of the 'Political' in the middle of the European discourse. There are visible signs that the CJEU is more ready than ever to embark on an unknown journey—compensating not only for the social deficit of the EU but also for the political deficit. However, the CJEU runs a high risk. It can only succeed in promoting a European identity and a European society if it accepts a role similar to the GCC, which served the German citizens as a substitute for politically incorrect patriotism. Habermas[85] coined the term *Verfassungspatriotismus*—constitutional patriotism.

Are we observing a similar move by the CJEU or at least a move in that direction? This is what some of the contributions tell us—Comandé with regard to the compensation of the political deficit, Colombi Ciacchi, Bell, Cherednychenko, and Mak with regard to the compensation of the social deficit. They all emphasize the downside of the development. But let us assume for a moment that the findings and the predictions confirm a general trend. It would mean that the CJEU is becoming ever more intrusive and would narrow considerably the leeway granted to national courts in applying the authoritative interpretation of EU law to the facts of the case. So far, the CJEU has stayed away, in the aftermath of *Barber* and *Heininger*, from 'solving' the social problems presented to it via the preliminary reference procedure by way of a European top-down decision. *Barber* had a clear human rights dimension—violation of the equality principle; this was less visible in *Heininger*, although one could easily build bridges to the famous *Bürgschafts* judgment of the GCC. *Mohamed Aziz* could turn into a litmus test for the CJEU. Its judgment raised high expectations by those Spanish citizens who lost their homes in the aftermath of the crisis. What if the Spanish courts and the Spanish authorities, the national government and the national Parliament are unwilling to accept the guidance provided by the CJEU on how the respective EU rules should be interpreted—to remedy unjustified evictions? What if it comes to nothing in the end? In *Barber*, as in *Heininger*, a forceful and—seen through the eyes of the victims—powerful support for their position vanished in the haze of follow-up references that tried to receive judicial confirmation from the CJEU, which looked all too promising. In the end, high hopes ended in deep disappointment and disillusionment. At least the Equal Opportunities Commission in the UK learnt its lesson. In *Heininger*, only a few consumers were compensated by the German courts. The majority ended in a deadlock—a nice looking European remedy which could not be enforced nationally, or, if enforced, would put them in an even worse situation.

If the CJEU were to give up its reluctance and intrude ever deeper into Spanish procedural law and not only this, if it also provided ever stronger guidance on what the Spanish government, or even broader the Spanish state, would be obliged to do in light of the (quasi-)constitutionalized private law rules—quasi because so far neither the Advocate General nor the CJEU refer directly to the Charter on Fundamental Rights—, the political implications of such a judicial success would be more than ambiguous. If the evictions were revoked, if the evicted could return to their homes, the CJEU would certainly be regarded by those who benefit from such judicial activism as having rescued their belief in a just society. What a wonderful result for European identity and society building! But at what a price! Not an authoritative but an authoritarian judgment would have struck down all the careful boundaries that the Treaties of Rome until Lisbon had erected, endlessly confirmed and defended in the national political fora. Crossing these boundaries would endanger the whole architecture of the EU Treaties. Justice would

[85] D. Sternberger and J. Habermas, *Verfassungspatriotismus. Eine vergleichende Darstellung der Begriffsbestimmung* (2010).

be achieved through a non-democratic authoritarian court which claims to be just and more legitimate than the national parliaments and governments.

It is hard to imagine that the CJEU would overstep these boundaries in a hard case like *Mohamed Aziz*, where the unheard voices of those who suffer most from the economic and Euro crisis have found a forum. There is no alternative to a political process, however difficult, burdensome, and slow it might be. This conclusion, if it is correct, has far-reaching consequences on the role and function of the constitutionalization of private law via human rights and fundamental rights, via national and European courts, operating in tandem or even side by side in the building of a European identity and in developing a social Europe. The CJEU may take strong positions, but the prime addressees of judgments are and should be the member states, their courts and their competent bodies in charge of 'applying' the European rules to the case at issue. Even the best and most promising 'just' constitutionalized rulings require the national enforcement authorities and courts to awaken the European rulings to life.[86] This might not be a very satisfying result, at least not for those who identify courts as the appropriate rule-makers in the multilevel structure of the EU. However, if the 'political' should not be sacrificed to the benefit of the judicial, there is no other way out of the dilemma.

B. Merging Constitutional Traditions and General Principles of Civil Law

It is tempting to strive for a kind of structure in the constitutionalized European private law, either horizontally cutting across the various fields or by designing a constitutionalized employment contract, consumer contract, or financial services contract. The key question would remain the same: What should the place be for such a constitutionalized private law in the overall edifice of European Union Law?

The CJEU has referred in a number of cases to the '(general) principles of civil law' (not private law), a development which has led to a real flood of publications.[87] Whether the CJEU will continue down this path is still open. After a series of decisions with varying references to the 'general principles of civil law',[88] it seems as if the CJEU has become more reluctant to utilize this technique, and may even be rethinking how to position the 'general principles of civil law'. A possible way out might be to line up the 'constitutional traditions common to the Member States'[89] with the 'general principles of civil law' in the search for a common denominator in the ongoing constitutionalization of private law. What if only those principles of civil law which enjoy a quasi-constitutional status via their upgrading through human rights and fundamental rights could be termed 'general' principles or even 'principles' at all?

[86] See De Witte, 'The Nature of the Legal Order', in P. Craig and G. de Burca (eds), *The Evolution of EU Law* (1999) 177, at 209.

[87] Hesselink, 'The General Principles of Civil Law: Their Nature, Roles and Legitimacy', in D. Leczykiewicz and S. Weatherill (eds), *The Involvement of EU Law in Private Law Relationships* (2013) 131.

[88] In ECJ, 10 April 2008, Case C-412/06, *Hamilton* [2008] ECR I-2382, Rec. 42: 'general principles of civil law'; Case C-489/07, *Messner* [2009] ECR I-7315, Rec. 29: 'general rules of civil law'; also opinion of AG Trstenjak, at paras 91 and 108; C-101/08, *Audiolux* [2009] ECR I-9823, Rec. 52: 'general principle of equal treatment of minority shareholders'; opinion of the AG: 'general principles of equal treatment of shareholders'.

[89] ECJ Case 44/79, *Hauer* [1979] ECR I-3727, at 15.

Such an understanding could, if feasible, solve two problems: (a) clarifying the *role and function* of the general principles of civil law in the overall structure of European private law as a safety net for the already existing European private law acquis and (b) concretizing the *substance* of the 'general' 'principles'. The 'merger' would allow for reducing possible elements of the 'general principles', thereby implicitly upgrading their importance. Giving the 'general principles of civil law' a constitutional twist could build a barrier against attempts to turn each and every open question in European private law into a matter of 'general principle' and/or into a constitutional, i.e. human and fundamental rights, issue. Such an approach could equally avoid the awkward debate around the different positioning of 'the general principles' in continental codified law and common law.[90]

C. Key Elements of a Constitutionalized European Private Law

On the basis of the different contributions in this volume it seems feasible to outline a set of elements which deserve to be studied in greater depth.[91] The intention, however, is not to try to show the potential in using fundamental rights with regard to certain identifiable key constitutional elements of private law in the future, but to describe the state of the art—the development as it stands at present. These key elements might form the basis of concretizing 'constitutional principles of European private law'.

1. *Status*—in private law, there is usually no connection between the legal subject and his citizenship. As long as the parties to a contract are operating within the same legal order, nationality does not matter. If it is a cross-border transaction, the well-settled mechanisms of international private law come into play. EU law prohibits any discrimination in private law transactions based on nationality.[92] Bell has raised the question whether there is a human/fundamental right *to be treated as a worker*. This would imply the feasibility to design key constitutional elements of how a worker can be distinguished from a self-employed entrepreneur. His question could easily be extended to whether there is a right *to be treated as a consumer*, in particular if European Union law imposes obligations on the consumer which she realistically cannot fulfil. Can the consumer argue under reference to fundamental rights that the status of a consumer implies a structural weakness in the sense that the GCC did in the famous *Bürgschafts* judgment? The same logic must apply to questions on the constitutional characteristics *of an employer, a company or a supplier, an SME*? Comandé adds an additional layer to the discussion by taking all the rhetoric of the consumer citizen—and in parallel the worker citizen, the employer citizen, and the supplier citizen—seriously.[93] Tying the economic activity in employment or consumer relations to what he calls *shadow citizenship* grants the status of the parties to a contract of whatever type a constitutional dimension, as they are part of the identity and society building.

In hard legal terms, the problems usually show up when legal rights are bound to a particular predefined status—the personal scope of application. This is a typical approach of secondary EU law, which finds its deeper reasons in the doctrine of enumerated powers. In employment law, the findings are mixed. The CJEU seems ready to use fundamental

[90] More generally Lord Goff, 'The Future of the Common Law', 46 *International and Comparative Law Quarterly (ICLQ)* (1997) 745.

[91] See Reich, 'General Principles of European Union Civil Law' (2013, forthcoming).

[92] See ECJ Case C-281/98, *Agnonese* [2000] ECR I-4139.

[93] Everson and Joerges, *supra* note 57; Davies, *supra* note 57.

rights to broaden the notion of the worker when she is in need of protection because the principle of equal treatment has been violated. In consumer law, the CJEU, quite to the contrary, starts from a rather narrow concept, which might make sense in the Brussels Regulation but not necessarily in substantive consumer law.[94] One reason might be that EU law leaves the decision on the personal scope of consumer protection either implicitly, via minimum protection rules, or explicitly, as in the Consumer Rights Directive,[95] to the member states. The strange consequence then is that only full harmonization of the personal scope of application of consumer law allows the CJEU to infer fundamental rights as a means of extending the scope of application.

2. *Access to services*—in a more traditional understanding of private law, accessibility is a matter for public or administrative legislation. In the EU context, access to services gains a more prominent position. Access is a necessary precondition in order to be able to participate in the benefits of the Internal Market. *Access* to *shadow citizenship* for persons not bearing the correct name—access to the labour market for women, handicapped workers, students, *access* to financial consumer services, to a bank account, to consumer credit, *access* to universal services more broadly, *access* to information barred via intellectual property rights, *access* to justice if one understands justice as a service which has to be delivered by practising lawyers or by out-of-court settlement bodies—all these 'access issues' can easily be identified as a strong common denominator throughout the contributions. In *Sky Austria*[96] the CJEU upgraded access to information to the constitutional level.

3. *Information, transparency, accountability*—European private law has heavily promoted the ideology that information serves as an appropriate means to compensate for the asymmetry between the parties to a contract, less so in labour law, much more in consumer law and financial services. So far, however, it seems that setting access to services aside where information might be needed to participate in the Internal Market, there is no evidence in the case law of the CJEU to upgrade information or at least a certain type of information to a higher constitutional level. Law and economics, behavioural economics, and bounded rationality could be used to distinguish relevant from irrelevant information. Some information might be so relevant for the contracting parties that it could be reconstructed in fundamental rights language.

Transparency, quite to the contrary, has gained importance in the CJEU case law not only but in particular in the field of contract terms.[97] Transparency, however, has remained so far at the 'normal' level of private law. The CJEU limits itself to taking transparency seriously so that it provides valuable information to the parties to the contract, which allows them to make effective use of their rights and remedies built into the contract. Similar to the information paradigm, clarification would be needed as to what kind of transparency we are talking about—competition or contractual transparency[98] —and once we are clear, whether transparency can be graded. Disclosure of information has thin borderlines.

[94] See, on the case law of the CJEU, N. Reich, *supra* note 39.

[95] Directive 2011/83/EU, OJ 2011 L 304/64, Rec. 13.

[96] Reich, 'Consumer/Citizen Access to Information—A new Fundamental Right under the EU Charter Case C-283/11 Österreich v. Österreichischer Rundfunk, Judgment of the Grand Chamber of 22.11.2013', in E. Terryn, G. Straetmans, and V. Colaert (eds), *Landmark Cases of EU Consumer Law: in Honour of Jules Stuyck* (2013) 35.

[97] ECJ Case C-92/11, *RWE Vertrieb v Verbraucherzentrale NRW*, judgment of 21 March 2013, not yet published.

[98] Micklitz, *supra* note 39, at 3.18.

Accountability would affect the making of the law, in particular when it comes to rules, which are developed by private or semi-private bodies[99] in the field of health and safety or in the fields of financial transactions. However, such cases have not yet reached the CJEU, at least not from the angle of accountability.

4. *Anti-discrimination and basic needs*—the principle of anti-discrimination or the principle of equality has found a well-settled place in employment law and employment contracts. Its transfer from employment contracts to insurance contracts in *Test-Achats*[100] and maybe to consumer law in fighting economic discrimination of the most vulnerable consumers raises much deeper questions on the relationship between contract law—where discrimination might lead to highly doubtful results—and competition law—which presupposes the legality and the legitimacy of economic discrimination.[101] Lifting anti-discrimination to the status of a general principle via human and fundamental rights inevitably leads to the question of what the economic constitution of the EU should look like. This then is indeed a constitutional issue of a higher level.

In *Messner*, the CJEU referred to 'good faith' as one of the general principles of civil law. It is hard to imagine that good faith could be given a constitutional standing in bridging the gap between the 'general principles of civil law' and 'the constitutional traditions common to the Member States'. What remains, however, can be observed in *Mohamed Aziz*,[102] where the CJEU did not refer explicitly to the Charter of Fundamental Rights, but used the 'right to housing' in the Charter as a means to interpret the fairness of standard terms in mortgage contracts. This is an elegant way to instrumentalize fundamental rights without explicitly granting supremacy of the Charter over contract law.

5. *Remedies*—a far-reaching consequence of the EUCFR would be to link the violation of a human or fundamental right to a right to claim compensation, as the Italian Constitutional Court has done.[103] The question then would be what kind of fundamental right in private law relations exists which could trigger such a claim for compensation. The well-known *Kadi* judgment, the freezing of financial resources of individuals and entities associated with Al-Qaeda, also touches upon private law matters.[104] Does an eventual violation of the right to be heard lead to a claim for compensation if Mr. Kadi is barred from making use of his—in so far illegally frozen—assets? What about Mr. Alassini, if he were barred from going to court? The CJEU recognized in that judgment the right of access to the court. In *Aziz*, the CJEU invented the right to injunctive relief, which obliges the Spanish state to make remedies available that allow for connecting enforcement and declaratory proceedings. Can Mr. Aziz claim compensation because that right did not exist and therefore he had to leave his house? Who is the addressee of such a claim, if it exists—is it always the public authority, the state or can it be that an eventual remedy could also address the wrongdoer directly, if as in the case of Spain the Caixa bank belongs de facto to the Spanish state?

[99] ECJ Case C-171/11, *Frabo*, judgment of 31 December 2012, not yet published.

[100] ECJ Case C-236/09, *Test-Achats* [2011] ECR I-773.

[101] Inaugural lecture by H. Schweitzer, 'Diskriminierungsverbote im Privat- und Wettbewerbsrecht' (25 February 2011), inaugural lecture at the University of Mannheim (*Antrittsvorlesung an der Universität Mannheim*), unpublished.

[102] ECJ Case C-415/11, *Aziz*, judgment of 14 March 2013, not yet published.

[103] See the reference in the contribution of A. Colombi Ciacchi in this volume.

[104] This is an important observation by C. Mak in her contribution.

2

On the (In)compatibility of Human Rights Discourse and Private Law

Hugh Collins

1. Introduction

Are human rights and private law compatible? Can respect for human rights be seamlessly integrated into the doctrines of private law? Or, like oil and water, will the fundamental rights declared in constitutions and international conventions never mix properly with private law? And if integration or coherence of legal doctrine is unattainable, does that incompatibility mean that we should resist the temptation to harness the human rights bandwagon to the august steeds of private law? All these questions about the application of human rights law to private law provoke puzzlement and controversy in equal measure.

The puzzle is how human rights law can have any application to the fields of private law, such as contract, tort, and property. The rights protected in leading conventions on human rights and national constitutions focus on civil liberties and political freedoms. In most instances their original purpose was to protect individuals and groups against the abuse of power by governments. The rights secure individual liberty against oppressive measures such as detention without trial and slavery; and they protect the right to form political associations, freedom of speech, and other essential conditions of a democratic system of government. The puzzle is how these civil and political rights might have any connection to such mundane matters as the enforcement of a guarantee of a loan to a business, the commission of a wrong causing injury to another, the dismissal of a worker for misconduct, or the divestment of property rights by a will. Yet human rights discourse and legal reasoning has played a decisive role in judicial decisions in such cases.[1] In Europe, we are currently witnessing in many jurisdictions a transplant of the human rights discourses of constitutional and public law into private law. Surely, it may be asked, the doctrines of private law will reject this transplant of human rights law as an alien species of legal reasoning with incompatible values and legal concepts?

As for the controversy that the insertion of human rights law into private law often provokes, the objections of the critics vary in their emphasis according to the particularities of national legal traditions. Many of the concerns voiced in civil law systems are summed up well by Oliver Gerstenberg (before he disagrees with them):

> The extension of fundamental rights between and among private (non-state) actors would thus: (i) pose a threat to private law's libertarian core of private autonomy (by placing private actors, by way of *judicial fiat*, under the same duties as public bodies acting in the common

[1] *Bürgschaft*, BVerfG 19 October 1993, BVerf 89, 214 (business loan); *Campbell v MGN Ltd* [2004] UKHL 22, [2004] 2 AC 457 (civil wrong); *Palomo Sánchez v Spain*, ECHR (2011) *Reports* 2011,1319; *Pla and Puncernau v Andorra*, ECHR (2004) 42 EHRR (2006) 25 (interpretation of a will).

interest); and, at the same time, (ii) result (if carried to a logical endpoint) in a sweeping judicial usurpation of legislative prerogatives in determining the boundaries of spheres of private autonomy, thereby displacing or even overriding the policy choices of [the] statutory legislator; and (iii) shift authority to interpret private law's core concepts such as property, contract, tort from ordinary (and specialised) courts to constitutional (and generalist) courts, and thereby render private law redundant and superfluous...[2]

In these criticisms there is a combination of concerns about the imposition of unwelcome (illiberal) values by forcing individuals to comply with public standards of political correctness, an overreaching by the judiciary into a field properly left to a democratic legislatures and a question about the competence of judges who have expertise in constitutional and human rights law to refashion private law. There may even be an underlying concern that public law and human rights law is swallowing up private law. If so, not only will the distinctive methods and traditions of private law be undermined or even obliterated, but the imperialism of human rights lawyers may lead eventually to the demise of separate departments of private law in some European universities. Though sharing some of those concerns, in the common law tradition critics emphasize the potential disruption to the settled rules and principles of private law that may be provoked by the transplantation of human rights law into the laws of contract, tort, and property.

While both the puzzle and the controversy described above give voice to valid concerns about the compatibility between human rights law and private law, further reflection on the issue reduces the force of the stark oppositions commonly drawn between human rights and private law. Private law is surely not opposed to the values and principles embodied in the terse statements of human or fundamental rights found in constitutions, conventions, and charters. On the contrary, many of those values influenced the doctrines of private law. The individual right to liberty may be discovered at the core of such key ideas of private law as freedom of contract and protections in tort against injury to the person. Similarly, private law provides most of the rules that protect the interest in or right to peaceful enjoyment of possessions; and tort law protects vital interests such as the right to privacy and through the law of defamation sets the limits on the misuse of the right to freedom of expression. It is certainly possible to argue that private law should be understood as an earlier embodiment of many of the values that also inspired declarations of human rights.[3]

That claim about the similarity of values (though not the mode of expression in the discourses of human rights) can be true even when we acknowledge that there is a significant difference in the way in which human rights function in public and private law. In a public law context, the rights are granted to individuals and associations; the law requires the government and agencies of the state to comply with those rights in the absence of compelling reasons to the contrary such as national security. Rights are never accorded to the state. In a private law context, however, both parties to a dispute are private individuals or organized groups, so both parties can appeal to the values underlying human rights such as individual liberty and dignity, respect for private property, and the protection of private life from interference. So there is a sharp difference in the function of rights in the

[2] Gerstenberg, 'Private Law and the New European Constitutional Settlement', 10 *ELJ* (2004) 766, at 769.

[3] E.g. Barak, 'Constitutional Human Rights and Private Law', in D. Friedmann and D. Barak-Erez (eds), *Human Rights in Private Law* (2001) 13, at 21–22; Smits, 'Private Law and Fundamental Rights: A Sceptical View', in T. Barkhuysen and S. Lindenbergh (eds), *Constitutionalisation of Private Law* (2006) 9; R. Stevens, *Torts and Rights* (2007).

two branches of the legal system: in public law rights serve principally as a defensive weapon against infringements by the state; in private law rights (often described as interests) are positive claims that must be balanced between the parties. Nevertheless, with apparently only minor changes in terminology, private law can be viewed plausibly as a branch of the law where, through the learning of centuries, the competing interests and rights of individuals have been reconciled into a settled scheme of codes in civil law systems and judicial precedents in the common law countries.

It may be the case that private law has traditionally shunned any explicit reference to the discourse of human rights because it originated in the one-sided claims of public law and therefore seemed unsuitable to the need for a balancing of the competing interests and rights of two formally equal parties. Yet such discomfort with the language of human rights does not contradict the view that the same values that prioritize individual interests and liberties underpin both public law and private law. The relation between human rights law and private law is closer than is commonly supposed by lawyers, but the connection is not a simple conduit. Human rights influence the content of private law through a network of connections that transmit and diffuse impulses.

Furthermore, to acknowledge that common values concerning the importance of individual interests or rights have informed both public law and private law is not to say that private law can be reduced to an articulation of individual rights. Rights may have influenced private law, but they are not the sole source of principles. Indeed, univocal theories of private law or parts of private law that attempt to explain the entire corpus of legal rules by reference to a single idea, whether it be rights, wealth maximization, or some other moral principle, inevitably fail to account for the complexity and richness of the law. All of these incommensurable discourses have probably played a part in shaping legal doctrine, including the ideas of liberty, dignity, and equal treatment that form the backbone of claims for human rights. To understand both the compatibility and the incompatibility of human rights with private law, we need to accept the rich tapestry of private law as it stands, not diminish it by reductionist interpretations that conveniently confine its role to the protection of individual rights.

This investigation of the compatibility of human rights with private law commences with a brief survey of how in many jurisdictions private law has fallen under the searching examination of the spotlight of human rights law (section 2). We then examine more closely why the introduction of explicit discussions of human rights into private law relations provokes such puzzlement. We call this: 'the puzzle of horizontality' (section 3). That discussion leads to the need to consider different theories regarding the structural relation within a legal system between public and private law. Part of the puzzle of horizontality derives from uncertainty about the location of fundamental rights in the architecture of a legal system and the consequent relation between those rights and other branches of the law. Are fundamental rights located in public law, private law, both, or somewhere else entirely (section 4)? The next step by which to discern the structure of the connections is to understand the reasons for the distinction that is commonly drawn between the direct effectiveness of fundamental rights in the sphere of public law and their limitation to indirect effect in the context of private law. Why is it that in private law it is usually asserted that fundamental rights, if they are effective at all, will only have an indirect effect on the law (section 5)?

Answers those questions permit us to return to the puzzle of horizontality with a clearer perspective and analysis. We can reconsider some of the criticisms and puzzles posed about the insertion of fundamental rights into private law. In particular, will the application of fundamental rights to private law disrupt legal doctrines with unforeseeable and probably unwelcome results? How can the competing rights of individuals be reconciled if not through the traditional doctrines of private law (section 6)? We can then address a problem of translation that arises during the transplant of constitutional and human rights into private law: should these fundamental rights mean different things according to whether they arise in a public law or a private law context (section 7)?

Whether or not the core meaning of the rights remains constant in the context of private law, it is evident that some practical differences will necessarily arise. In the first place, when rights are qualified by reference to other legitimate interests, such as other rights or legitimate goals of public policy, how should the test of justification be formulated in private law? Is the normal public law approach of the test of proportionality compatible with the mode of reasoning in private law (section 8)? A further difference may emerge when we consider the paradoxical challenge mentioned above that the insertion of human rights into private law will force the imposition of illiberal values on private actors rather than according them a wide margin of liberty (section 9)? We can also address the relevance of derogation or consent to the withdrawal or sacrifice of rights in a private law context, which appears rather different from the traditional rejection of derogations in public law (section 10). Finally, we should consider what contribution, if any, the application of fundamental rights to private law will make to ensuring fairness between the parties in a private law context. In public law the aim of rights is to protect the weaker party, the ordinary citizen, against the greater, collectivized power of the state. Does this protection of a weaker party also apply to the application of human rights to private law (section 11)?

In the conclusion, the central claim that will be advanced is that the application of rights in a private law context demands a shift in the emphasis of the underlying philosophical foundations of rights. Using the distinction commonly drawn between negative liberties and positive liberty or autonomy, the argument is that whilst liberal theories of the state tend to employ both sorts of foundations for theories of rights, both negative and positive liberty, in public law the context usually requires a focus on the values of negative liberty, whereas in private law the emphasis tends towards a more positive conception of liberty or autonomy. That contrast ultimately explains, it is suggested, the different way that rights function in the different contexts of public law and private law (section 12). It also explains how human rights or fundamental rights are simultaneously compatible and incompatible with private law.

2. The Growing Impact of Human Rights on Private Law

A. National Constitutions

Since there are several excellent studies of the increasing frequency and range of the application of human rights law to private law in many European countries,[4] there is no need here to rehearse in detail the extent of this jurisprudence. Most European countries

[4] E.g. D. Oliver and J. Fedtke (eds), *Human Rights and the Private Sphere: A Comparative Study* (2007); C. Mak, *Fundamental Rights in European Contract Law: A Comparison of the Impact of Fundamental Rights on Contractual Relationships in Germany, the Netherlands, Italy and England* (2008); S. Grundmann (ed), *Constitutional Values and European Contract Law* (2008); G. Brüggemeier, A. Columbi Ciacchi, and G. Comandé (eds), *Fundamental Rights and Private Law in the European Union. Volume 1: A Comparative Overview* (2010); O. O. Cherednychenko, *Fundamental Rights, Contract Law and the Protection of the Weaker Party: A Comparative Analysis of the Constitutionalisaton of*

acknowledge the existence of some potential impact of human rights law on private law, even if the effect is very weak. In many European jurisdictions, such as Denmark, Italy, and Greece, the national constitution provides explicitly that rights that may be inserted into private law and have horizontal effect between individuals. More commonly, the impact of human rights law contained in national constitutions and similar documents is derived indirectly, by the courts acknowledging that those values and fundamental rights should have a 'radiating effect' (to use the German phrase)[5] on the entire legal system. That radiating effect may steer courts towards a particular interpretation of the rules, principles, and general clauses of private law, or it may require a court to credit those values and rights with special weight when carrying out a balancing exercise between the competing rights of the parties. We will consider many examples of such insertions of human rights law into private law below.

B. European Convention on Human Rights

In addition to national constitutions, in all jurisdictions in Europe the European Convention on Human Rights (ECHR) of the Council of Europe has an impact on private law.[6] This impact may occur because of the 'monist' view that international instruments form part of the national legal system (as in France), or less directly, as in Germany, because judges will respect decisions of the European Court of Human Rights (ECtHR) by means of compatible interpretations of domestic law. The impact of the ECHR is strengthened in some countries such as the United Kingdom by its express incorporation into national law and the imposition of a duty on all public authorities, including courts, to make decisions that are compatible with the ECHR.[7]

Given this influential role of the ECHR in guiding the application of human rights to private law, the approach of the ECtHR is pivotal. As an international court with a jurisdiction confined to the application of the ECHR to national governments, at first sight the ECtHR appears unlikely to become involved in domestic private law disputes. But the ECtHR may establish jurisdiction over such disputes by insisting that in accordance with Article 1 ECHR, which imposes an obligation on states to secure the protected rights and freedoms, national courts have a duty to protect the observance of convention rights by national law, so that any decision of a national court must be compliant with those rights.[8] Although a human rights issue is unlikely to arise in the ordinary run of private law cases, when a national court resolves a property dispute or provides an interpretation of a contract, as an agency of the state that must uphold the ECHR, a court must provide a resolution that conforms to the protected rights.

Contract Law, with Emphasis on Risky Financial Transactions (2007); D. Hoffman (ed), *The Impact of the UK Human Rights Act on Private Law* (2011); C. Busch and H. Schulte-Nölke (eds), *Fundamental Rights and Private Law* (2011); and the works cited above, *supra* note 3.

[5] This is the phrase used in some German constitutional theory to describe the influence of the Basic Law (and its rights) on all aspects of the legal system. See Kumm, 'Who is Afraid of the Total Constitution? Constitutional Rights as Principles and the Constitutionalization of Private Law', 7 *German Law Journal* (2006) 341; Fedtke, 'Germany: *Drittwirkung* in Germany', in D. Oliver and J. Fedtke (eds), *Human Rights and the Private Sphere: A Comparative Study* (2007) 125.

[6] As well as applying to all the member states of the European Union, the Convention applies to a further 20 states including Russia and Turkey.

[7] Human Rights Act 1998.

[8] Spielmann, 'The European Convention on Human Rights: The European Court of Human Rights', in D. Oliver and J. Fedtke (eds), *Human Rights and the Private Sphere: A Comparative Study* (2007) 427.

The question at the heart of *Pla and Puncernau v Andorra*,[9] for instance, concerned the interpretation of a will. Notwithstanding the deference that the ECtHR would normally show to national courts to determine the content of obligations under national private law, it insisted that the interpretation of the will by the national court, as part of the state, should be compatible with the convention rights. By this technique of reviewing decisions of national courts for fulfilment of the duty to ensure compliance of their judgments with convention rights, the ECtHR can in practice intervene in any private dispute once there has been a judgment by a national court.

The jurisdiction of the ECtHR is extended to governmental administrative actions and omissions, when the applicant argues that a failure of the government to take the measures which may be legitimately expected has resulted in a failure by the state to protect his or her convention rights from other private individuals.[10] In the case of environmental torts, for example, when an individual claims an interference by a private business with the right to privacy because the noise or fumes emitted by the business pose a risk to the health of the applicant, the ECtHR establishes jurisdiction when it is demonstrated that the public authorities have failed to take appropriate protective action,[11] or have failed to enforce the applicable environmental laws.[12] In such cases the ECtHR does not appear to require more from public authorities than for them to comply assiduously with domestic laws, so that the Convention is not used to create new private law rights but rather to uphold existing legal standards.[13]

C. Charter of Fundamental Rights of the European Union

Article 6 of the Treaty on European Union (TEU) declares that the Charter of Fundamental Rights of the European Union (EUCFR)[14] shall have the same legal effect as a Treaty between the member states. The EUCFR duplicates the civil and political rights of the ECHR, but also contains a list of social and economic rights that is strongly influenced by the European Social Charter of the Council of Europe. Yet Article 6 also insists that the Charter will not extend the competences of the European Union (EU), which suggests that, while respect for human rights is a condition of the lawfulness of EU acts including decisions on EU law by courts, individuals cannot invoke the Charter as an independent basis for a legal claim. Article 6 TEU adds that the EU will accede to the ECHR and that those convention rights, together with the constitutional traditions of member states, constitute general principles of EU law. From these complex and nuanced provisions,[15] it is evident that any court, including the Court of Justice of the EU (CJEU, formerly ECJ) and national courts, when applying any aspect of EU law, should interpret that EU provision in a manner that is compatible with the EUCFR,

[9] ECHR (2004) 42 EHRR (2006) 25.

[10] *Cyprus v Turkey*, ECHR (2001) *Reports* 2001-IV, 331; *Öneryildiz v Turkey*, ECHR (2004) 41 EHRR (2005) 325.

[11] *López-Ostra v Spain*, ECHR (1994) Series A, No. 330-C, 20 EHRR (1994) 277; *Guerra v Italy*, ECHR (1998) *Reports* 1998-I, 26 EHRR (1998) 357.

[12] *Moreno Gómez v Spain*, ECHR (2004) *Reports* 2004-X, 41 EHRR (2005) 40; *Fadeyeva v Russia*, ECHR (2005) *Reports* 2005-IV, 45 EHRR (2007) 10; *Giacomelli v Italy*, ECHR (2006) *Reports* 2006-XII, 45 EHRR (2007) 38.

[13] Nolan, 'Nuisance', in D. Hoffman (ed), *The Impact of the UK Human Rights Act on Private Law* (2011) 165, at 173.

[14] OJ 2007 C 303/1.

[15] In more detail: D. Chalmers, G. Davies, and G. Monti, *European Union Law* (2nd ed.; 2010), chapter 6.

including appropriate deference to the decisions of the ECtHR on similar rights in the ECHR.[16]

Although the EU lacks formal competence in the field of private law, there has been a creeping invasion of the field through legislation ostensibly designed to help to remove barriers to trade within the Internal Market.[17] Most noticeably, minimum standards of consumer protection law have been established with a view to encouraging consumers to purchase goods across borders.[18] The European Commission is now edging towards uniform consumer law or full harmonization, as in the proposed Regulation for an optional consumer sales law.[19] Similarly, patchy regulation has been applied to employment, initially with a view to avoiding unfair competition in capital markets, but more recently to provide workers with basic legal rights to protect them against the risks of social dumping.[20]

Even if European private law is not directly involved, more general market regulation may have consequences in private relations. Any national regulation of markets may be subject to challenge on the ground that it interferes with the fundamental market freedoms of the EU and competition law. Such challenges often raise questions about the enforceability of contracts. For the purpose of interpreting EU regulation of markets and what national constraints on the fundamental freedoms may be permitted, the CJEU can turn to the EUCFR and other human rights documents. The general principle applied is that where a member state tries to justify rules that are likely to interfere with the exercise of the fundamental freedoms, the justification in accordance with Community law must be interpreted in the light of general principles and fundamental rights.[21] For instance, in the *Omega* case,[22] the ECJ relied upon the protection of human rights and in particular the right to dignity to uphold a German restriction on the marketing of computer games containing simulated acts of violence against persons (even though the marketing of the games was perfectly lawful in their country of origin).

D. Social and Economic Rights

The analysis in this chapter concentrates on the civil and political rights protected by the ECHR and duplicated almost verbatim in the EUCFR. These rights are likely to have the greatest impact on private law because they are usually given legal force in national constitutions at least in the context of relations between a citizen and the state. Many jurisdictions also recognize to some extent social and economic rights, such as rights to health care, education, and workers' rights.[23] Many of these rights are included in the EUCFR, though often in guarded terms that curtail the substance of those rights to the

[16] EUCFR Art. 52(3) specifies this connection. Cf. Case C-540/03, *Parliament v Council (family reunification)* [2006] ECR I-5769, for remarkable deference to the ECtHR.

[17] E.g. L. Miller, *The Emergence of EU Contract Law: Exploring Europeanization* (2011); C. Twigg-Flesner, *The Europeanisation of Contract Law* (2008).

[18] E.g. Directive 2011/83, OJ 2011 L 304/64 on consumer rights.

[19] E.g. S. Weatherill, *EU Consumer Law and Policy* (2005).

[20] E.g. C. Barnard, *EC Employment Law*, (3rd ed.; 2006); B. Bercusson, *European Labour Law* (2nd ed.; 2009); A. C. L. Davies, *EU Labour Law* (2012).

[21] Case C-260/89, *Elliniki Radiophonia Tileorassi AE v Dimotiki Etairia Pliroforissis* [1991] ECR I-2925.

[22] Case C-36/02, *Omega Spielhallen- und Automatenaufstellungs-GmbH v Oberbürgermesterin der Bundesstadt Bonn* [2004] ECR I-9609.

[23] 'In fact, twenty-five out of the twenty-nine constitutions of the countries which now form the EU (or aspire to become members) have social rights.' Fabre, 'Social Rights in European Constitutions', in G. de Búrca and B. de Witte (eds), *Social Rights in Europe* (2005).

standard, no matter how inadequate, set by national legislation. At EU level there is also the declaration of the European Council of the Community Charter of the Fundamental Social Rights of Workers.[24]

In some national constitutions and in the EUCFR, some social and economic rights are expressed not as rights but as guiding or directive principles, which are expected to influence the interpretation of the law but not provide the basis for any individual claims. In the German *Bürgschaft* case,[25] for instance, which concerned a surety agreement to facilitate a loan to a business, the reference to a 'social state' in the Constitution as a directive principle was significant in the determination of the case by favouring the naive surety against the bank. The importance of the inclusion of directive principles in a constitution is that, even in the absence of constitutional protection of social and economic rights, the directive principles create the potential to augment the impact of social and economic concerns in the interpretation of private law by the mechanism of indirect effect.

Although the ECHR does not contain social and economic rights for the most part,[26] the ECtHR has used the European Social Charter of the Council of Europe as a point of reference in its interpretation of the rights protected by the ECHR. The ECtHR promotes an integrated approach by which the meaning of the rights protected by the ECHR should be compatible with other international conventions including the European Social Charter.[27]

These social and economic rights or equivalent guiding principles have considerable potential to influence the development of private law relationships. At the level of the EU, the *Jaeger* case illustrates how the presence of a right steered the ECJ towards a rigid enforcement of protective legislation.[28] In that case, a collective agreement that fixed the hours of work and rest periods of hospital doctors was effectively invalidated on the ground that it provided inadequate rest periods. The Court relied on the entitlement to a rest period contained in the working time Directive,[29] but also strengthened its interpretation of the entitlement by reference to the Community Charter of the Fundamental Social Rights of Workers, which, though not legally binding in itself, declared the right to a daily period of rest to be fundamental. Similarly, when an issue is considered by the ECtHR, a Convention right may receive a broad interpretation in order to align its meaning with the rights protected in the soft law of the European Social Charter. For instance, Article 11 ECHR has been interpreted to include not only the right to be a member of a trade union, but also a right to effective mechanisms for collective representation of the interests of workers, which may include, in appropriate circumstances, the right to strike for the purposes of protecting the interest in collective representation through collective bargaining.[30]

[24] 9 December 1989. [25] *Bürgschaft*, BVerfG 19 October 1993, BVerf 89, 214.

[26] There are some exceptions: e.g. the right to be a member of a trade union and to have it represent a worker is protected in Art. 11 (freedom of association).

[27] Mantouvalou, 'Work and Private Life: *Sidabras and Dziantas v. Lithuania*', 30 *European Law Review (ELRev)* (2005) 573; Nickel, 'Rethinking Indivisibility: Towards a Theory of Supporting Relations between Human Rights', 30 *Human Rights Quarterly* (2008) 984; Scott, 'Reaching Beyond (Without Abandoning) the Category of "Economic, Social and Cultural Rights"', 21 *Human Rights Quarterly* (1999) 633.

[28] Case C-151/02, *Landeshauptstadt Kiel v Jaeger* [2003] ECR I-8389.

[29] Directive 93/104, OJ 1993 L 307/18.

[30] Ewing and Hendy, 'The Dramatic Implications of *Demir* and *Baykara*', 39 *Industrial Law Journal* (2010) 2.

3. The Puzzle of Horizontality

What are the risks of seeking to insert ideas of human rights discourse into private law? At first sight, it seems attractive to suggest that ordinary citizens should respect the ideals of human rights when conducting their ordinary dealings with others. Principles such as respect for liberty and for the dignity of individuals should no doubt infuse the entire legal order and influence all social relations. In a contract of employment, for instance, those values should ideally play an important role in the fabric of the relationship. At a certain level of restrictions on the freedom of the worker, the contract of employment becomes a contract of servitude, through which the worker is bound inextricably to a master in a subservient manner. Similarly, workers need to be protected from harassment and other kinds of demeaning treatment that deny them dignity and respect as autonomous individuals: labour is not a commodity. Through these and similar examples in relationships between citizens, it is possible to detect the importance attached to certain values or principles such as dignity and liberty throughout a liberal legal system, whether one looks in the constitution or in the details of private law governing contracts, property rights, wrongs, and family relations.

Yet there is a difference between saying that common values may infuse every aspect of a society and its legal system and proposing that fundamental rights or human rights should function to shape private relationships through law. The latter proposal suggests that the fundamental rights articulated in the constitution or bill of rights of a state should provide legal arguments that can determine the outcome of private law disputes and shape the development of the law. This proposal would suggest, for instance, that in the case of servitude, the worker should be able to challenge this condition and find a remedy through arguments based upon fundamental or constitutional rights rather than merely on the basis of the contractual relationship and other employment law measures. Similarly, in the case of demeaning treatment such as abusive language, the proposal seems to mean that the worker should be able to make a legal claim based upon a constitutional right to dignity rather than a claim based on breach of contract or a violation of some specific labour right. In short, the proposal for using fundamental rights to determine the rules governing private relationships breaks down the traditional legal demarcation between the rules of public law, which govern the relation between the citizen and the state, and the rules of private law, which regulate private relations between citizens and business associations.

The categories of public law and private law are perhaps legal constructions that may not matter very much in themselves. A blurring of those boundaries may not create serious risks for a legal system. But the boundaries are not pointless. They have evolved as a functional response to practical problems of government and adjudication. In the case of fundamental rights, this aspect of public law was developed in response to actual and potential abuses of power by public authorities. Constitutional rights protect individuals against the misuse of power by both the executive and the legislature. The content and character of those rights has evolved to combat the different kinds of abuse of power encountered in that context, whether it be the imposition of restrictions on liberty by a majority in the legislature in the name of some particular values or religion, or the misuse of coercive powers by executive agencies such as the police. These origins of constitutional rights in protecting civil liberties and a liberal democratic system of government have emphasized the importance of protecting civil and political rights. Although analogous problems of abuse of power may occur in a private law context, as in the above examples concerning employment contracts, similar problems are not, generally speaking, a central concern of private law. Private law is more oriented towards the protection of economic interests of individuals against harms caused by other individuals, whether through the commission of wrongs against those interests or breaches of contractual undertakings and other promises. It is, however, possible to restate private law in the language of individual rights, particularly property rights and individual liberty. But in so doing, one notices both that the list of the rights that appear to be significant differs between public law and private law and that the rights mentioned in the discourses of private law, if referred to at all, appear to weigh less heavily than those protected in the context of public law.

To make the same point in a technical way, in public law fundamental rights are conceived as having direct vertical effect. An individual exercises rights by bringing a claim for breach of those rights directly against a state authority. To use those same rights in a private law context would be to accord them horizontal effect against other individuals, a function outside their original scope and purpose. Consider, for instance, the right to a fair trial. The right was conceived in the context of a state exercising coercive powers. The right ensures that the individual receives a fair hearing before an independent court, with legal representation, and an unbiased determination of the issues before any punishment is imposed. How can such a right be transferred to the context of private law relations such as contracts? The shift in context does not deprive the right of any meaning, but to make sense of the right to a fair trial in a private context it is necessary to engage in a reshaping of the content of the right. One meaning that can be given to the right in horizontal relations between citizens is to insist that it imposes a positive duty on the state to provide adequate and effective civil courts and access to those courts for the resolution of disputes. This translation requires a shift from a negative right to be protected from arbitrary or biased adjudication to a positive obligation on the state to provide a professional service of civil courts. Another meaning that can be given to the right to a fair trial in a private law context is that it may affect the interpretation of private obligations. In a commercial contract that contains an arbitration clause, for instance, the right might be interpreted to create an implied contractual obligation for the arbitrator to conduct a fair hearing. In a contract of employment, the right to a fair trial might be narrowed to exclude the concern that a manager might be biased against an employee when deciding to make a dismissal and the employee's interest in legal representation, whilst preserving the element of fairness that grants the employee a fair chance to respond to criticisms and allegations of misconduct. Through either the construction of positive duties or the insertion of implied obligations, the right to a fair trial can be accorded meaning in the context of private law, but in crossing the border between public law and private law or moving from vertical effect to horizontal effect, the meaning of the right shifts. Some content of the right is lost in the translation, but new meanings are added.

Furthermore, in public law, generally speaking, fundamental rights are regarded as mandatory and inalienable. A citizen cannot give up constitutional rights to liberty and democracy by agreement: signing a contract that gives the authorities the power to detain a person indefinitely without trial would surely have no legal effect. Whilst these civil and political liberties can be qualified by reference to the protection of other rights or the rights of others and strong public policy considerations such as national security, these limitations arise not from consent given by an individual but by virtue of a closely patrolled test of justification, such as the legal test of proportionality, in which the relevance of consent will be closely monitored and in many cases excluded altogether. In contrast, in private law, the power of individual choice and consent, though not paramount, plays a pivotal role. The right to the peaceful enjoyment of private property, for instance, can be relinquished by a contract in private law, whereas in public law a state would have to find a strong justification to permit the seizing of private property (as well as having to pay compensation). Whilst there are limits to the power of individuals to consent to the abrogation of rights, such as the invalidity of a contract of slavery, these outer boundaries leave a wide range of choices for the exercise of individual discretion to qualify or forfeit individual rights.

To sum up these observations: whilst it seems likely that the values that underlie fundamental rights in a public law context will infuse the whole legal order including relations governed by private law such as contracts, the change to a private law context requires a double transformation. First, the rights have to be translated to fit their new context of private law: a simple transplant will be rejected. Second, the rights must become substantially alienable or derogable rather than mandatory. In public law, rights are clubs to defend oneself against the abuse of power, with clubs having been accorded trumping power by the constitution or bill of rights,[31] whereas in private law rights are diamonds to be traded with others or discarded by choice.

These differences provide the underlying reason for doubt about the practicability and appropriateness of inserting fundamental rights into private law. They indicate that there is a risk that such a transplant of rights will cause a perturbation in private law doctrines that will result in misunderstanding and distortion. Incompatible public law conceptions of rights will be applied to private law. This interpretation of the risks of inserting fundamental rights relies upon a view of the internal structures of a legal system. This view of the division between pubic and private law must now be interrogated in order to assess how far it determines the concern about the compatibility of fundamental rights and private law.

4. The Structural Relation between Public and Private Law

In order to approach the puzzle of horizontality, it is helpful to draw a distinction between two theories of the structural relation between private law, on the one hand, and constitutional rights and principles, on the other. On one view of this relation, private law and constitutional law resemble semi-detached houses: independent homes, but joined by a common wall. The two houses of public and private law lean on each other for support, but can be inhabited entirely separately. In the development of legal doctrine, each system of law, both public and private, develops its own autonomous integrity and coherence. On another view of this relation, constitutional laws, or at least the basic constitutional principles such as the fundamental rights, provide the common foundations for what is ultimately a single structure. The foundational rights support both the edifice of public law and private law. On this latter view, legal doctrine requires for its coherence and integrity that all the dimensions of law, both public and private, should be ultimately united into a single edifice. The former view may be labelled the mutual support structure and the latter view the single source structure.[32] What is the practical difference between these metaphorical structures?

On both views, there is a communication between the fundamental rights and private law: neither structure provides impermeable insulation. In the mutual support structure, the communication may be described as one in which both sides of the joining

[31] R. Dworkin, *Taking Rights Seriously* (1977) (for the metaphor of rights as trumps).

[32] Cf. Collins, 'The Constitutionalization of European Private Law as a Path to Social Justice?', in H.-W. Micklitz (ed), *The Many Concepts of Social Justice in European Private Law* (2011) 133.

wall, like considerate neighbours, have to take into account the interests of the other. In other words, in developing private law, it is important that lawyers ensure that the rules do not violate basic principles and rights of constitutional law, that is, do not greatly disturb the neighbours. Equally, the public lawyers should not disrupt the normal processes of private law. The structure requires harmonization, mutual respect, but there is no relation of dependence. In the single source structure, in contrast, the rules of private law are regarded as being ultimately derived from the same fundamental principles and rights of the constitution. It is possible on this view to regard private law as a detailed articulation of constitutional rights. For instance, freedom of contract as a principle in private law will be regarded as being based on or as representing a more practical expression of the constitutional principles of liberty, dignity, autonomy, and freedom of association. The content of Civil Codes and the common law can be analysed as a careful, often incremental, development of legal rules and principles that seek to balance or accommodate the different rights of citizens to property, liberty, dignity, equality, and so forth. In daily practice private lawyers may not refer explicitly to the underlying constitutional principles, but key constitutional ideas such as respect for proprietary interests, respect for the dignity of others, and protection of individual liberty exert a constant influence on private law doctrines.

The main difference between the two structures for a legal system lies in the contrast between the proposition that private law should not be permitted to subvert constitutional rights and the proposition that private law is ultimately derived from constitutional rights.[33] With regard to the systematic coherence of the law, whilst the single source structure requires all law, both public and private, to fit into a coherent body of legal doctrine, the mutual support structure only requires coherence within the autonomous spheres of public and private law, subject only to the constraint of abstention from interference with the principles of the other. It should be noted that this contrast is not a claim about historical origin or antecedence: the idea of private law antedates ideas of constitutional rights in most European countries. It is rather a claim about constitutional theory and the theoretical relation between private law and constitutional law.

The contrast between the mutual support theory and the single source theory is designed to highlight an ambiguity in conceptions of the legal system and the place of fundamental rights within it. It is probably possible to interpret any national legal system in both lights. What the contrast does emphasize is that the advent of the application of human rights law to private law does signal the growing strength of the single source structure as a theory of the arrangement of the internal divisions of a legal system. It is still possible, of course, to argue consistently with the mutual support structure that what is happening is that the dividing wall between public law and private law has proved far more permeable then previously expected. But as interventions based on human rights proliferate in national private law jurisdictions, the single source structure becomes increasingly plausible as an account of the architecture of a legal system. In turn, this adoption of the single source structure encourages the view that fundamental rights should have direct effect in private law between non-state actors. If the single source structure does justify or at least promote the direct effect of fundamental rights

[33] A similar contrast between a subordinate relationship and a complementary relationship between fundamental rights and private law is drawn in Cherednychenko, 'Fundamental Rights and Private Law: A Relationship of Subordination or Complementarity?', 3 *Utrecht Law Review* (2007) 1, <http://www.utrechtlawreview.org>.

in private law, it heightens concerns about the risks of incompatibility between human rights and private law.

5. The Controversy over Direct Effect

Beyond any terminological issues, there are two initial difficulties in assessing the controversy over direct and indirect horizontal effect.[34] One difficulty concerns the distinction at a conceptual level: what exactly is the difference in theory and in practice? The second requires an examination of the constitutional context in which the distinction is employed, because the significance of the distinction varies according to the institutional framework of the particular legal system.

A. Conceptual Distinction

On its face, the distinction between direct and indirect horizontal effect appears simple. If there is direct horizontal effect, an individual (A) can bring a private law claim against another private individual (B) on the ground that that B has unjustifiably interfered with A's rights, as set out in the relevant constitution or convention on fundamental rights. The violation of the fundamental right is itself a sufficient condition for A to have a cause of action against B. In contrast, for indirect horizontal effect, no such claim is available. A must argue instead that B has broken a private law obligation owed to A, but that claim is buttressed by the further argument that the content of that obligation should be determined in a way that is compatible with applicable fundamental rights. In both cases, the fundamental rights are applicable to the dispute between the parties, but only in the former do they create the claim.

The distinction can be restated in formal Hohfeldian terms.[35] Under direct horizontal effect, A has a claim-right based on the fundamental constitutional or convention right, and B has a correlative obligation. Under indirect horizontal effect, A has a claim right based upon private law, and B has a correlative private law obligation, but simultaneously A has a liberty-right (or privilege) that A's fundamental rights should not be unjustifiably interfered with. The role of the court in both cases is to enforce A's rights by imposing appropriate duties on B. For direct effect, the court vindicates A's fundamental right by enforcing the correlative duty imposed on B. For indirect effect, the court vindicates A's private law right by enforcing a correlative private law duty on B, but the interpretation of the respective private law rights and duties must simultaneously avoid unjustifiable interference A's liberty-right protected by the constitution or convention. In the case of indirect horizontal effect, the sole duty imposed on B arises from private law and is correlative with A's claim-right; a court, however, is obliged to respect liberty-rights in its decisions, so that its interpretation of private law must be adjusted appropriately.[36]

[34] The distinction is also expressed as one of unmediated and mediated effect (or application) following the German legal distinction between *unmittelbare* and *mittelbare Drittwirkung*.

[35] Hohfeld, 'Fundamental Legal Conceptions: as applied in Judicial Reasoning', 23 *Yale Law Journal* (1913) 16.

[36] For a similar analysis: Beyleveld and Pattison, 'Horizontal Applicability and Horizontal Effect', 118 *Law Quarterly Review (LQR)* (2002) 623, at 626. But those authors suggest (at 628), inconsistently with the Hohfeldian scheme, that in cases of indirect horizontal effect B owes two duties, a private law duty to A and a public law duty to the state to observe human rights. In Hohfeldian terminology, however, a liberty right (or privilege) does not impose a duty on B but rather (if on anyone) on the state and its courts.

Although the conceptual difference between direct and indirect horizontal effect is reasonably clear, the practical difference is paper thin. Consider the case of Naomi Campbell, the supermodel, who complained of an invasion of her privacy when a newspaper published a photograph of her leaving a rehabilitation clinic.[37] She attended the clinic to address her drug problem, the existence of which she had repeatedly denied to the press. If she could rely upon Article 8 ECHR directly, her claim-right would be the newspaper's unjustifiable interference with her right to respect for her private life; if she could only rely on the right indirectly, she would have to bring a suitable tort claim (breach of confidence under English law) and a court, when interpreting the scope of her right in tort, would have to ensure that it protected her Article 8 right adequately. In either case, the result would be that the newspaper would be liable if it had unjustifiably interfered with Campbell's Article 8 right, because the content of the private law right in tort would have to be developed so that it was compatible or consistent with Article 8.

No significant difference in outcome between direct and indirect horizontal effect is likely to arise unless there is no available private law claim on which to found an action in the first place. Given the sophistication and flexibility of private lawyers in developing new kinds of claims, such a situation seems almost inconceivable today. In the past, rules about status, such as one preventing a wife from suing her husband, may have created gaps in the coverage of private law claims, but those gaps have been filled no doubt in part for the reason that these differentiations by status are inconsistent with the commitment to equality before the law found explicitly or implicitly in all human rights documents. The Naomi Campbell case was alleged to fall into a gap in the law with respect to the protection of privacy against press intrusion, but eventually the gap was filled (or said not to exist) by the tort claim for breach of confidence being interpreted in a suitable way to comply with the requirements of Article 8. There will remain some areas, such as family life, where private law causes of action may not be recognized owing to the absence of an intention to create legal relations or to adjust proprietary interests. If I tell my children to stop making a racket and be silent for the rest of the evening because I am trying to write an article, I may have unjustifiably interfered with their right to freedom of expression, but surely no private law claim would arise in this family context. Even in a legal system that accords fundamental rights direct horizontal effect, it seems unlikely that a court would want to intervene in the domestic sphere and defend the children's rights. If there is no practical difference between direct and indirect horizontal effect in the outcome of cases, why does the conceptual difference matter and provoke such controversy?

B. Institutional Context

The labels of direct and indirect horizontal effect can be misleading owing to the differences in national court structures. Direct and indirect effect can appear virtually identical in a legal system with a constitutional court that is separate from the private law system, as in Germany, because to acquire jurisdiction over the matter the court must assert that a constitutional right of the claimant is engaged and consider whether private law interferes with it. Although the German constitutional court is widely interpreted since its decision in *Lüth*[38] as confining the role of constitutional rights to an indirect effect on private law, for the constitutional court to exercise its jurisdiction at all, it must insist

[37] *Campbell v MGN Ltd* [2004] UKHL 22, [2004] 2 AC 457.

[38] BVerfG 15 January 1958, B VerfGE 7, 198 (LÜTH).

that a fundamental right (or some other constitutional provision) is engaged. A claimant before the court must rely on the fundamental right in much the same way as in a case of direct horizontal effect. In the context of a separate constitutional court with supervisory powers over all other courts, the distinction between, on the one hand, interpreting a private law doctrine in an innovative way in the light of a constitutional right (indirect effect), and on the other, simply enforcing the constitutional right (direct effect), can appear rather technical, a distinction without a substantive difference.[39] The fig leaf of preserving the integrity of private law by suggesting that the constitutional court is merely interpreting a general clause in the Civil Code cannot disguise the reality that the court's reasoning relies entirely on an interpretation of constitutional rights and principles.

In contrast, in legal systems such as France and the United Kingdom, the highest court claims jurisdiction in private law matters and at the same time insists that it must ensure, so far as possible, that its decisions are compatible with the ECHR. Within this latter institutional framework, the court can achieve all that it needs to do to secure compliance with the ECHR through granting indirect horizontal effect. Invoking a fundamental right is unnecessary to secure jurisdiction. Nor is a reference to a fundamental right even necessary to achieve a judgment that complies with those rights, for compliance can be achieved by manipulation of private law doctrines within the traditions of private law. Furthermore, it seems probable that a unified court structure tends to weaken the impact of fundamental rights on private law, because a court will be reluctant to disrupt its own settled principles and rules on private law.[40]

Given these differing institutional frameworks, why then, as in the opening quotation from Oliver Gerstenberg, does the distinction between direct and indirect horizontal effect generate such controversy? In each legal system, the debate is often rooted in the separation of powers and the relation between different parts of the court structure. In the case of Germany for instance, the allegation can be made that the constitutional court should not engage in adjudicating over private law disputes for two reasons. First, it is quite possible that the members of the constitutional court will not have developed suitable expertise in private law, because the lawyers who make up the judges are likely to have specialized in public law. Equally, and this applies to France, the problem of competence arises in the opposite way: the *Cour de Cassation* is familiar with the civil code, but may have little experience of the ECHR. None of these criticisms carry much weight in the United Kingdom, because the higher courts have general jurisdiction in both public and private law. This argument about competence, if it seems relevant to the particular legal system, tends to encourage a cautious approach to the insertion of fundamental rights into private law: if it is to happen at all, it is said, the insertion should be done by the private law experts and then only by giving fundamental rights indirect effect.

Beyond the issue of competence lies the issue of the separation of powers. Whenever judges use fundamental rights to challenge settled interpretations of private law, the question arises whether they are overstepping their powers. Where private law has been developed primarily by the legislature, as in the case of codified systems of law such as France and Germany, judicial revisions of private law doctrines are regarded as prima

[39] Kumm, *supra* note 5, at 352: 'The practical difference between indirect and direct effect, however, is negligeable. [sic] It concerns merely the formal construction of the legal issue and has no implications whatsoever for questions relating to substantive outcomes or institutional competence.'

[40] For a similar assessment of practice in the Netherlands: Cherednychencko, 'Subordinating Contract Law to Fundamental Rights: Towards a Major Breakthrough or towards Walking in Circles?', in Stefan Grundmann (ed), *Constitutional Values and European Contract Law* (2008) 35, at 50.

facie invasions of a sphere properly left to democratic decisions through the legislature. It is said that the democratic legislature has devised a civil code that balances the competing interests and rights of private individuals and it is not appropriate for a court to adjust that balance by appeals to fundamental rights. For this reason, granting direct horizontal effect to constitutional and convention rights can be presented as an arrogation of power by the judiciary that undermines democratic government. The position is slightly different in common law countries, where private law is largely the creation of judges. Those judges are expected to develop the common law in an evolutionary manner as society changes, so adjustments and revisions at the margins are a normal part of the judicial function. So the objection based on the separation of powers and the democratic legitimacy of the legislature has much less relevance in common law systems. Even so, limiting the role of fundamental rights to indirect horizontal effect has the attraction in common law systems that it is likely to appear far more gradual and evolutionary than the sudden insertion into the private law system of directly effective human rights. In the *Campbell* case mentioned above, for instance, some of the judges protected her right to privacy by acknowledging that the law of tort needed to be slightly adjusted in order to make it compatible with Article 8 ECHR,[41] but other members of the court simply revised the scope of the tort and professed it unnecessary to invoke any convention right.[42]

C. A Unifying Theory?

These institutional considerations regarding the choice between direct and indirect horizontal effect probably mask a more fundamental jurisprudential dispute. Lord Neuberger has observed in this context that the issue will not be resolved without a 'grand unifying theory'.[43] By this phrase he is probably referring to what was described above as a single source theory of the structure of a legal system. On this view, all the law, both private and public, rests ultimately on the core protection of fundamental rights. If the single source theory is correct, it may then be suggested that there can be no objection in principle to granting direct horizontal effect to fundamental rights, because private law, so understood, is ultimately grounded in those fundamental rights. The development of private law can be understood as a process of 'reflective equilibrium',[44] in which detailed legal rules are developed by the legislature and the judiciary to express the fundamental rights, but their concrete application can always be reconsidered in the light of interpretations of the underlying fundamental rights. Such reinterpretations are necessary to achieve consistency and coherence for the legal system, essential ingredients, according to Dworkin,[45] of its integrity and legitimacy. On this view of a grand unifying theory, the single source structure provides the necessary justification and mandate for grating direct horizontal effect to human rights.

The logic of this argument is, however, flawed. A grand unifying theory (or single source structure) is a necessary but not a sufficient condition for granting direct horizontal effect to fundamental rights. It is probably necessary in order to establish the

[41] E.g. Baroness Hale. 'The 1998 Act does not create any new cause of action between private persons. But if there is a relevant cause of action applicable, the court as a public authority must act compatibly with both parties' Convention rights.'

[42] E.g. Lord Nicholls and Lord Hoffmann. For criticism of this approach: Morgan, 'Privacy in the House of Lords, Again', 120 *LQR* (2004) 563.

[43] Neuberger, 'Foreword', in D. Hoffmann (ed), *The Impact of the UK Human Rights Act on Private Law* (2011) xiii.

[44] J. Rawls, *A Theory of Justice* (1972), at 20.

[45] R. Dworkin, *Law's Empire* (1986).

proposition that human rights have a profound 'radiating effect' on all branches of the law, whether private or public. But it is not a sufficient condition, because even with a conception of a single source structure for the architecture of a legal system, there may be important additional considerations that dictate that the influence of fundamental rights in private law should be limited to indirect horizontal effect. Those additional considerations include, but are not limited to, the factors mentioned above concerning the institutional structures of legal systems. A single source structure or unifying theory is equally compatible with a practice of indirect horizontal effect. We should therefore consider in more detail these additional considerations in favour of judicial use of indirect horizontal effect as opposed to direct horizontal effect. These additional considerations were briefly described above as aspects of the puzzle of horizontality. Here we concentrate on the most salient issues: doctrinal integrity; the modification of the meanings of rights; the balancing of competing rights; the illiberal constraints of public law standards; consensual derogation from rights; and the protective function of rights.

6. Doctrinal Integrity

The most striking concern is that direct horizontal effect might turn out to be seriously disruptive to private law and therefore generate unpredictability and a consequent problem for businesses and citizens seeking to rely on the law in conducting their affairs. Settled doctrine on which the parties have relied in their dealings with each other might be bypassed by a direct constitutional claim. Not everyone shares that concern about unpredictability: for instance Viviane Reding, the Vice President of the European Commission, has asserted that the requirement for all courts when applying EU law to conform to the EUCFR will ensure a more efficient and coherent interpretation of the existing EU legislation in the field of private law.[46] Whilst it may be true that in a field like EU private law, where rules and guiding principles are sparse and opaque, extra guidance is always welcome, even if it takes the form of abstract entitlements, this is not the problem in national private law systems, where complex and detailed doctrinal systems exist already.

Even if one takes the single source structure view of the relation between private law and constitutional law, this concern about disruption and unpredictability remains pertinent. On that view, the significance of the introduction of constitutional arguments into private law is not that wholly new types of considerations are being voiced, but rather that the existing balance struck by private law between the rights of individuals needs to be adjusted. In a case concerning a contract, for instance, the argument based on constitutional rights may either be pressing for greater weight to be given to the interest of private autonomy and freedom of contract or for greater protection to be accorded to a weaker party on such grounds as the need to respect principles of dignity and equality. The threat posed by the application of the technique of direct horizontal effect to constitutional rights in a sphere already occupied by private law is that it may pay insufficient

[46] 'Foreword', in C. Busch and H. Schulte-Nölke (eds), *Fundamental Rights and Private Law* (2011) vii; cf. Mak, 'Harmonising Effects of Fundamental Rights in European Contract Law', 1 *Erasmus Law Review* (2007) 59; Colombi Ciacchi, 'Non-Legislative Harmonisation of Private Law under the European Constitution: The Case of Unfair Suretyships', *European Review of Private Law* (2005) 285; for a more sceptical assessment of the potential of fundamental rights in the harmonization project: Cherednychenko, 'The Harmonisation of Contract Law in Europe by Means of the Horizontal Effect of Fundamental Rights?', 1 *Erasmus Law Review* (2007) 37.

attention to the way in which private law has already sought to balance competing rights through its legal doctrines and rules and the way that people have ordered their affairs in reliance on these rules. Indirect horizontal effect seems superior in this respect, for it insists that any claims based on rights should be integrated into the existing, carefully considered, settlement between competing rights in private law, which has effectively been tested for generations through litigation in the courts and parliamentary debates.

This argument for the superiority of indirect horizontal effect makes certain assumptions about private law. It assumes that private law has already fully subsumed the human rights values that are proclaimed in constitutions or conventions into its legal doctrines. A second assumption is that the introduction of direct effect threatens to disrupt the coherence of private law and its elaborate doctrines that reconcile the competing rights of individuals. This second point requires a perception of private law that holds that it comprises a systematic and integrated set of rules. Given these assumptions about the qualities of private law, the introduction of novel claims based on directly effective fundamental rights will reopen, at the very least, the underlying claims of rights and values.

For instance, if a celebrity claims an invasion of the right to respect for privacy by a newspaper, the legal presentation of the argument for a directly effective right requires a court to engage in an explicit balancing exercise between the celebrity's right to privacy and the newspaper's freedom of expression. Not only will the reconfiguration of the arguments at a higher level of abstraction not help to resolve the underlying problem of the tension between privacy and freedom of the press, but there is a danger that, if judicial decisions pay less attention to the existing doctrines of private law, they will weaken the coherence of private law. The technique of indirect horizontal effect appears superior in this respect to direct effect, because it reduces the disruptive potential of the insertion of human rights into private law. As in the theory of the mutual support structure of the relation between public and private law, the method of indirect horizontal effect enables private lawyers to hear the voices of proponents of human rights next door, but permits them to choose their own way to respond and accommodate those concerns. In the terminology of systems theory,[47] indirect horizontal effect protects the autopoietic character of a private law system of law, whilst acknowledging that the system must respond to its changing environment, in this instance the growing importance attached to human rights in public discourses and values.

Although this argument for avoiding a revisiting of conflicts of basic values is intended to support the use of indirect horizontal effect against direct effect, its implication seems stronger. It suggests that courts would be well advised to steer clear of any discussion of fundamental rights when applying private law rules. Indeed, the introduction of basic rights discourses into commercial matters does not always seem to help to reach a convincing resolution of a dispute. This feature is highlighted, for instance, by German court decisions in connection with an advertising campaign used by Benetton, in which shocking pictures were used to heighten perception of the brand name. A picture in the campaign, which displayed a human's buttocks, stamped in bold letters with the letters 'HIV—Positive', was challenged by representatives of competitors under the German law of unfair competition. The Federal Supreme Court took the view that the advert violated unfair competition law because it was 'indecent', and that it was not protected

[47] For a critical discussion of this position from the perspective of systems theory, see Gerstenberg, 'Private Law and the New European Constitutional Settlement', 10 *ELJ* (2004) 766, at 774. It should be added that Gerstenberg doubts the coherence of this position, calling it 'inadequate and seriously misleading' (at 775).

by the constitutional right to freedom of expression because it violated the constitutional right to dignity of sufferers from Aids.[48] In contrast, the Federal Constitutional Court permitted a constitutional challenge to that decision on the ground of press freedom and rejected the view that the advertisement was an affront to human dignity, because the image of the sufferer had been used sympathetically, albeit for a commercial purpose.[49] Whatever one's view of the outcome, the point is that it is unclear how useful it was for the courts to invoke the abstract rights to dignity and freedom of expression, which both effectively ignored the legislative standard of 'indecency', thereby causing unpredictability, and which at the same time proved unsuitable and unhelpful in the resolution of the issue. The commercialization of other people's suffering for gain is unsavoury, but that is in effect what news media also do in some of their coverage of events such as wars and famines. If the courts had stuck to the legislative test of indecency, it would have been clear that even if the advertisement was in bad taste, it did not pass the threshold of indecency.

These arguments about the superiority of indirect horizontal effect with regard to the preservation of the normative coherence and predictability of private law can be challenged by testing their assumptions. What if the existing private law system has not fully subsumed the values of human rights documents, but instead remains locked into a scheme of nineteenth century values that are hard to shift and revise? For instance, where does one find in the civil codes and the common law of contract a prohibition on discrimination on the basis of race, sex, and other protected characteristics? Similarly, has private law adequately adapted its protection of privacy in view of modern technologies, starting with the camera in the nineteenth century and now with the threats to privacy posed by the vast technologies of covert surveillance? Even though the point that the introduction of directly effective rights may prove disruptive to existing private law rules may be valid, the disruption may appear, at least sometimes, to be beneficial in the sense of updating the law to modern values and its social context.

The second assumption regarding the coherence (and autopoietic character) of private law doctrines is, of course, also open to challenge from an American Legal Realist perspective and other sceptical positions. From those perspectives, the legal doctrines and concepts play a part in the ostensible justification for judicial decisions, but in reality the outcomes of cases will be determined by the application of often unacknowledged extra legal policy considerations. If so, the putative damage to the integrity of legal doctrines caused by the insertion of directly effective human rights should not be a matter of serious concern, because the courts use doctrines, drawn from both public and private law, instrumentally to achieve their preferred policy goals. On this sceptical view, the only difference that the insertion of directly effective fundamental rights into private law will make is that it will add to the available justificatory devices for the judges, though it is unlikely to affect the outcomes of the decisions. One need not go so far as to regard legal rules as 'pretty playthings',[50] in order to acknowledge that direct horizontal effect is unlikely either to obstruct or to facilitate judges in achieving the results that they regard as just and appropriate in the circumstances of a particular case.

Although these sceptical points suggest that concerns about the integrity of private law under the onslaught of directly effective fundamental rights are overstated, the problem

[48] *Stern v Benetton*, 6 December 2001, I ZR 284/00; this case (and the next) is translated in H.-W. Micklitz, J. Stuyck, and E. Terry (eds), *Cases, Materials and Text on Consumer Law* (2010) 80.

[49] *Stern v Benetton*, 11 March 2003, *Gewerblicher Rechtsschutz und Urheberrecht* (2003) 442.

[50] K. Llewellyn, *The Bramble Bush* (1930).

remains that the balance of interests contained in private law may be disrupted by directly effective human rights. This problem is bound to arise because of the great weight customarily accorded to fundamental rights in public law. Rights prioritize the interests of individuals, even if they can be subsequently modified by restrictions imposed to achieve legitimate goals and to protect the rights of others. When that strong value attached to rights is transposed to private law, it may unsettle rules that function to put collective interests ahead of individual rights. One example in English law where this system of values may apply concerns the duty of the occupier of premises to take reasonable care to protect the health and safety of any persons on the premises, whether they are employees, visitors, or even trespassers. This duty seems to be aimed at encouraging occupiers to make their land and buildings safe for everyone, even a burglar. The rights of an occupier to peaceful possession of property and privacy do not seem to figure in the creation of this tort duty.[51] Another example of the risk to private law of according strong priority to rights arose in an English case concerning a consumer credit transaction: *Wilson v First County Trust Ltd (No 2)*.[52] The consumer took out a short-term, high-interest loan, pledging her car as security. On default, the lender claimed the outstanding sum and asserted entitlement to the car in part satisfaction of the debt. But the courts decided that the paperwork for the transaction failed to comply with regulatory requirements of transparency by not correctly stating the amount and price of the loan. The statutory sanction for this defect in the documentation was the invalidity of the entire transaction, which apparently deprived the creditor of any remedy whatsoever. The creditor claimed that the statutory regulation interfered with its right to peaceful enjoyment of possessions. The House of Lords held that although there had been an interference with that right, the consumer protection measure was for a legitimate purpose and, granting deference to the decision of parliament, was appropriate. If this justification of the aim and methods of the legislation had not succeeded, the priority accorded to the right to property could have seriously undermined the protections afforded to consumers when dealing with loan sharks.

These examples illustrate the point made earlier that, even though respect for fundamental rights or interests may have informed the creation of many principles of private law, these principles cannot be reduced to a scheme of rights, because other values have shaped private law. The values that represent collective interests or public goods can only be restated in terms of aggregations of individual rights with considerable artificiality. It follows, therefore, that even if private law may be compatible with many claims framed as fundamental rights that are directly effective, that will not always prove to be the case. Where collective interests are concerned, as for example in making premises safe for all users or in cleansing the market of duplicitous loan sharks, assertions of claims based on fundamental rights, such as the right to peaceful enjoyment of property, are liable to defeat or subvert social or collective goals that have been embraced by private law. To that extent, direct horizontal effect of fundamental rights is likely to prove incompatible with private law.

[51] R. Bagshaw, 'Tort Design and Human Rights Thinking', in D. Hoffman (ed), *The Impact of the UK Human Rights Act on Private Law* (2011) 110, at 113.
[52] *Wilson v First County Trust Ltd (No 2)* [2003] UKHL 40, [2004] 1 AC 816.

7. The Translation of Transplanted Rights

As noted earlier, civil and political rights were formulated in the context of relations between the citizen and the state with a view to protecting the citizen against abuse of power by the legislature or the executive. In the context of relations between citizens, however, the detailed conception of these rights often needs to be adjusted to accommodate the issues presented in horizontal relations.[53] Even if private law is ultimately founded on the same set of rights, the meaning and emphasis of those rights is likely to differ in response to the context of competing rights between citizens. This consideration that points to a risk arising from giving direct horizontal effect to fundamental rights was introduced above with the illustration of the right to a fair trial, but it applies more broadly to civil and political rights.

Consider the right to privacy: for the purpose of considering whether agencies of the state have invaded the privacy of individuals, it often makes sense to draw a line between actions taken by citizens in public places and those in their own homes. Whereas the state may be entitled in general to observe and to control what occurs in public places without violating privacy rights (though the state may be violating other liberty rights), attempts to observe and to control what takes place in the home are likely to be regarded as an interference with privacy, which will require strong justification. In contrast, in the relations of civil society, this particular spatial distinction between public and private places seems less significant.[54] Instead, what seems more important is the protection of the confidentiality of personal information and the preservation of boundaries between public roles and private and personal life.

For instance, in *Pay v UK*,[55] the employer had dismissed a probation officer when he refused to give up or alter his outside work activities. In the evenings and at weekends, he ran a business selling bondage and sadomasochistic garments and implements. The business was advertised on the Internet, which featured a picture of the claimant wearing a mask that illustrated the products for sale. The products were also marketed at private clubs, where he performed a show. The employer, the probation service that assists convicted criminals to reintegrate into society, was concerned that Mr Pay's activities would embarrass the service and would be perceived as inappropriate for a person who sometimes supervised convicted sex offenders. The UK tribunal rejected Mr Pay's claim against his employer that he had been unfairly dismissed from his job. The tribunal accepted that the dismissal would have been unfair if it had involved an unjustifiable interference with his right to privacy. Following an earlier decision of the English Court of Appeal,[56] the domestic courts concluded, however, that as the activities took place in public, on the Internet, and in clubs to which the public had access, those activities were outside the scope of the protection of privacy established by Article 8 ECHR. When Mr Pay took his case to the ECtHR in Strasbourg, a different view was taken of the scope of Article 8 in this context. The fact that the activities took place in public or in places that the public could access did not necessarily lead to the conclusion that they were no longer within the scope of Article 8. A person's sexuality and sexual preferences are

[53] H. Collins, *Justice in Dismissal* (1992), at 198.

[54] Mantouvalou, 'Human Rights and Unfair Dismissal: Private Acts in Public Spaces', 71 *Modern Law Review (MLR)* (2008) 912 (who rejects the spatial conception of privacy in both public and private spheres); see also Freedland, 'Privacy, Employment and the Human Rights Act 1988', in K. S. Ziegler (ed), *Human Rights and Private Law: Privacy as Autonomy* (2007) 141.

[55] *Pay v UK*, ECHR (2008) Appl. No. 32792/05, decision of 16 September 2008, [2009] IRLR 139.

[56] *X v Y* [2004] EWCA Civ 662, [2004] ICR 1634.

important dimensions of Article 8, so in this instance Mr Pay had an arguable case. The Court eventually decided, however, that the claim was 'inadmissible', because on the assumption that Article 8 applied, the employer's decision to dismiss the employee was nevertheless justifiable, because Mr Pay was unwilling to alter his activities at all in order to prevent members of the public from linking his business to the probation service.

This case is interesting both for its different interpretation of the concept of privacy in a horizontal context, where the fact that actions take place in public is not regarded as a crucial factor by the ECtHR (unlike the UK courts), and for its interpretation of what counts as a suitable justification, because the employer was required to satisfy a test of proportionality (rather than the weaker test of reasonableness applied by UK courts).[57] The UK courts have persistently made the error of applying the public law conception of privacy involving a spatial dimension to private law disputes. This mistake has arisen even though the courts use the method of indirect horizontal effect.

Similarly, the spatial distinction between the public and private spheres may not be appropriate in the context of concerns about the privacy of celebrities when they go about their ordinary everyday lives. The privacy of such a person might be invaded in the street or another public place, as in *Von Hannover v Germany* for instance, where newspaper photographers constantly followed a celebrity around while she went about her ordinary affairs such as shopping.[58] The right to privacy has also been applied in France to invalidate an employer's contractual right to determine where a worker and his family should make their home.[59] In the obverse case, a worker using remote access from home to the employer's computer network, the employee is physically in a private space, but the employer is surely correct to regard the misuse of the computer, by for example sending offensive emails to colleagues, to be not a private matter but rather something of legitimate concern to the business. Equally, if the worker is at the workplace, but during a lunchbreak is sending emails marked private, there is support in a French case for the view that an employer's attempt to read those messages would be an invasion of the right to privacy.[60] The spatial distinction between public and private spheres, which in general provides a workable guide to the scope of Article 8 ECHR in the context of vertical relations between state and citizen, is evidently inappropriate for horizontal relations between citizens. Although Article 8 is certainly relevant to private law, its application depends not on physical location but on the kinds of information about a person at stake.

There is also a transformation of the right to freedom of expression, but this adjustment of meaning is more layered and nuanced. When Article 10 ECHR is applied in a public context, the right to freedom of expression has few permitted limitations, because in a democratic society the voicing of almost any kind of political view, even one that is offensive to the majority, is likely to be vigorously protected by the law. In a private context, however, the right to freedom of expression is likely to be regarded as much weaker, easily restricted by consensual derogations, and likely to be outweighed by competing interests of other individuals. The degree of protection for freedom of speech in a private

[57] Mantouvalou and Collins, 'Private Life and Dismissal', 38 *Industrial Law Journal* (2009) 133.

[58] *Von Hannover v Germany*, ECHR (2004) *Reports* 2004-VI, (2005) 40 EHRR 1; (2006) 43 EHRR 7; *Von Hannover v Germany (No 2)*, ECHR (2012) *Reports* 2012, 228.

[59] Cass. Soc. 12 January 1999, *Spielers v SARL Omni Pac, D* 1999, 635.

[60] Soc. 2 October 2001, *Société Nikon France SA v M Onof, D* 2001, 3148 note P.-Y. Gautier. In France, the horizontal effect of fundamental rights in employment is greatly assisted, however, by Art. L120-2 of the Labour Code, which states that any limits placed by an employer on the rights and freedoms of an employee must be justified by the nature of the tasks to be accomplished and proportionate to the goal pursued.

law context is also likely to be strongly influenced by the content of the speech. In appropriate circumstances, the law is likely to be much less tolerant of speech that others find offensive or critical. It is this weakening of the right in the private context that is the key ingredient in the translation.

In the context of employment, for instance, an employer is usually entitled to a contractual duty of loyalty from employees. This duty may be broken in many different ways including the case where an employee denigrates the employer's product or service to others. For instance, the shop assistant who worked in an Apple store who texted his friends to say that his iPhone was rubbish was justifiably dismissed and was accorded no protection on the ground of freedom of speech.[61] Although criticism of a government of a similar nature (e.g. the minister is incompetent) would normally be protected by the right to freedom of expression, a similar criticism of a manager would probably be unacceptable to an employer and result in a justifiable dismissal, without any protection from Article 10 or equivalent constitutional provisions.

As well as being weaker in a private law context, unlike a public law context, protection for freedom of expression is likely to be variable according to the content of the speech. In the case of whistleblowers, for instance, employees are protected by Article 10 if they can demonstrate that the speech was in the public interest, as for example where the speech exposes corruption or criminal behaviour. Courts must determine what kinds of speech are in the public interest in order to determine the scope of the protection for whistleblowers.[62] The content of the speech is also important in the employment relation where it concerns trade union activities. Almost certainly there would be a violation of a combination of Articles 10 and 11 ECHR if an employer disciplined a worker for advocating membership of a trade union and support for collective bargaining. But that special protection for freedom of expression will not apply, according to a controversial decision of the ECtHR, when the style of expression is deeply offensive.[63] In a public context, however, not involving the relation between an employer and an employee or a trade union official, the same style of expression would almost certainly be protected in liberal European states without careful scrutiny of its content.

In view of this need to translate fundamental rights when they are applied in a private law context, there is evidently a danger presented by the technique of direct horizontal effect that it may enable claims based upon public law meanings of rights to be advanced to regulate the different social context of civil society, where slightly different interpretations of those basic values such as privacy have evolved. Equally, notions of those rights developed in a private law context may be transplanted into a public law context with inappropriate results. That risk is not avoided entirely by the technique of indirect effect, as we noted in the context of the application of the right to privacy by UK courts. On the contrary, the danger is always present whenever constitutional discourse formed in vertical relations between state and citizen is transplanted into horizontal relations between citizens and businesses. The technique of indirect effect merely places some constraint on the misuse of transplants by compelling legal reasoning to measure its outcomes against the existing doctrinal interpretation of rights and fundamental principles developed in private law and social regulation.

[61] *Crisp v Apple Retail (UK) Ltd*, ET/1500258/11 (22 November 2011).
[62] *Guja v Moldova*, ECHR (2008) *Reports* 2008, 144.
[63] *Palomo Sánchez v Spain*, ECHR (2011) *Reports* 2011, 1319.

8. Double Proportionality: 'The Ultimate Balancing Test'

In public law, many fundamental rights can be qualified or modified on grounds of public policy according to some version of a test of proportionality. The test of proportionality can be formulated in slightly different ways, but its focus is on the issue of whether the policy reason for an interference with a protected fundamental right is of sufficient strength to justify the interference. In order to make that assessment, the first step is to establish whether the policy being pursued is a legitimate aim for government action. An aim that on careful analysis was merely designed to fill the pockets of the ruling elite or to cover up corruption in government would not satisfy that requirement. The second stage is an assessment of whether the means chosen are appropriate for the achievement of the goal in the sense that the goal is likely to be achieved. If there is evidence that that means chosen will not in fact promote the goal to any significant extent, the measure is likely to fall at this second hurdle. The third stage asks whether the measure is necessary in the sense that it questions whether other measures that interfere with fundamental rights to a lesser extent could be employed instead and nevertheless achieve the legitimate goal. The final step in the analysis tries to weigh the benefits of the achievement of the legitimate aim against the harm caused to the individual in having to sacrifice a fundamental right. This last stage often takes on the appearance of a cost–benefit analysis, though of course the values at stake are not usually commensurable. For instance, in the case of a ban on a public protest, the legitimate aim of protecting law and order on the streets has to be measured against the individual's right to freedom of assembly and freedom of expression. To balance these interests against each other is far from straightforward. In truth, the test of proportionality provides a useful structure for a legal analysis of the justifiability of interferences with fundamental rights, but ultimately it requires a court to engage in a difficult balancing exercise between incommensurable values.

The balancing exercise in private law often assumes a rather different character. This change results from the problem that in many cases both parties can claim that their fundamental rights are at stake. It is not a matter of assessing whether the government's case for the need to override a right in the pursuit of a compelling public interest is established, but rather how to measure competing rights against each other. There are likely to be both rights and policy considerations on both sides of the argument. This structure prevents the application of the familiar test of proportionality, because this transplant will not function to provide a procedure by which all the different relevant considerations are measured against each other. As Chantal Mak observes, 'the application of "limitation clauses", which constitutionally regulate the manner and situations in which certain fundamental rights may be restricted, seem difficult to transplant as such from the constitutional level to contract law disputes'.[64]

Again, direct horizontal effect presents a risk in this respect. This technique may induce courts to conceive of the necessary reasoning process as one of determining whether policy considerations justify the limitation on the claimant's constitutional right, whereas the correct question to ask must involve the balancing of interests on both sides, taking into account both rights and policies. Admittedly, private law reasoning must also resort to indeterminate open-textured tests such as good faith and reasonableness to provide the mechanism for this necessary balancing process between the private

[64] Mak, *supra* note 4, at 48.

parties' rights and the policies underlying the legal rules. The point is not that some kind of process of accommodation like a test of proportionality is not needed, but rather that the normal test of proportionality in public law provides the wrong formula in this context owing to its assumption that only one party to the dispute has rights.

If the test of proportionality developed in public law is inappropriate in those cases where both parties to a private law dispute are protesting about an interference with their rights, what is the correct formulation of the test? The simple answer is that the rights need to be balanced against each other. But this answer is not as informative as one might hope. Given that there are competing interests, rights, and policies on both sides of the argument in a private law dispute, the correct approach appears to be a double proportionality test. In other words, the case for interference with the separate rights of each party needs to be assessed separately according to a test of proportionality. The legitimate aim that may justify such an interference with a fundamental right is likely in a private law context to include the protection of the fundamental right of the other party.

This application of a double proportionality test emerges most clearly in the context of the competition between the right to freedom of expression (Article 10 ECHR) and the right to respect for privacy (Article 8 ECHR). Here the right of the press to publish information and pictures about an individual is clearly in tension with the right of that individual to keep personal information about himself or herself secret and away from the public gaze. Since the tension between the competing rights is self-evident in such cases, courts have to formulate their method for resolving the issue. In a case concerning restrictions on media publication of court proceedings, and therefore a clash between Articles 8 and 10 ECHR, Lord Steyn in the UK House of Lords suggested that the following approach would be appropriate:

> First, neither Article has *as such* precedence over the other. Secondly, where the values under the two Articles are in conflict, an intense focus on the comparative importance of the specific rights being claimed in the individual case is necessary. Thirdly, the justifications for interfering with or restricting each right must be taken into account. Finally, the proportionality test must be applied to each. For convenience, I will call this the ultimate balancing test.[65]

The features of this 'ultimate balancing test' have been helpfully explained by Sir Mark Potter:

> [E]ach Article propounds a fundamental right which there is a pressing social need to protect. Equally, each Article qualifies the right it propounds so far as it may be lawful, necessary and proportionate to do so in order to accommodate the other. The exercise to be performed is one of parallel analysis in which the starting point is presumptive parity, in that neither Article has precedence over or 'trumps' the other. The exercise of parallel analysis requires the court to examine the justification for interfering with each right and the issue of proportionality is to be considered in respect of each. It is not a mechanical exercise to be decided upon the basis of rival generalities. An intense focus on the comparative importance of the specific rights being claimed in the individual case is necessary before the ultimate balancing test in terms of proportionality is carried out.[66]

As these remarks indicate, the 'ultimate balancing test' involves in fact a double application of the test of proportionality, in which the rights of each party are qualified according to the weight of the rights in a particular context. The double test of proportionality should also apply to a court's choice of remedy, as for example in the choice between an interim and a permanent injunction.[67]

[65] *Re: S (Identity: Restrictions on Publication)* [2004] UKHL 47, para. 17.
[66] *A Local Authority v W* [2005] EWHC 1564 (Fam).
[67] *Plon (Société) v France*, ECHR (2004) *Reports* 2004, 200.

The sharp difference between a single test of proportionality and a double one provides a further consideration for resisting the direct horizontal effect of fundamental rights. There is a risk that a court using the mechanism of direct horizontal effect might fail to appreciate the need to apply the 'ultimate balancing test'.

9. Public Virtue and Private Preference

Private law has traditionally respected a wide discretion for private choices. The law generally permits individuals to live their lives in ways that depart from the requirements of neutrality and equal concern and respect that in a liberal democracy should govern all the actions of the state.[68] An individual can choose without significant restriction (other than money) what goods and services he wishes to purchase, who to treat as friends and associates, and what cultural events to experience. Respect for the liberty and the privacy of the individual, as demanded in constitutional provisions, necessitates that private individuals acting in a sphere of private activity should not be held to the same high standards of probity or correctness in conduct as will be required from state agencies. The principle of freedom of contract in the sense of freedom to choose a contractual partner represents recognition in private law that liberty of the individual is of utmost importance.

It follows that direct application of constitutional rights to private actors might be inappropriate, because it would impose a degree of 'political correctness' that would be oppressive for private individuals. A person may decide, for instance, that he finds everyone exhibiting strong religious faith to be profoundly irritating and confused, so he decides not to befriend or purchase goods from anyone with those religious qualities. If government officials took a similar view about how they should conduct public administration, however, they would be quickly condemned for a material interference with the individual right to freedom of religion. This boundary between private autonomy and public responsibility is not fixed and has been challenged in particular contexts.

Anti-discrimination legislation in Europe has moved the boundary in such a way that businesses dealing with the public have to refrain from discrimination on grounds of sex,[69] and race.[70] Furthermore, in the case of employment and occupation, employers are prohibited from discriminating between applicants and employees on the same grounds and other protected characteristics such as age, religion or belief, sexual preference, and disability.[71] The force of these anti-discrimination principles has been strengthened by Article 14 ECHR, which contains a general anti-discrimination principle:

> The enjoyment of rights and freedoms set forth in this convention shall be secured without discrimination on any ground such as sex, race, colour, language, religion, political or other opinion, national or social origin, association with a national minority, property, birth or other status.

[68] Taylor, 'The Horizontal Effect of Human Rights Provisions, the German Model and its Applicability to Common-Law Jurisdictions', 13 *King's College Law Journal* (2002) 187, at 218.

[69] Directive 2004/113/EC, OJ 2004 L 373/37, implementing the principle of equal treatment between men and women in the access to and supply of goods and services.

[70] Directive 2000/43/EC, OJ 2000 L 180/22, implementing the principle of equal treatment between persons irrespective of racial or ethnic origin.

[71] Directive 2000/78/EC, OJ 2000 L 303/16, establishing a general framework for equal treatment in employment and occupation; Directive 2006/54/EC, OJ 2006 L 204/23 on the implementation of the principle of equal opportunities and equal treatment of men and women in matters of employment and occupation.

It is important to note that the provision is not restricted to a finite list of protected characteristics. On the other hand, to invoke Article 14, it is necessary to point to an interference with some other convention right. Usually the ECtHR will hold that a discriminatory interference with a convention right cannot be justified and will therefore violate the ECHR.

It is evident that anti-discrimination law places a significant limit on the freedom of individuals to select their contractual partner. In *Bull and Bull v Hall and Preddy*,[72] the proprietors of a small hotel decided to exclude homosexual couples from rooms with a double bed on the ground that the proprietors regarded such behaviour (as with all sexual intercourse outside marriage)[73] as immoral and contrary to the tenets of their religious beliefs. Should this decision be regarded as falling within the scope of the proprietors' liberty to choose a contractual partner, or does the public interest require that any exclusion of homosexual couples from the hotel should be unlawful? On the one hand, in addition to their demand for the freedom to choose a contractual partner, the proprietors can claim the support of other important rights such as freedom of religion and the right to exclude unwelcome people from their private property. On the other hand, the proprietors' action certainly denies equal respect to homosexual couples (and all unmarried partners), and in so doing strikes at the core ideas of individual dignity and liberty that underpin liberal democracies and human rights. English courts had little doubt that the anti-discrimination legislation restricted the freedom of the proprietors of the small hotel. In this context, the normal liberty respected in private law, the freedom to choose a contractual partner, was curtailed in order to uphold the importance of the rights of the customers of the hotel to equal treatment and respect.

But anti-discrimination laws do not always protect equality rights. Suppose that a potential customer of the hotel discovers that the proprietor manifests his or her religion in various ways in the decoration of the premises, by for instance placing a large crucifix and a bible prominently in every room. As an ardent atheist, the customer objects to all religious symbols and prefers a strictly secular environment, so he or she decides to find alternative accommodation. Can the customer's decision be challenged on the ground that it involves disrespect to the proprietor's religious beliefs and autonomy, or is the customer's preference within the proper scope of the freedom to choose one's contractual partner? This conduct falls outside the scope of the European laws against discrimination. In general, a worker or a consumer can lawfully discriminate against a business on grounds such as race, sex, religion, and disability. The requirement of equal treatment usually only applies to employers and businesses. Nevertheless, the anti-discrimination legislation does apply to anyone who offers goods or services to the public, so it is possible for an individual acting in a private capacity to fall within the scope of the legislation. For instance, if an individual puts used goods for sale on an Internet auction site, that offer to the public probably falls within the scope of the EU Directive.[74] Modern anti-discrimination legislation therefore preserves some scope for unfettered

[72] [2012] EWCA Civ 83, [2013] UKSC 73.

[73] Under UK law (at present) it is not possible for homosexual couples to marry, though they can form a 'civil partnership', which has the same legal incidents as marriage: Civil Partnership Act 2004 (c. 33).

[74] Art. 3(1) of Directive 2004/113/EC, OJ 2004 L 373/37. 'Within the limits of the powers conferred upon the community, this Directive shall apply to all persons who provide goods and services, which are available to the public irrespective of the person concerned as regards both the public and private sectors, including public bodies, and which are offered outside the area of private and family life and the transactions carried out in this context.'

private conduct. The difficult question becomes how to define the appropriate scope of this unrestricted sphere of private autonomy. The application of fundamental rights to this issue could easily eviscerate the scope of private autonomy, because any controversial choice might be criticized for a failure to respect the dignity of others, or for a discriminatory interference with some other right.

The ECtHR considered the proper scope of the application of anti-discrimination laws and private autonomy in private transactions in the context of a will. In *Pla Puncernau v Andorra*,[75] a case considered above, the precise question was whether a testator could discriminate in her the will against adopted children. If so, then distant cousins would inherit the property. When the adopted son took his case to Strasbourg, the ECtHR was divided. The majority held that both Article 8 (the right to respect for private and family life) and Article 14 were engaged. The Court held that the Andorra's High Court's interpretation of 'will' had a discriminatory effect against adopted children, contrary to Article 14, so that a will containing such a discriminatory provision would be invalid. The majority of the Court therefore treated the enforcement of a will as a kind of public act, so that a state is required to ensure that any interference with the rights of others, such as the right to respect for private and family life of the adopted son in this case, should not be conducted on a discriminatory basis. For the minority, Judge Garlicki insisted that a testator's right to dispose of her property as she wished was an aspect of the right to property and her right to privacy under Article 8. As a protected convention right, her freedom to make this personal decision could only be restricted in exceptional circumstances. Such exceptional circumstances would only arise where the disposition in the will was repugnant to the fundamental ideals of the Convention or aimed at the destruction of the protected rights and freedoms. In this case, however, Judge Garlicki maintained, by leaving property only to children born to the marriage and excluding illegitimate and adopted children, the testator had acted within her rights and liberties and the will should be enforced.

Although this case concerns a will rather than a contract, similar principles should surely apply. In private tenancies, for instance, legislation often grants succession rights to partners of the tenants, and the ECHR has been used to prevent discrimination by landlords against same-sex partners.[76] The majority of the ECtHR in *Pla and Puncernau* reduced the exclusion of private and family life from the scope of anti-discrimination laws almost to vanishing point. The testator was not acting in the course of business or making offers to the public. On the contrary, she was making a private decision about the distribution of her property among her relatives and descendants after her death. Nevertheless, the majority of the ECtHR does not accept that the anti-discrimination principle is so limited in the context of private transactions and the family. Indeed, the court is pushing the anti-discrimination principle into the heart of the family by requiring equal treatment for adopted children, and presumably, between the sexes.

Although the example discussed here is drawn from anti-discrimination law, it is evident that the application of fundamental rights to private law is likely to require a reconsideration of the boundaries of the private sphere where individuals enjoy liberty of choice without the constraints of constitutional standards. It illustrates the concern identified at the beginning by Oliver Gerstenberg that the constitutionalization of private law 'poses a threat to private law's libertarian core of private autonomy'. The use

[75] *Pla and Puncernau v Andorra*, ECHR (2004) *Reports* 2004-VIII, (2006) 42 EHRR 25.

[76] *Karner v Austria*, ECHR (2003) *Reports* 2003-IX, (2004) 38 EHRR; *Ghaidan v Godin-Mendoza* [2004] UKHL 30, [2004] 2 AC 557.

of the method of indirect horizontal effect will not prevent the risk of illiberal decisions, but it may assist the court in recognizing that whilst it is in general important for everyone to respect the dignity of others, there is also a value, emphasized strongly in private law, of permitting individuals a wide scope for unsupervised private autonomy.

10. Derogation in Private Law

In a public law context, it is usually no defence for a state to allege that an interference with a right was justifiable on the ground that the individual concerned had consented to the interference. This rejection of the defence of consent may be due in part to scepticism that any individual would freely part with his or her rights, so that there must be a suspicion that any forfeiture of rights was secured by force or fraud. But even if the state were to overcome the heavy burden of proof to demonstrate free consent to derogation from a right, the defence of consent would surely not be acceptable as a matter of principle, whether the alleged consent be given to slavery, torture, or denial of freedom of expression. The state must defend its interferences with rights according to a strict test of proportionality, under which it must demonstrate that it has a legitimate aim and has acted appropriately and only where necessary.

In contrast, in the private sphere, it is normal for fundamental rights to be sacrificed by agreement. For example, alienation of property and therefore the loss of property rights is usually achieved through a consensual transaction. Similarly, the right to keep information private under the right to respect for private life can be lost by agreement, as where an author agrees to publish memoirs about his or her scurrilous life. We noted earlier that in the clash between privacy and freedom of the press, outside matters of pressing public concern that are vital for a democracy, the right to freedom of expression is nuanced and may be qualified by a variety of considerations including the content of the speech and any consent to publication.

This potential to derogate from rights in the private sphere has even been applied where the presence of consent is far from clear. In a line of cases before the ECtHR, employees have tried to assert their right to manifest a religion under Article 9 ECHR when it appears incompatible with the hours of work demanded by an employer. The claims of employees have been denied not only when they decide that their hours of work are no longer compatible with their need to manifest their religion, as in *Ahmad v United Kingdom*,[77] but also when the employer imposes a change of hours on the employee for production or business reasons.[78] In these cases it is said that the restriction on the right to manifest a religion is purely consensual, either because the employee initially accepted the terms of employment or because the employee can always find another job that is compatible with his or her religious beliefs. Similar arguments have been applied to cases involving dress codes that interfere with apparel that is worn in order to symbolize religious faith. In *R (Begum) v Headteacher and Governors of Denbigh High School*,[79] a majority of the House of Lords held that there was no interference with Article 9 when a school insisted on a pupil wearing its uniform on the ground that she could have attended three other schools in the area that would have permitted her to wear the jilbab.

[77] ECmHR, 4 EHRR (1982) 126.

[78] *Stedman v United Kingdom*, 23 EHRR CD (1997) 168; *Copsey v WWB Devon Clays Ltd* [2005] ICR 1789.

[79] [2006] UKHL 15, [2007] 1 AC 100.

The distinction between public law and private law with regard to consensual derogations from fundamental rights is not always clear cut. In some of the cases concerning manifestation of religion mentioned above, the employee concerned worked for a state managed school and the governors of the school were permitted to rely in part on the employee's consent to the terms of employment to justify their stance. As in *Ahmad v United Kingdom*, the defence of the governors was invariably strengthened in such cases by a demonstration that the contractual requirement was appropriate for the job in the pursuit of a legitimate aim and that the needs of the employee could not be accommodated without great difficulty.

The appropriate scope for consensual derogation of rights in the private sphere was the key issue in the French case concerning the public entertainment of dwarf throwing. In this entertainment, these physically tiny people were thrown about like a ball. No doubt their treatment was undignified and the element of the commercialization of their treatment was regarded by French authorities as unlawful.[80] Yet the actors themselves wanted to continue with their jobs, because this was their principal source of income, which is an important part of their private life in the sense that work provides an income and helps social inclusion.[81] If the case is simply regarded as a contest between two rights—the right to be treated with dignity and respect and the right to respect for private life—a court will have to determine whether the interference with the former is justifiable by reference to the latter. But if we permit the issue of consensual derogation to enter into the discussion, the consent of the actors to this treatment in full knowledge of the circumstances may well undermine the concern about dignity altogether.

Private law has always attached considerable importance to consent in determining the lawfulness of conduct. Human rights law usually takes the opposite starting point. The potential problem with permitting directly effective human rights to determine the outcome of private law disputes is that this traditional and liberal respect paid to informed consent will be ignored or sidelined. Again, the method of indirect horizontal effect will not avoid this risk, but it may force a court to explain more carefully why it proposes to ignore the consensual nature of the activity just because it regards it as undignified, distasteful, or perverse.

11. Protective Effect

What impact will the introduction of fundamental rights into private law have on the standards of fairness or social justice applied in disputes arising between private parties? Will the rights serve to protect weaker parties such as employees, tenants, and consumers against harsh contracts and robust property rights? Or, on the contrary, will those rights be used strategically by strong businesses and property owners to defend their interests against challenges from protective legislation and equitable legal doctrines? Attitudes towards the insertion of fundamental rights into private law are coloured by perceptions of the likely effects on weaker parties. In turn, those predictions influence the enthusiasm with which directly effective fundamental rights are greeted.

It is certainly the case that in the context of public law the role of human rights has been to protect the weaker party, the individual citizen, against the power of the state. But will this protective effect also apply in the context of horizontal relations? Given

[80] C.E. Ass. 27 October 1995, *Lebon*, 372.

[81] *Sidabras v Lithuania*, ECHR (2004) *Reports* 2004-XIII, 42 EHRR (2006) 6.

that both parties to a dispute can claim rights, there is no apparent reason why the insertion of rights into private law should help weaker parties against stronger ones. The large corporation or bank can claim its rights to property, liberty, or to freedom of speech just as easily as the ordinary individual. As Ohla Cherednychenko points out, in the *Bürgschaft* case, the bank seeking to enforce the contract was able to reply equally on the protection for freedom of contract based on the right to the free development of one's personality.[82] Indeed, given the advantage of the disparity of resources in most litigation,[83] the stronger party may well be able to manipulate fundamental rights to its advantage. It seems unlikely, therefore, that the insertion of fundamental rights into private law will necessarily nudge the law in either direction decisively. We should expect a variegated pattern, with some additional protection for weaker parties, but also a robust defence of vested interests.

Legal history reveals many examples of constitutional courts declaring that social legislation designed to protect weaker parties is invalid under the constitution on the ground that it deprives the holders of rights, such as rights to property, of their entitlements. In particular, in the United States, both at federal and state level, in the past courts have manipulated the constitution to assist challenges to legislation designed to help weaker parties such as workers on the ground that legislation is a restriction on individual freedom or an interference with the right to private property.[84] Hirschl argues on the basis of some comparative studies outside Europe (Israel, Canada, New Zealand, South Africa), that new constitutions are typically constructed and relied upon by hegemonic elites that fear erosion of their position by new populist groups. He suggests that the new constitutional courts of these countries, staffed by fellow professional elites, typically safeguard a neoliberal economic order against redistributive political movements.[85] Such cross-country comparisons may be extremely misleading, of course, not least because the constitutions and legal processes to invoke them differ substantially. Even so, such studies provide worrying examples for those who believe that constitutionalization of private law may assist social justice. The conflict in those examples, it should be noted, is between entrenched constitutional rights and social regulation. The social regulation concerned is likely to interfere with freedom of contract and private property rights, because part of its justification is that the free market does not produce acceptable outcomes as in the example of hours of work that are unhealthily long. Similarly, where social legislation seeks to promote a public good such as the health of the nation, it may interfere with the market and freedom of speech, as in the Canadian case on tobacco advertising, where the business interests were successful in having the legislation struck down as a violation of the Charter.[86] The tension between constitutional protections of the market order and the market-correcting purposes of social regulation is evident and unavoidable. The important questions are rather where the balance should be drawn and, perhaps more crucially, who should draw it—the courts or the legislature. In this

[82] Cherednychenko, *supra* note 4, at 551.

[83] Galanter, 'Why the "Haves" Come Out Ahead: Speculations on the Limits of Legal Change', 9 *Law and Society Review* (1974–1975) 95.

[84] *Lochner v New York*, 198 US 45 (1905) (law limiting working hours); *Adair v United States*, 208 US 161 (1908) (law forbidding dismissal of workers for union membership); *Adkins v Children's Hospital*, 261 US 525 (1923) (minimum wage for women). This line of cases in the US Supreme Court was overruled in *West Coast Hotel Co v Parrish*, 300 US 379 (1937) (minimum wage law).

[85] R. Hirschl, *Towards Juristocracy: The Origins and Consequences of the New Constitutionalism* (2004).

[86] *RJR-MacDonald v Attorney General of Canada* [1995] SCR 199; cf. Ison, 'A Constitutional Bill of Rights—The Canadian Experience', 60 *MLR* (1997) 499, at 502.

context, the aim of fairness or social justice is likely to be secured by the courts showing deference to a democratic legislature rather than insisting upon constitutional rights.

In other types of cases, where social protective legislation is not directly involved, the introduction of fundamental rights into private law often invites a court to reconsider the basic ground rules of private law. A court will be asked to strengthen or enlarge the existing protection for fundamental rights, or strike a new balance between competing rights and interests. For instance, the constitutionalization of the private law of contract interrogates and adjusts the idea of freedom of contract itself in order to ask, for instance, whether or not the conditions necessary to exercise freedom of contract or to have full personal autonomy were present in the circumstances under which the contract was made. There is some evidence that the opportunity afforded by a review of basic principles of private law in the light of fundamental rights has been taken to adjust liberal principles of private law towards a more protective approach.

Reviewing case law from Germany and the Netherlands, Chantal Mak finds two themes in the cases: first, that the legal reasoning emphasizes the importance of party autonomy or freedom of contract, but this concept is understood in a broad sense to require genuine autonomy, which ensures that weaker parties have proper possibilities for self-determination, unconstrained by pressure or deficits in information; secondly, that the effect of this reasoning tends to assist the position of a weaker party or to redress a situation of structural inequality.[87] The leading example that supports this interpretation is the previously mentioned *Bürgschaft* case, where a potentially ruinous surety contract entered into by a family member had been upheld in the private law courts, but the German Constitutional Court insisted that relief should be given to the surety on the basis of her constitutional right to the free development of one's personality in conjunction with the principle of the 'social state'. Another example that supports the idea that fundamental rights tend to protect a weaker party concerns the case of a commercial agent who was able to avoid a term in his contract that restricted the agent from working for a competitor for two years following the agency agreement.[88] Reviewing the case law from France, in examples largely drawn from both employment[89] and landlord and tenant,[90] Myriam Hunter-Henin also identifies what can be seen as a pattern of protection of the weaker party.[91] In contrast, a search for similar protection for workers as a weaker party in the United Kingdom would prove unrewarding because, aside from cases in the ECtHR protecting the rights of members of trade unions,[92] no employee has so far successfully invoked the ECHR to improve his or her legal position against an employer.[93]

The absence of a clear pattern in favour of the protection of weaker parties in a private law context should not come as a surprise. In a public law context, the rationale for rights is the protection of the isolated individual against abuses of power by governments, so

[87] Mak, *supra* note 4, at 323; cf. Colombi Ciacchi, 'Party Autonomy as a Fundamental Rights in the European Union', 6 *ERCL* (2010) 303.

[88] BVerfGE 81, 242 (*Handelsvertreter*).

[89] Soc. 2 October 2001, *Société Nikon France SA v M Onof, D* 2001, 3148, note P.-Y. Gautier; C.E. Ass. 27 October 1995, *Lebon*, 372.

[90] Civ. 3eme 6 March 1996 *OPAC de la ville de Paris v Mme Me Yedei, D* 1997, 167, note B. de Lamy; Civ. 3eme 18 December 2002, Bull. Civ. III, no. 262.

[91] Hunter-Henin, 'France: Horizontal Application and the Triumph of the European Convention on Human Rights', in D. Oliver and J. Fedtke (eds), *Human Rights and the Private Sphere: A Comparative Study* (2007) 98.

[92] *Wilson and National Union of Journalists v United Kingdom*, ECHR (2002) *Reports* 2002-V, EHRR (2002) 20.

[93] H. Collins, K. D. Ewing, and A. McColgan, *Labour Law* (2012), chapter 11.

protection of the weaker party is part of the genetic make-up of rights. In the different context of relations between individuals, the principle of equality before the law should obstruct any systematic support for one kind of party against another. This verdict will disappoint those who foresee the potential in the application of rights to the private sphere of subjecting private power, based on wealth, to similar constraints to those that are applied to the state. Though not using physical force, corporate power can seem as manipulative and overbearing sometimes as any governmental action. Global capital markets that facilitate the transfer of investments quickly from country to country often put governments, even strong powers, at the beck and call of multinational enterprises for fear of disinvestment and economic decline. The idea of subjecting private business organizations to the same duties as governments have under human rights law has the appeal, at least symbolically, of taming those private powers. By abolishing the restriction of 'state action' that has for so long tended to exclude considerations of fundamental rights from the sphere of the market and personal relations,[94] the introduction of horizontal effect has some potential to protect dignity, liberty, and equality in all fields of social and economic life. Yet as long as business organizations can employ the same rights as individuals in order to protect their proprietary interests and freedom of contract, the insertion of human rights into private law, whether directly or indirectly, is unlikely to produce much in the way of the desired subjection of business interests to principles that normally protect weaker contractual partners.

12. Autonomy and Positive Freedom

This assessment of the potential problems arising from the application of fundamental rights to private law has suggested a number of tentative conclusions. In the first place, it has become apparent that concerns about the ability of the judiciary to cope with this innovation are probably overstated, either because in many jurisdictions the unified court structure has familiarized judges with the need to treat the division between public law and private law as permeable, or because the values expressed by fundamental constitutional rights are not dissimilar to those underlying private law. The heated controversy about direct horizontal effect exaggerates the difficulties. Nevertheless, there is a strong case for any court to map the principles of private law applicable to a situation before asking whether those principles need to be adjusted in the light of fundamental rights. This method of indirect horizontal effect should avoid unexpected and ill-considered shocks to the system of private law whilst at the same time leaving the door open to shifts in legal rules in the light of modern values contained in declarations of fundamental rights. Given that in a private law dispute both parties are likely to be able to clothe their legal arguments in terms of rights, it is a mistake for any court to think that an appeal to a single right is likely to be determinative of a dispute. Instead, what is necessary in most cases is the application of the 'ultimate balancing test', which is in effect a double application of the test of proportionality to both of the rights at stake.

The most serious concern raised here about the practice of inserting fundamental rights into private law has been the issue of the need to translate the traditional civil and political liberties when inserting them into private law. It would be a mistake for a court simply to take the meanings of a concept such as freedom of speech or privacy that

[94] Tushnet, 'The Issue of State Action/Horizontal Effect in Comparative Constitutional Law', 1 *International Journal of Constitutional Law* (2003) 79.

have been established in disputes between the state and the citizen and then apply them to the different context of a private law dispute. The need for a translation of concepts occurs because the idea of liberty or freedom differs between the contexts of public law and private law.

In public law, the protection afforded by human rights is aimed primarily at negative liberty. It is concerned with placing limits on state power in order to protect the freedom of the individual from abuse of power and to enable individuals and groups to participate in a democratic political process. In private law, in contrast, the notion of liberty is primarily concerned with a positive freedom to achieve one's goals. In this context, the idea of private autonomy expresses the ideal that individuals should have the ability to be the authors of their own lives. There is a perfectionist strand also in this idea of private autonomy, as explained by Joseph Raz.[95] The law assists people to make worthwhile choices, but deters or frustrates efforts to make unwise bargains that are not in their long-term interests. When freedom is not used for such worthwhile purposes, the individual steps outside the constitutional protection for private autonomy. If this freedom is used, for instance, to harm the dignity of another, to invade another's privacy, or to exploit the weakness of another, or (more controversially) to harm oneself, it is arguably not serving a worthwhile purpose.

This contrast mirrors the famous distinction drawn by Isaiah Berlin between negative and positive liberty.[96] Berlin favoured negative liberty and distrusted the idea that individuals should be free only to do what the government believed to be worthwhile activities, no doubt on the valid ground that this concept of positive liberty had been used by totalitarian governments to destroy individuality and autonomy altogether. But if we shift the focus from public law to private law, a positive approach to liberty appears more appropriate and a more accurate description of the evolution of the law. The law of contract, for instance, enables individuals to pursue their goals by making binding transactions. But the law does not enforce every promise that is made. It selects between promises and agreements on various grounds. Was there a good reason for entering the transaction (consideration in the common law, *causa* in Romanistic civil law systems)? Was the consent given to the contract vitiated by force, fraud or undue influence so that it does not really constitute a valid and considered exercise of private autonomy? Does the contract involve illegality or an unjustifiable restraint on the freedom to enter other market transactions, in which case it is unlikely to amount to a worthwhile choice? All these questions and many more constitute an assessment of whether a contract is likely to augment the positive freedom of an individual. In answering such questions, private law needs to develop a positive and perfectionist view of freedom and private autonomy.[97]

This use of human rights to support a positive conception of freedom in private law may be challenged on the ground that it involves a misuse of the concept of human rights, which was invented primarily to protect the negative liberty of individuals. It is questionable whether this view is historically accurate. After all, the great statement of human rights in the Declaration of Human Rights of 1948, shortly after the foundation of the United Nations, was not confined to the protection of civil and political liberties, but included social, economic, and cultural rights. These rights such as the right to education, to health care, and to work, though containing a negative element that forbids

[95] J. Raz, *The Morality of Freedom* (1986).
[96] Berlin, 'Two Concepts of Liberty', in I. Berlin, *Four Essays on Liberty* (1968) 124.
[97] Collins, 'Utility and Rights in Common Law Reasoning: Rebalancing Private Law Through Constitutionalization', 30 *Dalhousie Law Journal* (2007) 1.

restrictions by the state, clearly contribute to a positive conception of autonomy, in which individuals should enjoy fair opportunities in life. Theories of human rights can certainly be constructed on the foundation of a more elaborate idea of private autonomy, which goes beyond negative freedom from interference, to place a duty on the state to promote conditions that enable individuals to realize their own conceptions of a worthwhile life. Human rights function within a perfectionist theory to guide the extremely difficult decisions about when freedom is not being exercised for a worthwhile purpose. The protection of rights within such a theory perhaps need not be linked to this perfectionist approach,[98] though the question of what conditions are essential, what interests need to be protected, or what constitutional rights citizens should have surely needs and deserves a more determinate and objective answer than statements like 'any rights that they feel they need for their well-being'.

If this interpretation of the need for translation when fundamental rights are inserted into private law is correct, it explains the source of the concern that it may involve the imposition of illiberal values by forcing individuals to comply with public standards of political correctness. But to describe these values as illiberal is to use the criterion of negative liberty and to assert that private law has hitherto developed its foundations in negative liberty. If private law is better interpreted as always having expressed a positive conception of liberty, including a perfectionist strand, the insertion of fundamental rights with this kind of 'radiating effect' will not cause a seismic shift in legal doctrine. What it will require, however, is a reconsideration of the requirements of positive freedom in the light of modern values. We observed how this transition has occurred dramatically in the context of anti-discrimination laws. It can also be detected in the *Bürgschaft* case, where the action of the bank that demands a surety from a family member, regardless of that person's comprehension of the transaction or ability to repay the loan, is regarded by the constitutional court as a misuse of the bank's freedom of contract because it necessarily involves inducing the surety to make a choice that cannot possibly be in her own best interests.

[98] J. Griffin, *On Human Rights* (2008); Tasioulas, 'The Moral Reality of Human Rights', in T. Pogge (ed), *Freedom From Poverty as a Human Right* (2007) 75; Moller, 'Two Conceptions of Positive Liberty: Towards an Autonomy-based Theory of Constitutional rights', 29 *Oxford Journal of Legal Studies* (2009) 757.

3

The Fifth European Union Freedom

Aggregating Citizenship . . . around Private Law

Giovanni Comandé

1. Introduction: The Fifth Freedom between Fundamental Rights and Fundamental Boundaries

European Union citizenship is increasingly assuming the role of, what we coin here, the fifth freedom of the Union. This has important consequences not only for the creation of a stateless civic polity, but also for the redefinition of the fundamental boundaries and rights enjoyed by all communities of the European multilevel architecture. Technically operating as an economic freedom, it expands and redefines the scope of fundamental rights by aggregating new bundles of rights around a shadow citizenship. This process necessitates interplay with all involved polities consequently promoting a new type of political allegiance, the final outcome of which is difficult to foresee. The phenomena of which we speak are principally identifiable in the field of private law coupled with traditional models of expanding the role of EU law. That being said, the impact of this process reaches beyond EU competences since it makes use of a particular interplay—the use of member states' private law as a tool to aggregate shadow citizenship in the everyday lives of EU citizens.[1]

Our modest, albeit unconventional, claim in this chapter is limited in scope. Specifically, we suggest that an unorthodox notion of citizenship, the essence of which extends beyond the creation of a novel form of supra/transnational state,[2] is culminating within the framework of the EU. We express the materialization of a notion that the current debate on postnational state-making or citizenship is unable to fully capture[3] and which can be found expressing itself within the realm of private law. We can go no further at present than to suggest that the EU construction process produces important and relevant side effects relating to the empowerment of EU citizens.[4] As a knock on

[1] It must be stated from the outset that the thoughts underlying the present contribution have been integrated into a much broader research project concerning the role of private law in shaping community identities and in the capacity of private law to strengthen democracy and empower citizens against both public and private actors within and across nation states. I am grateful to Hans-W. Micklitz for his critical challenges to earlier versions of this manuscript. Of course, all the views expressed in this chapter remain my own, and I am solely responsible for any errors it may contain.

[2] V. A. Schmidt, *Democracy in Europe: The EU and National Polities* (2006), who sees the EU as a regional state.

[3] For a simple but effective discussion of the current debate on citizenship and the role of national, supranational, transnational states and globalization see Dominique, 'Citizenship', in E. N. Zalta (ed), *The Stanford Encyclopedia of Philosophy* (Fall 2011), available online at <http://plato.stanford.edu/archives/fall2011/entries/citizenship/> (last accessed 28 March 2013) and the literature quoted therein.

[4] The concept of citizen's empowerment is a complex one, especially because it is cast as a connector between private law rules and democracy and certainly touches upon the fact that private law rules can

effect, rights emanating from this process reach beyond the positive laws of the member states despite any consensus surrounding their recognition or the span of protection they offer. In light of this hypothesis, we claim that the supranational legal layer strengthens its position, as, albeit paradoxically, the supposed democratic gap of the EU nurtures a new dimension of civic aggregation and political engagement from the bottom up in each member state. From the outset, we observe that this process levitates both within the framework of EU competences (i.e. the interplay between fundamental rights and fundamental freedoms) as well as *beyond* them, deeply influencing the overall structure of member states' legal systems and creating ruptures in their private law.

The underlying idea is that a plurality of agents, institutions, and legal dynamics is relentlessly aggregating a European citizenship. Conceptually speaking, we refer to this phenomenon as shadow citizenship. This shadow citizenship we speak of acquires its essence not only from the official one (i.e. those rights and liberties enshrined in the different layers of international treaties and the CJEU case law) but also—and more importantly—from the impact the fluid structure of the EU has, well beyond the competences debate, upon the private laws of member states and their scope.

In calling to mind the more traditional understanding of supranational entities, our uptake of the evolution of citizenship in addition to the role that private law plays, and more importantly potentially could play (not only in Europe), may well be construed as 'American-like'. In a sense, the perception of being not only a citizen of the State of Connecticut, for instance, but also a citizen of the USA has emerged via the expansion of the scope of so-called private law rights.[5] Indeed, it is even possible that in early times, after independence, citizens of the single States (the young former colonies) perceived the USA as more of a supranational entity rather than a national one according to the post-Westphalian understanding.[6] Yet, the potential of the parallel drawn between the two sides of the Atlantic (at least according to our investigation to date) ends here. This can be attributed to a number of factors, including the evolving features of the European treaties and the peculiar legal arena they shape according to CJEU jurisprudence; the history of European countries which, when examined, highlights a more evolved social dimension; the European fundamental rights parley that has managed to nestle human rights utterances within private law discourse, a process that is normally left to the devices of international human rights, in effect embedding fundamental rights in the daily lives

regulate private institutions acting as intermediaries between individuals and the state empowering the enjoyment of rights which would not otherwise be protected. However, this point is beyond the scope of this publication and we can only make reference to it here. In a different setting, examples from the US and China would be useful. They would offer two very specific references to patterns like those we are now witnessing in Europe. A retrospective one (USA) which illustrates (*mutatis mutandis*) that EU member state citizens find recognition for some private law rights (even in their own member state) only when they exercise their economic freedoms moving across borders; a partially prospective one (China) demonstrating that the private law tools used in Europe can produce similar effects of 'empowerment' in other legal systems much different from ours and which are often considered less 'democratic'. In this perspective traditional private law tools can silently empower citizens in facing their individual or business interplay within their legal order.

[5] For a normative reference see, for instance, USC Title 42, Chapter 21, Subchapter I § 1981.

[6] As a note of caution, however, we must note that perhaps the notion of state, nation, citizenship and their correspondent prefixes (trans, inter, supranational) are unable to fully capture the phenomenon (see in general Scott, '"Transnational Law" as Proto-Concept: Three Conceptions', 10 *German Law Journal* (2009) 877; CLPE Research Paper No. 32/2009, available online at <http://ssrn.com/abstract=1488245> or <http://dx.doi.org/10.2139/ssrn.1488245> (last accessed 28 March 2013)). Henceforth, we use the expression transnational, or supranational according to the limited meaning of non-national in the sense of the post-Westphalia nation state. Therefore, a cross-border element is not necessary to define the content of a transnational phenomenon.

of citizens.[7] As a result and in consideration of the EU dimension, we can safely say that there is no room for placing 'thicker' human rights in contraposition with a 'thinner' citizenship.[8] As we shall see, their relationship to each other is more harmonious with fundamental rights nurturing the shadow citizenship in many ways.

We must also admit that our understanding of citizenship does not perfectly fit within the confines of the ongoing debate concerning the notion. Our understanding cannot simply be located within the debate between liberal nationalists and post nationalists. Indeed, the shadow citizenship we are concerned with is characterized by being anchored in a non-nation state (the European Union). Hence, somehow it draws from both the republican model and the liberal idea of citizenship. From the former, it extracts the idea that engagement in the public sphere contributes to the very shaping of identity (the civic self-rule of Rousseau[9]) and from the latter it derives the notion of protection of the private individual sphere (citizenship as a legal status, a bundle of rights shared among members of the same community). This process, essentially conducted via aggregation, renders the appearance of the novel notion of European shadow citizenship as somehow liquid and incoherent: political participation in the republican conception of citizenship takes the path of individual rights assertion under the shadow of fundamental rights and economic freedoms. The cultivation of this aggregating citizenship does not necessarily give way to inclusion or identity since it reflects a rather diverse array of values and readings of fundamental rights. Such diversity is incoherent, as well, with 'differentiated citizenship'[10] since the only acknowledged 'group' aggregating citizenship is EU citizens, EU citizens who represent a variety of values and rights of such multitude and complexity that the notion of common constitutional traditions has been rendered inefficient or simply incapable of dealing with them. For this reason, attention has inevitably shifted to the EU Charter of Fundamental Rights as an alternative, or better, a foundation for the shadow citizenship we speak of.

For these reasons, the interplay between fundamental freedoms and fundamental rights proves to be an important factor that when analysed, demonstrates, in a paradoxical way, the ongoing transformation of the latter's underdog position to a more elevated and commanding stance. We must be mindful however, that the emerging content of fundamental rights in relation to the shaping of the shadow citizenship does not coincide entirely with the content embedded in member state constitutions.[11]

[7] H. Collins, *The European Civil Code: The Way Forward* (2008).

[8] See, in particular, Chapter III of C. Joppke, *Citizenship and Immigration* (2010).

[9] J. J. Rousseau, *On the Social Contract: with Geneva Manuscript and Political Economy* (1978), at 56.

[10] The term was first used by I. M. Young in Young, 'Polity and Group Difference: A Critique of the Ideal of Universal Citizenship', 99 *Ethics* (1989) 250. See, for recent accounts, Kymlicka, 'Citizenship in Culturally Diverse Societies: Issues, Contexts, Concepts', in W. Kymlicka and W. Norman (eds), *Citizenship in Diverse Societies* (2000) 1. Yet we are aware that, while it enables this liquid aggregation of shadow citizenship, the process we analyse runs the risks of leading to an unwanted 'differentiated citizenship' in which individuals are accommodated also according to their belonging to particular groups and consequently their rights partially depend on the group. 'From this perspective, the danger of... differentiated citizenship is that the emphasis [it] place[s] on the recognition and institutionalization of difference could undermine the conditions that make a sense of common identification and thus mutuality possible.' See J. H. Carens, *Culture, Citizenship, and Community: A Contextual Exploration of Justice as Evenhandedness* (2000), at 193.

[11] See the Opinion of AG Bot in Case C-283/11, *Sky Österreich GmbH v Österreichischer Rundfunk*, where at para. 80 it is stated that 'fundamental rights within the Union must be protected within the framework of its structure and objectives. It follows that the weighing of the different fundamental rights at stake does not necessarily call for the same response at national or EU level'. AG Bot supports the argument also by referring to early cases of the Court, particularly Case 11/70, *Internationale Handelsgesellschaft* [1970] ECR 1125, Rec. 4.

From a more practical point of view, our thesis suggests that the EU building process may actually be in the course of creating a modern form of state, silently forging its very own identity by gathering and depicting values informed by the legal systems and the legal input of the member states. This creation of a multifaceted identity is a visible result of the aggregating role of the shadow citizenship. From such a framework, a double link to democratic considerations appears vivid. On the one hand, not only does this process accommodate more than a minority or identity position, avoiding 'differentiated citizenship', but it also empowers a true European citizen as such (attracting loyalty to the EU polity beyond any understanding of it as a national or postnational state). On the other hand, it offers a tangible solution to the often-criticized fixes proposed to overcome the democratic deficit affiliated with the building and governance of the EU. Technically, the legal path we make reference to finds its roots in the original approach of the (then) ECJ when it came to empowering individuals and lower courts to force their governments to abide by their international commitments, in other words, the idea advocated by the *Van Gend & Loos* direct applicability notion.[12]

Ever since the early days of the Internal Market building endeavour, empowering economic freedoms and polishing the Internal Market were the main driving forces behind the institutional construction of what is, today, the EU polity. The original idea was to build a community by applying mutual recognition principles and dismantling regulatory barriers in 'broadly similar private law systems'.[13] Over time, these goals have irradiated most aspects of the EU edifice, including the role played by private law to this end. This has remained so even though the protection of fundamental rights stemming from Brussels (EU law as interpreted by the ECJ) and Strasbourg (interpreting the ECHR) has begun to illuminate the entire field of European private law. In other words, the dominating legal technique remains the enforcement of the economic freedoms even where reference to them or their actual exercise[14] became less of a substantive requirement and more a formal one.[15]

In light of the above, sections 2 and 3 illustrate, on one side of the coin, the interplay between fundamental rights and the allocation of competences as components of the EU polity. On the other side, they discuss how the language of private law and of the protection of the EU economic freedoms renders the emergence of the shadow citizenship (or, a supranational state in contemporary discourse), in defining its fundamental bonds to member state citizens in everyday relationships, less political and axiological. Building upon these considerations, sections 4 and 5 explore the theoretical and historical bases from which the shadow citizenship emerges, arguing that offering relevance to the rights of EU citizens and forging EU fundamental rights protection through the language and technical processes—usually adopted with regard to the protection of the fundamental freedoms—has proved an important and characterizing feature of EU law and for its identity shaping process. While anchoring the overall thesis to examples of CJEU cases, the final section problematically sets out the role this technique of 'disguised' fundamental rights protection can still have in expanding the scope of EU citizens' rights if we elaborate the notion of EU citizenship just as if it were the fifth economic freedom of the EU under which the official and the shadow notions of citizenship merge.

[12] Case 32/84, *Van Gend & Loos NV v Inspecteur der Invoerrechten en Accijnzen* [1985] Reports of Cases 779. See also A. M. Slaughter, 'Judicial Globalization', 40 *Virginia Journal of International Law* (2000) 1005.

[13] Collins, *supra* note 7, at 22.

[14] See *infra*, notes 212 and 213 and accompanying text.

[15] See sections 4 and 5 on the necessary community connection.

2. The Perceived Role of Human Rights in Modern Societies and...

In our modern societies, fundamental rights[16] protection has taken a stance concerning the protection of rights related to the guarantees of a functioning democracy,[17] the fostering of the principle of equality,[18] and the fight against all discrimination.[19] That being said, the interplay between democracy and human rights may appear paradoxical at times,[20] generating tensions within a given legal order and between national and supranational legal orders.[21] Resolving these tensions sets new equilibria within and among legal orders. The confrontation between these tensions in the European multilevel system of governance is shaping a civic identity that is proving difficult to frame in traditional ways since it is emerging based on both conventional and non-conventional patterns.[22]

As these processes continue to develop, we can assert that effective rights protection reinforces the possibility of democratic involvement well beyond electoral participation.[23] In addition, we can assume that the effective protection of daily life rights encompasses that which ordinary citizens discern to be the icon of democracy and of participation in it. The perceived guarantee of these rights clearly contributes to a sense of belonging to a democratic community equivalent to the feeling of security conjured by the protection of fundamental rights in post-World War II European constitutions. Most of these rights are defined in the so-called private law domain (e.g. performance of contractual

[16] Although not entirely clear-cut, a definition of fundamental rights appears to emerge as those rights which the state cannot limit without following specific 'aggravated processes', if it can at all. These rights are usually enshrined in constitutional and/or supranational texts and tend to shape the evolution of rights and duties both between citizens and states and among citizens themselves.

[17] The EU, according to Art. 2 TEU, 'is founded on the values of respect for human dignity, freedom, democracy, equality, the rule of law and respect for human rights'.

[18] For a problematic reading of the interplay between the notion of EU citizenship and the principle of equality, see for instance, D. Kochenov, 'Citizenship without Respect: The EU's Troubled Equality Ideal' (2010), Jean Monnet Working Papers 8, <http://centers.law.nyu.edu/jeanmonnet/papers/10/100801.html> (last accessed 28 March 2013).

[19] Weiler, 'Human Rights, Constitutionalism, and Integration: Iconography and Fetishism', in R. Kastoryano (eds), *An Identity for Europe, The Relevance of Multiculturalism in EU Construction* (2009) 73.

[20] See A. Clapham, *Human Rights Obligations of Non-State Actors* (2006), stressing at 533 that: 'Democracy may demand a wide-ranging circulation of ideas, even at the expense of absolute respect for private property and private relations. But democracy also demands that rules are made in a way as there is accountability to those who are governed by those rules.'

[21] For an overview of the difficult interplay and potential conflicts that can arise between constitutional and EU fundamental rights at both the national level and at the CJEU see A. T. Pérez, *Conflicts of Rights in the European Union: A Theory of Supranational Adjudication* (2009).

[22] On the attempts made to describe and measure the interplay between democracy and European identity, see, for instance, O. Brzezińska et al. (eds), 'Identity and Democracy in the New Europe: The Next Generation Finds Its Way' (2012), RECON Report No. 18.

[23] 'Universal suffrage has not put an end to inequalities in the capacity of citizens to exercise and influence state power, because that capacity is affected by disparities in society. Subordinate socio-economic statuses tend to reinforce, and be reinforced by, political marginalization. Efforts to ensure political and civil rights must therefore go hand in hand with moves to secure respect for social, economic and cultural rights. Finally the homogeneity of the democratic "people" cannot be assumed. Since the social disparities which affect participation in public processes are systematically correlated (*inter alia*) to divisions of gender, ethnicity, and other group affiliation, political equality must not be understood in terms of (a particular) identity. Rather it must be approached in terms of the need to ensure that differences among citizens do not operate as disadvantages. Democracy must be conceived as requiring that all citizens have the chance to participate in decision-making which affects them all.' S. Marks, *The Riddle of all Constitutions: International Law, Democracy and the Critique of Ideology* (2003), at 59–60.

or work-related obligations and family relationships).[24] This holds true even when the counterpart in the private relationship is a public authority, and is even more evident as a result of the deregulation and privatization processes fostered at the turn of the last century.

Still, we wonder if shifting from the language of human rights and its universality claims[25] to the language of fundamental rights (in the sense of positively acknowledged rights in constitutional orders and now in the EU) can offer more room for pursuing the protection of individual dignity and a corresponding strengthening of democracy.[26] For instance, the nature of human rights, especially those contained in international instruments, and moreover their characterization based on historical considerations, may not suffice in offering a complete protection of human dignity across the board coupled with a strengthening of democracy. However, their general nature, in the sense that they attempt to be so far-reaching, could be overcome if fundamental rights were already entrenched in national settings and expansive interpretative techniques, from elsewhere if needs be, were adopted.[27] In this sense, fundamental rights[28] protection and in general the protection of the private sphere not only serves the scope of individual/group protection but also the strengthening of democracy while simultaneously assisting individuals to challenge public and private abuses averse to their (fundamental) rights.[29]

In addition, and by way of further introduction, we must note that the same paradigm of reference to fundamental rights and freedoms can foster different patterns of legal evolution and different ways of perceiving democracy and shaping allegiance to citizenship.[30] It is also true that, for instance, the protection of the private sphere has legitimized—by

[24] This can be noted as a shared opinion. See, for instance, Collins, *supra* note 7, at 6: 'The evolving rules of ownership, trade and personal status contained in private law described the structure and scope of a community. Legal discourses weave their own distinctive interpretations of the standards that should govern relations in civil society and how those standards are connected to broader political principles such as the protection of individual rights and the obligations of membership of a community. Reliance on the rules implies a common identity and membership in a community. Without such an implicit common identity and membership, it seems impossible to imagine a single polity, an association of all the peoples of Europe.'

[25] For a challenging analysis, see E. Brems, *Human Rights: Universality and Diversity* (2001).

[26] Concerns have, however, been raised in relation to the potential negative impact the incorporation of a bill of rights, such as the Charter of Fundamental Rights, may have in the European scenario. A. Gruber, 'La Charte des Droits Fondamentaux de l'Union Européenne: Un Message Clair Hautement Symbolique', *Petites Affiches: La Loi*, 22 January 2001, No. 15, 4, at 16.

[27] To exemplify, we can make reference to the expansive reading of the right to education embedded in the Chinese constitution and its direct application via the general principles of private law; a process somehow mirroring the third party effect used in several European countries. From 2001 to 2009 (when the No. 25 Judicial Interpretation of the Supreme People's Court of China was repealed) the right to education enumerated in the Chinese constitution was used to award compensation for its infringement in conjunction with the general principles of private law. See Zhu L., 'The Right to Education Proceedings before the Chinese Courts: To what Extent the Law in Paper has been Realised in Practice?' (2012), available online at: <http://rwi.lu.se/wp-content/uploads/2012/04/The-Right-to-Education-Proceedings-before-the-Chinese-Courts-Zhu-Lijiang.pdf> (last accessed 14 December 2012).

[28] For the sake of our argument here, we use the term fundamental rights in reference to those embedded in state constitutions or international covenants.

[29] What could be termed as democratic empowerment: enabling individuals to counter private and public powers.

[30] For an anthropological analysis of the development of citizens' rights in contemporary societies, see Riccio and Scandurra, 'Citizenship: Anthropological Approaches to Migration and Social Exclusion', in K. De Feyter and G. Pavlakos (eds), *The Tension between Group Rights and Human Rights* (2008) 207. We should also note that the adoption of the concept of European citizenship has been sometimes read with great scepticism on the basis that it is not capable of adding anything substantial to the field, not even in the domain of immigration and circulation of people. See T. Kostakopoulou, *Citizenship, Identity and Immigration in the European Union: Between Past and Future* (2001), at 66. See

way of claiming no interference in the private sphere itself—domestic violence, rape within marriage, and racially exclusive clubs and associations, to highlight but a few examples.[31] In other terms, it is true that fundamental rights and liberties have served quite different 'masters' by way of purporting different legal approaches or claiming protection of different fundamental rights in opposition to one another.[32] More generally, the idea that courts had enhanced democracy[33] by 'uphold[ing] such non political rights as rights of property, procreation, parental authority, marital privacy, travel, and personal security' is not new at all[34] since they can have both progressive and regressive outcomes.

In general, these assumptions are verifiable in relation to any legal order, be it national or supranational, in circumstances where they function 'internally' in any given legal system. However, the situation becomes more convoluted when, considering the interplay between the EU and member states, different readings of (even the same) fundamental rights define different polities and their internal balances which must cohabit. As we

also D. Kochenov, '*Ius Tractum* of Many Faces: European Citizenship and the Difficult Relationship between Status and Rights', 2 *Columbia Journal of European Law* (2009) 173.

[31] Clapham, *supra* note 20, *passim*.

[32] A non-European example may be useful here. For quite different approaches in the same legal system one can think of the affirmation of private law rights in the American experience attached to the reading of state and federal law in light of the US constitution. For better or worse, at different moments in time the basic tenets of the (common) law anchored in the US Constitution have been used to foster fundamental principles. Take for example the cases of *Loving v Virginia* (388 US 1 (1967)) and *Lochner v New York* (198 US 45 (1905)) from which it is evident that two completely different conceptions underpin the reasoning in the respective cases. In one direction, *Loving v Virginia* can be characterized by the vein of anti-discrimination running through the reasoning: 'Marriage is one of the "basic civil rights of man", fundamental to our very existence and survival.... To deny this fundamental freedom on so unsupportable a basis as the racial classifications embodied in these statutes, classifications so directly subversive of the principle of equality at the heart of the Fourteenth Amendment, is surely to deprive all the State's citizens of liberty without due process of law. The Fourteenth Amendment requires that the freedom of choice to marry not be restricted by invidious racial discrimination. Under our Constitution, the freedom to marry, or not marry, a person of another race resides with the individual and cannot be infringed by the State.' In a different tone, albeit from the same era, the *Lochner* case can be taken as an example of the potential of using fundamental rights and freedoms arguments for the strengthening of private law rights, in this instance freedom of contract, of sustaining the empowerment of a democratic state under the banners of the rule of law and what—at a given moment in legal history—is perceived as a private law right. We can point, for instance, to freedom of contract vs union organization activities and collective bargaining as exemplified by the history of 'labour injunctions' (for more information, see F. Frankfurter and N. Green, *The Labor Injunction* (1930). For a discussion of the state of the art both prior and post the Norris-La Guardia Act, see L. M. Friedman, *A History of American Law* (1973). On the parallel between *Lochner* and the evolution of EU law see Caruso, 'Lochner In Europe: A Comment On Keith Whittington's "Congress Before The Lochner Court" ', 85 *Boston University Law Review* (2005) 867).

[33] On the democracy enhancing role of transnational dialogue among national judges in fostering and stifling the national and political debate in a context of expanded relocation of regulatory policy-making power from the domestic to the international sphere, see Benvenisti and Downs, 'The Democratizing Effects of Transjudicial Coordination', 8 *Utrecht Law Review* (2012) 158, where it is argued that such a role can promote accountability to diverse democratic concerns by providing opportunities for national legislatures and civil society to weigh in on matters subject to executive discretion or international regulation: 'The national courts' main asset in this regard is their ability to influence the character of the domestic political and institutional response to the actions of the executive. Their intervention generates information that alerts additional domestic actors such as the domestic legislature, opposition parties and voters that a potential problem exists and enables these actors to weigh in on the matters under review that they otherwise might have ignored. By so doing, the courts' intervention activates and empowers domestic actors that executives have often sought to bypass, and establishes the basis of coalition that can potentially succeed in limiting executive discretion.' (at 160–161).

[34] Selznick, 'Communitarian Jurisprudence', in D. Carney (ed), *To Promote the General Welfare* (1999) 29.

shall see, in these instances the language of (fundamental) rights sometimes requires some exercise of (formal or linguistic) disguise so as to offer effective protection. In other words, the effective protection of the fundamental right must be achieved via an indirect path, i.e. the protection must appear as a side effect of protecting a different legal interest (e.g. economic freedoms). Accordingly, we must investigate whether effective participation in democratic life can only be attained via the possibility for citizens to reaffirm their rights and obtain effective protection without risking discrimination or whether there is another viable way.

This approach of 'disguising' the legal protection of fundamental rights and its interference with national private law, essentially causing a rupturing effect, appears to be, in our opinion, a characteristic of the European multilevel system in that it permits the system to avoid openly confronting the coexistence of so many different polities and sets of values rooted in the private laws of member states. Indeed, despite its apparent obviousness, a shared definition of fundamental rights is difficult to find, even within the same legal order at any given moment in time, as scholars, courts, and constitutions do not always converge on one definition.[35] The main distinctions among fundamental rights reflect the 'traditional' taxonomies among different generations of rights, for instance differences between 'classical' and 'social' fundamental rights.[36] In relation to this, it is fair to say that the social reception of particular fundamental rights can be rather divergent in the various member states, exacerbating the rhetorical character of the reference to common constitutional traditions. That being said, the historical evolution of the balance between conflicting rights and powers—at every level of governance—largely boils down to the unstable nature of fundamental rights.[37]

In principle, fundamental rights are 'inherent to the person and cannot be modified by either the ordinary legislator, the constitutional legislator, or the communitarian legislator'.[38] In reality, however, fundamental rights can generally be restricted or interfered with, but this is subject to certain conditions (usually the protection of other legally protected rights) and, sometimes, legislative reservation is also required. In any event, it undoubtedly appears that the core of fundamental rights—human dignity—cannot be affected in modern western societies whatever the temporary balance between fundamental rights and their possible limits.[39] That being said, a limit to dignity in one country might not necessarily constitute a limit in another.[40] Moreover, assuming the universal (or otherwise) nature of human rights, their historical and political dimension

[35] Differences in terminology are found everywhere. For instance, in Sweden, the Constitution is referred to as the *Grundlagen* (fundamental law), while fundamental rights may be translated as *grundläggande rättighter, civila rättighter*, or *medborgerliga rättighter*.

[36] See Palombella, 'From Human Rights to Fundamental Rights—Consequences of a Conceptual Distinction', 93 *Archiv für Rechts- und Sozialphilosophie* (2007) 396, and quoted literature.

[37] Of course, some key features of fundamental rights can be highlighted such as the special legislative procedure (e.g. an aggravated process of constitutional review) designed to deal with interferences and/or their non-modifiability by the legislature.

[38] Comandé, 'Comparative remarks', in G. Brüggemeier, A. Colombi Ciacchi, and G. Comandé (eds), *Fundamental Rights and Private Law in the European Union. Volume 1: A Comparative Overview* (2010) 707.

[39] That being said, the notion of dignity can be described in very different ways. See J. Q. Whitman, 'The Two Western Cultures of Privacy: Dignity versus Liberty' (2004), Faculty Scholarship Series, Paper 649, available online at: <http://digitalcommons.law.yale.edu/fss_papers/649> (last accessed 14 December 2012).

[40] Pérez, *supra* note 21, at 80 where it is argued that '[a]s a consequence of the process of European integration, a supranational legal order has emerged, in which rights are protected and interpreted by a supranational court. The interpretation of fundamental rights, owing to their open texture and essentially contested content, is highly controversial. Additionally, they may conflict with public interests or

can have quite different legal implications envisaging them as absolute limits to state and individual actions or as rights whose essence is regulated by the constitutional settings acknowledging them.

These understandings and multiform techniques of legal protection appear to be shared patrimony both at member state and at EU level. However, since in the EU a common set of notions (including on dignity itself) does not exist, a dynamic equilibrium is created, one much more unstable than that 'naturally' found in every national legal system. For instance, there are different conceptions of dignity[41] and they often sustain one or another legal and/or political option.[42] For example, in the EU a large number of anti-discrimination directives enshrine the notion of dignity in defining the discrimination referred to. Indeed, in EU law the notion of dignity is quite often entrenched in the fight against any form of discrimination.[43] Thus, in the EU the equilibrium appears both precarious internally, showing inconsistencies due, as well, to the interplay between fundamental rights and the economic freedoms, and precarious externally—vis-à-vis the various member states—so as not to appear to be endorsing a single member state polity's acknowledgement of fundamental rights.[44]

other fundamental rights. The balance between them may be legitimately resolved differently in diverse legal systems. Since it is uncertain whether there is only one "correct" interpretation, and even if there is, there is no agreement on how to reach it, diverse political communities might "reasonably disagree" about the meaning of fundamental rights'.

[41] See Brownsword, 'Freedom of Contract, Human Rights and Human Dignity', in D. Friedmann and D. Barak-Erez (eds), *Human Rights In Private Law* (2001) 181, at 193–194 who explains two concepts of human dignity. According to him, human dignity in its empowerment function supports individual autonomy but it can also act as a constraint on individual autonomy itself. Yet, at the core of any concept of human dignity we can find the Kantian conception: 'Every human being has a legitimate claim to respect from his fellow human beings and is in turn bound to respect every other. Humanity itself is a dignity: for a human being cannot be used merely as means by any human being (either by others or even by himself) but always be used at the same time as an end. It is just in this that this dignity (personality) consists, by which he raises himself above all other beings in the world that are not human beings and yet can be used, and so over all things. But just as he cannot be himself away for any price (this would conflict with his duty of self-esteem), so neither can he act contrary to the equally necessary self-esteem of others, as human beings, that is, he is under obligation to acknowledge, in a practical way, the dignity of humanity in every other human being. Hence there rests on him a duty regarding the respect that must be shown to every other human being.' I. Kant, *The Metaphysics of Morals* (1797, translation 1996), at 186–209.

[42] See Rao, 'Three Concepts of Dignity in Constitutional Law', 86 *Notre Dame Law Review* (2011) 183.

[43] 'Human dignity, as a *raison d'être* for human rights, is reflected, not only in international instruments, but also in various constitutional orders'. In this regard, see Clapham, *supra* note 20, at 533.

[44] This instability is convoluted and complicated further, especially in consideration of our hypothesis here, when we consider the development of the shadow citizenship alongside the interplay between national courts, the CJEU and the ECHR. See, the Grand Chamber in case C-617/10, *Åklagaren v Hans Åkerberg Fransson*, judgment of 26 February 2013, not yet published, at Rec. 45 where it is stated that with regard to 'the conclusions to be drawn by a national court from a conflict between provisions of domestic law and rights guaranteed by the Charter, it is settled case-law that a national court which is called upon, within the exercise of its jurisdiction, to apply provisions of European Union law is under a duty to give full effect to those provisions, if necessary refusing of its own motion to apply any conflicting provision of national legislation, even if adopted subsequently, and it is not necessary for the court to request or await the prior setting aside of such a provision by legislative or other constitutional means (Case 106/77 *Simmenthal* [1978] ECR 629, paragraphs 21 and 24; Case C-314/08 *Filipiak* [2009] ECR I-11049, paragraph 81; and Joined Cases C-188/10 and C-189/10 *Melki and Abdeli* [2010] ECR I-5667, paragraph 43)'. Indeed the court recalled that '[s]ince the fundamental rights guaranteed by the Charter must therefore be complied with where national legislation falls within the scope of European Union law, situations cannot exist which are covered in that way by European Union law without those fundamental rights being applicable. The applicability of European Union law entails applicability of

This unstable ambiguity offers fertile ground upon which the shadow citizenship can flourish. It empowers individuals and legal entities to protect their interests according to one or other status (national or EU) considering the given circumstances and to foster—in legal terms—their political participation. The ability to shift between allegiances, for instance, in claiming that EU law infringes upon national values and member state citizens' rights[45] or that EU law prevents member state law to treat EU *citizens* as *subjects*, somehow contributes to an understanding of the EU shadow citizenship as positively propitious. It enables individuals (including legal entities) to play the game of pondering which of the two citizenships available to them is more in line with their wishes/needs/interests/values, thereby transforming legal action into political democratic participation. This game ultimately permits dressing a specific political idea in legal clothes, clothes that were unavailable in the national context. Of course, the game is relatively new and is only beginning to expropriate the language of 'protection of citizens'. In addition, the legal tools employed by the game-players are different. However, the invention of the supremacy of EU law[46] and the expansive mechanism of building the Internal Market in accordance with the fundamental economic freedoms have been of paramount importance.

In addition, we may note that across different parallels, meridians, and of course with the passing of time, different societies have been following different patterns—in relation to the definition of fundamental rights—according to predominant and/or emerging views.[47] Indeed, this holds true also in consideration of different generations of fundamental rights[48] and the notion of dignity underlying them.[49] The issue concerning

the fundamental rights guaranteed by the Charter' (Rec. 25). This is so even if 'the national legislation...has not been adopted to transpose' (at Rec. 28) a directive and bearing in mind that 'here a court of a Member State is called upon to review whether fundamental rights are complied with by a national provision or measure which, in a situation where action of the Member States is not entirely determined by European Union law, implements the latter for the purposes of Article 51(1) of the Charter, national authorities and courts remain free to apply national standards of protection of fundamental rights, *provided that the level of protection provided for by the Charter, as interpreted by the Court, and the primacy, unity and effectiveness of European Union law are not thereby compromised* (see, in relation to the latter aspect, Case C-399/11 *Melloni* [2013] ECR I-0000, paragraph 60)' (Rec. 29, emphasis added). However, once again the Court does not offer clear guidance that national judges may follow.

[45] Perhaps by simply highlighting a situation whereby the EU exceeds its competences.

[46] To cite the words of A. M. Slaughter and W. Mattli, one effect of the shadow citizenship is 'the power to promote certain substantive policies through law. In other words, where European law and national law promote different policies or have different distributional effects with respect to a particular class of litigants, a national judge may have the opportunity to achieve the result that she favours through the application of European Law'. Slaughter and Mattli, 'The Role of National Courts in the Process of European Integration: Accounting for Judicial Preferences and Constraints', in A. M. Slaughter, A. S. Sweet, and J. H. H. Weiler (eds), *The European Courts And National Courts: Doctrine And Jurisprudence* (1997) 258.

[47] For an insightful analysis of the ambiguities that arose concerning the early applications of the human rights rhetoric see, M. Callari Galli, 'Human Rights and the Anthropological Perspectives on the Dynamics of Cultural Differences', in K. De Feyter and G. Pavlakos (eds), *The Tension Between Group Rights And Human Rights: A Multidisciplinary Approach* (2008) 73.

[48] Indeed, the two follow-up covenants of the Universal Declaration of Human Rights (UDHR) divide rights into two distinct classes: civil and political rights; and economic, social, and cultural rights. See the International Covenant on Civil and Political Rights (ICCPR), 19 December 1966, 999 UNTS 171 (entered into force 23 March 1976) and the International Covenant on Economic, Social and Cultural Rights (ICESCR), 19 December 1966, 993 UNTS 3 (entered into force 3 January 1976). For a discussion of the reasons behind the split, see Keller, 'The Indivisibility of Economic and Political Rights', 1 *Human Rights & Human Welfare* (2001) 9 (reviewing A. Sen, *Development as Freedom* (1999), available online at <http://www.du.edu/korbel/hrhw/volumes/2001/1-3/keller-sen.pdf> (last accessed 14 December 2012)). However, no clear division is made among them (cf. UDHR Arts 22–27). See Keller, 'The American Rejection of Economic Rights as Human Rights and the Declaration of Independence: Does the Pursuit of Happiness Require Basic Economic Rights?', 19 *New York Law School Journal of Human Rights* (2003), 557.

[49] On the various notions of dignity, see notes 27, 41 and followings with accompanying text. See also Rao, *supra* note 42, at 183–271.

the analytical dimension according to which the progressive acknowledgement of the fundamentality of a right in a legal system contributes to shape the democratic dimension of the state and to define the identity of the group(s)[50] pertaining to the given legal system that potentially enjoy(s) the rights, cannot be fully explored here. Suffice it to say that the level of protection accorded to fundamental human rights at any given moment in time contributes in defining the perception of one's community as a democracy[51] and allegiance to it since it contributes to limiting the (private or public) powers that can potentially infringe upon them. Indeed, against this backdrop and although the very notion of human rights[52] and their level of protection—beyond a certain core—is not common in the western legal tradition, the idea of upholding rights, rights that are so 'fundamental' they cannot be stripped away by any authority, remains at the centre of the cherished notion of the rule of law and a key rhetorical element that constitutes a democracy and the feeling of belonging to it.

Whatever conception of society is accepted (e.g. liberal, communitarian, etc.), the protection of the rights of individuals and legal entities is perceived as the basis for maintaining a healthy society and restricting public—and more recently—private powers.[53] At the EU level, 'commitment to fundamental human rights as a unifying ideal, one of the core values around which the people and peoples of Europe may coalesce'[54] is a mantra to which everybody refers,[55] at least implicitly since the first intervention of the ECJ.[56] Yet, beyond this intuitive understanding, the delineation of a common set

[50] Clapham, *supra* note 20, at 311, stating that '[t]alking about human rights may sometimes bestow identity on Community citizens'.

[51] Weiler, *supra* note 19, at 107, where he notes that 'our constitutions are said to encapsulate fundamental values of the polity and this, in turn, is said to be a reflection of our collective identity as a people, as a nation, as a state, as a community, as a Union'.

[52] On several occasions, alternative definitions are used in each legal system (for example, '*diritto fondamentale*' and '*diritto inviolabile*' (inviolable right), 'human rights', or 'citizen's rights'). Though often used as synonyms, those expressions do not always convey the same legal concept and rather refer to subsets of fundamental rights, or to those rights acknowledged by constitutions, or those which receive their fundamental character through constitutional recognition (such as when referring to constitutional rights, '*diritti costituzionali*', etc.). 'Human right' is a formula often used as a synonym of fundamental right and refers to rights that people possess merely because they are part of human society and/or are enshrined in international charters. Yet, human rights are often related to natural law, while civil rights and liberties are related to positive law and therefore they can be used as leverage for innovation and democratic empowerment well beyond any claim of universality. In any event, from an historical point of view, two different conceptions of fundamental rights are often present (at least) in the European legal systems: the conception according to which fundamental rights pre-dated the state, and the conception requiring the recognition of these fundamental rights by the state for their very existence.

[53] See, for instance, the proposed EU Regulation on Data Protection, COM(2012) 11 final. On the quest concerning the extension of human rights to non-state actors see Clapham, *supra* note 20, *passim*.

[54] Weiler, 'Fundamental Rights and Fundamental Boundaries: Common Standards and Conflicting Values in the Protection of Human Rights in European Space', in R. Kastoryano (ed), *An Identity for Europe: The Relevance of Multiculturalism in EU Construction* (2009), 73.

[55] See, for instance, the opinion of AG Sharpston in Case C-34/09, *Gerardo Ruiz Zambrano v Office national de l'emploi (ONEm)* [2011] ECR I-1177: 'Over succeeding years, the EU has reinforced its policy on fundamental rights through (for example) setting up a Fundamental Rights Agency, creating an independent portfolio within the Commission responsible for fundamental rights, supporting humanitarian projects throughout the world and transforming the Charter of Fundamental Rights of the EU, first proclaimed in 2000, from a non-binding text ("soft law") into primary law. Fundamental rights have thus become a core element in the development of the Union as a process of economic, legal and social integration aimed at providing peace and prosperity to all its citizens.' (para. 154).

[56] 'In safeguarding [fundamental rights, the Court] is bound to draw inspiration from constitutional traditions common to the Member States, so that measures which are incompatible with the fundamental rights recognized by the constitutions of those states are unacceptable in the Community.' Case C-44/79, *Liselotte Hauer v Land Rheinland-Pfalz* [1979] ECR 3727, 3728 (ECJ).

of values defining EU identity remains unclear since it is far from common and fairly resembles a basket of fruits picked from rather different trees. In addition, since private law is supposed to conform to the fundamental rights equilibrium reached in given constitutional settings and in turn, any constitutional interpretation must be informed by a deep understanding of private law rules by citizens,[57] interfering with one or the other inevitably impinges upon both.

In summary, beyond a minimal core, protection of fundamental rights as a unifying trait of EU identity rests more on a perception of sharing rather than an actual sharing of specific values and their meaning. Nevertheless, its rhetoric remains a powerful one in the gathering together of European peoples and—as we shall see—contributes to a shift in focus from the technical protection of economic freedoms to the creation of a shared identity via its interactions with daily life rights within the national legal orders.

3. . . . Creative Tensions in Defining the Boundaries of EU Multilevel Identity

As a flip side of the same coin, the projects or aims of a given polity at any given moment in time, shape the fundamental boundaries within which each community has the power to define their shared values without interference from other legal (national, supranational, international) orders.[58] This is still the case for member states vis-à-vis the EU but, to use Weiler's words, since 'human rights constitute . . . both a source of, and index for, cross-national differentiation and not only cross-national assimilation',[59] we should ask whether there is an identity shaping role for human rights at the EU supranational level at all.[60] We claim here that there is a role, one which is driven mainly, albeit not exclusively, by private law (a) with regards to the way the interplay, between EU and member state private law orders, has been shaped and (b) in relation to the intrinsic characteristics of private law language,[61] a language that has been borrowed by the economic freedoms rhetoric in EU regulation and can also be located in the CJEU case law. The identity shaping role stems from the possibility of purporting different visions of fundamental rights and their interplay with private law rules. This is what shapes EU identity in the mould of the legal process as opposed to a ready made, clear-cut bundle of

[57] Collins, *supra* note 7, at 105 notes 'the contributions of constitutional law and private law as two sides of the same coin. General constitutional principles protecting private property and freedom of contract should be seen as closely connected with private law rules about circulation and protection of property rights, so that they are mutually dependent parts of a broader scheme of social justice'.

[58] In a way, this is the rationale of EU law with respect to the criteria for establishing the nationality of member state citizens. See Case C-413/99, *Baumbast and R v Secretary of State for the Home Department* [2002] ECR I-7091; Case C-200/02, *Kunqian Catherine Zhu & Man Lavette Chen v Secretary of State for the Home Department* [2004] ECR I-9925.

[59] Weiler, *supra* note 19.

[60] On the changes concerning the idea of membership in postnational communities, postnational communities of which the actual EU is a sort of precursor, see Shaw, 'Postnational Constitutionalism in the European Union', 6 *Journal of European Policy* (1999) 579.

[61] Caruso, 'Private Law and State-Making in the Age of Globalization', 39 *New York University Journal of International Law and Politics* (2006–2007) 1, argues that 'traditional private law discourse facilitate the emergence of new forms of institutional sovereignty in the age of globalization' (at 6), claiming the EU is one of these examples. Caruso brilliantly illustrates how 'in its horizontal and apolitical dimension, private law can produce unassailable arguments and can change the nature of any dispute from hotly ideological to seemingly neutral and objective' (at 19). Here, we claim this process has a rebound effect on national private laws helping to shape in turn a dispersed identity.

fundamental rights (or reference to constitutional traditions). Differences and tensions in relation to values are then converted into occasions for dialogue and political participation in a novel way. Of course, the idea that technical discussion on private law rules can easily hide (or overcome) majoritarian political choices that are difficult to make in 'electoral and legislative contexts'[62] is not a new one.[63] However, it is claimed here that this process is actually sheltering the edification of an EU polity while mixing together—not necessarily in a coherent way—elements gathered from different understandings of fundamental—boundaries and—rights.

Internalizing the Treaty is a long judicial process. Although Article 6 TEU makes reference to fundamental rights 'guaranteed by the European Convention for the Protection of Human Rights and Fundamental Freedoms and as they result from the constitutional traditions common to the Member States', it is clear that this 'commonality' among member states' constitutions[64] is non-existent. Moreover, it is difficult to find a real common shared understanding of fundamental rights beyond the minimum common core enshrined in the ECHR and the level of protection actually accorded to it by the Strasbourg Court.

As anticipated, every polity demonstrates a continuously evolving equilibrium between (fundamental) rights and (fundamental) boundaries to private and public powers in the general interest. Such a balance reflects the core values of each polity at a given moment and helps to explain the diverging understandings of the protection of freedom of speech or privacy etc. within the same legal tradition.[65]

This latter consideration would also explain the tensions inherent in a multilevel system, such as the EU and member states. Moreover, the balance referred to should also, in principle, permit the supranational EU level to control only the shared (minimal) core of such a balance so as to avoid imposing one (member state) polity's view on the others. However, we claim that the EU is actually instigating changes that effect the core values of each member state and that this should not be understood as tampering with their fundamental boundaries[66] but rather as a forceful process of building a European identity, the boundaries of which still remain rather unclear. It can be seen as a process that presents immense identity shaping prospects and which is deeply entrenched in the creation process of European private law. Whichever path it takes (for instance, via the regulation of private law issues or defining EU fundamental rights) the results, we claim, converge in aggregating EU citizens' identity.

After all, such 'tampering' continuously, and even profoundly, occurs, forcing new balances between fundamental boundaries and rights upon the EU and member states via an affirmation of the economic fundamental freedoms. In a sense, this 'tampering' is at the core of the common critique of the creation of European private law as an edifice too heavily oriented towards market/economic freedoms and mostly oblivious to social justice.[67]

[62] Collins, *supra* note 7.

[63] See G. Comandé, *Risarcimento del Danno alla Persona e Alternative Istituzionali* (1999); Kennedy, 'The Political Stakes in "Merely Technical" Issues of Contract Law', 9 *European Review of Private Law* (2001) 7.

[64] Ekhardt and Kornack, 'Of Unity in Diversity and Inherent Tensions: Interpreting the European Union's New Architecture of Fundamental Rights', 16 *Columbia Journal of European Law* (2010) 92. See also Weiler, *supra* note 19 and *supra* note 54.

[65] Weiler, *supra* note 54.

[66] Weiler, *supra* note 19, at 78 who actually considers that '[b]eyond the agreed core, to foist a fundamental right on a society is, arguably, to tamper with its fundamental boundaries'.

[67] See, among other manifestos on social justice, M. W. Hesselink, *CFR & Social Justice* (2008). And yet, the court (Case C-283/11, *Sky Österreich GmbH v Österreichischer Rundfunk*, judgment of

Against this backdrop, we are inclined to think that reliance on the apparently neutral technicality of fostering economic freedoms, and on the need to remain within the EU enumerated competences, have devised clear patterns to build a European identity for polities whose majoritarian values are sometimes deeply different from each other. As counterintuitive as it may appear, the fact that EU fundamental rights protection is so deeply entrenched in—and even somehow dependent on—the protection of market economic freedoms and the legal reasoning that has developed around this very protection has made it possible to put the 'fruits'—to continue with the metaphor—, even those incompatible with each other, in the same basket. Up to now, such a result has been read in terms of 'competence distortion'[68] since it has actually contributed to the distortion and/or expansion of EU competences. With the insertion of the notion of EU citizenship in the Treaty and the ensuing case law, however, this process has begun to evade its apparent technical neutrality and instead mould itself in relation to the European Charter of Fundamental Rights.

It has been said, with reference to the international enforcement of human rights against states (and private entities),[69] that 'in at least some respect, the burden of proof has been shifted—in order to be validated, a purported human right must justify its contribution to a broader, market-based "vision" of the good society'.[70] Even though this is an assumption that cannot be fully tested here, it could nonetheless easily be claimed that a similar attitude towards the interplay between market vision(s) and human/fundamental rights has affected the evolution of the EU[71] as well as incrementally implementing processes that have resulted in a dilution of member state sovereignty. With reference to the latter, the unravelling of the economic freedoms has been driving the dilution of sovereignty.[72]

The outspoken language of the case law often revolves around the market and formal equality. Nevertheless, as we will see below, it is under this very shadow that an EU citizenship has begun to flourish.[73] Indeed, the market-oriented language driven by

22 January 2013, not yet published, Rec. 45) in remembering that 'the freedom to conduct a business is not absolute, but must be viewed in relation to its social function (see, to that effect, Joined Cases C-184/02 and C-223/02 *Spain and Finland* v *Parliament* and Council [2004] ECR I-7789, paragraphs 51 and 52, and Case C-544/10 *Deutsches Weintor* [2012] ECR I-0000, paragraph 54 and the case-law cited)' oriented its reasoning towards a social dimension considering the permissible constraints on fundamental rights and freedoms.

[68] This expression is used by Collins, *supra* note 7, at 30.

[69] Alston, 'The Myopia of the Handmaidens: International Lawyers and Globalization', 8 *European Journal of International Law (EJIL)* (1997) 435, at 442.

[70] It is worth remembering the words of I. Kant: 'But a human being regarded as a person, that is, the subject of a morally practical reason, is exalted above any price; for as a person he is not to be valued merely as a means to the ends of others or even to his own ends, but as an end in himself, that is, he possesses a dignity (an absolute inner worth) by which he exacts respect for himself from all other rational beings in the world. He can measure himself with every other being of this kind and value himself on a footing of equality with them.' See *supra* note 41, at 186.

[71] See for initial thoughts Comandé, 'Co-determining European Private Law(s) and Constitutionalization Process(es)', in S. Grundman (ed), *Constitutional Values and European Contract Law* (2008) 161.

[72] J. H. H. Weiler, *The Constitution of Europe* (1999), at 93, where he notes that the anti-discrimination treaty provisions and economic freedoms 'also serve to remove nationality and state affiliation of the individual, so divisive in the past, as the principal referent for transnational human intercourse'. In the language of other authors, for instance Slaughter, *supra* note 12, the result of such a process is a 'disaggregated sovereignty'.

[73] As it has been stressed 'through the notion of European citizenship, which is held alongside national citizenship, the European Union has encouraged the development of a rival social identity'. See Collins, *supra* note 7, at 127.

the fostering of the economic freedoms can be read—at least as well and perhaps even in a politically undesirable way—as an attempt to exploit the apparently politically neutral language of private law. The EU Commission mainly presents private legislation as re-regulation[74] (negative integration by removing regulatory barriers to trade[75] and positive integration by re-regulation) in an attempt to avoid offering systematic solutions and, in a sense, benefit from the legitimating role of 'neutral' private law regulation.[76] This strategy seems to pave the way to systemic—albeit erratic—case law building[77] even in the 'absence of an institutional competence to develop adequate principles of private law'.[78]

Even if we refuse these hypotheticals, the introduction of the notion of European citizenship has given new impulse to the protection of private law rights and opened the path to an identity building process, the outcome of which is still unclear.

In our understanding, the actual notions and levels of protection offered to fundamental rights are constituents of the democratic powers of our societies since fundamental boundaries are a 'metaphor of the principle of enumerated powers or limited competences that are designed to guarantee that in certain areas communities (rather than individuals) should be free to make their own social choices without interference from above'.[79] In societies as ours where, since after World War II, private law has had to be coherent with constitutional principles (that is the accepted balance between fundamental rights and fundamental boundaries), these notions and levels of protection of fundamental rights in any legal order (be it member states or the EU) are deeply related to the core of the tradition of private law, i.e. to the economic constitution of everyday life.[80] Therefore, hinging upon fundamental rights or hinging upon private law rights are just two ways of contributing to defining the identity of a polity. At the EU level, as we have noted, the EU polities are further shaped by tensions among different sets of values that make up 'the game' that is the EU legal process.

The CJEU, by way of protecting private law rights shaped by EU law and the protection of economic freedoms, interferes with the balancing of rights in the national domain and instead shapes a supranational balance. This in turn constitutes a process of

[74] The peculiar strategy of presenting private law legislation as re-regulation is clearly described by Collins, ibid., at 48.

[75] Case C-120/78, *Rewe-Zentrale AG v Bundesmonopolverwaltung für Branntwein (Cassis de Dijon)* [1979] ECR 649.

[76] See Caruso, *supra* note 61, at 32. According to her, 'private law can strangely depoliticize the context of human rights disputes and allow for otherwise unpalatable, ideologically-colored holdings'.

[77] This is in contradiction with the view of Collins, *supra* note 7, who emphasizes the oscillation of the CJEU in 'its willingness to construct rules of private law as the need arises for the purposes of interpreting European Directives' and denies this can be described as a sort of 'common law (i.e. judicial precedent) method of evolving principles of private law through precedents and careful elaboration of legal doctrines by the judges'.

[78] Ibid., at 61.

[79] Weiler, *supra* note 19.

[80] According to Collins, *supra* note 7, at 94: 'An Economic Constitution comprises the basic legal structure that shapes civil society. In its essential, it comprises property entitlements, familial rights and obligations, and rules governing transfers of assets.' The author further elaborates that '[t]he rules of property law, contract law, domestic relations and so forth provide the details of the scheme for a particular market order. Private law specifies, for instance, what kind of assets are susceptible to private ownership, and how possession of those assets can be vindicated. The law of contract defines the scope of freedom to enter transactions and to choose the terms, and provide mechanisms for the enforcement of voluntary undertakings including transfer of assets. The law of persons and capacity determines which individuals and organizations may own property, enter contracts and protect their interests. Particular branches of private law, such as employment law and consumer protection law, regulate and control operation of those segments of the market'.

building an identity for EU citizens as EU citizens, as 'individuals bound to a political community and protected by fundamental rights', beyond their function as 'mere economic factors of production'.[81] It is a bottom-up approach because the CJEU operates according to the impulses of the cases brought forward by individuals.

Considering fundamental rights in conjunction with private law[82] can be understood as being in apparent contrast with the classical economic theories. It forces one to cast the individual outside the consumerist attitude that modern economic development, accompanied by the idea of globalization, has created in regional areas and instead places the individual at the centre of attention. In giving preference to the human being as opposed to his or her economic resources ('having'[83]), we are offered a new paradigm according to which legal discourse revolves around human beings in their own right and not on their consumer, or more broadly, economic actor characteristics.[84] Whether this process should or should not delineate a different equilibrium between member states and the EU is a different issue. What we are concerned with here is describing the process and the direction it pursues (or might pursue), highlighting the fact that it is significantly altering national private law systems while simultaneously defining a European civic identity regardless of any political will in this regard.

At the EU level, this shift towards the individual and beyond his or her role as an economic actor has been technically set in motion by the notion of EU citizenship. In our view, this shift paves the way for a larger role for solidarity and social justice[85] in the building of European private law. In addition, it draws stronger attention to the weaker human being without solely focusing on economic weaknesses.[86] This process of reorientation can certainly be accelerated by deliberate choices concerning values that can be inserted, for instance, in a codification of principles.[87] However, such a pattern would

[81] Advocate General Sharpston in Case C-34/09, *Gerardo Ruiz Zambrano v Office national de l'emploi (ONEm)*, at para. 127.

[82] The notion and scope of private law within states (and among member states as well) is not a settled one.

[83] E. Fromm, *To Have or to Be* (1976).

[84] As noted by AG Sharpston in *Zambrano* (at para. 128) 'when citizens move, they do so as human beings, not as robots. They fall in love, marry and have families. The family unit, depending on circumstances, may be composed solely of EU citizens, or of EU citizens and third country nationals, closely linked to one another. If family members are not treated in the same way as the EU citizen exercising rights of free movement, the concept of freedom of movement becomes devoid of any real meaning'.

[85] Wilhelmsson, 'Varieties of Welfarism in European Contract Law', 10 *ELJ* (2004) 712, at 712: 'In analyses of what could be generally called social justice in contract law, the change [towards a greater inclusion in contract law of other social values than purely market-oriented, liberal ones] is often pictured with the help of dichotomies like freedom versus solidarity [referring to Unger, "The Critical Legal Studies Movement", 96 *Harvard Law Review* (1983) 561, at 616], individualism versus altruism [referring to Kennedy, "Form and Substance in Private Law Adjudication", 89 *Harvard Law Review* (1976), 1685], and market-individualism versus consumer-welfarism [J. Adams and R. Brownsword, *Understanding Contract Law* (1987), at 52]. The new phenomena have also been described with the help of concepts like "social contract law" and "contractual solidarity" as well as principles like "the principle of regard and fairness." '

[86] However, 'various visions of social justice may justify quite different results', cf. Wilhelmsson, ibid., at 713. Moreover, once translated into the domain of private law, this attitude towards the individual can impose outcomes that might appear contrary to any efficient achievement or rationale, contrary to the current understanding of a market economy.

[87] 'A Civil Code also initiates a process that leads to popular acceptance of this economic and social model. Every assertion of rights and obligations arising under the private law rules of the code implies an acceptance of its standards of justice and fairness. A complaint to a fishmonger by a customer that her mackerel tasted stale and bitter involves an acceptance of certain rules regarding sales of goods to consumers; any acknowledgement or response to the complaint also takes as a reference point those legal rules about contracts and their quality standards. Through such dialogues, multiplied by the

encounter the political hurdles of a deliberative choice that necessarily forces one polity's view on others. Our claim here is that such a reorientation is in silent, almost unnoticeable, motion laying the foundations for a deliberative process by amalgamating a variety of values under the apparently neutral, technical legal language and legal process of the Internal Market building endeavours.

Considering this, we should ask both whether the European multilevel system is at all prepared to speak out regarding such a shift and, if necessary, whether it is ready to reshape the balances between fundamental rights and fundamental boundaries openly. After all, the use of the human/fundamental rights language implies the existence of a political dimension in the legal discourse. However, the Court in Luxembourg has constantly tried to disguise this behind the (apparently) neutral technicalities[88] of building the Internal Market and depoliticizing the language of private law. The shadow citizenship is a side effect of precisely these attempts.

The legal techniques used over time can vary, evolving well beyond the equation of fundamental rights and constitutionally embedded rights (at the national level) which in fact has become incapable of capturing reality even in those legal systems in which this equation seems to rule on a descriptive/terminological level (as in the Netherlands). Indeed, through reference to constitutional articles, national courts have acknowledged rights, rights not explicitly enumerated in constitutional or international texts, as fundamental rights[89] and have been re-reading existing statutory provisions in light of these fundamental rights essentially expanding the scope of private law rights.[90] In adopting rather similar techniques, EU law uses the language of the economic freedoms to expand EU citizens' rights.

Indeed, against this backdrop, in reference to the legal systems of each member state, the EU itself has been developing a rather different relationship between fundamental rights and fundamental economic freedoms in an attempt to build a fully functional European Internal Market (in other words and in reference to the official aim, i.e. shaping the economic arena of member states without assuming the powers and role of a federal state).

This interplay has begun to impinge on the development of private law within the member states well beyond the competences[91] of the EU and the traditional interplay

near-infinite variety of interactions in civil society, the rules of private law are tested, refined and ultimately accepted as the legitimate ground rules. They become popularly accepted not by a momentary vote in a ballot but rather through the repeated use of the rules to guide behaviour and communications. The rules of civil law provide a shared basis for communications that enable trust and mutual understanding.' Collins, *supra* note 7, at 5. Indeed, according to him the objective of a European civil code finds a better justification 'in the quest for an Economic constitution and a post-national identity'.

[88] Kennedy, *supra* note 63. See also C. Mak, *Fundamental Rights in European Contract Law* (2008).

[89] See, e.g. the acknowledgment of a general personality right ('*algemeen persoonlijkheidsrecht*') by the Dutch Supreme Court in the 1994 *Valkenhorst* case (HR 15 April 1994, NJ 1994, 608).

[90] See, for instance, the evolution of personal injury damages in Italy. See. Comandé, 'Towards a Global Model for Adjudicating Personal Injury Damages: Bridging Europe and the United States', 19 *Temple International & Comparative Law Journal* (2005) 241, and Comandé, 'Doing Away with Inequality in Loss of Enjoyment of Life', in J. Ward and R. Thornton (eds), *Personal Injury and Wrongful Death Damages Calculations: Transatlantic Dialogue* (2009) 255.

[91] On the competences of the EU with reference to private law, see Van Gerven, 'Codifying European Private Law: Top Down and Bottom Up', in S. Grundmann and J. Stuyck (eds), *An Academic Green Paper on European Contract Law* (2002) 405; Weatherill, 'Reflections on the EC's Competence to Develop a "European Contract Law"', 13 *European Review of Private Law* (2005) 405; Weatherill, 'Why Object to the Harmonization of Private Law by the EC?', 12 *European Review of Private Law* (2004) 633. Note that a parallel comparative analysis with the US would prove significantly intriguing since the notion of citizenship in both the US and the EU requires national citizenship before the higher level

between state private law and fundamental rights. As an example of such intervention, we may recall the right to use one's name in all member states so that one can fully enjoy citizenship of the Union—the 'fundamental status of nationals of the Member States'[92]—thereby attributing real meaning to the rights that flow from EU citizenship. However, and more importantly, the establishment of the right to use one's name in all member states, be it under the banner of either freedom of movement or EU citizenship and in both cases beyond the technical rhetoric of reverse discrimination,[93] deeply impinges upon both national understandings of the private law of family relationships and of personality rights: it gives content to 'the genuine enjoyment of the substance of the rights conferred by virtue of their status as citizens of the Union'.[94]

4. Aggregating European Citizenship from the Internal Market Building Process

The assertion here is that the EU private law legislative endeavours[95] coupled with the case law of the CJEU—mostly after the insertion of official EU citizenship into the primary law of the Union—are together shaping a transnational[96] shadow citizenship by way of establishing private law rights sustained by the fundamental economic freedoms and their interaction with fundamental rights. Technically, EU (official) citizenship is being treated as a sort of 'fifth economic freedom'. This innovative notion of citizenship is being constructed based upon the leading role assumed by those citizens actively enjoying[97] European internal mobility granted by the establishment of the EU. It is

(EU–US) citizenship can be rendered possible. In addition, at least historically, rights enjoyed pertaining to EU or US citizenship are not automatically granted at the state level.

[92] Case C-184/99, *Grzelczyk v Centre public d'aide sociale d'Ottignies-Louvain-la-Neuve* [2001] ECR I-6193, Rec. 31; Case C-413/99, *Baumbast and R v Secretary of State for the Home Department* [2002] ECR I-7091, Rec. 82; Case C-148/02, *Carlos Garcia Avello v Belgian State* [2003] ECR I-11613, [2004] 1 CMLR 1, Rec. 22; Case C-200/02, *Chen and Zhu v Secretary of State for the Home Department* [2004] ECR I-9925, [2004] 3 CMLR 48, Rec. 25; and Case C-135/08, *Janko Rottmann v Freistaat Bayern* [2010] ECR I-1449, Rec. 43.

[93] AG Sharpston in Case C-353/06, *Grunkin-Paul v Standesamt Niebüll* [2008] ECR I-7639, at para. 45 stated '[a]nd, given the increasing mobility of citizens throughout the territory of the European Union, which is not merely a single market but a single area of freedom, security and justice, it is clear that conflicts of interest involving the determination and use of personal names can (and probably will) arise with increasing frequency unless and until some adequate solution is found. Such a solution should be fully and systematically thought out, with due regard to all its implications for all the legal systems involved'.

[94] See the *Zambrano* case at Rec. 42 according to which 'Article 20 TFEU precludes national measures which have the effect of depriving citizens of the Union of the genuine enjoyment of the substance of the rights conferred by virtue of their status as citizens of the Union'.

[95] However, here we must limit ourselves to scraping the surface of the judicial component of this process.

[96] For criticisms stressing the lack of a real transnational civil society in the EU see Collins, *supra* note 7, at 2: 'The European Union, however, lacks such a dense set of connections between peoples. It has failed to establish an integrated transnational civil society out of which a common European identity could be constructed. The protection of fundamental economic freedoms by the European Treaties—the free movement of goods, services, capital and labour—created elements of a European civil society by giving citizens the right to engage in commerce across borders. The additional regulatory interventions of the Single Market initiative reduced further the barriers between national communities. These measures removed some of the most conspicuous obstacles to cross-border trade such as quotas, tariffs and prohibitions. But a more comprehensive and inclusive transnational civil society requires more extensive support.'

[97] By way of exercising their freedoms of movement.

only with the expanding scope of EU citizenship that citizens as individuals, regardless of their actual exercise of the freedoms of movement,[98] have come within the ambit of protection. For this reason, the endeavour in itself may even be perceived as elitist. Nevertheless, enabling every EU citizen or legal entity to fight for their rights using the EU legal arena creates an area of political engagement in an environment characterized by substantive fluid principles, yet clear legal procedures.

The process we describe operates along two strata. First, it gives more weight to EU citizens' rights outside their own nation/member state, initially by way of economic freedoms and subsequently via EU citizenship as such. This first layer reduces the differences among citizens of different member states facilitating an aggregation of them under the umbrella of EU citizenship. Such a process clearly relies more on the expansion of anti-discrimination rights as opposed to a positive development of multicultural claims.[99] Secondly, the process attributes significance to citizens' rights in their own nation/member state by redefining the rights citizens enjoy in their nation/member state. This is conducted in such a way so as to avoid any contradiction of national citizenship and rather focuses on reinforcing national ties remodelling the set of reference values. Initially, this transpired, technically speaking, via a relaxation on the part of the ECJ in relation to the rule that protection could only be afforded to those who had actually exercised their economic freedoms[100] and later (the result of which is yet to be exposed in its entirety) relying on EU citizenship and the bundle of fundamental rights it incrementally encompasses.[101]

There are at least two categories of CJEU cases that illustrate these phenomena. One clearly expands the scope of protection of fundamental rights under EU law by way of defending the enjoyment of EU citizenship and the ensuing rights thereof. The other expands the same scope by way of (officially) protecting the enjoyment of economic freedoms or redefining their scope according to the proportionality test. We should note, however, that cases cannot always be easily categorized and some overlap occurs on occasion.

What we can certainly note from the CJEU case law, however, is a profound and sometimes creeping shift in interpretation, a shift that has moved from recognizing individuals as economic actors (subjects) to individuals as citizens of the EU polity.[102] This movement is characterized by an oscillation between the settled—and somehow accepted—use of the economic freedoms rhetoric on the one hand, and explicit reference to EU citizenship and the Charter on the other.

Our analysis has already been cast within the broader framework concerning the unstable equilibria of the European multilevel system[103] and within the multiform understanding of fundamental rights. Therefore, it is not necessary to repeat here that the battlefield of both lines of cases is often technically focused on defining the competences of the EU and the core values of reference for defining them. Cases such as

[98] Indeed, *Garcia Avello, Zhu and Chen*, and *Rottmann* illustrate that the existing case law already allows certain citizenship rights to be invoked independently of prior transborder movement by the EU citizen in question.

[99] See Joppke, *supra* note 8. See also Weiler, *supra* note 72, at 93 where he states that anti-discrimination treaty provisions and economic freedoms 'also serve to remove nationality and state affiliation of the individual, so divisive in the past, as the principal referent for transnational human intercourse'.

[100] For reference to the specific cases, see the discussion *infra*, sections 6 and 7.

[101] Ibid.

[102] See Case C-413/99, *Baumbast and R v Secretary of State for the Home Department* [2002] ECR I-7091.

[103] See for instance C. Joerges, 'On the Legitimacy of Europeanising Private Law: Considerations on a Justice-making Law for the EU Multi-level System', 7 *Electronic Journal Of Comparative Law* (2003), available online at <http://www.ejcl.org/73/art73-3.html> (last accessed 28 March 2013).

Konstantinidis demonstrate that defining which equilibrium of competence prevails sets out not only the respective competences of the CJEU and national courts (and of the EU and member states respectively) but also delineates the core values which occasionally prevail in European (private) law.[104] This can be expressed directly in terms of a redefinition of competences between the Union and the states,[105] diluting the requirements so as to facilitate a more simplified linkage to EU law,[106] or in terms of a newly reached equilibrium between the economic freedoms and a commonly shared (according to the CJEU) set of fundamental rights enjoyed by EU citizens.[107]

However, it might also be the case that the promotion of a right is not necessarily expressed through the language of fundamental rights but rather disguised through the reaffirmation of economic freedoms, loosely linking a practical situation to them. Again our claim here is that this process, due to technical constraints, is silently aggregating a non-national identity and should not be disregarded despite the confusion and incertitude it creates. After all, it might not always be possible to claim (although it would be more intellectually linear), in line with Advocate General Jacobs in *Konstantinidis* (even though his view was rejected by the Court) that 'a Community national who goes to another Member State as a worker or self-employed person under Articles [39, 43 or 49] of the Treaty is entitled not just to pursue his trade or profession and to enjoy the same living and working conditions as nationals of the host State; he is in addition entitled to assume that, wherever he goes to earn his living in the European Community, he will be treated in accordance with a common code of fundamental values, in particular those laid down in the European Convention on Human Rights . . . in other words, he is entitled to say "civis europeus sum" and to invoke that status in order to oppose any violation of his fundamental rights'.[108]

This pronouncement was somehow prophetic considering the fact that it was asserted well before the notion of European citizenship was implanted in the Treaty and, in addition, prior to the casting out of the idea that moving and residing are not necessarily consequent rights.[109] Nevertheless, AG Jacobs' statement presupposes the status of a crystallized bundle of rights, something that in actual fact only exists in rhetorical terms. Our claim here is that the political participation enabled by individual litigation fosters an ever evolving bundle of rights moving the system beyond the limits suggested by AG Jacobs and moving towards the construction of a conception of a civic European citizenship that is actually functional in the daily lives of individuals acting

[104] Comandé, *supra* note 71.

[105] Yet, this would require difficult political negotiations and commitments.

[106] See *infra*, note 212 and cited text.

[107] See *infra*, note 213 and cited text. This seems to be the approach of the Court in areas of law different from private law. See, for instance, *Åklagaren v Hans Åkerberg Fransson, supra* note 44.

[108] See the Opinion of AG Jacobs in the Case C-168/91, *Konstantinidis v Stadt Altensteig, Standesamt, and Landratsamt Calw, Ordnungsamt* [1993] ECR I-1191, at para. 46.

[109] See the Opinion of AG Sharpston in Case C-34/09, *Gerardo Ruiz Zambrano v Office national de l'emploi (ONEm)*, where it is concluded 'that Articles 20 and 21 TFEU are to be interpreted as conferring a right of residence in the territory of the Member States, based on citizenship of the Union, that is independent of the right to move between Member States. Those provisions do not preclude a Member State from refusing to grant a derivative right of residence to an ascendant relative of a citizen of the Union who is a national of the Member State concerned and who has not yet exercised rights of free movement, provided that that decision complies with the principle of proportionality' (at para. 122). Yet, AG Sharpston (in para. 84) sustained that EU fundamental rights can be relied upon 'when exercising an economic right to free movement as a worker, or when national law comes within the scope of the Treaty . . . or when invoking EU secondary legislation . . . , but [not] when merely "residing" in that Member State'.

mainly in accordance with national private law rules. Accordingly, the 'traditional' mode of exchange between national and supranational protection of fundamental rights expands upon rights habitually held under national private law. The acceptance of EU citizenship is slowly building a framework within which individual entitlements, emanating from private law rules that embody both identical and different values from national settings, can be properly construed and exercised in member states based on the novel reality that we are not only national citizens anymore but also European Union citizens. The astonishing intellectual merry-go-round can be articulated as follows: we are EU citizens as long as we are citizens of a member state and we enjoy some 'extra' rights—even in our national member state—by virtue of being EU citizens;[110] in other words, we are able to challenge the national set of values using our European allegiance and vice versa.

Throughout this process, the interplay between fundamental rights, private law rights, and the acknowledgement of the characteristics of a democracy has always been at the forefront. This process of institution building is creating a polity that does not correspond to any traditional classification proposed by political science. In other words, it is not entirely a supranational (even more afar a federal) state nor is it an intergovernmental entity.[111] Furthermore, this institution building is in line with modern unease concerning the notion of citizenship and group identity related to belonging to a given territory.[112] While the official characterization of EU citizenship corresponds to classical definitions, the shadow citizenship we are concerned with reflects the aggregation process of EU citizenship, a process that began well before the Treaty on European Union came into force in 1993. The first step in this process—in the eyes of a jurist of private law—can be pinpointed as the acknowledgment, by the ECJ as it then was, of the necessity for Community law to be in line with fundamental rights.[113] Indeed, this overarching acknowledgment of the role of fundamental rights protection as a key (and identity building) element among (originally western) European states dates back much earlier than the introduction of an official EU bill of rights. In fact, even though the Charter of Fundamental Rights of the European Union has only recently been incorporated into the Lisbon Treaty, the rhetoric of fundamental rights had already entered the DNA of the EU, setting the aggregation of the EU shadow citizenship in motion much earlier than one would imagine.

Although the sharing of a bill of rights—or at least a set of shared rights—is significantly symbolic in nature[114] and is to be welcomed, reference to controversial and highly

[110] Case C-135/08, *Rottmann* [2010] ECR I-1449.

[111] For references, see Sbragia, 'The European Community: A Balancing Act', 23 *Publius: the Journal of Federalism* (1993) 24.

[112] After all, the only requirement to enter the game of the EU legal process is possession of member state citizenship even if the litigating citizen was not born or has not lived in any part of the EU.

[113] See, for instance, Case C-11/70, *Internationale Handelsgesellschaft* [1970] ECR 1125; Case C-4/73, *Nold v Commission* [1974] ECR 491; Case C-44/79, *Hauer* [1979] ECR 3727; and Joined Cases 46/87 and 227/88, *Hoechst* v *Commission* [1989] ECR 2859. For a more detailed account see Krzeminska-Russo, 'The horizontal effect of fundamental rights and freedoms in European Union law', in G. Brüggemeier, A. Colombi Ciacchi, and G. Comandé (eds), *supra* note 38, 8.

[114] This has been stressed also with reference to the Charter of Fundamental Rights (Gruber, *supra* note 26) and in official documents (European Council Decision on the Drawing up of a Charter of Fundamental Rights of the European Union. Presidency Conclusions (annex X), Cologne, June 1999: 'There appears to be a need, at the present stage of the Union's development, to establish a Charter of fundamental rights in order to make their overriding importance and relevance more visible to the Union's citizens.')

political or morally oriented values may prove to be a divisive and sensitive issue.[115] For these reasons, simple reference to fundamental rights has not proved capable of fully serving the EU identity building process and the ECJ jurisprudence has, for some time now, focused on nurturing the EU's respect for fundamental rights as guaranteed by the European Convention on Human Rights and the constitutional traditions common to member states (the supposed lowest common denominator) without attempting to define the content of the rights. In addition, the Court habitually camouflages its discussion with the 'neutral' argumentation usually connected to the reasoning applied to cases concerning the economic freedoms.

These observations do not undermine the fact that, owing to the case law of the Court, fundamental rights have been recognized as general principles of Community law[116] and, in addition, all EU countries have ratified the European Convention on Human Rights. Nor do they underestimate that the ECJ's interpretation of the treaties and the notion of fundamental rights has taken these considerations on board by way of subjecting Community fundamental freedoms to the protection of fundamental rights and the common constitutional traditions of the member states (Article 6 TEU). Nor do they reject that direct or indirect reference to the Universal Declaration of Human Rights, the European Convention on Human Rights, and the jurisprudence of the Strasbourg Court are to be considered as cornerstones for the construction of a European judicial charter of fundamental rights based on the shared list of values delineated in the Charter of Nice and subsequent incorporation into the Lisbon Treaty.[117] Indeed, these events mark the framework for a more constrained evolution of the shadow citizenship owing to this generally shared (at least in the fact that they are documented) bundle of rights according to which jurists can exercise textual interpretation along common hermeneutical lines of reasoning and methodology. The abovementioned observations shed light on the limits these extremely valuable achievements can have since, as we discussed, the current understanding is that the shared achievements concerning the acknowledgement of rights, purported as common to all, are only really common on paper. In reality, the true acknowledgement of rights—rights that often do not exist in the member state of origin—is being forced by those citizens enjoying their economic freedoms and moving across member state borders.[118] In this direction, the sharing of a text (the EU Charter of Fundamental Rights incorporated in the Treaty assuming the status of general principles) is proving to be a forceful legal argument.[119]

In short, the endeavour of building the EU edifice under the official insignia of making a common (single) market is fostering the emergence of a new polity, a result

[115] Clapham, *supra* note 20, at 15 states that: 'they may well operate as a double edged sword. Not only are they a cohesive force but they may well be divisive. Should the Community move to tackle questions such as divorce, contraception, abortion, blasphemy, surrogacy, etc., rights might no longer be handy tools for integration but vehicles of division and disintegration'.

[116] The original formula of Art. 6 TEU was actually taken from the ECJ's original phrasing in the famous cases C-29/69, *Stauder* [1969] ECR 419, Rec. 7; Case C-11/70, *Internationale Handelsgesellschaft* [1970] ECR 1125; and Case C-4/73, *Nold* [1974] ECR 491, Recs 13 and 14.

[117] Even though the CJEU and scholars broadly share the understanding that the 'Charter does not require the institutions of the European Union, including the European Court of Justice, to respect these rights, and it insists that any derogation from them should only be permitted in European law if they are necessary, proportionate and genuinely meet objectives of general interest'. Collins, *supra* note 7.

[118] See *infra*, especially note 212.

[119] See for instance cases quoted *infra*, in notes 144, 208, and 209.

which goes beyond the political will sustaining any given innovation in the evolution towards today's European Union[120] and outside the common understanding of post-national identities and citizenship.

The need for legislative intervention with a view to fashioning a European civil society has been forecasted by scholarship.[121] Our claim here, however, differs in that we claim that many of the innovative characteristics of private law that have the potential of providing the foundations for a civil society are in fact emanating from the case law and, moreover, from areas that are not necessarily considered as traditional fields of private law understood according to its economic dimension (contract, property, tort).

We further argue that EU legislation aimed at incrementing single market and cross-border transactions, such as Directive 24/2011/EU, despite its fragmented nature,[122] will inevitably fuel this process. Sooner or later, the CJEU will be confronted with the contours of the fundamental right to health and the contractual relationships surrounding it. It will be called upon to shape, for instance, the content of the right 'to a written or electronic medical record of... treatment',[123] the actual implications of 'the principle of non-discrimination with regard to nationality', to forecast limits 'to what is necessary and proportionate and may not constitute a means of arbitrary discrimination'.[124] These hermeneutical interventions will influence deeply member states' national private law principles and rules and their interplay with national constitutional values and collective understandings of, for instance, the right to health and health care. The stance and directions these interventions take, will, in juxtaposition to consumer protection, contribute to a greater extent to the process of defining an EU civic identity. This is principally because any such intervention will 'tamper' with citizens' rights and individual perceptions of them, in effect doing away with the need for revered comprehensive codes or legislation.

The process thus far illustrated paves the way to an acknowledgment of the shadow European citizenship as a sort of side effect of the processes of guaranteeing the internal common market building endeavour and in conceiving of suitable forms of democratic participation in defining EU policies and legislation. While officially aiming to achieve a larger market, it is our opinion that below the surface an innovative notion of citizenship is beginning to emerge shaped by the interplay between fundamental rights protection and fundamental economic freedoms implementation. Thus, we may say that the official EU citizenship is being treated as the fifth (economic) freedom and is technically expanding its reach accordingly. It is our assumption that the political ideals behind the Treaty of Rome have silently been using these driving forces to devise a true *shadow EU citizenship*. This shadow citizenship coexists with and somehow emanates from the

[120] The argument for a full assimilation of social rights in the integration process has been made by Poiares Maduro, 'Striking The Elusive Balance Between Economic Freedom and Social Rights in the EU', in P. Craig and G. De Búrca (eds), *The Evolution of EU Law* (1999) 449, stating at 470: 'Free movement of persons and rights of participation and representation such as the freedom of association, the right to collective bargaining, and the right to collective action should be considered as instrumental to a fully functioning integrated market which can increase efficiency and wealth maximisation... the argument in favour of these fundamental social rights arises not from the need for a level playing field but from the need of the competition system itself to achieve the goal of efficiency... at the same time, such rights will enhance the concept of European citizenship by providing new forms of participation and representation in a European forum of decision-making which is normally ignored in the debates regarding the democratic deficit: the European common market.'

[121] Collins, *supra* note 7.

[122] A prominent scholar uses the metaphor of the European Directives as 'an archipelago of small islands in the wide seas of national private law systems'. See Collins, *supra* note 7, at 40.

[123] Directive 24/2011/EU, OJ 2011 L 88/45, Art. 4(2).

[124] Ibid., Art. 4(3).

EU's official one, as described for example by the Lamassoure Report[125] and further praised by the Monti Report,[126] with a view to strengthening a new consensus around the Single Market idea. Jointly with others,[127] these documents signal a turning point in the potential—albeit unintended—merging of EU *official citizenship* with its private law *shadow* alter ego, towards a *single* European *citizenship*.

Both technocratic analysis and academic scholarship have mostly focused on dismantling obstacles in the way of EU official citizenship, without exploring the interplay between the political dimension of the shadow citizenship and the increasing transnational character of private law rules. Also absent is an investigation into the way they mould together different European legal cultures and offer a unique model in a globalized world.[128] These issues cannot be analysed here in sufficient profundity, as we must confine ourselves to unearthing the links between the shadow citizenship and private law.

5. Defining the Contours of EU Citizenship: The Shadow Citizenship as a Metaphor

What constitutes this *shadow EU citizenship* then? It is the paradoxical result of the structuring of economic freedoms; it is the side effect of a market vision in which levelling the playing field for economic players trumps long lasting rules and sometimes values in member states; it is built upon the participation of forerunner citizens i.e. those who enjoy the mixed blessings of transnational living in a borderless single market. Notwithstanding this, the shadow citizenship must unavoidably confront itself with member states' private law and constitutional values even in cases where there is no EU law dealing with the legal issue at stake.

The shadow citizenship, even when fostering fundamental rights, often speaks the sole language of the market vision embedded in the fundamental economic freedoms. Sometimes it blends fundamental rights (e.g. privacy) and fundamental economic freedoms (e.g. to do business)[129] in a conceptual combination.[130] It is the actual and prospective catalyst for a European identity, stirring together the plurality of member

[125] A. Lamassoure, 'The Citizen and the Application of Community Law', Report to the President of the Republic, 8 June 2008.

[126] M. Monti, 'A New Strategy for the Single Market: At the Service of Europe's Economy and Society', Report to the President of the European Commission, J. M. Barroso, 9 May 2010.

[127] See for instance Horizon 2020—The EU Framework Programme for Research and Innovation, hereinafter 'Horizon 2020' and the Digital Agenda for Europe, note 40.

[128] See, however, the goals of Horizon 2020.

[129] Yet the CJEU clearly clarifies that '[t]hose freedoms are not absolute rights, however, but must be considered in relation to their social function. Consequently, restrictions may be imposed on their exercise, provided that the restrictions correspond to objectives of general interest and do not constitute in relation to the aim pursued a disproportionate and intolerable interference, impairing the very substance of the rights guaranteed' (Joined Cases C-184/02 and C-223/02, *Spain and Finland v Parliament And Council* [2004] ECR I-7789).

[130] A process helped by reference to both of them in the Charter. For an example of this, see Case C-544/10, *Deutsches Weintor eG v Land Rheinland-Pfalz*, judgment of 6 September 2012, not yet published, Rec. 45-47 in which the court stressed: 'it is important also to take into account the second sentence of Article 35 of the Charter, which requires that a high level of human health protection be ensured in the definition and implementation of all the European Union's policies and activities. As is apparent from recitals 1 and 18 in the preamble to Regulation No 1924/2006, health protection is among the principal aims of that regulation.... In those circumstances, the compatibility of the prohibition, without exception, of a claim of the kind at issue in the main proceedings must be assessed in

state legal systems in an actual transnational one, blending together (more or less) shared constitutional values and private law solutions.

Technically, it is the elitist citizenship of the relatively few member state citizens who exercise their freedom of movement;[131] hence it is mostly relevant only in light of its transnational component.[132] We call this phenomenon shadow citizenship also because it has grown within the haze of the *grands projets* attached to the EU's constitutional endeavour and the European civil code idea.

Even though these *grands projets* might, to some extent, be gradually fading away, they leave us with an important legacy: the shadow citizenship, the constituent elements of which will require further systemic investigation as they discretely unfold a set of transnational legal models acceptable among different legal and social cultures. We can highlight here, by way of example, the fact that the enjoyment of EU citizenship through the exercise of the economic freedoms is a way to reduce the possibility of assimilation by the majoritarian groups in one's own member state by way of recognizing '*droits différenciés*'.[133] It must be stressed that the fostering of these substantial innovations has not followed a pattern akin to accommodating[134] the minority and diversity but rather one of enabling rights within the framework offered by the EC/EU organization through empowering transnational citizens.

In other words, if regular normativity in the member state adopts, as its own, the predominant groups' vision of the world (e.g. male, heterosexual, Christian, middle class)[135] and relegates different views in a pattern of differentiated citizenship, one can theoretically escape these modes of assimilation by testing the limits of the post/supranational EU shadow citizenship.

As anticipated, and alongside this panorama, EU legislation and the CJEU case law have often fostered the reception of substantial—even radical—legal innovation into member state legal systems. These innovations constitute models already praised in different continents. For example, personal data protection and several consumer protection instruments can be described as seeds of EU law planted in member state legal systems laying down the foundations for a civic society. As such, they can be perceived

the light not only of the freedom to choose an occupation and the freedom to conduct a business, but also of the protection of health.... It follows from this that such an assessment must be carried out in accordance with the need to reconcile the requirements of the protection of those various fundamental rights protected by the Union legal order, and striking a fair balance between them (see, to that effect, Case C-275/06 *Promusicae* [2008] ECR I-271, paragraphs 65 and 66)'.

131 Case C-434/09, *McCarthy v Secretary of State for the Home Department* [2011] ECR I-3375, Rec. 56, concluding that 'Article 21 TFEU is not applicable to a Union citizen who has never exercised his right of free movement, who has always resided in a Member State of which he is a national and who is also a national of another Member State, provided that the situation of that citizen does not include the application of measures by a Member State that would have the effect of depriving him of the genuine enjoyment of the substance of the rights conferred by virtue of his status as a Union citizen or of impeding the exercise of his right of free movement and residence within the territory of the Member States'.

132 It is noteworthy that member state citizens who exercise their freedom of movement are a very special kind of migrant in postnational societies; they remain 'flexible' and automatically related to more than one polity. See A. Ong, *Flexible Citizenship: The Cultural Logics of Transnationality* (1999).

133 W. Kymlicka, *Multicultural Citizenship: A Liberal Theory of Minority Rights* (1995); W. Kymlicka, *La voie canadienne: Repenser le multiculturalisme* (2003), at 95.

134 Comandé, 'Discrimination and Reasonable Accommodation: "Insights" for a (Non) Zero Sum Game', 2 *Opinio Juris In Comparatione* (2010) 1.

135 See Young, 'Polity and Group Difference: A Critique of the Ideal Universal Citizenship', 99 *Ethics* (1989) 250. Of course this view does not buy the normative neutrality argument as presented by J. Rawls, *A Theory of Justice* (1971).

as immaterial components, pieces of a puzzle, of the dormant—albeit alive and well—*single EU citizenship*. Furthermore, and although not stemming directly from EU regulated areas of law, several changes in traditional legal solutions are clearly a significant result of the interplay between the shadow citizenship and MS national laws, particularly when viewed through the lenses of economic freedoms and the plural conception(s) of fundamental rights mentioned earlier.[136] These processes invite a deeper exploration and comprehension of the policy questions they entail and raise. In fact, the official EU citizenship is institutionally constrained in formalities,[137] whilst the shadow citizenship encounters problems in affirming itself by reason of the limited competences of the EU and the need to emerge mostly via the economic freedoms. Yet, while the official citizenship evokes the image of 'citizens as consumers',[138] the shadow citizenship, a much wider concept, rather encompasses EU women and men as citizens, distilled into a bundle of statuses within the margins of natural/legal persons dialectic (consumers, workers, elderly people, disadvantaged individuals, people with disabilities, students, residents, professionals, entrepreneurs, etc.) potentially overcoming future fragmented protection via the unified concept of EU citizenship.

Within this overall framework, we must investigate in which direction—along with the 'if', the 'why', and the 'how'—EU citizenship shall be construed in the future.[139]

Certainly, and according to the ambiguity that often accompanies fundamental rights protection, we need to further investigate whether EU citizenship will live in the shadow of individualism and self-empowered individual rights or, instead, in the penumbra of the solidarity principle (in a socially inclusive context of a reconstructed non-national civic membership).[140] The CJEU case law and scholars can certainly help to define the direction EU identity imbued in EU citizenship will take. Being profoundly embedded and oriented in the market rhetoric of the EU edifice, the notion of 'justice through access'[141] has the potential of trapping the expanding notion of citizenship within a concept

[136] E.g. C-148/02, *Garcia Avello*; C-456/02 *Trojani* [2004] ECR I-7573; C-200/02 *Zhu and Chen*; C-209/03, *Bidar* [2005] ECR I-2119.

[137] E.g. unless a member state citizen, one cannot be an EU citizen. Most individual rights find protection under economic freedoms although deeply rooted in fundamental rights.

[138] European Commission, EU Citizenship Report 2010: Dismantling the obstacles to EU citizens' rights, COM(2010) 603, at 10.

[139] After all, isn't it already emerging in the EU programmatic documents and legislations and/or from the CJEU case law?

[140] It is the traditionally inclusive role of a citizenship and the identity of a group. 'Europe rightly shies away from an ethnic, religious, or any other thick form of organic self-understanding and political identity. The only normatively acceptable construct is to conceive the polity as a community of values.... When one grasps for a content for such a community of values, the commitment to human rights becomes the most ready currency.' Weiler, *supra* note 19, at 106. In our understanding the reasoning of the CJEU that links social functions to some of the rights enshrined in the Charter does not fit similarly to national reasoning concerning the same issues, for instance a social reading of the Italian constitution (Art. 41). See for instance Case C-544/10, *Deutsches Weintor eG v Land Rheinland-Pfalz*, Rec. 54, arguing 'that, according to the case-law of the Court, the freedom to pursue a trade or profession, like the right to property, is not an absolute right but must be considered in relation to its social function (see, to that effect, Case C-210/03 *Swedish Match* [2004] ECR I-11893, paragraph 72). Consequently, restrictions may be imposed on the exercise of those freedoms, provided that those restrictions in fact correspond to objectives of general interest pursued by the European Union and do not constitute, with regard to the aim pursued, a disproportionate and intolerable interference, impairing the very substance of those rights (Case C-22/94 *Irish Farmers Association and Others* [1997] ECR I-1809, paragraph 27, and Joined Cases C-20/00 and C-64/00 *Booker Aquaculture and Hydro Seafood* [2003] ECR I-7411, paragraph 68)'.

[141] H.-W. Micklitz, *Social Justice and Access Justice in Private Law*, EUI Working Paper Law, 2011/02 (2011), available at SSRN: <http://papers.ssrn.com/sol3/papers.cfm?abstract_id=1824225> (last accessed 14 December 2012).

concerned with formal equality of rights. On the contrary, the interaction with member states' private law, their constitutional elements, and their multifarious traditions of social justice and individual rights protection (often enshrined in national constitutions) could propel the process forward, towards an ideal of substantial equal treatment in light of fundamental rights, thereby reclaiming a central role for human rights within EU borders and with reference to EU citizens. In this latter case, the identity-shaping role of the interplay between fundamental rights and private law would, once again, meet the democratic empowerment role.[142]

These processes require the research and design of new legal and linguistic hermeneutics[143] with a view to driving together the identity-shaping and the participative empowerment role of citizens that we illustrated at the beginning of this chapter. After all, several streams for convergence appear to be compatible with Article 2 TEU, newly introduced by the Lisbon Treaty. Most of what constitutes the shadow citizenship stems from the protection of individual rights and economic freedoms. Therefore, its configuration is not inherently shaped by the idea of protecting the weaker party in private law relationships, or by anti-discrimination principles.[144] Nevertheless, in the new political and legal dimension of EU citizenship, our hypothesis is that consumer welfare (official citizenship) and citizen welfare (shadow citizenship) are not antagonistic tools when it comes to economic and legal policy, but, quite to the contrary, two reinforcing sides of the same token protecting the human being.[145]

Coherently, our hypothesis is that a combined reading of Article 2 TEU and the Charter of Fundamental Rights of the European Union will coerce an amalgamation of the official and the shadow citizenship resulting in a materialization of the values and rights enumerated in Article 2.[146] As controversial as it may seem, to this end, there are already signs of such a movement in the case law. For instance, the fundamental rights penumbra is seemingly expanding and assuming a more significant stance in the digital market.[147] The mentioned phenomena involve several different layers so strictly intertwined that they demand the design of new linguistic and legal hermeneutics. For

[142] A modest though expanding role for fundamental rights in the understanding set forth by the new Art. 6 of the TFEU in reorienting private law interpretation at European and national law is acknowledged for instance by Collins, *supra* note 7, at 248.

[143] See *infra* in the text.

[144] See, however, e.g. Case C-236/09, *Association Belge des Consommateurs Test-Achats ASBL and Others v Conseil des Ministres* [2011] ECR I-773, [2011] 2 CMLR 38, prohibiting insurance companies to use gender as discriminating factor.

[145] Collins distinguishes between welfare and well-being and exemplifies the distinction with a neat example: 'the invalidity or ineffectiveness of contracts of slavery, servitude, prostitution and gambling seems to be best explained as the private law response to a perception that none of these transactions is likely to contribute to the well-being of the participants, even though they might improve the welfare of some' (at 161). According to Collins (at 171) 'despite their differences, national private law systems in Europe share this commitment to the development of a perfectionist discourse regarding the support and promotion of the values of well-being'. Collins, *supra* note 7.

[146] In line with other authors, we can note the reshaping potential of specific articles of the treaties (e.g. today, Art. 169 TFEU) in relation to private law. See Collins, *supra* note 7, at 248.

[147] In both Case C-70/10, *Scarlet Extended SA v Société belge des auteurs, compositeurs et éditeurs SCRL (SABAM)*, judgment of 24 November 2011, not yet published, and Case C-360/10, *Belgische Vereniging van Auteurs, Componisten en Uitgevers (SABAM) v Netlog*, judgment of 16 February 2012, not yet published, the CJEU denied the admissibility of a duty on internet service providers and social networks to place preventive filters on user-generated content. Such a duty would have run against 'the requirement that a fair balance be struck between the right to intellectual property, on the one hand, and the freedom to conduct business, the right to protection of personal data and the freedom to receive or impart information, on the other'. See also Case C-275/06, *Productores de Música de España (Promusicae) v Telefónica de España SAU* [2008] ECR I-271.

instance, one layer captures the interplay between fundamental rights and economic freedoms between EU and member state private laws.[148] Another layer focuses on the interactions emanating from EU citizenship(s) creeping out from the economic freedoms logic and language.

6. Echoes of the Fifth Freedom in Case Law

As discussed above, the notion of official EU citizenship 'added a new political dimension to the hitherto primarily economic nature of European integration'.[149] It has set the scene for a revision of the actual, well-documented gap between 'the social' dealt with at the member state level, and 'the economic framework' managed at the supranational EU level.[150] Introduced by the Treaty of Maastricht in 1992, citizenship of the EU has been strengthened by the CJEU's case law advocating non-discrimination in relation to the treatment of EU citizens as such and not as economic players. Accordingly, EU citizenship has become a source of free movement (private law) rights and not only vice versa.[151] This is a remarkable change, which has nonetheless been either ignored, or underestimated.[152]

Nevertheless, the mere fact that EU citizens are entitled (as such) to reside in another member state—in light of Article 21(1) TFEU—paves the way for legal problems unexpected by EU legislation.[153] This process is implicitly transforming the lives of member state citizens (from *subjects* recognized according to denizens)[154] by recognizing them according to individual rights—some of which can be classified as fundamental or human rights according to some legal systems—as opposed to recognition based on the exercise of their economic freedoms. The shadow citizenship phenomenon makes the overcoming of this impasse possible giving rise to the emergence of individual rights for (EU) citizens, politically described as a precondition 'for fully benefiting from the single market'[155] —again the language of economic freedoms—while simultaneously providing the ingredients for the *single civic citizenship* from which they stem.

Still, the transnational requisite for the enforcement of these rights[156] under the EU banner makes these new rights appear inchoate: 'orphan' rights leaving EU citizens to fend for themselves based on their status as denizens.[157] The theoretical casting of these

[148] E.g. in the domain of the right to health, or access to services.

[149] EU Citizenship Report (2010), *supra* note 114.

[150] See for instance the contribution on citizenship from Ianniello Saliceti, 'La protezione diplomatica e consolare dei cittadini dell'UE', in P. De Cesari (ed), *Trattato di diritto Privato dell'Unione europea, Persona e Famiglia* (2008) 149. See also Murray, 'Fundamental Rights in the European Community Legal Order', 32 *Fordham International Law Journal* (2008–2009) 531, and Weiler, 'Eurocracy and Distrust: Some Questions Concerning the role of the ECJ in the Protection of Fundamental Human Rights within the Legal Order of the European Communities', 61 *Washington Law Review* (1986) at 1103.

[151] See for examples Cases C-413/99 *Baumbast and R* [2002] ECR I-7091, Rec. 84, and C-200/02, *Zhu and Chen* [2004] ECR I-9925, Rec. 26.

[152] In fact, the very TFEU conceives it as 'the fundamental status of [member state] nationals' because 'it confers upon all EU citizens an *additional* set of rights, guaranteed by the EU Treaties' (Art. 20 TFEU) (emphasis added).

[153] E.g. the ones illustrated in the EU Citizens Report 2010.

[154] T. Hammar, *Democracy and the Nation State: Aliens, Denizens, and Citizens in a World of International Migration* (1990).

[155] See the Monti Report, *supra* note 126, at 74, referring to access to basic services of economic interest and particularly to a bank account.

[156] The sufficient link requirement in EU law. See cases quoted in the next paragraph.

[157] Although in some instances the CJEU has established that the status of Union citizen can be claimed against the member state of origin. See, for instance, Case C-434/09, *McCarty* [2011] ECR

rights in the language of economic freedoms and legal competences, while a useful technique for fostering them, limits the scope of these orphan rights. Oddly enough, this asymmetry—I virtually enjoy my EU-matrix right only (at least potentially[158] physically) away from 'home'[159]—somehow evokes the USA Constitution prior to the enactment of the XIVth amendment when States could consider their 'citizens' in a way that was inconceivable for the Union itself (*subjects* and even slaves instead of citizens!).[160] Yet, such a situation is better described in terms of the reverse discrimination problem[161] even though the CJEU has begun to tackle the issue not in terms of reverse discrimination but in terms of proportionate measures.[162] In Europe, this asymmetry creates—or shall create—a tension with the notion of fundamental rights, a tension which the new status of the ECHR in the EU legal system makes prospectively unbearable.[163] As a result, one's own fundamental rights remain cast in the logic and language of the market-oriented economic freedoms.[164] Hence emerges the paradoxical image of the protection of EU citizenship rights as the underdog of market creation.[165] After all, and through the voice of the CJEU, the EU has traditionally been at one end of the

I-3375, at Rec. 48 stating that '[a]s a national of at least one Member State, a person such as Mrs McCarthy enjoys the status of a Union citizen under Article 20(1) TFEU and may therefore rely on the rights pertaining to that status, including against his Member State of origin, in particular the right conferred by Article 21 TFEU to move and reside freely within the territory of the Member States (see Case C-33/07 *Jipa* [2008] ECR I-5157, paragraph 17 and case-law cited)'.

[158] See for instance, Case C-60/00, *Mary Carpenter v Secretary of State for the Home Department* [2002] ECR I-6279.

[159] When the required cross-border element is missing, EU law simply does not apply and my own member state can impair the same right I would enjoy if and when availing myself of the economic freedoms.

[160] As the case of *Loving v Virginia* illustrates, even the XIVth amendment by itself was not sufficient to grant equality of rights. Referring back to the EU, in her opinion in the case of *Zambrano*, AG Sharpston clearly stressed that '[i]t would be paradoxical (to say the least) if a citizen of the Union could rely on fundamental rights under EU law when exercising an economic right to free movement as a worker, or when national law comes within the scope of the Treaty... or when invoking EU secondary legislation..., but could not do so when merely "residing" in that Member State' (Opinion of AG Sharpston in Case C-34/09, *Gerardo Ruiz Zambrano v Office national de l'emploi (ONEm)*, para. 84.)

[161] The CJEU has consistently asserted that reverse discrimination issues ('Any difference in treatment between Union citizens...according to whether those Union citizens have previously exercised their right of freedom of movement') does not fall within the scope of EU law. See Case C-127/08, *Metock and Others* [2008] ECR I-6241, Recs 77–78.

[162] According to Case C-353/06, *Grunkin-Paul* [2008] ECR I-7639, Rec. 21: 'National legislation which places certain of the nationals of the Member State concerned at a disadvantage simply because they have exercised their freedom to move and to reside in another Member State is a restriction on the freedoms conferred by Article 18(1) EC on every citizen of the Union (see Case C-406/04 *De Cuyper* [2006] ECR I-6947, paragraph 39, and Case C-499/06 *Nerkowska* [2008] ECR I-0000, paragraph 32).' Indeed '[a]n obstacle to freedom of movement such as that resulting from the serious inconvenience described in paragraphs 23 to 28 of this judgment could be justified only if it was based on objective considerations and was proportionate to the legitimate aim pursued' (Rec. 29, quoting Case C-318/05, *Commission* v *Germany* [2007] ECR I-6957, Rec. 133, and the case law cited).

[163] For instance, it is difficult to explain to Lambda, an EU citizen, that she enjoys the right to bear the surnames of both parents if her own member state does not provide for it unless economic freedoms are actually at stake. The technical explanation for this odd result is nonetheless crystal clear: EU law simply does not apply and member states are sovereign since 'Citizenship of the Union shall be additional to and not replace national citizenship' (Art. 20(1) TFEU).

[164] See the reasoning of the Court (First Chamber) of 14 October 2004, Case C-36/02, *Omega Spielhallen- und Automatenaufstellungs-GmbH v Oberbürgermeisterin der Bundesstadt Bonn* [2004] ECR I-9609.

[165] In line with the reasoning in the text Collins, *supra* note 7, emphasizes that the acquis communitaire in private law is really an accidental byproduct of endeavours to do something else: to help the internal market to succeed. As a result, it is patchy, inconsistent, opaque, and often poorly justified.

ever growing tension between *the human rights tradition* (where rights are universal and dissociated from citizenship or at least membership in a community)[166] and the *modern tradition of citizenship* (where political participation in a nation state and rights are deeply intertwined).

Facing the abovementioned tensions, judicial intervention might not wait for an EU-like XIVth amendment. Indeed, even with the American XIVth amendment, judicial action was required to foster equal dignity of citizens as recalled in *Loving v Virginia.*[167]

In fact, as has been argued,

> [t]he creation of a supranational community to establish a form of collective action regarding certain subject matters does not itself justify homogenizing fundamental rights. Undeniably, citizens from all member states should receive the same protection from the EU legal order against the action of EU institutions. At the same time, standards of protection given to parallel constitutional rights might reasonably diverge from one state to the other. In the face of reasonable disagreement, other values, such as democratic self-government or political identity, might justify co-existing, differing interpretations. EU member states constitute democratic constitutional polities for the self-government of a group of people with a collective identity living under the same constitution. Thus, some degree of autonomy to interpret constitutional rights should be respected, even within the field of application of EU law. In short, equality does not require that state diversity be immediately rejected in favour of supranational uniformity.[168]

However, it would seem that this last argument is unable to cope with the fact that member state citizens would 'enjoy' EU protected rights in their own state of national citizenship if and only if they have made use of their economic freedoms and/or the CJEU considers this the case. This paradoxical shortcut—ultimately creating unequal citizenship[169]—attests to the conflict between collective identities, more particularly those identities present at both EU and member state levels and their interaction with the different citizenships. This conflict or tension proves difficult to solve for different reasons. One, and perhaps the most relevant here, is that EU identity is either non-existent[170] or is at least a fragmented one. It is emerging apparently randomly through CJEU case law and EU legislation coupled with the interplay of notions of European citizenships set out herein. It seems to differ significantly from national identity[171] reflecting political and social diversity among communities. Indeed, these different communities might influence the way essential public values and constitutional rights in particular are conceived in each

[166] For a definition of citizenship as the 'status bestowed on those who are full members of the community' and which includes civil, political, and social rights and obligations, see Th. Marshall, *Citizenship and Social Class* (1959), at 14.

[167] Indeed there is no economic due process as per the American style in Europe. See M. Poiares Maduro, *We, The Court: The European Court Of Justice & The European Economic Constitution* (1998). We can note here initial ideas, emanating from the judiciary, similar to an EU-like XIVth amendment. This initial reflex can be extracted from the case *Åklagaren v Hans Åkerberg Fransson, supra* note 44, where the undefined scope of Union law is seen to work as a tool of technical discretion for the Court allowing it to practise discretion when interpreting fundamental rights according to the Charter.

[168] Pérez, *supra* note 21, at 81.

[169] 'Unequal citizenship is an oxymoron, generating stigma and unease in the mistreated'. Kochenov, *supra* note 18. See also ibid., at 35: 'More economically active EU citizens are now enabled to benefit more from EU law provisions than ever before.'

[170] Grimm, 'Does Europe Need a Constitution?', 1 *ELJ* (1995) 297; Weiler, 'Does Europe Need a Constitution? Reflections on Demos, Telos and the German Maastricht Decision', 1 *ELJ* (1995) 219.

[171] Some might think this result is even desirable, see Weiler, *supra* note 72, at 341, where he states: 'It would be... ironic if the ethos which rejected the boundary abuse of the nation-state gave birth to a polity with the same potential for abuse.'

state. For instance, Scandinavian countries have proved to be quite progressive, adopting measures to advance equality on the basis of sex and sexual orientation. In short, diverse constitutional polities might bring about distinct interpretations of analogous fundamental rights. These political communities and corresponding constitutional understandings deserve a measure of respect as well as the possibility to develop further within a broader EU pluralist structure.[172]

The traditional response to such a diversity of values has historically been the migration of citizens to a community better suited to their preferences. The potential of European citizenship can be summarized in the possibility to offer EU non-Scandinavian nationals the possibility to enjoy Scandinavian progressive measures without having to move to a Scandinavian country to enjoy them. Strikingly, EU non-Scandinavian citizens might reach the result by virtually[173] exercising one of their economic freedoms or rights emanating from the status of EU citizen and basing any objections on the right of Union citizens to enjoy 'the substance of the rights conferred by virtue of that status or of impeding the exercise of their right of free movement and residence within the territory of the Member States'.[174]

The legal framework being constructed by the CJEU case law might, in fact, offer a greater level of protection at the EU level than that offered at national level,[175] enabling individuals to leverage for change both at national and EU levels. In any event, the possibility of channelling, using the language of the fundamental economic freedoms in conjunction with the EU citizenship rights, makes the EU, as opposed to the member states, a laboratory for innovation.[176] This result is the opposite of the US understanding of the interplay between state and national levels. To use the words of Justice Brennan in reference to the USA: 'As tempting as it may be to harmonize results under state and national constitutions, our federalism permits state courts to provide greater protection to individual civil rights and liberties.'[177] Within the EU it is the opposite and it operates in a non-national legal framework.

The multifarious and serpentine[178] set of cases surrounding the notion of EU citizenship is unearthing the identity of a truly European civil society[179] and, as Hugh Collins argues,

[172] Pérez, *supra* note 21, at 86.

[173] See for instance Case C-60/00, *Mary Carpenter and Secretary of State for the Home Department* [2002] ECR I-6279.

[174] See Case C-434/09, *McCarthy v Secretary of State for the Home Department* [2011] ECR I-3375, Rec. 53; Case C-34/09, *Gerardo Ruiz Zambrano v Office national de l'emploi (ONEm)* [2011] ECR I-1177, and Case C-148/02, *Carlos Garcia Avello v Belgian State* [2003] ECR I-11613.

[175] Still, the possible issues concerning abuses of rights may alter the results.

[176] The idea of 'states as laboratories' was introduced by Justice Brandeis in his dissent in *New State Ice Co. v Liebman*, 285 US 262 (1932).

[177] W. J. Brennan, Jr, 'The Bill of Rights and the States: The Revival of State Constitutions as Guardians of Individual Rights', 61 *New York University Law Review* (1986) 536, at 551, stating that after all, '[t]he existence of separate polities... when coupled with a reasonable degree of mobility, may significantly enhance individual freedom whenever a state acts against personal preferences'. See also D. L. Shapiro, *Federalism: A Dialogue* (1995), at 91–92 and 95–96.

[178] 'What was required of the Court was to come up with a just, convincing and logically justifiable test that would be universally applicable, to enable any citizen to know for sure, via application of a handful of simple and clear rules, which level of the law is to apply to her in each particular situation and why. Such a test should also avoid being overwhelmingly restrictive allowing as many citizens as possible to benefit from the liberating features of EU law, which they would invoke against the Member State... The ECJ largely failed this difficult task.' See Kochenov, *supra* note 18, at 40–41.

[179] The idea in itself is not new. See Weiler, *supra* note 170, arguing that there could/should be a European identity (he writes in terms of 'polity') that does not and does not need to displace the national identities.

business associations, social networks, technical standards bodies and scientific associations, together with long term family relations and more transient transactions such as package holidays are the building blocks of a transnational civil society in Europe. They open up the possibilities for transnational networks between citizens to become denser and form part of the routines of everyday life. These routines derive ultimately from mutual reliance and trust, but then themselves reinforce social solidarity, a sense of belonging to and owing loyalty towards a European community.[180]

It is plausible that the existing advocacy networks and structures, along with the expanding reach of interplay among the judiciaries and among judges, could work as 'substitutes' for a common language[181] helping to overcome[182] the scarcity of several elements of a democracy in the EU, of which a shared language is but one. Yet, those patterns may prove insufficient in moving participation beyond the threshold of formal equality. In fact, once the mutual recognition of the law of the member states[183] is balanced with the growing role of EU citizenship, we can note the shaping of a transnational civil society according to the rights emanating from cases. In this scenario, there is no need for an explicit, full, common set of private law rules or even principles, essentially permitting the process to avoid the political difficulties this may entail.

This eventual furthering of individual protection[184] via dual protection (at both national and EU levels) of fundamental rights and liberties can easily be exemplified by reference to the case law.[185] This in itself, however, causes paradoxical results since the results extracted from the case law (or a large number of them) are reached at the EU level before the national level. This in effect gives rise to reverse discrimination problems[186] and an inherent conflict of loyalties.

[180] Collins, *supra* note 7.

[181] Which political scientists often see as a necessary element for a democracy. See Kymlicka, 'Citizenship in an Era of Globalization: A Commentary on Held', in I. Shapiro and C. Hacker-Cordon (eds), *Democracy's Edges* (1999) 112, at 121.

[182] See the criticism of Kymlicka, 'New Forms of Citizenship', in T. J. Courchesne and D. J. Savoie, *The Art of the State: Governance in a World Without Frontiers* (2003) 265, at 291, where the reasons for his euroscepticism are clearly explicated. See also Kymlicka, 'Territorial Boundaries: A Liberal-Egalitarian Perspective', in D. Miller and S. H. Hashmi (eds), *Boundaries and Justice: Diverse Ethical Perspectives* (2001) 249, at 324–326.

[183] Once the principle is understood as 'the idea that each national legal system should respect the rules of others where they are more closely connected to the issue or dispute [it] exhibits the quality of the comity of nations' of the EU. Collins, *supra* note 7, at 13.

[184] Poiares Maduro, 'Las Formas del Poder Constitucional de la Unión Europea', 119 *Revista de Estudios Políticos* (2003) 11.

[185] Case C-177/88, *Elisabeth Johanna Pacifica Dekker v Stichting Vormingscentrum voor Jong Volwassenen Plus* [1990] ECR I-3941; Case C-32/93 *Carole Louise Webb v EMO Air Cargo (UK) Ltd* [1994] ECR I-3567.

[186] Some cases signal that the Court is in fact aware of these issues. We can look to the Opinion of AG Kokott in Case C-434/09, *McCarthy v Secretary of State for the Home Department*, at para. 42: 'It cannot of course be ruled out that the Court will review its case-law when the occasion arises and be led from then on to derive a prohibition on discrimination against one's own nationals from citizenship of the Union. Citizenship of the Union is after all destined to be "the fundamental status of nationals of the Member States, enabling those who find themselves in the same situation to receive the same treatment in law irrespective of their nationality, subject to such exceptions as are expressly provided for' " (quoting Case C-184/99, *Grzelczyk* [2001] ECR I-6193, Rec. 31, and Case C-524/06, *Huber* [2008] ECR I-9705, Rec. 69; Case C-300/04, *Eman and Sevinger* [2006] ECR I-8055, in particular Recs 57, 58, and 61; and in relation to citizenship of the Union as 'the fundamental status' quoting Case C-413/99, *Baumbast and R* [2002] ECR I-7091, Rec. 82; *Garcia Avello*, Rec. 22; and Case C-135/08, *Rottmann* [2010] ECR I-1449, Rec. 43).

Perhaps then, it is not without significance that the novel vocabulary of the Horizon 2020 research agenda of the Digital Agenda for Europe and the Monti Report, while all tackling a 'new impulse' of the Single Market endeavour, use a language increasingly closely connected to the relationship between rights, territory, and membership in a social dimension. Inclusion of the marginalized or rightless, protection of the vulnerable,[187] identity, and respect for diversity are but a few examples illustrating this paradigm shift.

Nevertheless, again the political agenda looks to economic rights while the shadow citizenship contributes to the EU citizenship identity aggregation purporting legal changes both traditionally out of the scope of EU legislation and mainly in civil, commercial, and family law.[188] Also for this reason, the emergence of a civic citizenship remains problematic since those targeted areas are highly sensitive; they are value driven at both national and sometimes even subnational and regional levels. As a result, the search for the European shared values it requires is difficult and can only be shaped on a case-by-case basis. Such a casuistic approach proceeds from the possibilities provided for by EU law in the daily life of individuals and takes the form of an emerging EU citizenship as a modelling concept of postnational (*rectius*: non-national) fragmented identity.[189] As anticipated, the underlying idea is that a plurality of agents, institutions and legal dynamics are relentlessly aggregating a European citizenship, shaped by the clash, and subsequent consequences, of either individual or socially orientated fundamental rights with legislation, policies, and rulings rooted in the economic freedoms. Indeed, transnational private law patterns to civic EU citizenship are emerging not only when rights are availed of 'beyond national borders'.[190] For instance, the necessity principle[191] which informs data protection, defines the structural limits of the software used and the way a business is organized regardless of the transnational nature of the transaction involved.[192] Yet the analysis of these legislative patterns cannot be pursued here and we should confine ourselves to some more detailed references to CJEU case law in the next concluding section.

7. Conclusions: Digging Back through the Cases for Insights into the Future

We have developed our discourse all the while making perfunctory reference to CJEU jurisprudence in many fields of law. We must now undertake a more thorough investigation of the case law so as to decipher the patterns that are emerging from the CJEU

[187] See the Monti Report, *supra* note 126, at 47 referring to consumers, but also Directive 2005/29, OJ 2005 L 149/22, on unfair commercial practices.

[188] Notably, areas such as family or tort law or even property are not among those the Commission feels comfortable to propose legislation for. See Collins, *supra* note 7, at 33.

[189] One characteristic of postnational citizenships, it has been said, is their fragmented character. See Bamyeh, 'Postnationalism', 3 *Bulletin of the Royal Institute for Inter-Faith Studies* 3 (2001).

[190] '[T]hrough travel, study, work, marriage, retirement, buying or inheriting property, voting, or just shopping online from companies established in other Member States' (EU Citizenship Report 2010, *supra* note 114).

[191] Art. 6(c) of the Data Protection Directive 95/46/EC, OJ 1995 L 281/31, and Directive 2002/58/EC, OJ 2002 L 201/37 on Privacy and Electronic Communications.

[192] Indeed, it has been affirming itself in primary and secondary legislation as a distinctive feature of EU private law legislation within a framework which makes it a cornerstone of EU data protection to which large and SME businesses should conform, setting the tone as to the protection EU citizens enjoy—as opposed to (e.g.) American ones—towards a more inclusive and trustworthy society.

declarations. Bearing in mind our metaphor concerning the merging of the shadow citizenship with the official citizenship to create a single borderless civic citizenship centred on fundamental rights, when we look to the CJEU cases it is possible to immediately distinguish two kinds of relevant case sets. As anticipated, on the one hand, we find the more traditional cases that expand the scope of fundamental rights indirectly by protecting the fundamental economic freedoms.[193] On the other hand, we can delineate cases[194] that directly or indirectly expand the scope of EU fundamental rights relying on EU citizenship.[195]

Both sets of cases influence private law in the relevant sectors in that they intercept in the situation/case at hand and hence beyond the discrete domain of EU competences.[196]

We can also note from both lines of reasoning that the minimum link to community law requirement retains importance in that the national measure at stake must be causing an inconvenience so substantial so as to affect the genuine enjoyment of freedoms and/or citizenship, along with the absence of an abuse of community law.

Yet, in the second line of cases, the CJEU, in deciding whether or not a given member state interference is 'depriving citizens of the Union of the genuine enjoyment of the substance of the rights conferred by virtue of their status as citizens of the Union',[197] has taken an approach that we can even quantitatively/qualitatively interpret. For example, the Court stated that '[t]he refusal of the host Member State to grant rights of entry and residence to the family members of a Union citizen is such as to discourage that citizen from moving to or residing in that Member State'.[198] It further extended the protection of family life to third country nationals entering illegally[199] on the condition they are 'married to a national of a Member State where he is able to prove his identity and the conjugal ties and there is no evidence to establish that he represents a risk to the requirements of public policy, public security or public health'.[200]

Further, and in reference to the field of contract law, in a case in no way characterized by transnational components, the Grand Chamber read Article 2(5) of Council Directive 2000/78/EC of 27 November 2000 as 'precluding rules of national law which recognise an age-limit of 60 for pilots established by collective agreement for the purposes of air safety'.[201] The court in deciding that 'national and international legislation considered that it was not necessary to prohibit pilots from acting as pilots after age 60 but merely

[193] See for instance, Case C-60/00, *Mary Carpenter v Secretary of State for the Home Department* [2002] ECR I-6279, expanding the fundamental right to family life via Ms Carpenter's economic freedoms.

[194] Case C-34/09 *Gerardo Ruiz Zambrano v Office national de l'emploi (ONEm)* [2011] ECR I-1177.

[195] See Case C-200/02, *Kunqian Catherine Zhu & Man Lavette Chen v Secretary of State for the Home Department* [2004] ECR I-9925, in which by virtue of Catherine's EU citizenship, residence rights were granted to both Catherine and her mother upholding the unity of the family.

[196] For instance, on the impact on areas such as family law of cases such as *Zambrano* or *Dereci* see Van Elsuwege and Kochenov, 'On the Limits of Judicial Intervention: EU Citizenship and Family Reunification Rights', 4 *European Journal of Migration and Law* (2011) 443.

[197] See Case C-34/09, *Gerardo Ruiz Zambrano v Office national de l'emploi (ONEm)*, Rec. 42. See also Kochenov, 'A Real European Citizenship; a New Jurisdiction Test; a Novel Chapter in the Development of the Union in Europe', 1 *Columbia Journal of European Law* (2012) 55.

[198] Case C-127/08, *Blaise Baheten Metock and Others v Minister for Justice, Equality and Law Reform* [2008] ECR I-6241, Rec. 64.

[199] It has been stressed that human rights tend to protect non-citizens in postnational states. See Y. N. Soyal, *Limits of Citizenship: Migrant and Postnational Membership in Europe* (1994).

[200] Case C-459/99, *Mouvement contre le racisme, l'antisémitisme et la xénophobie ASBL (MRAX) v Belgian State* [2002] ECR I-6591, Recs 61–62.

[201] Case C-447/09, *Reinhard Prigge, Michael Fromm, Volker Lambach v Deutsche Lufthansa* [2011] ECR I-8003, Rec. 36.

to restrain those activities' effectively rewrote the equality principle in the German (and in all member states') legal setting. More specifically, it limited the freedom of contract of social parties. The result of the Court's reasoning, i.e. that 'the prohibition on piloting after that age, contained in the measure at issue in the main proceedings, was not necessary for the achievement of the pursued objective'[202] de facto grants a more significant protection to EU citizens than that accorded by the national law in question. The legal implications move beyond the actual case and clearly evidence both the civic engagement we have been referring to thus far, and the aggregation of a novel civic allegiance: the boundaries for public and private actors in the member states are redefined as an outcome of individual participation in the EU legal order and in light of their citizenship. Indeed, the underlying principle for the decision was that 'the prohibition of all discrimination on grounds, inter alia, of age is incorporated in Article 21 of the Charter of Fundamental Rights of the European Union ("the Charter"), which, from 1 December 2009, has the same legal status as the treaties'.[203] Furthermore, it is clearly espoused that it is the responsibility of the Court to balance the rights acknowledged in the Charter.[204]

Similarly, in the *Sky Österreich* case, a contractual clause was struck down when the Court reasoned that 'an established legal position on a broadcaster, protected by Article 17(1) of the Charter, enabling it to exercise its broadcasting right autonomously... in the sense that it could demand compensation exceeding the additional costs directly incurred in providing access to the signal, [is] contrary to the mandatory provisions of Directive 2007/65'. The necessary balance between the rights and the freedoms at issue in the particular case[205] was struck in a way allowing the Court to consider 'the fundamental freedom to receive information and to promote pluralism of the media', as guaranteed by the Charter, and ultimately the balancing act permitted the Court to grant prevalence to the latter mentioned, Charter specific, right.[206]

In addition, rights to annual leave and paid holidays are deeply entrenched in contractual rules and are often granted clear constitutional protection.[207] To some extent, those rights can even be said to form part of the heart of every modern polity. Yet, according to the CJEU, these rights for EU citizens might be more widely protected by

[202] Rec. 63.

[203] See Rec. 38. Indeed, the Grand Chamber stresses the fact that such a principle has already been recognized by case law, but now has acquired a higher legal status.

[204] See reference to Art. 28 and collective negotiation for instance at Rec. 47. In another case (also, Case C-275/06, *Promusicae* [2008] ECR I-271, para. 56, referring to Case C-101/01, *Lindqvist* [2003] ECR I-12971, Rec. 87), AG Kokot noted: 'The balance between the relevant fundamental rights must first be struck by the Community legislature and, in the interpretation of Community law, by the Court.' Yet in agreeing with the AG the Court went on to establish (Rec. 70) that: 'Community law requires that, when transposing those directives, the Member States take care to rely on an interpretation of them which allows a fair balance to be struck between the various fundamental rights protected by the Community legal order. Further, when implementing the measures transposing those directives, the authorities and courts of the Member States must not only interpret their national law in a manner consistent with those directives but also make sure that they do not rely on an interpretation of them which would be in conflict with those fundamental rights or with the other general principles of Community law, such as the principle of proportionality.'

[205] See Case C-283/11, *Sky Österreich GmbH v Österreichischer Rundfunk*, judgment of 22 January 2013, not yet published, Recs 59–60 in which is it noted that 'the European Union legislature was required to strike a balance between the freedom to conduct a business, on the one hand, and the fundamental freedom of citizens of the European Union to receive information and the freedom and pluralism of the media, on the other. Where several rights and fundamental freedoms protected by the European Union legal order are at issue, the assessment of the possible disproportionate nature of a provision of European Union law must be carried out with a view to reconciling the requirements of the protection of those different rights and freedoms and a fair balance between them'.

[206] See Rec. 66.

[207] See, for instance, Art. 36 of the Italian Constitution.

relying on their EU allegiance as opposed to their nation state affiliation, since Article 7(1) of Directive 2003/88/EC of the European Parliament and of the Council of 4 November 2003 concerning certain aspects of the organization of working time 'must be interpreted as precluding national provisions under which a worker who becomes unfit for work during a period of paid annual leave is not entitled subsequently to the paid annual leave which coincided with the period of unfitness for work'. It is important to point out here that the Court particularly stressed the fact that 'the right to paid annual leave is, as a principle of European Union social law, not only particularly important, *but is also expressly laid down in Article 31(2) of the Charter of Fundamental Rights of the European Union, which Article 6(1) TEU recognises as having the same legal value as the Treaties*'.[208] We can thereby note the Court's escalating tendency to relate rules and principles to the text of the Charter of the Fundamental Rights and additionally, its will to clearly express that when legislation makes explicit reference to the rights in the Charter, the validity of that legislation 'must be assessed in the light of those provisions'.[209]

In other decisions, the Court has begun to develop what might be termed a 'level of inconvenience' test, for which objective criteria have yet to be delineated.[210] In short, in order to satisfy the test, it must be established that a measure is 'liable to cause serious inconvenience for the Union citizens concerned that constituted an obstacle to freedom of movement that could be justified only if it was based on objective considerations and was proportionate to the legitimate aim pursued'.[211] However, no clear guidance has been offered as of yet with a view to facilitating the determination of what exactly qualifies as a 'serious inconvenience' or as a measure 'proportionate to the legitimate aim pursued'. Therefore, the Court has been left with much room for manoeuvre.

Furthermore, the requirement of a link to EU law has been interpreted in different ways by the CJEU. In our understanding, the frequent use of the economic freedoms language has assisted the court in both restricting and enlarging its scope. Hence, in establishing a sufficient connection, the fact that an athlete participated in a competition in a member state other than that in which he was established[212] was considered adequate. In addition, we can make reference to a case according to which proof that the citizen offered 'correspondence services [comprising] services where there is no change of place by the provider and recipient of the service but the services themselves are provided across a frontier'[213] was also considered satisfactory.

Interestingly, especially for our purposes here, the Court, in *Garcia Avello*, seemed ready to acknowledge a sufficient link by mere virtue of possessing EU citizenship.[214]

[208] Case C-78/11, *Asociación Nacional de Grandes Empresas de Distribución (ANGED) v Federación de Asociaciones Sindicales (FASGA) and Others*, judgment of 21 June 2012, not yet published, at Recs 17 and 24 respectively. Emphasis added. This phrase is increasingly repeated in CJEU cases.

[209] Case C-236/09, *Association Belge des Consommateurs Test-Achats ASBL and Others v Conseil des Ministres* [2011] ECR I-773, Rec. 17 quoting to this effect Joined Cases C-92/09 and C-93/09 *Volker und Markus Schecke and Eifert* [2010] ECR I-11063, Rec. 46.

[210] See the Opinion of AG Sharpston in *Grunkin-Paul, supra* note 162, at para. 73, where is it argued that '[s]uch inconvenience is in no way lessened by the fact that a person has the nationality of only one of the Member States concerned. It stems, in practical terms, not from the possession of more than one nationality but from the fact of moving, as a citizen of the Union, between Member States and successively living, studying, working, seeking benefits, completing administrative formalities, opening bank accounts and carrying out the many other transactions of everyday life in each of them'.

[211] Case C-434/09, *McCarthy v Secretary of State for the Home Department*, at Rec. 53 quoting *Grunkin-Paul*, Recs 23, 24, and 29 on proportionality.

[212] Joined Cases C-51/96 and C-191/97, *Deliège* [2000] ECR I-2549, Rec. 58.

[213] Joined Cases C-34/95, C-35/95, and C-36/95, *De Agostini mid TV-Shop* [1997] ECR I-3843. See also Case C-60/00, *Mary Carpenter and Secretary of State for the Home Department.*

[214] Case C-148/02, *Garcia Avello*, Rec. 26: '[s]uch a link with Community law does, however, exist in regard to . . . nationals of one Member State lawfully resident in the territory of another Member

Indeed, in these cases the 'purely internal situation' doctrine, developed by the CJEU to cast outside the scope of EU law any case that was considered wholly internal to a member state,[215] is questioned by reference to the fifth freedom (EU citizenship) and by those cases[216] which directly or indirectly revolve around the notion of European Citizenship and its protected rights.

The cases mentioned below illustrate the need to and possibility of expanding the scope of protection of fundamental rights beyond the traditional results of the CJEU[217] using EU citizenship as a fifth (non) economic freedom since it has the capacity to expand the scope *ratione personae* of EU law by virtue of its potential to reach 'every person holding the nationality of a Member State'.[218]

Thus, cases such as *Grunkin-Paul*,[219] for instance, can be interpreted as a way to empower citizens (against the public administration or private counterparts) by virtue of simply being an EU citizen. With specific reference to private law, even though 'as Community law stands at present, the rules governing a person's surname are matters coming within the competence of the Member States, the latter must none the less, when exercising that competence, comply with Community law unless what is involved is an internal situation which has no link with Community law'.[220] That being said, the Court[221] was unwilling to accept 'internal discrimination' vis-à-vis one's own nationality in light of a violation of fundamental rights when citizenship was in play. This is very important in our analysis since *Grunkin-Paul* basically rests solely upon EU citizenship reasoning.[222]

The artificial creation of a favourable situation interpreted as an abuse of EU law remains a possible gatekeeper. However, the judgment in *Zhu and Chen*[223] downplayed the argument that the place of birth was deliberately chosen for the sole purpose of acquiring nationality, questioning the gatekeeping function referred to above:[224] 'to speak of an abuse of law, there must . . . also be an underlying "combination of objective circumstances" in which "despite formal observance of the conditions laid down by the Community rules, the purpose of those rules has not been achieved" '.[225] Indeed, there is much room for discretion and some confusion concerning the requirements that need to be satisfied before a practice can be considered abusive. In addition, we can also note confusion regarding the potential disputability of virtually any national law—even those not falling within the scope of EU competences—thereby encompassing most private law rules.

State'. And, as added by AG Tizzano in Case C-200/02, *Kunqian Catherine Zhu & Man Lavette Chen v Secretary of State for the Home Department*, at para. 33 'that is the case regardless of whether they have exercised the freedom of movement provided for by the Treaty or, as in that case, had lived since birth in the territory of the host Member State'.

[215] For a critical analysis see Hanf, ' "Reverse Discrimination" in EU Law: Constitutional Aberration, Constitutional Necessity, or Judicial Choice', 2 *Maastricht Journal of European and Comparative Law* (2011) 29.

[216] For instance *Rottmann, Ruiz Zambrano*, and *McCarthy*.

[217] In Case C-159/90, *The Society for the Protection of Unborn Children Ireland Ltd. v Stephen Grogan and Others* ECR [1991] I-4685, Recs 24–27 and 31, the Court opined that the link between students distributing information and abortion clinics was too tenuous.

[218] Case C-224/98, *D'Hoop* [2002] ECR I-6191, Rec. 27.

[219] Case C-353/06, *Grunkin-Paul*.

[220] See Rec. 16. Actually the quote comes from the *Garcia Avello* case which continues at Rec. 25 referring to 'in particular the Treaty provisions on the freedom of every citizen of the Union to move and reside in the territory of the Member States'.

[221] See Rec. 20.

[222] See Rec. 21.

[223] See Rec. 34 et seq.

[224] See the Opinion of AG Sharpston in *Grunkin-Paul*, para. 86.

[225] Case C-212/97, *Centros* [1999] ECR I-1459, Rec. 24.

It has been argued that the profound persistent character of private law assumes a constitutional role for societies.[226] Although we agree with this view concerning the role of private law in nation state building,[227] it seems clear that it has a foundational/constitutional role as well in more or less explicit 'revolutionary' moments, moments in which a rupture occurs in the system, either caused by private law or occurring within private law.[228] This is actually how the Napoleonic Civil Code came into existence, for instance, and this is partially, we claim, the case concerning the changes directly or indirectly fostered by EU law. Importantly, discrete but visible changes in national legal systems, adopted via self-presented[229] re-regulation of discrete areas of private law in conjunction with the significant impact of the economic freedoms and the significant potential of EU citizenship, are creating silent ruptures in the national legal systems and planting the seeds for a borderless European identity. EU citizenship imposes an increasing level of national (private and public) law conformity on European law that could not be achieved by a code of principles. It is developing a decentralized mode of constructing civic networks and civic identity. Paradoxical as it might sound, this process might be less laborious politically speaking because the expansion of individual rights under the EU banners occurs formally in a decentralized way, by way of casuistic case law.

In addition, it has been argued that 'the principles of civil law articulate moral and social values'.[230] However, once the principles (or better, some rules emanating from them) are altered in case law by the force of EU citizenship, a silent fracture is created in national legal systems. Once we take into account that '[a]t the core of the [Luxembourg] Court's historical success lies its ability to "constitutionalize" the project of economic integration without ever seeming to blur the line between law and politics, or between supranational powers and states' sovereignty, or between common policies and individual rights',[231] we can clearly play the same 'game' according to the same rules but taking an alternative direction, i.e. using the language of economic freedoms to sustain a fundamental rights-based, identity-shaping process which does not endorse one polity's set of values but, occasionally, picks them from different polities and redefines them in a dialectic which continuously changes the equilibrium of fundamental rights and boundaries at every level of the EU and member state polities.

Such a process can quickly overturn the idea that 'citizenship of the Union' is limited to the existing Treaty right of free movement and residence especially when read in light of the further bolstering of these rights in secondary EU law. On the contrary, the construction of new EU citizens' rights on the shoulder of economic freedoms might permit a less confrontational development.

The case law mentioned and the understanding flowing from the decisions ought to overcome the interpretation of Article 6 TEU[232] as constituting 'at most an instruction

[226] Collins, *supra* note 7.

[227] For an acute and challenging reconstruction applied to supranational institutions see Caruso, *supra* note 61.

[228] However, see Collins, *supra* note 7, at 103; Schepel, 'The Enforcement of EC Law in Contractual Relations: Case Studies in How Not to "Constitutionalise" Private Law', 12 *European Review of Private Law* (2004) 661.

[229] See *supra* note 74.

[230] Collins, *supra* note 7.

[231] See Caruso, *supra* note 61, at 873. See also Poiares Maduro, *supra* note 185, at 20–21 where he states: 'What is remarkable in the Court's case law is that the conflicts of values inherent in the exercise of discretion and the choices made thereon are not made explicit, but remain hidden behind formal reasoning.'

[232] Which states that '[t]he Union shall respect fundamental rights, as guaranteed by the European Convention for the Protection of Human Rights and Fundamental Freedoms... and as they result from the constitutional traditions common to the Member States, as general principles of Community law'.

to the European Court of Justice to bear these principles in mind in its interpretation of community law'.[233] On the contrary, the process we are concerned with here is in fact, as delineated throughout this contribution, an aggregation of a truly common bundle of rights, rights that are not at all common to the member states' constitutional traditions, around the notion of EU citizenship.

A reading of EU citizenship anchored in fundamental rights—inherently including the diverse tensions they create—even when made through the lenses of fundamental freedoms would actually provide 'a method for citizens to assert their rights and freedoms directly before a court'.[234] After all, Article 20 TFEU[235] rights have been incorporated in Title V of the Charter and can certainly be claimed by individual citizens, as the CJEU constantly recalls. However, it is not yet clear if all EU fundamental rights in the Charter are citizenship rights rendering them directly applicable also in purely internal situations[236] even though, in the same vein, it has been argued that the only applicability requirement is nationality.[237]

It is clear from the foregoing that we can surrender to the idea that the provisions on EU citizenship are more than mere declaratory statements contained in the treaties and rather succumb to the new notion presented here, i.e. that their provisions can be understood as the fifth economic freedom of the EU. Using the same kind of arguments that the CJEU has developed over time in expanding its role, the scope of European private law might, at the very least, expand leading to an application of EU fundamental rights in 'purely' internal situations at least by way of expanding the scope of the 'other' four freedoms or in loosening the required link to EU law.

Once one novel solution is achieved and accepted under the umbrella of European private law, regardless of its re-regulatory or principle-establishing character, Pandora's box is open and the *Marleasing*[238] rule that requests national courts to interpret national

[233] Collins, *supra* note 7, at 97. [234] In contradiction, see Collins, *supra* note 7, at 97.

[235] Art. 20 TFEU (ex Art. 17 TEC):

1. Citizenship of the Union is hereby established. Every person holding the nationality of a Member State shall be a citizen of the Union. Citizenship of the Union shall be additional to and not replace national citizenship.
2. Citizens of the Union shall enjoy the rights and be subject to the duties provided for in the Treaties. They shall have, inter alia:
   (a) the right to move and reside freely within the territory of the Member States;
   (b) the right to vote and to stand as candidates in elections to the European Parliament and in municipal elections in their Member State of residence, under the same conditions as nationals of that State;
   (c) the right to enjoy, in the territory of a third country in which the Member State of which they are nationals is not represented, the protection of the diplomatic and consular authorities of any Member State on the same conditions as the nationals of that State;
   (d) the right to petition the European Parliament, to apply to the European Ombudsman, and to address the institutions and advisory bodies of the Union in any of the Treaty languages and to obtain a reply in the same language.

These rights shall be exercised in accordance with the conditions and limits defined by the Treaties and by the measures adopted thereunder.

[236] On this reading, see Hailbronner and Thym, 'Case C-34/09, *Gerardo Ruiz Zambrano v. Office national de l'emploi (ONEm)*, Judgment of the Court of Justice (Grand Chamber) of 8 Mar. 2011', 48 *Common Market Law Review* (*CMLRev*) (2011) 1258.

[237] '[T]here is no mention in that Article of the need to satisfy any other requirement but that of nationality of a Member State before being able to claim citizenship rights under the Treaty or secondary legislation.' In the same vein, see Spaventa, 'Seeing the Wood Despite the Trees? On the Scope of Union Citizenship and its Constitutional Effects', 45 *CMLRev* (2008) 13.

[238] Case C-106/89, *Marleasing v La Comercial Internacional de Alimentacion* [1990] ECR I-4135.

laws in a way which is compatible with European law, will, in the long run, expand the silent ruptures created in the system(s). To offer but one example, since the national rules on family names have been placed under the spotlight an entire host of change has become possible since national courts are obliged to give full effect to the rules of European Union law and, where appropriate, to disregard national law that conflicts with that law.[239]

What our analysis illustrates is not a creeping codification[240] but rather the muffled rising of a citizenship coupled with private law, the principles of which are forming in the metaphorical cauldron with an eventual view to developing a sort of transnational civil society. In taking a proactive attitude, this European private law is called upon to develop the European social model in a time of globalization, a time that necessitates the exploration of ways to expand internal production and consumption while simultaneously attempting to reach out to the disempowered and the marginalized. We are considering a period in time when such choices are politically difficult for parliaments. However, light can be shone on them by court judgments. Considering this, we may easily forecast developments in relation to health and its related services,[241] developments that could potentially arrive on the crest of the EU citizenship wave.

Since the gate-opener for new rights is European Union citizenship,[242] we think our analysis holds true even if we apply a very restrictive reading of the new Article 6 TFEU, according to which recognition of the 'rights, freedoms and principles set out in the Charter of Fundamental Rights of the European Union' would be literally incapable of extending 'in any way the competences of the Union as defined in the Treaties' and where, although becoming 'general principles of the Union's law', fundamental rights do 'not affect the Union's competences as defined in the Treaties'. As we illustrated, it is unnecessary to formally expand EU competences with a view to positively creating ruptures in member states' private law and inserting new bundles of rights for citizens. On the contrary, a restrictive reading of the text of the Treaty would even strengthen the ability to continue developing EU citizenship rights relating them indirectly to fundamental rights[243] by way of disguising the process behind the curtains of economic freedoms. At the very least, it could prove a sustainable strategy suitable for the difficult political and economic times Europe finds itself in at present.

Certainly, the expanding role of the EU citizenships and their ultimate mergence into, what we term, the fifth EU freedom could make it more attractive for EU citizens 'to seek protection of their social and economic positions against the forces of business and markets'[244] well before we reach the point of overcoming the limits of reverse

[239] Case C-434/10, *Aladzhov*, judgment of 17 November 2011, not yet published, Recs 31–32. See also the illuminating implications of *Åklagaren v Hans Åkerberg Fransson, supra* note 44.

[240] Berger, 'The Principles of European Private Law and the concept of the "*Creeping Codification*" of Law', 9 *European Review of Private Law* (2001) 21.

[241] See the above-mentioned example of Directive 24/2011/EU.

[242] Spaventa, *supra* note 237.

[243] Van den Brink, 'EU Citizenship and EU Fundamental Rights: Taking EU Citizenship Rights Seriously?', 39 *Legal Issues of Economic Integration* (2012) 273. For an application, see the *Carpenter* case at Rec. 46.

[244] Collins, *supra* note 7, arguing that the CJEU has not been such a forum due to 'the absence of concrete statements of social and economic rights, as opposed to the grandiloquent statements about the general objectives of the European Union'. However, here we rather claim with others that it is (should be) the role of the CJEU to give 'meaning, specificity, and value to [citizenship], thereby establishing new institutional norms which will impact on and modify national legal cultures'. See also Kostakopoulou, 'Ideas, Norms and European Citizenship: Explaining Institutional Change', 2 *MLR* (2005) 263.

discrimination.[245] To use the words of AG Sharpston in *Grunkin-Paul* referring to the German choice of law rule in question: 'This is clearly an area in which it behoves the Court to tread softly, and with care. But just because it must tread softly, that does not mean that it must fear to tread at all.'[246]

[245] On the interplay between reverse discrimination and national discrimination see A. Tryfonidou, *Reverse Discrimination in EC Law* (2009); Tryfonidou, 'Reverse Discrimination in Purely Internal Situations: An Incongruity in a Citizens' Europe', 35 *Legal Issues of Economic Integration* (2008) 43; Van Elsuwege and Stanislas, 'The Limits of Constitutional Dialogue for the Prevention of Reverse Discrimination', 5 *European Constitutional Law Review* (2009) 327.

[246] Para. 41, Opinion of AG Sharpston, Case C-353/06 *Grunkin-Paul v Standesamt Niebüll.*

4

European Fundamental Rights, Private Law, and Judicial Governance

Aurelia Colombi Ciacchi

1. Introduction

This chapter intends to analyse how and for which societal governance purposes fundamental rights are applied by national and European courts in cases concerning litigation between private parties. The perspective of this chapter is both analytical and normative. After having analysed how the horizontal effect of national and EU fundamental rights works and which policy goals it serves, this chapter attempts to answer the question whether this use of fundamental rights is legitimate and desirable.

Section 2 clarifies how this chapter uses the terms 'European fundamental rights' and 'private law'. Section 3 explains the difference between vertical and horizontal effect, and section 4 the difference between direct and indirect horizontal effect of fundamental rights. In section 5 this chapter takes position in favour of a normative individualistic understanding of fundamental rights.

Section 6 provides a macro-comparative overview of five models of fundamental rights horizontality recognizable at the national level. These five models correspond to five groups of EU member states. Section 7 identifies nine common fact patterns of horizontal application of fundamental rights at the national level. Sections 8 and 9 provide examples and fact patterns of direct and indirect horizontal effect of fundamental rights at the national level (section 8) and the EU level (section 9).

Section 10 analyses the horizontal effect of the Charter of Fundamental Rights of the European Union (EUCFR), with particular regard to the jurisprudence of the Court of Justice (CJEU, formerly ECJ). In this section, a new doctrine is proposed: the double indirect horizontal effect of fundamental rights. This doctrine serves two functions. First of all, it helps explain the horizontal impact of EU fundamental rights on private relationships in the European multilevel system of judicial governance. Secondly, it provides a tool with which the Court of Justice could develop its jurisprudence towards a better consideration of the non-economic human interests protected by EU fundamental rights.

Section 11 explains why the horizontal effect of fundamental rights can be seen as a form of judicial governance. This chapter does not focus on the institutional dimension of governance, but rather on its operative function: governance as policy-making with or without the government. It looks at how courts contribute to the governance of society through policy-making, by accommodating and balancing conflicting interests of different actors.

Sections 12 and 13 analyse the societal governance policies related to the horizontal effect of fundamental rights at the national level (section 12) and the EU level (section 13). Section 14 attempts to answer the question whether the pursuit of these societal governance policies through court adjudication constitutes a legitimate use or an illegitimate instrumentalization of fundamental rights. This section assesses the extent to which both the national and European fact patterns of horizontal effect correspond to the normative individualistic perspective outlined in section 5.

The conclusive section 15 summarizes the results of the analysis carried out by this chapter in eight points.

2. 'European Fundamental Rights' and 'Private Law'

The concept of 'fundamental rights' referred to in this chapter embraces the following groups of rights:

- human rights;
- rights enshrined in the Charter of Fundamental Rights of the European Union;
- rights enshrined in the common constitutional traditions of the EU member states;
- rights enshrined in the constitutions or in the constitutional traditions of individual states; and
- rights otherwise generally acknowledged as fundamental in a national or supranational legal system.

The concept of 'European fundamental rights' is much older than the Charter of Fundamental Rights of the European Union. In the 1960s–1970s, the European Court of Justice introduced and progressively developed the rule according to which international human rights and fundamental rights enshrined in the common constitutional traditions of the member states are to be observed as general principles of Community law.[1] This rule became established jurisprudence of the ECJ. It was then codified in the Maastricht Treaty and maintained in all successive treaties.

Fundamental rights have an impact on every field of law. This chapter deals with their impact on substantive private law.[2] The concept of 'private law' used in this chapter embraces all legal rules concerning relationships between private parties, including commercial relationships between undertakings. A private party can be generally defined as a natural or legal person other than a public authority: an individual citizen, a privately owned commercial undertaking, a non-governmental organization, a trade union, or even (within a democratic system) a political party.

[1] See ECJ Case C-29/69, *Stauder* [1969] ECR 1-419: '... the fundamental human rights enshrined in the general principles of Community law and protected by the Court'; ECJ Case C-4/73, *Nold v European Commission* [1974] ECR 372: '...fundamental rights form an integral part of the general principles of law, the observance of which [the Court] ensures. In safeguarding these rights, the Court is bound to draw inspiration from constitutional tradition common to the Member States.... Similarly, international Treaties for the protection of human rights on which the Member States have collaborated or of which they are signatories, can supply guidelines which should be followed within the framework of community law'.

[2] The impact of fundamental rights on civil procedure is a different phenomenon, which cannot be dealt with in this chapter.

3. Vertical Effect of Fundamental Rights

One may distinguish between a vertical and a horizontal effect (or application) of fundamental rights in private law. On the one hand, one may see the relationship between a private party and a public authority as 'vertical', and the relationship between two private parties as 'horizontal'. On the other hand, one may consider the impact of fundamental rights on the enactment, abolition, and formal amendment of legislative rules as 'vertical', while the impact of fundamental rights on the interpretation and application of formally unchanged rules could be considered as a 'horizontal'.

Classic examples of vertical effect of fundamental rights are:

- legislative reforms realized for the purpose of complying with fundamental rights;
- declarations of unconstitutionality of legislative rules; and
- condemnations of states by supranational courts on ground of non-compliance with human rights.

4. Horizontal Effect of Fundamental Rights

The concept of horizontal effect of fundamental rights or constitutional principles generally refers to the recourse had to those rights and principles in order to determine or specify the entitlements or obligations of the parties of a private relationship. In most cases, such references are made by courts while adjudicating private litigation.

A. Direct Horizontal Effect

In many cases, courts have based a private law remedy (e.g. the invalidation of a contract clause, or the award of damages) directly on a fundamental right or a constitutional principle. This phenomenon is known as 'direct horizontal effect'.[3] It means on a practical level that some entitlements and obligations within a private relationship directly descend from a fundamental right or constitutional principle, without the intermediation of a classic private law rule. On a theoretical level, this may imply that the fundamental right or constitutional principle in question is not only binding upon public authorities, but to some extent also upon private parties.

B. Indirect Horizontal Effect

Fundamental rights or constitutional principles may also affect the rights and duties of the parties of a private relationship indirectly, through the medium of the application of classic private law rules. This phenomenon is known as 'indirect horizontal effect'.[4] This means on a practical level that a private law remedy is based on a private law rule which is interpreted and applied in the light of a fundamental right or constitutional

[3] Brüggemeier, Colombi Ciacchi, and Comandé, 'Introduction: Fundamental rights and private law in the European Union: concepts and methodology of a research project', in G. Brüggemeier, A. Colombi Ciacchi, and G. Comandé (eds), *Fundamental Rights and Private Law in the European Union. Volume 1: A Comparative Overview* (2010) 1.

[4] Ibid.

principle. On a theoretical level, this may imply that the fundamental right or constitutional principle in question is only binding upon public authorities who have the duty to ensure and protect it.

5. A Normative Individualistic Understanding of Fundamental Rights

The legal-philosophical understanding of fundamental rights that underlies this chapter is based on an approach conceptualized by Dietmar von der Pfordten as 'normative individualism'.[5] According to this approach, legal and political decisions are to be justified in the last instance with reference to all individuals concerned. What ultimately matters, are the individuals concerned with their aims, interests, and wishes. Normative individualism is therefore the opposite of normative collectivism, i.e. the justification of legal and political decisions with reference to a collective: state, society, economy, societal subsystem etc.[6]

Human rights were conceived by Enlightenment thinkers as natural rights to liberty and equality, on the basis of which human beings are licensed to preserve themselves from their 'fellow creatures', i.e. other individuals.[7] At the time of the Enlightenment, the freedom and equality of individuals were endangered not only by other individuals and public powers, but also by corporative associations and other *pouvoirs intermédiaires* of the *ancien régime*. Arguably, this function of fundamental/human rights has once again become important in present times. Following the crisis and/or transformation of nation states, the contemporary situation is characterized by an intricate growth of public, private, and public–private forms of regulation in complex correlation with each other. Thus today we arguably need fundamental rights that operate erga omnes and protect every single individual against violations and abuses of power coming from either other individuals or collective entities (public and private powers, rule makers, corporations, functionally differentiated societal subsystems, anonymous matrices,[8] and others).

This normative-individualistic perspective of course does not exclude the existence of fundamental rights of collective entities. Fundamental rights protect not only individuals but also individual associations, corporations, trade unions etc. from violations and abuses coming from larger and more powerful collectives. However, it is submitted that the protection of fundamental rights of collective entities can only be justified with reference to the basic interests of the individuals directly concerned, such as the individual members of an association, or the individual workers affected by the measure to which a trade union's action pertains.

[5] Von der Pfordten, 'Normativer Individualismus und das Recht', *JZ* (2005) 1069. On the other descriptions in which the main thought of normative individualism emerges ('humanism', 'legitimatory individualism', 'subjectism', 'self-determination', 'autonomy', 'individuality', 'individual value', 'individual', etc.) see ibid., 1069 with further references.

[6] Ibid.

[7] Cf. T. Hobbes, *Leviathan* (1651). See also <http://science.jrank.org/pages/9663/Human-Rights-Classic-Theories-Hobbes-Locke.html>.

[8] Teubner, 'The Anonymous Matrix: Human Rights Violations by "Private" Transnational Actors', 69 *MLR* (2006) 327.

6. Models of Fundamental Rights Horizontality in the EU Member States

Some kind of horizontal effect of fundamental rights is acknowledged in the private laws of most member states. From the viewpoint of macro-comparative law, a distinction can be made between four groups of countries.

A. The Constitutional Court Model

In several continental European legal systems with a written constitution, such as Germany, Italy, Poland, Portugal, and Spain, a constitutional court is competent not only to control the constitutionality of statutes in the abstract, but also to adjudicate on the correct interpretation and application of the Constitution in concrete private law cases brought before the civil courts. In each of the countries mentioned above, after the fall of a totalitarian regime and the enactment of a new democratic constitution, both the civil courts and the constitutional court soon began to apply the constitution horizontally in private law cases.[9] Therefore, this phenomenon is as old as their new democratic constitutions: more than 50 years in Italy[10] and Germany,[11] more than 20 years in Portugal[12] and Spain,[13] and less than ten years in Poland.[14]

Within this group of countries, the horizontal effect of the national constitutions has a great practical relevance. Major changes in private law adjudication have often been initiated or consecrated by the constitutional courts. Sometimes the latter have forced the supreme courts to overrule their consolidated precedents in order to provide a better protection of certain fundamental rights or principles in specific private law cases.[15]

Curiously enough, this paramount role of the constitutional courts in private law development in those countries seems to be generally independent of the possibility

[9] For early cases see in Italy Trib. Firenze, 23 March 1948, (1949) *Monitore dei tribunali* n 18; in Germany BGH 10 June 1952, BGHZ 6, 360; in Spain, SSTC 2/1982 of 29 January 1982, FJ 2; in Portugal Ac TC n 198/85, DR II série, 15 February 1986; in Poland *Trybunal Konstytucyjny*, 19 February 2002, U 3/01, OTK-A 2002/1/3.

[10] See Mak et al., 'Italy', in G. Brüggemeier, A. Colombi Ciacchi, and G. Comandé (eds), *Fundamental Rights and Private Law in the European Union. Volume 1: A Comparative Overview* (2010) 325.

[11] See Beckmann et al., 'Germany', in G. Brüggemeier, A. Colombi Ciacchi, and G. Comandé (eds), *Fundamental Rights and Private Law in the European Union. Volume 1: A Comparative Overview* (2010) 253. For a comparative overview of the German and Italian discourse on this topic, see also H. Nießen, *Die Wirkung der Grundrechte im deutschen und italienischen Privatrecht* (2005).

[12] See Kern, 'Portugal', in G. Brüggemeier, A. Colombi Ciacchi, and G. Comandé (eds), *Fundamental Rights and Private Law in the European Union. Volume 1: A Comparative Overview* (2010) 547; Vieira de Andrade, 'Os Direitos Fundamentais nas Relações entre Particulares', 5 *Documentação e Direito Comparado* (1981) 181.

[13] See Ribot Igualada and Conrad, 'Spain', in G. Brüggemeier, A. Colombi Ciacchi, and G. Comandé (eds), *Fundamental Rights and Private Law in the European Union. Volume 1: A Comparative Overview* (2010) 610; García Rubio, 'La eficacia inter privatos (Drittwirkung) de los derechos fundamentales', in *Libro Homenaje a Ildefonso Sánchez Mera* (2002) 297.

[14] See Jańczuk and Krzemińska-Vamvaka, 'Poland', in G. Brüggemeier, A. Colombi Ciacchi, and G. Comandé (eds), *Fundamental Rights and Private Law in the European Union. Volume 1: A Comparative Overview* (2010) 485. On the horizontal dimension of Constitutional provisions in Poland see also Wojtyczek, 'Horyzontalny wymiar praw człowieka zagwarantowanych w Konstytucji', 2 *Kwartalnik Prawa Prywatnego* (1999) 225.

[15] See, for instance, in Italy *Corte Costituzionale* 14 July 1986, no. 184 (1986) *Foro it.* I 2053 (personal injury damage); in Germany BVerfGE 89, 214 and *Neue Juristische Wochenschrift* (1994) 36 (unfair suretyships).

of individual complaints of unconstitutionality. For example, Italian and Portuguese citizens have no direct access to the constitutional court, unlike German, Spanish, and Polish citizens. However, in Italy and Portugal indirect access to constitutional justice, through a question of constitutionality raised before a civil court and referred by the latter to the constitutional court,[16] seems to work as well. As far as it results from first comparative studies, the influence of the constitutional court on the interpretation and application of private law in Italy appears to be as strong as in Germany, and in Portugal as strong as in Spain.[17]

In those countries, the horizontal effect of international conventions such as the European Convention on Human Rights (ECHR) plays a small role, if any. References to the ECHR in private law judgments are quite rare and mostly redundant: the ECHR articles are quoted together with national constitutional provisions protecting the same rights, just to confirm the values expressed by the latter.[18] This is mainly due to the fact that all fundamental rights enshrined in those conventions find their counterpart in national constitutional provisions. Moreover, in these legal systems the international conventions are neither considered hierarchically superior to the national constitutions nor are they generally acknowledged to have constitutional rank.[19]

B. The French and Dutch Model

The French and Dutch legal systems are based on written constitutions, too. However, in the Netherlands neither a constitutional court exists, nor do civil courts have the competence to invalidate unconstitutional legislation.[20] In France there is a Constitutional

[16] On the Italian system of constitutional adjudication see R. Bin and G. Pitruzzella, *Diritto costituzionale* (2011); L. Paladin, *Diritto costituzionale* (3rd ed.; 1998) 772; for Portugal J. Bacelar Gouveia, *Manual de direito constitucional* (2011); J. Miranda, *Manual de direito constitucional. Vol. I—Preliminares* (3rd ed.; 2000) 260. On the Portuguese system, see also J. Sinde Monteiro et al., 'Portugal', in *International Encyclopedia of Comparative Law. Vol. I* (1996) 186.

[17] For a comparative study on the horizontal effect of fundamental rights in nine EU member states, see G. Brüggemeier, A. Colombi Ciacchi, and G. Comandé (eds), *Fundamental Rights and Private Law in the European Union. Volume 1: A Comparative Overview* and *Volume 2: Comparative Analyses of Selected Case Patterns* (2010).

[18] See, e.g. in Italy Cass 11 November 1986 n 6607, (1987) *Foro Italiano* I, 833 (Art. 8 ECHR); in Portugal STJ 9 January 1996, (1996) *Colectânea de Jurisprudência* I, 37 (Art. 2 ECHR). For an exception to this rule see the German case *AG Tauberbischofsheim, Neue Juristische Wochenschrift—Rechtsprechungsreport* 1992, 1098, where the reference to Art. 10 ECHR was decisive for the recognition of the right of a Turkish tenant to install a satellite dish against the landlord's will. However, two years later the German Federal Constitutional Court adjudicated the same matter without any reference to the Convention: the Court deduced the right of immigrant tenants to receive information via a satellite dish directly from Art. 5 German Constitution (freedom of opinion and information). See BVerfGE 90, 27 and *Neue Juristische Wochenschrift* 1994, 1147.

[19] Cf. in Germany C. Grabenwarter, *Europäische Menschenrechtskonvention* (5th ed.; 2012) 16 et seq. The scarce impact of the ECHR on private law adjudication in Germany was observed by Ellger, 'Europäische Menschenrechtskonvention und deutsches Privatrecht. Die Einwirkung von Art. 8 und 10 EMRK auf die deutsche Privatrechtsordnung', 63 *Rabels Zeitschrift für ausländisches und internationales Privatrecht* (1999) 625, at 661. On the relationship between Convention and Constitution in Italy, see Mori, 'Convenzione europea dei diritti dell'uomo, patto delle Nazioni Unite e costituzione italiana', *Rivista di diritto internazionale* (1983) 307. For Portugal, see Moura Ramos, 'A Convenção Europeia dos Direitos do Homem, sua posição no ordenamento jurídico portguês', 5 *Documentação do Direito Comparado* (1995) 163; for Spain Pérez Tremps, in L. López Guerra et al., *Derecho Constitucional Volumen I: El ordenamiento constitucional. Derechos y deberes de los ciudadanos* (6th ed.; 2003) 109.

[20] See de Vos, 'The Netherlands', in G. Brüggemeier, A. Colombi Ciacchi, and G. Comandé (eds), *Fundamental Rights and Private Law in the European Union. Volume 1: A Comparative Overview* (2010) 405; van Empel and de Jong, 'Constitution, International treaties, contracts and torts', 10 *European Review of Private Law* (2002) 287.

Council (*Conseil Constitutionnel*), which, however, until 2010 was not competent to decide on the application of the Constitution by ordinary courts in civil cases. Questions of constitutionality could only be raised in the abstract,[21] and about legislation which had not yet come into force. Contesting the constitutionality of legislation was a prerogative belonging to political organs: the President of the Republic, the Prime Minister, the Presidents of the Chambers of Parliament, or a group of members of Parliament (at least 60).[22] Only after a constitutional reform of 2008,[23] implemented through a legislative Act entered into force on 1 March 2010, now the ordinary judiciary can challenge the constitutionality of legislation in a special form of procedure called '*la question prioritaire de constitutionnalité*' (QPC).[24]

Independent of the possibilities of constitutional review of private law norms, in France and the Netherlands the horizontal effect of constitutional norms has been commonly acknowledged[25] and widely practised by the judiciary for several decades. French and Dutch courts have been referring to fundamental rights in deciding private law cases for half a century.[26] They have applied horizontally not only provisions of their national constitutions, but also—and to a great extent—the ECHR and other international conventions.[27] This phenomenon may be explained bearing in mind that in France and the Netherlands international law instruments such as the ECHR have supremacy over national law and are considered directly effective in so far as self-executing.[28]

[21] See Herrmann and Perfumi, 'France', in G. Brüggemeier, A. Colombi Ciacchi, and G. Comandé (eds), *Fundamental Rights and Private Law in the European Union. Volume 1: A Comparative Overview* (2010) 190; Molfessis, 'La dimension constitutionnelle des libertés et droits fondamentaux', in R. Cabrillac, M.-A. Frison-Roche, and T. Revet (eds), *Libertés et droits fondamentaux* (9th ed.; 2003) 69.

[22] Philip, 'L'enlargissement de la saisine du Conseil constitutionnel', *L'Actualité Juridique—Droit Administratif* (1975) 15.

[23] Loi constitutionnelle n° 2008-724 du 23 juillet 2008 de modernisation des institutions de la Ve République (see <http://www.legifrance.gouv.fr>).

[24] Loi organique n° 2009-1523 du 10 décembre 2009 relative à l'application de l'article 61-1 de la Constitution (see <http://www.legifrance.gouv.fr>). See X. Magnon, *QPC—La Question Prioritaire de Constituionnalité* (2011).

[25] See Herrmann and Perfumi, *supra* note 21; L. Favoreu et al., *Droit des libertés fondamentales* (2003) 157; de Vos, *supra* note 20; C. Mak, *Fundamental Rights in European Contract Law* (2008), at 83 et seq.; O. Cherednychenko, *Fundamental Rights, Contract Law and the Protection of the Weaker Party* (2007), at 115 et seq.; Cherednychenko, 'Fundamental Rights and Contract Law', *ERCL* (2006) 489; B. de Vos, *Horizontale werking van grondrechten. Een kritiek* (2010); L. F. M. Verhey, *Horizontale werking van grondrechten, in het bijzonder het recht op privacy* (1992), at 180; Nieuwenhuis, 'De constitutie van het burgerlijk recht', *Rechtsgeleerd Magazijn Themis* (2001) 203.

[26] For an early case of horizontal effect in France, see *Tribunal de la Seine*, 22 January 1947, *Dalloz* (1947) 126. A testamentary clause subject to the condition that the beneficiary does not get married to a Jew was deemed void on grounds of violation of the public order, to be defined in the light of the 1946 Constitution. A case slightly similar, but concerning contract law, was decided in the Netherlands in the same period of time: Ktr Arnhem, 25 October 1948, NJ 1949, 331 (invalidity of a clause of a farming lease contract on grounds of violation of freedom of religion). It must be noted, however, that some Dutch scholars have questioned the horizontal effect nature of this case, as the Court did not expressly refer to constitutional sources: de Graaf and de Haas, 'Horizontale werking van grondrechten: een heilloos leerstuk', *Nederlands Juristenblad* (1984) 1354.

[27] On the horizontal effect of the ECHR in the Netherlands, see de Vos, *supra* note 20; de Vos, *supra* note 25; Verhey, 'De horizontale werking van het EVRM', in A. W. Heringa, J. G. C. Schokkenbroek, and J. van der Velde (eds), *40 jaar Europees Verdrag voor de Rechten van de Mens* (1990) 19; for France, see Herrmann and Perfumi, *supra* note 21; J.-P. Marguénaud, *CEDH et droit privé* (2001).

[28] Marguénaud, 'Le droit civil français sous influence de la Convention européenne des droits de l'homme', *Revue trimestrielle de droit civil* (1996) 505; C. A. J. M. Kortmann and P. T. Bovend'Eert, *Dutch Constitutional Law* (2000), at 145.

The practical relevance of horizontal effect seems greater in the Netherlands than in France. Since the mid-1990s, however, French courts have also made an increasingly wide use of constitutional and convention norms in solving private (and contract) law cases.[29]

C. The Swedish Model

Sweden has a written constitution but it differs notably from the other European constitutions as it consists of four basic laws: the Act of Succession 1810, the Instrument of Government 1974, the Freedom of the Press Act 1949, and the Fundamental Law on Freedom of Expression 1991. There is no such thing as a constitutional court in Sweden. The competence of constitutional review lies with ordinary courts and administrative agencies, which, however, have made very little use of this power.[30]

National constitutional provisions are normally not provided with horizontal effect,[31] while the opposite is true for the ECHR.[32] However, the horizontal application of the ECHR is a fairly recent phenomenon as it was triggered by the 1994 Act incorporating the Convention into Swedish law.[33]

D. The British Model

In the United Kingdom there is neither a written constitution, nor institutions comparable to a constitutional court. Nevertheless, some kind of constitutionalization of private law has also taken place in this country. The ECHR was incorporated into national law with the Human Rights Act 1998 (HRA),[34] and this has sparked an intense debate on the impact of Convention rights in UK private law.[35] In academic literature it is still controversial whether and to what extent human rights can have horizontal effect.

[29] This impression arises from the case law materials collected in the framework of the project whose results are published in Brüggemeier, Colombi Ciacchi, and Comandé, note 17.

[30] See Lauer and Colombi Ciacchi, 'Sweden', in G. Brüggemeier, A. Colombi Ciacchi, and G. Comandé (eds), *Fundamental Rights and Private Law in the European Union. Volume 1: A Comparative Overview* (2010) 658; B. Bengtsson et al., *Swedish Law: A Survey* (1994); Cameron, 'Sweden', in R. Blackburn and J. Polakiewicz (eds), *Fundamental Rights in Europe. The European Convention on Human Rights and its Member States 1950–2000* (2001) 853.

[31] Scholars are divided on whether an exception could be made for the traditional unwritten fundamental right *Allemansrätt* (right of everybody). This is an old customary right to cross someone else's property. In favour of a horizontal effect of the *Allemansrätt*: Cameron, 'Protection of Constitutional Rights in Sweden', *Public Law* (1997) 488. See Lauer and Colombi Ciacchi, note 30, at 662 et seq.

[32] For an overview of the horizontality debate in Sweden see Lauer and Colombi Ciacchi, note 30, at 667 et seq.; J. Nergelius, *Konstitutionellt rättighetsskydd: svensk rätt i ett komparativ perspektiv* (1996).

[33] Lag 1994:1219 of 5 May 1994, entered into force on 1 January 1995.

[34] In force as of 2 October 2000.

[35] For an overview, see Gajdosova and Zehetner, 'England', in G. Brüggemeier, A. Colombi Ciacchi, and G. Comandé (eds), *Fundamental Rights and Private Law in the European Union. Volume 1: A Comparative Overview* (2010) 119; P. Craig, *Administrative Law* (5th ed.; 2003), at 599; see further Young, 'Human Rights, Horizontality and the Public/Private Divide: Towards a Holistic Approach', 2 *UCL Human Rights Law Review* (2009) 159; Hunt, 'The Horizontal Effect of the Human Rights Act', *Public Law* (1998) 429; Bamforth, 'The True "Horizontal Effect" of the Human Rights Act 1998', 117 *LQR* (2001) 3434; Buxton, 'The Human Rights Act and Private Law', 116 *LQR* (2000) 48; Wade, 'Horizon of Horizontality' 116 *LQR* (2000) 217. For discussion of the impact of the Human Rights Act on contracts, see Whittaker, 'The Human Rights Act 1998 and Contracts', in H.G. Beale (ed), *Chitty on Contracts* (29th ed.; 2004) 1-029.

However, at least a weak, indirect horizontality seems beyond doubt, in so far as the courts are, as 'public authorities' under section 6(3)(a) HRA, obliged to act in a way compatible with Convention rights.[36]

Since 1998, the civil courts have increasingly taken the Convention into account in solving private law cases. They have provided human rights with indirect horizontal effect, i.e. mediated through the application of a traditional private law instrument.[37] It should be noted, however, that human rights horizontality in the United Kingdom is older than the Human Rights Act: a few cases of horizontal application of Convention rights had already been decided before 1998.[38]

E. The Irish Model

Ireland follows a unique path of private law constitutionalization.[39] It has had a written Constitution since 1937. The judicial control of constitutionality lies in the competence of the Irish Supreme Court, which can also provide constitutional interpretation of statutory provisions or common law instruments in the field of private law. In the 1960s and 1970s, the Supreme Court acknowledged the doctrine of direct horizontal effect, establishing the principle that constitutional rights are directly applicable between private individuals.[40] However, the civil courts have made little use of this powerful tool. They prefer to ground private law judgments on established common law doctrines rather than on constitutional norms.[41]

The horizontal effect of the ECHR does not seem to have reached the Irish shores yet. This is mainly due to the fact that Ireland was the last country to formally adopt the Convention, with the European Convention of Human Rights Act 2003. Moreover, unlike the British courts, the Irish ones are exempted from 'organs of the State' in the sense of Section 1 ECHR Act and therefore do not seem to be under an obligation to act in accordance with the Convention.[42]

7. Common Fact Patterns of Horizontal Effect in the EU Member States

Significant convergence across the member states can be observed with regard to the specific private law topics subject to horizontal application of fundamental rights. This

[36] For an analysis of the models of horizontality proposed by UK scholars, see Young, 'Horizontality and the Human Rights Act 1998', in K. Ziegler (ed), *Human Rights and Private Law: Privacy* (2007) 35; Young, *supra* note 35.

[37] This is particularly evident in privacy cases: claims for damages against tabloids which had unlawfully published photographs or other information about the private life of celebrities were based not directly on the violation of a 'right to privacy', but on the traditional equitable doctrine of breach of confidence. See *Douglas v Hello* [2003] 3 All ER 996; *Campbell v MGN Ltd* [2004] UKHL 22.

[38] *Panesar v Nestle Co Ltd* [1980] IRLR 60, CA; *Spring v Guardian Assurance plc* [1995] 2 AC 296, [1994] 3 All ER 129.

[39] On the horizontal effect of constitutional rights in Ireland see O'Callaghan, 'Fundamental Rights and Private Law: The Approach of the Irish Courts', in A. Furrer (ed), *Europäisches Privatrecht im wissenschaftlichen Diskurs* (2006) 249.

[40] *Educational Co Ltd v Fitzpatrick (No 2)* [1961] IR 345; *Meskell v CIE* [1973] IR 121; *Glover v BLN Ltd* [1973] IR 388.

[41] O'Callaghan, *supra* note 39, at 249.

[42] Ibid., at 252.

enables us to detect recurrent 'fact patterns'.[43] Converging, fundamental rights based lines of reasoning in similar factual situations have concerned, inter alia:

(a) the conflict between freedom of speech, freedom of information and privacy rights (or other personal rights) in cases of unauthorized use of information concerning public[44] and non-public persons;[45]

(b) in particular, the unauthorized publication of photographs of celebrities[46] and ordinary people;[47]

[43] See Brüggemeier, Colombi Ciacchi, and Comandé, *supra* note 3; Colombi Ciacchi, 'Concluding Remarks', in G. Brüggemeier, A. Colombi Ciacchi, and G. Comandé (eds), *Fundamental Rights and Private Law in the European Union, Volume 2: Comparative Analyses of Selected Case Patterns* (2010) 421.

[44] For converging cases in England, France, Germany, Italy, and Portugal, see *Campbell v MGN Ltd* [2004] UKHL 22 (publication of the story of Naomi Campbell's attendance at Narcotics Anonymous meetings: balancing of conflicting rights under Arts 8 and 10 ECHR); Cass 14 December 1999, (2000) *D* 372 note B Beigner (publication of a book revealing details about former French President Mitterand's illness: balancing of conflicting rights of freedom of expression under Art. 10 ECHR and privacy under Art. 8 ECHR and Art. 9 French Civil Code); BGH 29 June 1999, (1999) *GRUR* 1034 (publication of the story of Prince von Hannover's love affairs and divorce: weighing of freedom of press under Art. 5(1) German Constitution against the general personality right under Arts 1(1) and 2(1) German Constitution); Cass 20 April 1963 no. 990, (1963) *Foro it.* I 877 (publication of embarrassing details about Mussolini's lover Clara Petacci and her family: award of damages for violation of the fundamental right to freely develop one's personality under Art. 2 Italian Constitution); STJ 19 November 2002 no. 02A2028, <http://www.stj.pt> (publication of true but defamatory facts about a famous lawyer: weighing freedom of expression and information under Art. 37 Portuguese Constitution against the right of honour, reputation, and own image under Arts 25 and 26 Portuguese Constitution). Cf. Krzemińska-Vamvaka and O'Callaghan, 'Mapping out a right to privacy in tort law', in G. Brüggemeier, A. Colombi Ciacchi, and G. Comandé (eds), *Fundamental Rights and Private Law in the European Union. Volume 2: Comparative Analyses of Selected Case Patterns* (2010).

[45] Cf. English, French, German, Italian, Dutch, Portuguese, and Spanish cases: e.g. *Venables and Thompson v Newsgroup Newspapers and Associated Newspapers Ltd* [2001] WLR 1038 (injunction restricting a publication which could endanger the life or physical integrity of two young men and former criminals: balancing of conflicting rights under Arts 2, 3, and 10 ECHR); Cass 9 July 2003, (2004) *D* 1634 (publication of a novel about the true story of a disappeared man, hurting the feelings of his relatives: balancing of conflicting rights under Arts 8, 10 ECHR and Art. 9 French Civil Code); BGH 25 May 1954, 13 BGHZ 334 (*Schacht-Leserbrief* case: acknowledgment of a general personality right based on Arts 1(1) and 2(1) German Constitution); Cass 22 June 1985 no. 3769, (1985) *Foro it.* I 2212 (acknowledgment of a right to personal identity directly based on Art. 2 Italian Constitution); HR 6 January 1995, NJ 1995, 422 (weighing free speech under Art. 10 ECHR against honour and reputation and the right to be left alone); STJ 18 April 2002 no. 02B3553, <http://www.stj.pt> (weighing freedom of expression and information under Art 37 Portuguese Constitution against personal integrity, honour and reputation under Arts 25 and 26 Portuguese Constitution); STS 23 April 1999 no. 330\1999, (1999) *RJ* 4248 (weighing freedom of expression and information against the right to honour, privacy and own image under Art. 18(1) Spanish Constitution).

[46] See the case law in England, France, Germany, Italy, the Netherlands, and Spain: e.g. *Douglas v Hello* [2003] 3 All ER 996; *Campbell v MGN Ltd* [2004] UKHL 22; Cass 30 June 2004, (2004) *JCP* II 10160 (*Elf affaire* case: balancing of conflicting rights under Arts 8, 10 ECHR and Art 9 French Code Civil); BVerfG 15 December 1999, 101 BVerfGE 361 (*Caroline of Monaco III* case: balancing of conflicting rights under Arts 1(1), 2(1), and 5(1) German Constitution); Cass 27 May 1975, (1975) *Foro it.* I 2895 (*Soraya* case: acknowledgment of the right to privacy as protected by Art. 2 and other provisions of the Italian Constitution); HR 4 March 1988, (1988) *Signaal Rechtspraak van de Week* 53 (*Princess Irene* case: balancing of conflicting rights under Arts 7, 10 Dutch Constitution and Arts 8, 10 ECHR); STS 28 October 1986, (1986) *RJ* 6015 (*Paquirri* case: balancing of conflicting rights under Arts 18(1) and 20(1)(d) Spanish Constitution).

[47] Cf. French, German, Italian, Dutch, Portuguese, and Spanish cases: e.g. Cass 20 February 2001 no. 98-23471, (2001) *D* 1199, note JP Gridel (balancing of conflicting rights under Art. 10 ECHR and Arts 9, 16 French Civil Code); BGH 14 February 1958, 26 BGHZ 349 (*Herrenreiter* case: protection of the general personality right enshrined in Arts 1, 2 German Constitution); Cass 20 April 1963 no. 990, (1963) *Foro it.* I 877 (acknowledgment of the right to personality development as an absolute right based on Art. 2 Italian Constitution); HR 1 July 1988, NJ 1988, 1000 (interpretation of Dutch private law in the light of Art. 8 ECHR), STJ 18 April 2002 no 02B3553, <http://www.stj.pt> (balancing of

(c) the landlord's obligation to cease emissions constituting intolerable nuisance, in consideration of the neighbours' fundamental rights to property, private life, health, and/or healthy environment;[48]

(d) the landlord's obligation to tolerate the installation of a satellite dish by a tenant, in consideration of the tenant's fundamental right to information;[49]

(e) the protection of tenants from termination of tenancy contracts;[50]

(f) adjustments of the content of imbalanced contracts through general principles of contract law, such as good faith or immorality, which are to be interpreted in the light of constitutional principles;[51]

(g) more specifically, the invalidity of clauses of employment or agency contracts excessively restricting the employee's or agent's freedom of profession[52] or the freedom to choose his or her own domicile;[53]

conflicting fundamental rights under Arts 25, 26, and 37 Portuguese Constitution); STC 8 November 1999 no. 202, (1999) *RTC* 202 (reference to Arts 18(1), 4, and 10 Spanish Constitution as legal bases of privacy protection).

[48] Cf. the case law in Italy, Poland, Portugal, and Spain: e.g. Cass civ sez un 9 March 1979 no. 5172, (1979) *Foro it.* I 2302 (acknowledgment of a fundamental right to a healthy environment enshrined in Art. 32 Italian Constitution); Postanowienie Sądu Najwyższego 19 December 2002 V CZ 162/02, OSNC 2004/2/31 (reference to Art. 8 ECHR to support a claim against harmful emissions by a quarry); STJ 9 January 1996 (recourse to Constitutional norms to protect the plaintiff against emissions from a butchery); STS 2 February 2001, (2001) *RJ* 1003 (application of the duty to defend and conserve natural resources and to enjoy them under Art. 45 Spanish Constitution to protect neighbours from pollutant emissions). See Sanchez Galera and Zehetner, 'Action against emissions: fundamental rights and the extension of the right to sue in private nuisance to non-owners', in G. Brüggemeier, A. Colombi Ciacchi, and G. Comandé (eds), *Fundamental Rights and Private Law in the European Union. Volume 2: Comparative Analyses of Selected Case Patterns* (2010) 298.

[49] On which there are major convergences in German, Italian, and Dutch cases. See 90 BVerfGE 27, (1994) NJW 1147, <http://www.servat.unibe.ch/dfr/bv090027.html> (application of Art. 5(1) German Constitution); Cass 16 September 1983 no. 7418, (1984) *Foro it.* I 415 (application of Art. 21 Italian Constitution); for the Netherlands, Ktr Assen, 25 March 1986, NJ 1987, 15 (application of Art. 10 ECHR).

[50] This can be observed in England, Italy, the Netherlands, and Portugal: *Shaws (EAL) Ltd v Walbert Pennycook* [2004] EWCA Civ 100, [2004] Ch 296; [2004] 2 All ER 665 (engagement of Protocol 1 Art. 1 ECHR in a case of deprivation of the right to renew a tenancy); Corte Cost 24 March 1988 no. 404, (1988) *Giur it* I 1627 note A Trabucchi (interpretation of the Italian tenancy law in light of the constitutional principle of solidarity); in the Netherlands, Court of Appeal Arnhem 25 October 1948, NJ 1949, 331; Court of Appeal Arnhem 24 June 1958, NJ 1959, 473 (termination of farming leases on ground of the lessee's new religion); STC 24 July 1992, (1992) *Acórdãos do TC* 21, 495 (indirect application of the right of housing under Art. 65 Portuguese Constitution).

[51] Cf. in Germany and Italy 81 BVerfGE 242 = (1990) NJW 1469; 89 BVerfGE 214 = (1994) NJW 36; Cass 20 April 1994 no 3775, (1994) *Giust civ* I 2169; Cass 28 January 1998 no 831, (1998) *Foro it.* I 770 (both the latter Italian judgment and the German judgment 89 BVerfGE 214 concern suretyships). Cf. C. Mak, 'Harmonising Effect of Fundamental Rights in European Contract Law', 1 *Erasmus Law Review* (2007) 60.

[52] For convergence in France, Germany, and Portugal, see Cass Soc 11 July 2000, (2000) *JCP* IV, 2556 (employment contract, reference to the Preamble of the French Constitution); 81 BVerfGE 242, (1990) NJW 1469 (agency contract, application of Art. 12(1) German Constitution); STJ 12 January 1994 no. 084387, <http://www.stj.pt> (employment contract, direct application of Art. 47(1) Portuguese Constitution). See C. Mak, *The Lion, the Fox and the Workplace: Fundamental Rights and the Politics of Long-Term Contractual Relationships*, Centre for the Study of European Contract Law Working Paper Series, 2009/08 (2009) available at <http://papers.ssrn.com/sol3/papers.cfm?abstract_id=1437601>.

[53] Cf. in France and Germany Cass Soc 12 January 1999, (1999) *D* 645 notes JP Marguenaud and J Mouly (application of Art. 8 ECHR to an employment contract); Landesarbeitsgericht Nürnberg 24 June 2003, <http://www.arbg.bayern.de/lagn/6sa676.2htm> (application of Art. 2(1) in connection with Art. 1(2) German Constitution to an employment contract). See Perfumi and Mak, 'The Impact of Fundamental Rights on the Content of Contracts: Determining Limits to Freedom of Contract in Family and Employment Relations', in G. Brüggemeier, A. Colombi Ciacchi, and G. Comandé (eds),

(h) the protection of freedom of religion in employment relationships;[54] and
(i) the equal treatment of women and men in employment relationships.[55]

8. Direct Horizontal Effect in the Jurisprudence of National and European Courts

Examples of direct horizontal effect can be found in the jurisprudence of both national and European courts.

A. National Level

A large part of the cases in which national courts have given direct horizontal application to fundamental rights or constitutional principles concerns labour law. For example, labour courts in Germany and Italy found clauses of employment contracts or dismissals from employment invalid on grounds of their non-conformity with fundamental rights or other constitutionally protected rights.[56]

In Germany, the direct horizontal effect doctrine was rejected later by the Federal Constitutional Court (*Bundesverfassungsgericht*, BVerfG).[57] Italian jurisprudence, on the contrary, has never challenged this doctrine.

B. EU Level

1. *Fundamental Rights*

The Court of Justice has not yet applied classic fundamental rights (human rights of the first generation[58]) directly to a private relationship. However, since the 1970s the Court

Fundamental Rights and Private Law in the European Union. Volume 2: Comparative Analyses of Selected Case Patterns (2010) 33.

54 For similar lines of reasoning in France, Germany, and Italy, see Cass Soc 24 March 1998, (1998) *Bull civ* V no. 171, 125 (application of Arts 1 and 75 French Constitution to the case of a Muslim employee in a grocery refusing to come into contact with pork meat); for Germany, BVerfG 30 July 2003 (2003) NJW 2815 (application of Arts 4 and 12(1) German Constitution to declare unlawful the dismissal of a Muslim vendor because she insisted on wearing a veil at work); for Italy, Cass 16 June 1994 no. 5832, (1995) *Foro it.* I 875 (balancing between freedom of opinion and religion and freedom of education, all protected by the Italian Constitution, in a case where a gymnastics teacher was dismissed from a Catholic school because she was not married in a church).

55 See the case law in Germany, Italy, Portugal, and Spain: e.g. BVerfG 28 January 1992, 85 BVerfGE 191 (application of Art. 3 German Constitution); in Italy, Cass 25 September 2002 no. 13942, (2002) Dir e giustizia 37, 32 (application of Art. 37 Italian Constitution); in Portugal, STJ 25 July 1896 no. 001412, <http://www.stj.pt> (application of Art. 13 Portuguese Constitution); in Spain, STS 10 April 1999, (1999) RJ 1877 (application of Art. 14 Spanish Constitution).

56 See, in Germany, ArbG Bamberg, 7 November 1950, RdA 1951, 118: the Court found a dismissal from employment due to the employee's membership of the Communist Party invalid on ground of violation of the fundamental right to freedom of expression of political opinions enshrined in Art. 5(1) of the German Constitution. In Italy, see Trib. Firenze, 23 March 1948, Mon. trib. 1949 no. 18: the Court held that the stipulation of a too low remuneration in an individual labour contract was invalid on ground of violation of Art. 36 of the Italian Constitution, which establishes the right to a remuneration sufficient to ensure a free and dignified existence for employees and their families.

57 BVerfG 15 January 1958, BVerfGE 7, 198 (Lüth).

58 For the metaphor of the three generations of human rights see Vasak, 'A 30-Year Struggle', *The UNESCO Courier* (November 1977) 29; Cf. also K. Vasak (ed), *The International Dimensions of Human*

has regularly given direct horizontal effect to human rights of the second generation such as equality and non-discrimination, enshrined in the Treaty provisions prohibiting discrimination on ground of nationality,[59] or establishing the right to equal pay for men and women.[60] Moreover, in the recent *Tyrolean Airways* case,[61] the CJEU was faced with the question of direct horizontal effect of the fundamental right to non-discrimination, enshrined inter alia in Article 21 of the Charter of Fundamental Rights of the European Union. For a detailed discussion of this case, see section 10(B).

2. *Fundamental Freedoms*

The Court has often held that the freedom of movement of workers[62] and the freedom to provide services[63] directly apply to relationships between private parties. The same direct horizontal effect principle was confirmed in the *Viking* case[64] with regard to freedom of establishment.[65]

3. *Freedom of Competition*

Freedom of competition is neither a classic fundamental right, nor it is a fundamental freedom in the strict sense. Nevertheless, it belongs to the fundamental principles of the European economic constitution, which may be—and indeed has been—applied horizontally. In several cases, the Court of Justice has given direct horizontal effect to the prohibitions of restriction of competition enshrined in the Treaty. According to the Court's established jurisprudence, these prohibitions have direct effect in relations

Rights (1982). For extensive discussion on, and examples of, human rights of first, second, and third generations, see C. Tomuschat, *Human Rights Between Idealism and Realism* (2003), at 24 et seq.

[59] See ECJ Case C-36/74, *B.N.O. Walrave and L.J.N. Koch v Association Union cycliste internationale, Koninklijke Nederlandsche Wielren Unie and Federación Española Ciclismo* [1974] ECR 1405: 'Prohibition of discrimination does not only apply to the action of public authorities but extends likewise to rules of any other nature aimed at regulating in a collective manner gainful employment and the provision of services' (in the case at stake, rules of sporting organizations discriminated against employees on ground of nationality).

[60] See, e.g. ECJ Case C-43/75, *Gabrielle Defrenne v Société anonyme belge de navigation aérienne Sabena* [1976] ECR 455: direct effect of the principle of equal pay for men and women on employment relationships.

[61] CJEU Case C-132/11, *Tyrolean Airways Tiroler Luftfahrt Gesellschaft mbH v Betriebsrat Bord der Tyrolean Airways Tiroler Luftfahrt Gesellschaft mbH*, judgment of 7 June 2012, not yet published.

[62] See, e.g. ECJ Case C-415/93, *Union royale belge des sociétés de football association ASBL v Jean-Marc Bosman, Royal club liégeois SA v Jean-Marc Bosman and others* and *Union des associations européennes de football (UEFA) v Jean-Marc Bosman* [1995] ECR I-4921: direct effect of the freedom of movement of workers on the business relationship between football clubs; ECJ Case C-281/98, *Roman Angonese v Cassa di Risparmio di Bolzano SpA* [2000] ECR I-4139: direct effect of the freedom of movement of workers on employment requirements stipulated by a private bank.

[63] See, e.g. ECJ joined cases C-51/96 and C-191/97, *Christelle Deliège v Ligue francophone de judo et disciplines associées ASBL, Ligue belge de judo ASBL, Union européenne de judo (C-51/96) and François Pacquée (C-191/97)* [2000] ECR I-02549: direct effect of the freedom to provide services on private sport rules; ECJ Case C-341/05 *Laval* [2007] ECR I-11767 (for a discussion of this case, see section 9(B) below).

[64] ECJ Case C-438/05, *ITJ* (*Viking Line*) [2007] ECR I-10778. For a discussion of this case, see section 9(B) below.

[65] For a critical analysis of the direct horizontal effect of the free movement provisions, see Schepel, 'Constitutionalising the Market, Marketising the Constitution, and to Tell the Difference: On the Horizontal Application of the Free Movement Provisions in EU Law', 18 *ELJ* (2012) 177.

between individuals and confer on interested parties' rights which national courts must safeguard.[66]

9. Indirect Horizontal Effect in the Jurisprudence of National and European Courts

Examples of indirect horizontal effect can be found in the jurisprudence of both national and European courts.

A. National Level

National cases of indirect horizontal effect of fundamental rights or constitutional principles touch upon a broad spectrum of private law matters, from contract law to family law, from tort law to property law.[67] A typical litigation pattern in tort law, which in several member states is dealt with on the basis of balancing different fundamental rights, is the conflict between the freedom of the press and privacy interests of celebrities. For example, in the United Kingdom the House of Lords reinterpreted the common law doctrine of breach of confidence in the light of Article 8 ECHR in order to enable the award of damages to celebrities whose privacy was intruded upon by the yellow press.[68]

B. EU Level

1. Liberty Rights

Classic fundamental rights, i.e. liberty rights such as the right to property, the right to private and family life, freedom of profession, and freedom of expression and assembly, have been given indirect horizontal application in several cases decided by the Court of Justice. The horizontal effect of the right to private life, the right to protection of personal data, freedom of profession, and intellectual property rights, was dealt with in *Promusicae*,[69] *Scarlet Extended*,[70] and *SABAM v Netlog*.[71] Moreover, an example of indirect horizontal effect of the right to private and family life and the fundamental rights of the child is *J. McB. v L. E.*.[72] All four decisions will be discussed in detail in section 10(C) below.

[66] See ECJ Case C-127/73, *Belgische Radio en Televisie v SV SABAM and NV Fonior* [1974] ECR 51; ECJ Case C-37/79, *Anne Marty SA v Estée Lauder SA* [1980] ECR 2481; ECJ Case C-179/90, *Merci convenzionali porto di Genova SpA v Siderurgica Gabrielli SpA* [1991] ECR 5889.

[67] For an overview and a discussion of typical case patterns see Brüggemeier, Colombi Ciacchi, and Comandé, *supra* note 17.

[68] *Campbell v Mirror Group Newspapers* [2004] 2 AC 457; [2004] 2 WLR 1232; [2004] 2 All ER 995.

[69] ECJ Case C-275/06, *Productores de Música de España (Promusicae) v Telefónica de España SAU* [2008] ECR I-271.

[70] CJEU Case C-70/10, *Scarlet Extended SA v Société belge des auteurs, compositeurs et éditeurs SCRL (SABAM)* [2011] ECR I-11959.

[71] CJEU Case C-360/10, *Belgische Vereniging van Auteurs, Componisten en Uitgevers CVBA (SABAM) v Netlog NV*, judgment of 16 February 2012, not yet published.

[72] CJEU Case C-400/10 PPU, *J. McB. v L. E.* [2010] ECR I-8965.

Good examples of indirect effect of the freedom of expression and assembly are the cases *Commission v France*[73] and *Schmidberger.*[74] In both cases, private demonstrations amounted to a restriction of free movement of goods. These demonstrations could be seen as an exercise of the fundamental rights to freedom of expression and assembly. These fundamental rights found indirect effect through the interpretation and application of the Treaty provision allowing for derogation from the four freedoms on public policy grounds. The question was whether the exercise of these fundamental rights could be seen as a legitimate public policy ground for derogation from the fundamental freedom concerned. In *Commission v France,* given the illegality of the protest actions undertaken by French farmers, no legitimate public policy ground was found. On the contrary, in *Schmidberger*, the lawfulness and peacefulness of the demonstrations enabled the Court to acknowledge a legitimate public policy ground for derogation from the free movement of goods.

It is questionable, however, whether *Commission v France* and *Schmidberger* could be considered *horizontal* effect cases. On the one hand, both the holders of the fundamental rights in question (the demonstrators) and the entities affected by the restriction of free movement of goods (business firms) are private actors. On the other hand, however, the proceedings from which the preliminary references were brought before the Court were not litigation between private parties.

2. *Socio-economic Rights*

Human rights of the second generation, i.e. socio-economic rights, have found indirect effect in the controversial *Viking,*[75] *Laval,*[76] and *Rüffert*[77] decisions of the Court of Justice. This chapter will only touch upon the first two, which are cases of litigation between private parties (labour unions against private employers). *Rüffert* is clearly not a horizontal effect case because it deals with procedures on the award of public work contracts by a public authority (the *Land* Niedersächsen).

In the *Viking* case, trade unions took collective action against a Finnish ferry operator who intended to reflag a vessel to Estonia. The vessel was running at a loss as a result of direct competition from Estonian vessels operating on the same route with lower wage costs. According to the Court of Justice, this trade union action constituted a restriction of freedom of establishment. This restriction could be in principle justified by overriding reasons of public interest (such as the protection of fundamental rights and interests of workers), if suitable for ensuring the attainment of the legitimate objective pursued and not going beyond what is necessary to achieve that objective. However, in the case at stake, the Court held that the restrictions went beyond what was necessary to protect the jobs or conditions of employment of the trade union's members who were liable to be affected by the reflagging of the vessel.

[73] ECJ Case C-265/95, *Commission v France* [1997] ECR I-6959.

[74] ECJ Case C-112/00, *Eugen Schmidberger, Internationale Transporte und Planzüge v Republic of Austria* [2003] ECR I-5659.

[75] ECJ Case C-438/05, *ITJ* (*Viking Line*) [2007] ECR I-10778.

[76] ECJ Case C-341/05, *Laval* [2007] ECR I-11767. On *Viking* and *Laval* see C. Joerges and F. Rödl, 'Von der Entformalisierung europäischer Politik und dem Formalismus europäischer Rechtsprechung im Umgang mit dem "sozialen Defizit" des Integrationsprojekts' (2008), ZERP-Diskussionspapier 2/2008.

[77] ECJ Case C-346/06, *Rüffert* [2008] ECR I-1989. On this case, see C. Schmid, *Die Instrumentalisierung des Privatrechts durch die Europäische Union* (2010), at 355 et seq.

In the *Laval* case, a Latvian company posted Latvian workers to Sweden to work on building sites operated by a Swedish construction firm. Swedish trade unions undertook collective action in order to force Laval to sign a collective agreement guaranteeing certain levels of pay to the posted workers. The Court reiterated the *Viking* principles and held that this restriction of the freedom to provide services could not be justified because it went beyond what was allowed by Directive 96/71 on the employment of posted workers.

In both *Viking* and *Laval*, fundamental rights found indirect horizontal application through the interpretation and application of the public policy derogations from the four freedoms. Some commentators argued that these judgments have made the freedom of enterprise, as manifested in the freedom of establishment and the freedom to provide services, into a fundamental freedom which is not just equal to social fundamental rights, but prevails over them.[78]

This chapter does not share such a generalized criticism. The Court did not rank the four freedoms higher than the fundamental rights of trade unions. It just clarified that fundamental freedoms may be limited by fundamental rights and vice versa. Each of the two may prevail over the other, depending on the circumstances of the case.[79]

3. *Fundamental Freedoms*

As for the indirect horizontal effect of the four freedoms as such (i.e. independent of their interaction with EU fundamental rights), the free movement of goods[80] and free movement of capital[81] have mostly only had indirect horizontal effect in the Court's jurisprudence. In the Court's reasoning, it is a duty of the member states to adequately protect these freedoms through their legislation.

Thus the Court seems to make a distinction between fundamental freedoms which directly confer rights upon individuals or undertakings (freedom of movement of persons, freedom of establishment, and freedom to provide services), and fundamental freedoms which do not (free movement of goods and capital).

4. *Freedom of Competition*

In some cases, the prohibitions of restriction of competition enshrined in the Treaty have found indirect horizontal application.[82]

[78] A. Somek, *Juridikum* (3/2008) 118–125. Cf. also Reich, 'Free Movement v. Social Rights in an Enlarged Union—the *Laval* and *Viking* cases before the ECJ', 9 *German Law Journal* (2008) 125; Moreau, 'Labour relations and the concept of social justice in the European Union', in H.-W. Micklitz (ed), *The Many Concepts of Social Justice in European Private Law* (2011) 303. See also the criticism of Schmid, note 77, at 350 et seq. with further references.

[79] For a critical comment on the mainstream opinion and a new perspective on the *Viking* and *Laval* cases, see H.-W. Micklitz, 'Three Questions to the Opponents of the *Viking* and *Laval* Judgments' (2012), OSE Opinion Paper no. 8.

[80] ECJ joined cases C-177/82 and C-178/82, *Jan van de Haar and Kaveka de Meern BV* [1984] ECR 1797; ECJ Case 311/85, *Vereniging van Vlaamse Reisbureaus v VZW Sociale Dienst* [1987] ECR 3801; ECJ Case C-112/00, *Eugen Schmidberger, Internationale Transporte und Planzüge v Republic of Austria* [2003] ECR I-5659.

[81] ECJ Case C-213/04, *Ewald Burtscher v Josef Stauderer* [2005] ECR I-10309.

[82] ECJ Case C-66/86, *Ahmed Saeed Flugreisen and Silver* [1996] ECR I-5457.

10. The Horizontal Application of the Charter of Fundamental Rights of the European Union

A. Impact of the Charter on National Case Law

Between its proclamation in 2000 and its entry into force on 1 December 2009, the Charter of Fundamental Rights of the European Union has been referred to by national courts in a number of cases concerning private parties. Such references can be found in German,[83] Italian,[84] Polish,[85] and English[86] case law. The main purpose of such references was to reaffirm that a certain fundamental right or principle was generally recognized throughout Europe.

Interestingly, such references seem to have been more frequent in England than in other European countries. English judges however explicitly stated that the Charter was not a source of law in the strict sense but could be 'consulted in so far as it proclaimed, reaffirmed or elucidated the content of those human rights that are generally recognised throughout the European family of nations'.[87]

A clearly negative statement on the effect of the Charter was pronounced by the Polish Supreme Court in 2005. The Court held that the Charter could not constitute a sole source of individual rights asserted before national courts, nor could it be regarded as an appropriate basis for reviewing the conformity of national law with the fundamental rights incorporated in the Charter.[88]

This position could be still defended after 1 December 2009 for Poland and the United Kingdom, which opted out from the Charter. For the other member states, however, the situation will be clearly different: the Charter provisions will have quite a significant impact on national law.

The question of whether national courts could put aside domestic legislation which is inconsistent with provisions of the Charter has already arisen.[89] This is, however, a question of vertical effect, not of horizontal effect.

Article 51(1) EUCFR does not mention private parties among those being bound by the Charter. This has led some scholars to deny the direct horizontal effect of the Charter.[90]

[83] See Amtsgericht Garmisch-Partenkirchen 16 December 2007, 1 F 293/07, which refers to Art. 24 EUCFR. Cf. Busch, 'Fundamental Rights and Private Law in the EU Member States'. in C. Busch and H. Schulte-Nölke (eds), *EU Compendium Fundamental Rights and Private Law: A Comparative Casebook* (2010) 17.

[84] See App. Roma (ordinanza) 11 April 2002, <http://www.dirittiuomo.it>. Cf. Mak et al., *supra* note 10, at 386.

[85] Judgment of the Supreme Court of 17 March 2005, III PK 83/2004, (2006) 1-2 OSNP [1]. Cf. Jańczuk and Krzemińska-Vamvaka, *supra* note 14, at 532.

[86] *R (on the application of Robertson) v Wakefield MDC* [2002] QB 1052; [2002] 2 WLR 889; *R v Secretary of State for the Home Department, ex parte Howard League for Penal Reform* [2003] 1 FLR 484.

[87] Mr Justice Munby in *R v Secretary of State for the Home Department, ex parte Howard League for Penal Reform* [2003] 1 FLR 484. See also *R (on the application of Robertson) v Wakefield MDC* [2002] QB 1052; [2002] 2 WLR 889, where Mr Justice Maurice Jay cited Art. 8 EUCFR, which confers the right to protection of personal data. The case related to the commercial selling of electoral registers. Cf. Gajdosova and Zehetner, 'England', in G. Brüggemeier, A. Colombi Ciacchi, and G. Comandé (eds), *Fundamental Rights and Private Law in the European Union. Volume 1: A Comparative Overview* (2010) 119, at 173.

[88] Judgment of the Supreme Court of 17 March 2005, III PK 83/2004, (2006) 1-2 OSNP [1]. Cf. Jańczuk and Krzemińska-Vamvaka, *supra* note 14, at 532.

[89] ECJ Case C-555/07, *Kücükdeveci* [2010] ECR I-365.

[90] Cartabia, 'Article 51', in R. Bifulco, M. Cartabia, and A. Celotto (eds), *L'Europa dei diritti. Commento alla Carta dei diritti fondamentali dell'Unione Europea* (2001) 345; Magiera, 'Die

Other scholars however have pointed out that many provisions of the Charter are drafted in a manner which suggests their capability of being applied directly to relationships between private parties. This is true for Articles 24, 29, 30, and 32 of the Charter.[91] Furthermore, Article 3(2) and Article 5 could be also given direct horizontal effect, on ground of the particularly strong need of protection of those interests.[92] Potentially capable of producing direct horizontal effect are also Articles 27, 28, 30, 31(1) and (2), and 33(2).[93]

B. Direct Horizontal Effect of the Charter in the Jurisprudence of the Court of Justice

A good and recent example of direct horizontal effect of fundamental rights enshrined in the Charter is the *Tyrolean Airways* case.[94] Here, two questions were referred to the CJEU for preliminary ruling.

The first question was whether Article 21 EUCFR (in conjunction with Article 6(1) TEU), the general legal principle of European law (Article 6(3) TEU) relating to the prohibition of age discrimination, and Articles 1, 2, and 6 of Directive 2000/78[95] had to be interpreted as precluding a provision of a collective agreement which takes into account, for the purposes of grading in the employment categories provided for in that agreement and, therefore, determination of the level of pay, only the professional experience acquired as a cabin crew member of a specific airline, while excluding substantively identical experience acquired in the service of another airline belonging to the same group of companies.

The second question was whether a national court could treat as void and disapply a clause of an individual employment contract which indirectly infringes Article 21 EUCFR, the general legal principle of European Union law relating to the prohibition of age discrimination, and/or Articles 1, 2, and 6 of Directive 2000/78, 'on grounds of the horizontal direct effect of the fundamental rights of the European Union'.[96]

The Court came to the conclusion that Article 2(2)(b) of Directive 2000/78 must be interpreted as not precluding such a provision of a collective agreement. Consequently, there was no need to decide on the second question. However, the mere fact that the issue of direct horizontal effect of fundamental rights was explicitly recognized and mentioned by the CJEU is noteworthy.

Grundrechtecharta der Europäischen Union', *Die Öffenliche Verwaltung* (*DÖV*) (2000) 1017, at 1025; Kingreen, 'Art. 51 GRCh' in C. Calliess and M. Ruffert, *Kommentar des Vertrages über die Europäische Union und des Vertrages zur Gründung der Europäischen Gemeinschaft—EUV/EGV* (2007), No. 18. On this discussion, see Busch, 'Fundamental Rights and Private Law in the EU Member States', in C. Busch and H. Schulte-Nölke (eds), *EU Compendium Fundamental Rights and Private Law: A Comparative Casebook* (2010) 18.

[91] Nowak, 'Allgemeiner Teil, § 6', in S. Heselhaus and C. Nowak (eds), *Handbuch der Europäischen Grundrechte* (2006), at paras 57–59.

[92] Ibid., para. 59. [93] Ibid.

[94] CJEU Case C-132/11, *Tyrolean Airways Tiroler Luftfahrt Gesellschaft mbH v Betriebsrat Bord der Tyrolean Airways Tiroler Luftfahrt Gesellschaft mbH*, judgment of 7 June 2012, not yet published.

[95] Council Directive 2000/78/EC, OJ 2000 L 303/16, establishing a general framework for equal treatment in employment and occupation.

[96] See *Tyrolean Airways*, note 94 at para. 20.

C. Indirect Horizontal Effect of the Charter in the Jurisprudence of the Court of Justice

1. *J. McB. v L. E.*

A classic example of indirect horizontal effect of the Charter is the CJEU decision *J. McB. v L. E.*.[97] It concerns an international child abduction case in which the Irish Supreme Court referred a question to the Court of Justice for preliminary ruling. Mr J. McB., an Irish national, and Mrs L. E., a British national, lived together as an unmarried couple for more than ten years in England, Australia, Northern Ireland, and Ireland. They had three children together. After the couple's relationship deteriorated, the mother, alleging aggressive behaviour on the part of the father, fled on several occasions, with her children, to a women's shelter. Eventually, she fled with them to England. The father's claims before English and Irish courts, seeking the return of the children to Ireland, failed on the ground that the father had no rights of custody in respect of the children at the time of their removal, and consequently the removal was not wrongful within the meaning of either the 1980 Hague Convention on the civil aspects of international child abduction, or Regulation 2201/2003.[98]

The father did not accept that the removal of a child by its mother without the knowledge of its natural father was not wrongful under the 1980 Hague Convention and Regulation 2201/2003, even though the father lived with his child, and with the child's mother though not married to her, and played an active part in bringing up that child.

The question referred by the Irish Supreme Court was whether Regulation 2201/2003 had to be interpreted, pursuant to Article 7 EUCFR or otherwise, as precluding a member state from providing by law that the acquisition of rights of custody by a child's father, where he is not married to the child's mother, is dependent on the father's obtaining a judgment from a national court with jurisdiction awarding such rights of custody to him, on the basis of which the removal of the child by its mother or the retention of that child may be considered wrongful, within the meaning of Article 2(11) of that regulation.

The Court of Justice answered this question in the negative. It acknowledged (by referring inter alia to the interpretations of Article 8 ECHR given by the European Court of Human Rights) that neither the right to private and family life enshrined in Article 7 EUCFR nor the child's fundamental rights laid down in Article 24 EUCFR precluded a situation where, for the purposes of applying Regulation 2201/2003, rights of custody are granted, as a general rule, exclusively to the mother and a natural father possesses rights of custody only as the result of a court judgment.

J. McB. v L. E. is a quite simple case of indirect horizontal effect, in which the EU law applicable to a private litigation is to be interpreted in light of fundamental rights enshrined in the Charter and the ECHR. This means that the rights and duties of the private parties in the family relationship in question are indirectly shaped by EU fundamental rights.

[97] CJEU Case C-400/10 PPU, *J. McB. v L. E.* [2010] ECR I-8965.

[98] Council Regulation (EC) 2201/2003, OJ 2003 L 338/1, concerning jurisdiction and the recognition and enforcement of judgments in matrimonial matters and the matters of parental responsibility.

2. *Promusicae*

Less simple cases of indirect horizontal effect are the ones in which both national and European courts need to accommodate conflicting fundamental rights of different private parties and balance them against each other, in order to interpret both national and EU law in conformity with those fundamental rights. In this regard, interesting examples of indirect horizontal effect of Charter provisions are the ECJ/CJEU copyright cases *Promusicae*,[99] *Scarlet Extended*,[100] and *SABAM v Netlog*.[101] In all three cases, the Court decided on questions referred for preliminary rulings by civil courts that were to adjudicate private litigation on copyright matters.[102]

In *Promusicae*, the question for preliminary ruling was referred by a Spanish civil court which asked whether the E-Commerce Directive,[103] the Directive on the harmonisation of copyright and related rights in the information society,[104] the Directive on the enforcement of intellectual property rights,[105] and Articles 17(2) and 47 EUCFR required member states to lay down, in order to ensure effective protection of copyright, an obligation to communicate personal data in the context of civil proceedings. The Court's argumentation concerning the fundamental rights enshrined in the Charter could be divided into three steps:

(1) In the case at stake, the requirements of the protection of different fundamental rights, namely the right to respect for private life (Articles 7 and 8 EUCFR and Article 8 ECHR) on the one hand and the rights to protection of property (Article 17 of the Charter) and to an effective remedy (Article 47 EUCFR) on the other, needed to be reconciled.[106]

(2) The three aforementioned directives include rules which leave the member states with the necessary discretion to define transposition measures which may be adapted to the various situations possible. They do not require the member states to lay down an obligation to communicate personal data in order to ensure effective protection of copyright in the context of civil proceedings.[107]

(3) However, Community law requires that, when transposing those directives, the member states take care to rely on an interpretation of them which allows a fair balance to be struck between the various fundamental rights protected by the Community legal order. Further, when implementing the measures transposing

[99] ECJ Case C-275/06, *Productores de Música de España (Promusicae) v Telefónica de España SAU* [2008] ECR I-271.

[100] CJEU Case C-70/10, *Scarlet Extended SA v Société belge des auteurs, compositeurs et éditeurs SCRL (SABAM)*, judgment of 24 November 2011, ECR 2011 I-11959.

[101] CJEU Case C-360/10, *Belgische Vereniging van Auteurs, Componisten en Uitgevers CVBA (SABAM) v Netlog NV*, judgment of 16 February 2012, not yet published.

[102] Another recent case in which the Court decided on a similar copyright matter was *Airfield* (CJEU joined cases C-431/09 and C-432/09, *Airfield NV, Canal Digitaal BV v Belgische Vereniging van Auteurs, Componisten en Uitgevers CVBA (Sabam) and Airfield NV v Agicoa Belgium BVBA* [2011] ECR I-09363). This decision is not commented on in this chapter because it does not contain any reference to fundamental rights.

[103] Directive 2000/31/EC of the European Parliament and of the Council of 8 June 2000, OJ 2000 L 178/1, on certain legal aspects of information society services, in particular electronic commerce, in the Internal Market.

[104] Directive 2001/29/EC of the European Parliament and of the Council of 22 May 2001, OJ 2001 L 167/10 on the harmonisation of certain aspects of copyright and related rights in the information society.

[105] Directive 2004/48/EC of the European Parliament and of the Council of 29 April 2004, OJ 2004 L 157 on the enforcement of intellectual property rights.

[106] *Promusicae, supra* note 99, paras 61–65. [107] Ibid., paras 67–70.

> those directives, the authorities and courts of the member states must not only interpret their national law in a manner consistent with those directives but also make sure that they do not rely on an interpretation of them which would be in conflict with those fundamental rights or with the other general principles of Community law, such as the principle of proportionality.[108]

3. *Scarlet Extended and SABAM v Netlog*

In *Scarlet Extended* and *SABAM v Netlog*, the questions for preliminary rulings were referred by Belgian civil courts. They asked inter alia whether an injunction imposed by a member state's court on an internet service provider (ISP) requiring it to install a filtering system to prevent illegal downloading would be compatible with EU law, read in the light of the ECHR. The CJEU found in favour of the internet service provider. Its reasoning can be summarized as follows:

(1) Confirming the principles already stated in *Promusicae*,[109] the Court acknowledged that national authorities and courts must strike a fair balance between the protection of the intellectual property right enjoyed by copyright holders and the protection of the fundamental rights of individuals who would be affected by the installation of the contested filtering system.

(2) The injunction to install the filtering system would result in a serious infringement of the freedom of the ISP concerned to conduct its business enjoyed by operators such as ISPs pursuant to Article 16 EUCFR.[110] That injunction would also infringe the fundamental rights of that ISP's customers, namely their right to protection of their personal data (Article 8 EUCFR) and their freedom to receive or impart information (Article 11 EUCFR).[111]

(3) Consequently, in adopting the injunction requiring the ISP to install the contested filtering system, the national court concerned would not be respecting the requirement that a fair balance be struck between the right to intellectual property, on the one hand, and the freedom to conduct business, the right to protection of personal data, and the freedom to receive or impart information, on the other. Therefore, Directives 2000/31, 2001/29, 2004/48, 95/46, and 2002/58, read together and construed in the light of the requirements stemming from the protection of the applicable fundamental rights, must be interpreted as precluding an injunction made against an ISP which requires it to install the contested filtering system.[112]

4. *'Double Horizontal Effect' of EU Fundamental Rights*

The *Promusicae, Scarlet Extended*, and *SABAM v Netlog* cases discussed above are very good examples of what this chapter calls 'double indirect horizontal effect' of EU fundamental rights. Double indirect horizontal effect means that the rights and duties of the parties of a private relationship are shaped by EU fundamental

[108] Ibid., paras 68, 70. [109] Ibid.

[110] *Scarlet Extended, supra* note 100, at paras 45–49; *SABAM v Netlog, supra* note 101, at paras 43–47.

[111] *Scarlet Extended, supra* note 100, at paras 50–52; *SABAM v Netlog, supra* note 101, at paras 48–50.

[112] *Scarlet Extended, supra* note 100, at paras 53–54; *SABAM v Netlog, supra* note 101, at paras 51–52.

rights through two layers of indirect horizontal effect. The first layer is the CJEU interpretation of the relevant EU Directives in the light of EU fundamental rights. The second layer is the interpretation by national civil courts of the national rules implementing those directives, and their application to the private relationship in question. In this interpretation and application, national courts must not only interpret the national law in a manner consistent with those directives but also make sure that they do not rely on an interpretation of them which would be in conflict with those fundamental rights.

As concerns the application in practice of the new doctrine of double indirect horizontal effect, a significant difference can be noted between *Promusicae* on the one hand, and *Scarlet Extended* and *SABAM v Netlog* on the other. In *Promusicae,* the first layer of indirect horizontal effect was dealt with only very briefly, whereas the Court concentrated itself on the second layer. Indeed, regarding the first layer, the Court first stressed the need to reconcile the relevant conflicting fundamental rights and then came to the conclusion that the directives could not be interpreted as requiring the member states to lay down such an obligation to communicate personal data in order to ensure effective protection of copyright. However, the needed balancing of all conflicting European fundamental rights was not operated explicitly by the Court itself: the task was entrusted to the national lawmakers and courts (second layer).

Taking a contrary approach, in *Scarlet Extended* and *SABAM v Netlog* the Court itself performed the needed balancing of all conflicting European fundamental rights, in the framework of the first layer of indirect horizontal effect. Here, the Court finally took the responsibility to give a clear statement of policy: it considered the business-related fundamental rights and interests of the ISP and the fundamental rights of its customers to privacy and protection of personal data as prevailing over the intellectual property rights.

Such clear balancing of conflicting fundamental rights and interests and such clear statements of policy by the Court of Justice should be welcomed. In the years to come, the Charter's binding force could and arguably should help the Court to considerably extend the scope of the horizontal effect of fundamental rights in its jurisprudence. This development would be necessary and desirable. It is submitted that the double horizontal effect of fundamental rights represents a suitable means to foster such a development.

Hence, the new doctrine of double indirect horizontal effect proposed in this chapter serves two purposes. First of all, it represents an analytical model that helps to understand how EU fundamental rights impact private relationships in the European multilevel system of judicial governance. Secondly, it is a tool that could and arguably should be used more extensively by the Court of Justice in order to develop its jurisprudence towards a better consideration also of the non-economic interests protected by EU fundamental rights.

The statement, right at the beginning of the new EU Treaty, that the Union is founded on the respect of human dignity and the protection of fundamental rights (Article 2 TEU), should inspire the Court of Justice to evolve its jurisprudence towards an equally sensitive consideration of economic and non-economic human interests. The double indirect horizontal effect framework leaves considerable leeway for national law and interpretations by national courts, thus it could not be seen as an illegitimate intrusion of the European court into national sovereignty.

11. The Horizontal Application of Fundamental Rights and Judicial Governance

At both the national and the European level, the horizontal effect of fundamental rights may be seen as a form of judicial governance.[113] Despite the variety of meanings the concept of governance has acquired in different academic disciplines, one can identify a minimum content, a common core: governance may be understood as decision and policy making within a group of persons or within an institution, or within a system of institutions.[114] It is, so to say, governing with or without a government, policy making with or without politics.[115]

Governance is not a synonym of regulation. First, not all that can be regulated, can also be object of governance. Only societies, societal groups, collective entities, and human relationships in general can be the object of governance. Secondly, governance can be performed through other means than regulation, such as politics or more informal deliberative processes.

Governance structures are often multilayered. Governance at the local level coexists and interacts with governance at the state level, and these coexist and interact with governance at the supranational, international, and global level.[116] The relationship between the layers of such a multilevel system of governance is often a non-hierarchical one. Thus the concept of governance often refers to non-hierarchical relationships between decisionmakers, and to forms of coordination of societal actors other than command and control.[117]

One of the most important goals in governing both private and public institutions (corporations, owner's associations, religious communities, states, supranational entities etc.) is that the interests of all participants are well represented and realized. Governance is more than organization, management, and coordination: it involves policy. Policies are common interests and goals pursued by a group or institution. Policies are a plurality of interests which can come into conflict with each other. Thus governance as policy-making implies dealing with different interests and policy objectives, which can be public interests, semi-public interests (i.e. collective or societal interests not necessarily endorsed by public powers), or private interests.

[113] For a governance perspective on the adjudication of conflicts concerning the European economic (and societal) constitution, see S. Frerichs, *Judicial Governance in der Europäischen Rechtsgemeinschaft. Integration durch Recht jenseits des Staates* (2008). Frerich's systems theory approach is, however, radically different from the normative-individualistic approach of the present chapter.

[114] Colombi Ciacchi, 'Governance Meets Law: Background and Methodology of a Research Project', in A. Colombi Ciacchi (ed), *Governance Meets Law* (2014, forthcoming).

[115] Rosenau and Czempiel, 'Governance without Government: Order and Change in World Politics', 20 *Cambridge Studies in International Relations* (1991); Rhodes, 'The New Governance: Governing without Government', 44 *Political Studies* (1996) 465; A. Kazancigil, 'Governance and science: market-like modes of managing society and producing knowledge', 50 *International Social Science Journal* (1998) 69. Cf. P. Westerman, 'Governing by Goals: Governance as a Legal Style', 1 *Legisprudence* (2007) 51 and Frerichs, *supra* note 113.

[116] See H. Enderlein, S. Wälti, and M. Zürn (eds), *Handbook on Multi-Level Governance* (2010); L. Hooghe and Gary Marks, *Multi-Level Governance and European Integration* (2001); C. Joerges and E.-U. Petersmann (eds), *Constitutionalism, Multilevel Trade Governance and International Economic Law* (2011).

[117] See M. Zürn and C. Joerges (eds), *Law and Governance in Postnational Europe: Compliance Beyond the Nation-State* (2005); P. Kjaer, *Between Governing and Governance: On the Emergence, Function and Form of Europe's Post-National Constellation* (2010), both with further references. See also F. Cafaggi and H. Muir-Watt, *Making European Private Law. Governance Design* (2008); C. Joerges, 'Integration through de-legalisation?', 33 *ELRev* (2008) 291.

Policy aspects may concern:

- the policy reasons which have led to a certain regulatory setting;
- the policy arguments which speak pro or contra a certain interpretation/application of a certain regulatory setting;
- the (intended or unintended) social, political, and economic consequences of a certain regulatory setting.

Policy aspects can be economic and non-economic interests of human beings or collective entities, efficiency goals, democracy, human rights, or constitutional values, etc. A large number of those interests are protected at a national, European, or constitutional level as fundamental rights or constitutional principles.

Speaking of good (or better) governance, four aspects play a major role: efficiency, democracy, rule of law, and protection of fundamental rights. The best governance is ideally at the same time the most efficient and the most democratic one, and the one which best respects the rule of law and fundamental rights.

One may argue that the horizontal application of fundamental rights in private litigation is a form of judicial governance. Through this practice, the judiciary opens up the private law legal discourse to embrace the constitutional and international law discourse as well. In doing so, it enables legal actors to deal with the balancing of conflicting interests and policies in private relationships more explicitly, under a broader and supranational perspective. The substantive core of judicial reasoning becomes more transparent, more suitable to cross-border comparison and mutual learning processes.[118]

In this chapter, the concept of 'judicial governance' is *not* used to describe the institutional framework of coordination and interaction between national and European courts. Instead, in this chapter, this concept refers to *societal governance through policy-making* in the adjudication of private litigation by courts. Governance as policy-making implies accommodating and balancing different policy objectives and interests of different actors. The following sections will analyse how national and European courts contribute to the governance of society while deciding on private relationships through the application of fundamental rights. A number of societal governance policies will be identified, which underlie the use of fundamental rights in the adjudication of private litigation.

12. Policies of Horizontal Application of Fundamental Rights: National Level

The horizontal effect of fundamental rights in civil jurisprudence of the member states does not depict a neutral legal policy phenomenon.[119] If one were to attempt to systematize the different policy trends that seem to result from the constellations of horizontal effect

[118] In favour of the (horizontal) constitutionalization of private law, see Gerstenberg, 'Private Law and the New European Constitutional Settlement', 11 *ELJ* (2004) 766, and Gerstenberg, 'What Constitutions Can Do (but Courts Sometimes Don't): Property, Speech, and the Influence of Constitutional Norms on Private Law', 17 *Canadian Journal of Law and Jurisprudence* (2004) 61; Brüggemeier, 'Constitutionalisation of private law—the German perspective', in: T. Barkhuysen and S. Lindenbergh (eds), *Constitutionalisation of Private Law* (2006) 59, at 82; C. Mak, 'Judges in Utopia. Fundamental Rights as Constitutive Elements of a European Private Legal Culture' (2012), available at <http://ssrn.com/abstract=2127137>. In favour of the horizontal effect of fundamental rights in contract cases, see C. Mak, *Fundamental Rights in European Contract Law* (2008).

[119] Along the same lines concerning contract law, Mak, 'Harmonising Effect of Fundamental Rights in European Contract Law', 1 *Erasmus Law Review* (2007) 60; C. Mak, *Fundamental Rights in European Contract Law* (2008), at 193 et seq.

on fundamental rights in Germany, England, France, Italy, the Netherlands, Poland, Portugal, Sweden, and Spain, then one would recognize above all six tendencies.

A. Protection of the Weaker Party in Contract Law

The first tendency is the protection of weaker parties or rather the correction of unequal levels of power in contract law. The courts consistently fall back to fundamental rights to protect the interests of employees against employers, small businesses against bigger corporations, tenants against landlords, patients against doctors, hospitals, etc., further than they would be protected in an ordinary application of private law.[120]

Through this special emphasis on the interests of weaker parties by judges in the consideration of colliding interests and fundamental rights positions, it is attempted to compensate for structural inequalities in the bargaining abilities and socio-economic relations of private individuals.[121] This fits without a doubt in the material paradigm: the socially unsatisfactory consequences of a formal application of contract law are being corrected by new, material interpretations which take into account the actual socio-economic situation of the contracting parties. Indeed, it would also be theoretically possible to achieve these new interpretations without falling back on fundamental rights. The use of fundamental rights argumentation offers, however, two important advantages. First, it creates a new doctrine of civil law which deviates from the consolidated jurisprudence, is more legitimate and is protected from non-fundamental rights argumentation. Second, through the reference to fundamental rights it is made clear that in the handling of conflicting fundamental rights between private parties by legislation and jurisprudence to date, the interests of one party were cut too short, which is why an adjustment is now necessary.[122]

B. Reduction of Discrimination

The second policy trend in regard to the horizontal effect of fundamental rights is the reduction of discrimination. Since the end of World War II and still today, courts have been using fundamental rights to a large degree to counter unequal treatment (i.e. between men and women,[123] Jews and Christians,[124] legitimate and non-legitimate children,[125] or homosexuals and heterosexuals[126]).

[120] A. Colombi Ciacchi, 'The Constitutionalisation of European Contract Law: Judicial Convergence and Social Justice', 2 *ERCL* (2006), 167, at 175 ff. with further references; Perfumi and Mak, *supra* note 53, with further references; Gagliardi and Sukhova, 'Contractual Duties of Care: Confidence and Cooperation in the Context of Fundamental Rights and Constitutional Principles', in G. Brüggemeier, A. Colombi Ciacchi, and G. Comandé (eds), *Fundamental Rights and Private Law in the European Union. Volume 2: Comparative Analyses of Selected Case Patterns* (2010) 7, with further references.

[121] Cf. Colombi Ciacchi, *supra* note 43, at 427.

[122] Cf. A. Colombi Ciacchi, 'Non-Legislative Harmonisation of Private Law under the European Constitution: The Case of Unfair Suretyships', 13 *European Review of Private Law* (2005), 285–308.

[123] H. C. Nipperdey, 'Gleicher Lohn der Frau für gleiche Leistung', *Recht der Arbeit* (1950) 121. For Italian jurisprudence see Cass. 25. September 2002 No. 13942, Dir. e giust. 202, 32 with a comment by Grassi.

[124] See, in France Tribunal de la Seine 22 January 1947, *D* 1947, 126. The court found a clause of a testament which eliminates rights to inheritance for a person who marries a Jew to be invalid because of a violation of public policy (Art. 900 Code Civil). There, the term public policy was interpreted in the light of the French constitution of 1946. For this, see Herrmann and Perfumi, *supra* note 21, at 218 et seq.

[125] See, in Portugal, Tribunal Constitucional Ac. TC 99/88 DR, II série, 22 August 1988. For this, see Kern, *supra* note 12, at 577 et seq.

[126] I.e. in *Ghaidan v Godin-Mendozy* [2004] UKHL 30. The House of Lords affirmed a right of abode of the spouse of a man after his death based on a new interpretation of the Rent Act of 1977

On the one hand, one could see the fight against discrimination in private law matters as a materialization of private law:[127] the formalistic understanding of freedom and equality is, at least partially, replaced by a material understanding, which recognizes and attempts to compensate for human 'unfreedom' and inequality. On the other hand, anti-discrimination policy is compatible with neoliberal market liberalism and with a non-solidary society, as Alexander Somek has argued convincingly.[128]

C. Economic Upgrade of the Interests of the Individual and Social Equality in Tort Law

Usually, the horizontal application of fundamental rights in tort law serves the purpose of enabling or improving the ability to compensate for personal damage. Here, personal damage means injury to the body, health, or person, rather than conventional property damage.

Consequences in tort law of to infringements of one's person (including privacy) are the most frequent cases of horizontal effect of fundamental rights in German, English, French, Italian, Dutch, Portuguese, Polish, Spanish, and Swedish law.[129] In this way, the economic value of personal interests that were not or only to a limited extent compensable in pre-constitutional tort law has been recognized.

Other damages which have gained relevance through the horizontal effect of fundamental rights are non-property damages caused by bodily or health infractions. In Germany, this has only very seldom resulted in further liability: using the constitutional protection of the personal enabled, for instance, granting compensation to people who could no longer feel pain (because of damage to the nervous system) due to the tortious act.[130]

In Italy, the consequences of this tendency went much further. This is due to two revolutions in liability law. The first was the recognition of compensation for bodily and health damages per se, completely independent of the existence of economic loss.[131] This principle, according to the Italian *Corte Costituzionale* (Constitutional Court) in 1986, follows the constitutionally anchored fundamental right to health (Article 32 of the Italian Constitution).[132] However, thoughts on social equality and personal dignity also fostered this doctrine: it was found unjust and incompatible with the equality of all

in the light of Arts 8 and 14 ECHR. For this, see Favilli and Ferreira, 'Different Legal Treatment of Married and Unmarried Couples in the European Union', in G. Brüggemeier, A. Colombi Ciacchi, and G. Comandé (eds), *Fundamental Rights and Private Law in the European Union. Volume 2: Comparative Analyses of Selected Case Patterns* (2010) 347, at 349 et seq.

[127] On 'material' private law see Schmid, *supra* note 77, at 27 ff. with further references.

[128] A. Somek, 'Das europäische Sozialmodell: Diskriminierungsschutz und Wettbewerb', 3 *Juridikum* (2008) 118.

[129] See Krzeminska-Vamvaka and O'Callaghan, 'Mapping out a Right of Privacy in Tort Law', in G. Brüggemeier, A. Colombi Ciacchi, and G. Comandé (eds), *Fundamental Rights and Private Law in the European Union. Volume 2: Comparative Analyses of Selected Case Patterns* (2010) 111; Colombi Ciacchi, *supra* note 43, at 423 et seq.

[130] See BGH 13 October 1992, BGHZ 120 1, NJW 1993, 781 with a comment by E. Deutsch, JZ 1993, 516 with a comment by D. Giesen (Compensation because of a brain injury caused by a doctor's mistake, which is equal to destruction of personality). For a reinterpretation of monetary compensation as civil compensation see G. Brüggemeier, *Haftungsrecht. Struktur, Prinzipien, Schutzbereich: Ein Beitrag zur Europäisierung des Privatrechts* (2006), at 575 et seq.

[131] G. Brüggemeier advocates compensation for personal damages (injuries to physical or mental integrity that cannot be restituted), see ibid., at 557 et seq.

[132] Corte Costituzionale 14 July 1986 No. 184, *Foro it.* 1986 I 2053, with a comment by Giulio Ponzanelli.

persons if, for example, two school children were injured by the same unlawful act, with the parents of the one belonging to the upper class and the other's being poor workers, and they were compensated differently based on their future income potentials.[133]

In Italian literature and jurisprudence, this doctrine was called *danno biologico* (biological damage).[134] This is the most frequent and also best-known constellation of horizontal effect of fundamental rights in Italian civil jurisprudence.[135]

Finally, the second revolution was brought about by jurisprudence of the highest Italian judges, a principle overcoming the traditional legal system of very limited compensation of non-material damages. With a set of decisions in 2003, the *Corte di Cassazione* (Court of Cassation) and the *Corte Costituzionale* created a new principle, which states that all violations of fundamental rights establish a right, per se, to compensation.[136]

The principle of per se compensation of violations of fundamental rights has the potential to become a pan-European principle of law.[137] One could see it as a national level equivalent to the right to an effective remedy in the case of human rights violations in accordance with Article 13 ECHR. At any rate, all of the aforementioned developments of member state jurisprudence show a materialization of tort law. As in contract law, the horizontal effect of fundamental rights opens the door to a more flexible and better consideration of social and human needs in the application of private law.

D. Control of the Power of the Media

A fourth policy dimension of the horizontal effect of fundamental rights can be seen in cases of conflict between personality rights on the one hand and freedom of opinion and information on the other.[138] This is the most common constellation of horizontal effect in Germany, England, France, Italy, the Netherlands, Poland, Portugal, Sweden, and Spain.[139]

Here, falling back on fundamental rights serves not only the materialization of private law: the plural-procedural paradigm also plays a role in this constellation. On the one hand, it is a matter of protecting constitutionally safeguarded interests of natural persons

[133] This argument was triggered by the *Gennarino* case during the 1970s: when the child of a simple worker was the victim of an accident, the Milan court (*Trib. Milano* 18 January 1971) calculated the extent of the compensation based on the assumption that the child would pursue the same career as his father. This decision was heavily criticized as class justice. See Galoppini, 'Il caso Gennarino, ovvero quanto vale il figlio dell'operaio', *Democrazia e diritto* (1971) 255, who provocatively asks how much a worker's child is worth.

[134] F. Busnelli, *Il danno biologico. Dal 'diritto vivente' al 'diritto vigente'* (2001); G. Alpa, *Il danno biologico. Percorso di un'idea* (2003).

[135] For the 'Europeanization of *danno biologico*' or rather for the relation between this doctrine and the tort law provisions of the Draft Common Frame of Reference, see Brüggemeier, 'Gemeinsamer Referenzrahmen (Entwurf), Buch VI: "Außervertragliche Haftung für die Schädigung anderer"—eine kritische Stellungnahme', in H.-J. Ahrens et al. (eds), *Festschrift für Erwin Deutsch zum 80. Geburtstag* (2009) 749.

[136] Cass. 31 May 2003 No. 8827 and 8828; Corte cost. 11 July 2003 No. 233, *Foro it.* 2003 I 2201. For this, see G. Ponzanelli (ed), *Il 'nuovo' danno non patrimoniale* (2004).

[137] In the Draft Common Frame of Reference (DCFR), a per se damage (injury as such, Art. 6:204 DCFR) can also lead to compensation in cases other than violations of fundamental rights. For a commentary on this norm, see C. von Bar (ed), *Non-contractual liability arising out of damage caused to another (PEL Liab. Dam.)* (2009), at 986–990.

[138] See the cases referred to *supra* note 44.

[139] See Krzeminska-Vamvaka and O'Callaghan, *supra* note 129; Colombi Ciacchi, *supra* note 43, at 423 et seq.

from abuses of power by non-state actors (the media). On the other hand, it is also an issue of procedural control of processes considered political in a broad sense: with their decisions, the courts help to define the borderline between private and public matters or rather to determine some rules of political discourse.

E. Exercise of Political Rights in Privately Managed Spaces

A fifth policy dimension of the horizontal effect of fundamental rights is even more strongly characterized by plural-procedural elements: the exercise of political rights in spaces that are private property but open to the public. In several European states, courts are often confronted with suits by people who were banned by the operators of shopping centres, sports stadiums, or airports from handing out flyers or practising other forms of political activism.[140] This is primarily a matter of setting the borderline between the private and the public, and the rules of political discourse.[141]

F. Environmental Protection

A sixth policy dimension of horizontal application of constitutional principles is environmental protection. In several European countries, constitutional rules were applied along with private law instruments, especially property law, to protect the neighbours of lots of land and the environment itself from harmful emissions.[142]

13. Policies of Horizontal Application of Fundamental Rights: EU Level

Different and conflicting societal policies support the different possible outcomes of the horizontal application of fundamental rights at the EU level. The main four policies underlying the horizontal effect cases decided by the ECJ/CJEU seem to

[140] In Germany, BGH NJW 2006, 1054 (protests against the German deportation practice on the premises of the Fraport AG). On this see Fischer Lescano and Maurer, 'Grundrechtsbindung von privaten Betreibern öffentlicher Räume', *NJW* (2006) 1394. A political activist filed a constitutional complaint against this BGH decision, where famous Frankfurt professors Günter Frankenberg and Gunther Teubner were delegated for the process. On 22 February 2011, the BVerfG decided this case in favour of the complainant. It held the prohibition of political demonstrations issued by the Fraport AG to be disproportionate and it declared the unconstitutionality of the BGH decision which considered this prohibition lawful. A classic case of mall litigation, which dealt with the handing out of flyers for a citizens' initiative in an English shopping centre, even required the intervention of the European Court of Human Rights: *Appleby v United Kingdom*, ECHR (2003) 37 EHRR 38. For this, see Gerstenberg, 'Private Law and the New European Constitutional Settlement', 11 *ELJ* (2004) 766. In Italy, see Trib. Verona 7 July 1999, *Il diritto dell'informazione e dell'informatica* (1999) VI, 1059 (distribution of political flyers in a shopping centre). In Sweden, see NJA 1971, 571; in Spain, STS 7 November 2001, RJ 2001/1025. See Gajdosova and Banakas, 'Private property, public access and the access to information—a comparative analysis', in G. Brüggemeier, A. Colombi Ciacchi, and G. Comandé (eds), *Fundamental Rights and Private Law in the European Union. Volume 2: Comparative Analyses of Selected Case Patterns* (2010) 281.

[141] See Gerstenberg, 'Private Law and the New European Constitutional Settlement', 11 *ELJ* (2004) 766.

[142] See S. Patti, *La tutela civile dell'ambiente* (1979). For a detailed comparative study of this subject matter see B. Pozzo (ed), *Property and Environment* (2007). See also Sánchez Galera and Zehetner, *supra* note 48.

be the reduction of discrimination on grounds of gender, age, and nationality; the realization of the Internal Market through the protection of the freedom of movement of workers, the freedom of establishment, the freedom to provide services, and the freedom to conduct a business; the freedom of information; and the protection of privacy.

A. Reduction of Discrimination on Ground of Gender or Age

Examples:

(1) ECJ Case C-43/75, *Gabrielle Defrenne v Société anonyme belge de navigation aérienne Sabena* [1976] ECR 455.
(2) CJEU Case C-132/11, *Tyrolean Airways Tiroler Luftfahrt Gesellschaft mbH v Betriebsrat Bord der Tyrolean Airways Tiroler Luftfahrt Gesellschaft mbH*, judgment of 7 June 2012, not yet published.

B. Reduction of Discrimination on Ground of Nationality; Protection of Freedom of Movement of Workers

Examples:

(1) ECJ Case C-36/74, *B.N.O. Walrave and L.J.N. Koch v Association Union cycliste internationale, Koninklijke Nederlandsche Wielren Unie et Federación Española Ciclismo* [1974] ECR 1405.
(2) ECJ Case C-415/93, *Union royale belge des sociétés de football association ASBL v Jean-Marc Bosman, Royal club liégeois SA v Jean-Marc Bosman and others* and *Union des associations européennes de football (UEFA) v Jean-Marc Bosman* [1995] ECR I-4921.
(3) ECJ Case C-281/98, *Roman Angonese v Cassa di Risparmio di Bolzano SpA* [2000] ECR I-4139.

C. Protection of Freedom of Establishment and Freedom to Provide Services

Examples:

(1) ECJ joined cases C-51/96 and C-191/97, *Christelle Deliège v Ligue francophone de judo et disciplines associées ASBL, Ligue belge de judo ASBL, Union européenne de judo (C-51/96) and François Pacquée (C-191/97)* [2000] ECR I-2549.
(2) ECJ Case C-438/05, *ITJ* (*Viking Line*) [2007] ECR I-10778.
(3) ECJ Case C-341/05, *Laval* [2007] ECR I-11767.

D. Protection of Privacy, Freedom of Information and Freedom to Conduct Business

Examples:

(1) ECJ Case C-275/06, *Productores de Música de España (Promusicae) v Telefónica de España SAU* [2008] ECR I-271.
(2) CJEU Case C-70/10, *Scarlet Extended SA v Société belge des auteurs, compositeurs et éditeurs SCRL (SABAM)* [2011] ECR I-11959.

(3) CJEU Case C-360/10, *Belgische Vereniging van Auteurs, Componisten en Uitgevers CVBA (SABAM) v Netlog NV*, judgment of 16 February 2012, not yet published.

14. Legitimate Legal Policy or Fundamental Rights Instrumentalization?

The policy trends mentioned in the previous sections of this chapter do not represent a complete list. One could insert more examples. For the purpose of this chapter, however, this is not necessary. The question now arises whether and to what extent the recourse to fundamental rights in order to achieve policy goals in the adjudication of private relationships presents an unacceptable instrumentalization of fundamental rights.

As stated in section 5, this chapter understands fundamental rights in the perspective of normative individualism.[143] Accordingly, a fundamental rights argumentation is more convincing and legitimate the more closely it comes to the basic interests of the concerned individuals. Therefore, a policy orientation of the horizontal effect of fundamental rights should not be considered an unacceptable instrumentalization as long as the constellation of horizontal effects in question strengthens the consideration of basic interests of the concerned individuals.

A. National Level

With regard to the six aforementioned policy trends recognizable in the member states' case law, the following observations can be made.

1. Protection of the Weaker Party in Contract Law

The leading cases exemplifying the policy trend of protection of weaker parties in contract law[144] reveal that, before the horizontal application of fundamental rights, an unjustified imbalance existed in the legal treatment of the basic interests of the contract parties concerned. The prevalent judicial interpretations of the applicable private law took proper consideration of the basic interests of some parties (the economic and self-determination interests of lenders, landlords, employers, etc.), while it neglected some basic interests of the counterparties: the self-determination interests of personal guarantors, the tenants' interests to freedom of information, the employee's political rights, etc. The courts have taken fundamental rights as a justification for the need to change those prevalent interpretations.[145] Hence, the horizontal application of fundamental rights has given a voice to those basic interests of the contract parties which had not been taken into account under the previous state of private law. This has

[143] See, also for references to D. von der Pforten's works on normative individualism, *supra*, section 5.

[144] See *supra*, section 12(A).

[145] See, in Germany, the leading cases of the Federal Constitutional Court on agency contracts (BVerfG 7 February 1990, BVerfGE 81, 242), suretyship contracts (BVerfG 19 October 1993, BVerfGE 89, 214), marriage contracts (BVerfG 6 February 2001, BVerfGE 103, 89) and insurance contracts (BVerfG 26 July 2005, 1 BvR 782/94 and 1 BvR 957/96; BVerfG 26 July 2005, 1 BvR 80/95). For further discussion on these five cases see Colombi Ciacchi, 'Party Autonomy as a Fundamental Right in the European Union', 6 *ERCL* (2010) 303.

strengthened the consideration of the basic interests of some categories of individuals, without, however, weakening the consideration of the basic interests of their counterparties. Since the courts have become aware of the need to take all relevant fundamental rights of the contract parties into account, and balancing them where necessary, one may argue that the horizontal effect of fundamental rights has strengthened the consideration of all basic interests of the directly concerned individuals.

2. *Reduction of Discrimination*

The same applies to the anti-discrimination policy trend. Before the fundamental right to equality and non-discrimination was first applied horizontally in the adjudication of labour litigation, tenancy litigation, etc., the correspondent basic interests of the concerned parties (i.e. the individuals discriminated against) were not adequately taken into account in the prevalent interpretations of the applicable law. The practice of horizontal effect tried to correct this imbalance and widened the range of basic interests of the directly concerned individuals that ought to be respected in the adjudication of private litigation.

3. *Economic Upgrade of the Interests of the Individual and Social Equality in Tort Law; Control of the Power of the Media*

Also in tort law, the horizontal application of fundamental rights has given a voice to those basic interests of the directly concerned individuals (the tort victims) that previously did not enjoy adequate consideration. This is true for both the compensation of non-economic loss in personal injury cases, and for the compensation of economic and non-economic loss in cases of infringement of privacy and personality rights (coming from abuses of power of the media).

4. *Protection of Political Rights in Privately Owned Spaces*

Also, the policy trend of protection of political rights in privately owned but publicly accessible spaces goes along with the strengthening of basic interests of the individuals concerned. Here, the horizontal effect of fundamental rights has given a voice precisely to those individuals who have claimed the acknowledgment of their freedom of speech, political opinion, and association vis-à-vis the owners of publicly accessible spaces. Without the horizontal application of fundamental rights, the corresponding basic interests of the individuals concerned would have remained neglected under the traditional interpretations of property law.

5. *Protection against Environmental Pollution*

Similarly, the recourse to fundamental rights has helped the courts revise traditional interpretations of property law concerning harmful emissions, in order to better protect the basic interests of the directly concerned neighbours of polluting plants. At least in Italy, the fundamental principle applied horizontally by the courts was not the state's duty to protect the environment, but the fundamental right to health of the concerned individuals. The interpretation of the right to health was extended to the right to live in a healthy environment, but the basic interests concerned remained the ones of the single individuals living near the sources of pollution.

6. *Preliminary Conclusion*

It must be concluded that, at least in the six fields analysed above, the horizontal application of fundamental rights by national courts does not constitute an unacceptable instrumentalization of these rights. Despite its use (also) for purposes of the materialization of private law, despite its plural and procedural dimension, the horizontal effect of fundamental rights normally leads to a better consideration of all basic interests of the individuals concerned. These interests, such as the actual self-determination of weaker contractual parties, or the exercise of freedom of expression and political activism in 'mall litigation' cases, were not adequately considered before their breakthrough in the respective private law cases. The interests of the counterparties, however, such as the economic freedom of banks, were already adequately protected by the private law instrumentarium. Thus some fundamental rights were favoured, while other fundamental rights were neglected without a compelling reason. Exactly this imbalance is being corrected by the horizontal effect of fundamental rights. One may argue that courts invoke fundamental rights in adjudicating private litigation in order to protect the individuals whose interests had not been fought for by a powerful lobby at the legislative level.

In summary, it must be noted that the horizontal effect of fundamental rights is not neutral from a legal policy viewpoint. Yet, the policy orientation of this horizontal effect in the case law of national civil courts (at least in the six analysed fields) does not amount to an unacceptable instrumentalization of fundamental rights. In fact, in these fields the genuine content of fundamental rights and basic interests of individuals has been actualized. The horizontal application of fundamental rights by member states' courts is therefore a very positive phenomenon.[146]

B. EU Level

The policy of European integration and full realization of the Internal Market underlies most ECJ/CJEU decisions in the field of private law.[147] Therefore, the policies of fundamental rights horizontality at the EU level clearly differ from the ones recognizable at the national level. Only at the national level, the horizontal effect of fundamental rights is used to address typical social justice concerns such as the inequality of bargaining power in contract cases, or the unequal treatment of poor and rich tort victims in personal injury cases. At the EU level, a different model of justice emerges, which challenges the national models of social justice in private law.[148]

146 In the same direction, see recently Mak, 'Judges in Utopia', *supra* note 118. For contract law, see also Mak, *Fundamental Rights, supra* note 118. For criticism of the horizontal application of fundamental rights in civil cases see Cherednychenko, 'Fundamental Rights, Policy Issues and the Draft Common Frame of Reference for European Private Law', 6 *ERCL* (2010) 39; Cherednychenko, 'Fundamental Rights and Private Law: A Relationship of Subordination or Complementarity?', 3 *Utrecht Law Review* (2007) 1; Cherednychenko, 'Subordinating Contract Law to Fundamental Rights: Towards a Major Breakthrough or towards Walking in Circles?', in S. Grundmann (ed), *Constitutional Values and European Contract Law* (2008) 35; Cherednychenko, 'The Constitutionalization of Contract Law: Something New under the Sun?', 8 *Electronic Journal of Comparative Law* (2004) 1; B. de Vos, *Horizontale werking van grondrechten. Een kritiek* (2010).

147 For a detailed analysis see Schmid, *supra* note 77.

148 On this, see H.-W. Micklitz, 'Social Justice and Access Justice in Private Law', EUI Working Paper Law, 2011/02 (2011) <http://papers.ssrn.com/sol3/papers.cfm?abstract_id=1824225>, with further references; H.-W. Micklitz (ed), *The Many Concepts of Social Justice in European Private Law* (2011).

However, this difference between the national and EU policies of fundamental rights adjudication arguably does not substantially influence the extent to which the national or EU case patterns of fundamental rights horizontality are compatible with a normative individualistic perspective. It is submitted that in the cases of horizontal effect of fundamental rights discussed above, EU market integration policy has gone hand in hand with the strengthening of basic interests of individual persons, workers, and businesses against the opposite interests of larger collectives, such as sport federations, trade unions, and national states. This perfectly corresponds to a normative individualistic approach. The following subsections will substantiate this claim with reference to the policies of adjudication enumerated in section 13.

1. *Reduction of Discrimination; Protection of Freedom of Movement of Workers*

In several cases where an individual worker litigated against his or her employer and/or another collective entity, the Court of Justice let the rights of the former prevail against the rights of the latter. More precisely, the basic interests of individual workers to non-discrimination and freedom of movement prevailed over the interests of their collective counterparties in saving money, favouring male employees (in equal pay litigations such as the *Defrenne* case[149]), employing locals (such as in the *Angonese* case[150]), or restricting the freedom of individual athletes to change their affiliation (such as in the *Bosman* case[151]). Thus the direct horizontal applications of both the fundamental right to non-discrimination and the fundamental freedom of movement for workers have strengthened the rights and interests of the individual workers directly concerned in the litigation. This arguably confirms the normative-individualistic paradigm.

2. *Protection of Freedom of Establishment and Freedom to Provide Services*

The horizontal effect of fundamental rights and fundamental freedoms in the *Viking*[152] and *Laval*[153] cases has certainly strengthened the rights and interests of the directly concerned individual businesses against the national and corporative interests of trade unions. As for the rights and interests of the directly concerned individual workers (not just the ones employed by Viking and Laval), different opinions may be defended equally well. One may argue that all individual workers concerned would be better off if the trade unions were empowered to force the applicability of the higher salaries of western member states against the competition of cheaper Eastern European labour. However, one may also argue that the *Viking* and *Laval* decision saved the jobs of both the directly concerned employees and a countless number of other European workers, which would be endangered if an inflexibly high level of salary made certain industrial activities in certain member states less competitive.

Anyway, it is noteworthy that, while giving horizontal application to fundamental rights and freedoms in *Viking* and *Laval,* the Court opted for an interpretation of the public policy derogation according to which the trade union's action can only reasonably fall within the objective of protecting workers if it is appropriate for securing the

[149] ECJ Case C-43/75, *Gabrielle Defrenne v Société anonyme belge de navigation aérienne Sabena* [1976] ECR 455.

[150] ECJ Case C-281/98, *Roman Angonese v Cassa di Risparmio di Bolzano SpA* [2000] ECR I-4139.

[151] ECJ Case C-415/93, *supra* note 62.

[152] ECJ Case C-438/05, *supra* note 75.

[153] ECJ Case C-341/05, *supra* note 76.

attainment of this objective and not going beyond what is necessary in order to attain that objective. It is submitted that this reflects a normative-individualistic perspective. The decisive weight given by the Court in *Viking* to the existence of a jeopardy or serious threat to 'the jobs or conditions of employment of that trade union's members who are liable to be affected by the reflagging of the vessel' corresponds to the normative-individualistic consideration of the interests of all individuals directly concerned by the decision.

Certainly a positive effect of the *Viking* and *Laval* judgments consists in that national courts are put under a duty to take into account, in their application of the public policy derogation to fundamental freedoms, all conflicting fundamental rights of individuals: the directly concerned employers, the directly concerned employees, *and* the individual members of the directly concerned trade unions. Thus one may say that in these cases the horizontal application of fundamental rights has weakened the rights and interests of collectives but has strengthened the basic rights and interests of all directly concerned individuals.[154]

3. *Protection of Privacy, Freedom of Information, and Freedom to Conduct Business*

In *Promusicae*,[155] *Scarlet Extended*,[156] and *SABAM v Netlog*,[157] the Court of Justice recognized extensively all conflicting fundamental rights and interests that need to be balanced against each other in these types of cases. Here, the author's intellectual property rights clash not only with the ISP's freedom of enterprise, but also with the rights of the ISP's clients to privacy and protection of personal data, and with the freedom of ISP's clients to receive or impart information. In requiring the balancing of these conflicting rights, the Court did not refer to the rights of abstract collectives, but to the rights of the directly concerned authors, the directly concerned ISP's, and their clients. This evidences once again a normative-individualistic perspective.

15. Conclusion

From the analysis performed in the previous sections, one can draw the following conclusions:

(1) At both the national and the European level, the horizontal application of fundamental rights is a form of judicial governance.

(2) In applying fundamental rights horizontally to a specific litigation pattern, both the Court of Justice and the national courts require and/or operate a balancing of all conflicting fundamental rights that play a role in that litigation pattern.

(3) In requiring or exercising the balancing of conflicting fundamental rights, the Court of Justice and the national courts do not give weight to rights and interests of abstract entities and collectives (such as 'the state', 'the Swedish workers', 'the natural environment'), but to rights and interests of the directly concerned individuals. These may include the individual members of an individual

[154] Cf. H.-W. Micklitz, 'Three Questions to the Opponents of the *Viking* and *Laval* Judgments', OSE Opinion Paper no. 8, May 2012, 7, where the author comments—in the light of Durkheim's thought—on the 'shaping of the European legal order by the ECJ through the extension of subjective rights, thereby indirectly turning down collective rights'.

[155] *Supra* note 99. [156] *Supra* note 100. [157] *Supra* note 101.

collective entity, such as a trade union or a business firm. Thus one can say that the normative-individualistic paradigm shines through all types of cases of horizontal effect of fundamental rights.

(4) At both the national and the European level, the horizontal effect of fundamental rights in a specific litigation pattern may strengthen the rights and interests of some individuals. This does not necessarily mean that the conflicting rights and opposite interests of other individuals are weakened. The vast majority of cases deal with conflicting fundamental rights of equal rank. These rights must be balanced according to all circumstances of the case. In the same litigation pattern, changed circumstances may let the fundamental rights and basic interests of either party prevail.

(5) At both the national and the European level, the leading cases of a horizontal effect of fundamental rights have caused a revolution in private law, when they required giving weight to a certain fundamental right of one litigating party which had not been given sufficient weight in a previous balancing operated by either the judiciary or the legislature in regulating the same litigation pattern.

(6) At both the national and the EU level, the horizontal application of fundamental rights is not a neutral phenomenon from a legal policy viewpoint. In applying fundamental rights horizontally, both the Court of Justice and the national courts seem to regularly give preference to certain societal policies over others.

(7) However, this preference does not amount to any unacceptable instrumentalization of fundamental rights. Pursuing certain policies in certain litigation patterns goes hand in hand with the strengthening of the basic interests of all individuals directly concerned. Hence, the fundamental rights in question are not instrumentalized but, on the contrary, actualized.

(8) To summarize: at both the national and the EU level, the horizontal application of fundamental rights is a positive phenomenon. It requires the courts to explicitly discuss and balance all conflicting fundamental rights and interests affected by the litigation. This strengthens not only the basic interests of all directly concerned individuals, but also the constitutional legitimacy of the adjudication of private law cases.

5

Constitutionalization and EU Employment Law

Mark Bell

1. Introduction

One of the evident trends in European Union employment law has been a gradual shift towards the constitutionalization of key workers' rights. There are multiple interpretations of the term 'constitutionalization', but it can be linked to processes that seek to entrench certain legal norms and to attribute them with a higher status.[1] This typically has the consequence that those provisions that have been constitutionalized become more difficult to amend or repeal. Moreover, if there is a conflict with other legal norms, then those that have been constitutionalized should prevail or should be accorded greater weight based on their elevated status. The process of constitutionalization is often made visible through the proclamation or adoption of legal texts that are given a special value. Most obviously, this occurs when a constitution is adopted. It can extend to other instruments that lack the label of a 'constitution', but which receive the hierarchically superior status associated with such documents. In relation to the EU, its efforts to adopt a document with the formal title of constitution may have withered, but it is clear that the founding Treaties have a constitutional function in the Union's legal order. The Treaties also illustrate the role of courts in the process of constitutionalization. The Court of Justice has described the Treaties as a 'constitutional Charter'[2] and it has used them as a foundation for identifying rights that should be treated as 'fundamental' within the EU legal order, such as the rights of EU citizenship.[3] The activism of the Court of Justice also reveals how courts may be inventors of constitutionalization even in the absence of formal legal texts pursuing this objective.[4] An example that will be considered in this chapter is the constitutional role of the unwritten general principles of EU law, which have been constructed over time by the Court of Justice.

The idea that certain rights relating to the workplace should be recognized as possessing a fundamental or constitutional character is not particularly novel. For example, the Council of Europe's 1961 European Social Charter might be described

[1] Arthurs, 'The Constitutionalization of Employment Relations: Multiple Models, Pernicious Problems', 19 *Social and Legal Studies* (2010) 403, at 405; Christodoulisdis and Dukes, 'Labour, Constitution and *A Sense of Measure*: a Debate with Alain Supiot', 19 *Social and Legal Studies* (2010) 217, at 218.

[2] *Opinion 1/91 on the draft agreement between the Community, on the one hand, and the countries of the European Free Trade Association, on the other, relating to the creation of the European Economic Area* [1991] ECR I-6079, Rec. 1 of judgment.

[3] Shaw, 'Citizenship: Contrasting Dynamics at the Interface of Integration and Constitutionalism', in P. Craig and G. de Búrca (eds), *The Evolution of EU Law* (2011) 574.

[4] Fudge, 'Constitutionalizing Labour Rights in Europe', in T. Campbell and K. Ewing (eds), *The Legal Protection of Human Rights* (2011) 244.

as reflecting a form of constitutionalization; the signatories agreed to adhere to a set of minimum standards in terms of workers' rights, thereby fettering their discretion to alter employment law in a manner that dipped below the catalogue of rights guaranteed by the Charter (at least in principle if not in practice). In relation to the EU, a clear signal of the trajectory towards the constitutionalization of employment rights can be found in the 1989 Community Charter of the Fundamental Social Rights of Workers. The preamble of this document describes it as a 'solemn proclamation', but it is not legally binding. Nevertheless, the decision by the member states[5] to cloak the revitalization of European social policy in the language of a 'Charter', and its reference to 'fundamental' rights, has been subsequently interpreted by the Court of Justice as an indication of its special legal value. The Court has deployed the 1989 Charter as a means of identifying employment rights that warrant extra protection, or more intense judicial scrutiny of any departures from these rights.[6] The idea of enshrining fundamental workers' rights in a document of constitutional significance is reflected even more forcefully in the EU Charter of Fundamental Rights,[7] which now enjoys the same legal status as the Treaties.[8]

This chapter explores the process and effects of constitutionalization within EU employment law and reflects upon its impact on the substantive content of this area of law. The first section begins by examining how constitutionalization has evolved. It considers the tension between constitutionalization and the autonomy of parties to the contract of employment, as well as the reasons for the tendency to embody certain workers' rights with a higher legal status. The second section looks at a specific example of constitutionalization within employment law: the case of EU equality law. This is an area where both the courts and the legislator have recognized that the legal norms engage fundamental principles of law, including the protection of human rights. This impacts upon the Court's interpretation of equality legislation, with some recent decisions emphasizing that the constitutional rights and principles are superior and free-standing sources of law, which reach beyond the contents of the equality directives. The final section of this chapter considers an area of employment law where the engagement of constitutional rights is more ambiguous: the personal scope of employment rights. In order to access most employment rights, it must first be recognized that the activity performed was in the context of an employment relationship. In short, many employment rights are only extended to those deemed to be 'workers' or falling into associated categories.[9] The person who is genuinely self-employed will, in most cases, not be entitled to the protection of employment law. The apparent simplicity of this binary divide is misleading; disentangling the complexity of modern working relationships is a conundrum that challenges most European legal systems.[10] The final section of this chapter re-examines this issue through the lens of constitutionalization. This is an aspect of employment law that is not commonly associated

[5] The Charter was originally signed by only 11 of the then 12 member states (the UK being the exception).

[6] See further section 2 of this chapter.

[7] OJ 2010 C 83/389.

[8] Art. 6(1) TEU.

[9] Legal systems adopt different terminology in this field. For example, in the UK, there is an important legal distinction between 'employees' and 'workers'. For the purposes of this chapter, 'worker' will be adopted as a generic term to capture broadly the personal performance of work; it is not intended to reflect any particular national definition of this legal category.

[10] Veneziani, 'The Employment Relationship', in B. Hepple and B. Veneziani (eds), *The Transformation of Labour Law in Europe* (2009) 99.

with fundamental rights; the notion of a right to be treated as a worker is not expressly found in most fundamental rights instruments. Therefore, this section will explore whether the process of constitutionalization has relevance or effect even where there is the absence of a clearly applicable fundamental social right.

2. Constitutionalization and the Employment Relationship

The pace with which constitutionalization has established itself within the sphere of employment means that there is a temptation to take it for granted that the employment relationship is an appropriate venue for the application of constitutional rights and principles. Yet standing back from current legal developments, this is not immediately obvious. Private law typically views the employment relationship through the prism of the contract of employment. Broadly speaking, the contract is an agreement between the worker and the employer for the provision of labour in exchange for remuneration and the acceptance by the worker of some degree of subordination to the managerial requirements of the employer.[11] Classically, the private law perspective on the employment contract begins with the principle of freedom of contract; the employer and worker are free to negotiate the terms of their agreement without external interference.[12] Freedom of contract in the employment sphere disguises, however, the inequality of bargaining power between the two parties. In most cases, the potential worker has a greater dependence on the employer than vice versa. The employer may be able to offer contractual terms on a 'take it or leave it' basis, with no genuine possibility for the worker to renegotiate the terms. The economic power of the employer, especially in sectors where the supply of workers exceeds demand from employers, creates a risk of exploitation on the part of the dominant party to the contract and this has resulted in legal intervention to rebalance the bargaining power of the parties. Notably, there has been statutory intervention to regulate working conditions; workplace health and safety was often an initial field where the state felt it was not sufficient to rely on freedom of contract in order to secure adequate protection of workers' interests.[13] Collins suggests that the extensiveness of social regulation of employment now tends to overshadow its private law origins.[14] At the same time, state intervention has often been directed towards strengthening the negotiating power of workers by facilitating their collective organization through trade unions and encouraging processes of collective bargaining. In the light of such interventions, it is clear that the 'privacy' of the employment contract has long been subject to direct or indirect intrusion by the state. Indeed, contemporary debates about the extensiveness of EU employment law tend to be more dominated by concern for the economic consequences of further regulation rather than principled objections to the erosion of the freedom of contract.

While state intervention in the employment relationship is commonplace, this can be distinguished from the trend towards constitutionalization. Not all forms of legal

[11] While the approach to defining the employment relationship varies across member states, these two elements are the focus of the approach of the Court of Justice to whether someone enjoys the status of 'worker': e.g. Case C-232/09, *Danosa v LKB Līzings SIA*, judgment of 11 November 2010, not yet published, Rec. 39.

[12] Collins, 'Justifications and Techniques of Legal Regulation of the Employment Relation', in H. Collins, P. Davies, and R. Rideout (eds), *Legal Regulation of the Employment Relation* (2000) 3, at 6.

[13] E.g. P. Davies and M. Freedland, *Labour Legislation and Public Policy* (1993), at 35.

[14] Collins, *supra* note 12, at 7.

intervention have the character of constitutionalization; it would be an overextension of this concept to suggest that any legislation that impinged upon the employment relationship implied constitutionalization. There is, therefore, a distinction to be drawn between 'ordinary' legislation and that which has been constitutionalized. Where the rights at stake are housed within a constitutional-type document, the bifurcation is visible; within the EU context, there is an evident intention that the employment rights located in the Charter of Fundamental Rights should receive a higher legal status than employment rights found only in secondary legislation, such as regulations and directives. The Court has already annulled elements of secondary legislation in conflict with the Charter, illustrating its hierarchical superiority.[15] Nevertheless, it would be too simplistic to view constitutionalization purely in terms of the location of legal provisions. Through the interpretation of the courts, it may be possible that elements of secondary legislation are deemed to have a special legal significance, which leads, in effect, to a constitutionalization of these norms. Mantouvalou links this to the extent to which economic considerations are deemed to be a legitimate basis for the restriction of the protection of workers; where rights have been constitutionalized, then this should counter arguments that seek to curtail rights based on cost considerations.[16] An example of this type of reasoning can be found within the Court's case law on gender equality at work, where it has opposed the argument that economic factors may form an explicit basis for restricting equal treatment:

> to concede that budgetary considerations may justify a difference of treatment between men and women which would otherwise constitute indirect discrimination on grounds of sex would mean that the application and scope of a rule of Community law as fundamental as that of equal treatment between men and women might vary in time and place according to the state of the public finances of Member States.[17]

The prohibition of indirect discrimination was only expressly found within secondary legislation, but this did not prevent the Court from attributing it with a higher legal status due to its connection to one of the fundamental principles of EU law (equal treatment of women and men).

While gender equality is an obvious example of constitutionalization within the Court's reasoning, it is also clear that there are some areas of EU employment law where the Court has not identified a nexus with the protection of fundamental rights and where economic reasons for restricting rights are not overtly excluded. The Acquired Rights Directive[18] offers an example in this regard. Hepple has argued that the approach of the Court in this area has been conservative in comparison to its gender equality case law.[19] While there is acknowledgement of the protective objectives of the legislation,[20]

[15] Case C-236/09, *Association Belge des Consommateurs Test-Achats ASBL and Others v Conseil des ministres*, judgment of 1 March 2011, not yet published.

[16] Mantouvalou, 'Human Rights for Precarious Workers: the Legislative Precariousness of Domestic Labour', 33 *Comparative Labor Law and Policy Journal* (2012) 133.

[17] Case C-226/98, *Jørgensen v Foreningen af Speciallæger and Sygesikringens Forhandlingssugvalg* [2000] ECR I-2447, Rec. 39 of judgment. See further, Schiek, 'Indirect Discrimination', in D. Schiek, L. Waddington, and M. Bell (eds), *Cases, Materials and Text on National, Supranational and International Non-Discrimination Law* (2007) 323, at 453.

[18] Council Directive 2001/23, OJ 2001 L 82/16, on the approximation of the laws of the Member States relating to the safeguarding of employees' rights in the event of transfers of undertakings, businesses or parts of undertakings or businesses.

[19] Hepple, 'The Implementation of the Community Charter of Fundamental Social Rights', 53 *MLR* (1990) 643, at 649.

[20] E.g. Case C-392/92, *Schmidt v Spar- und Leihkasse der fruheren Amter Bordesholm, Kiel und Cronshagen* [1994] ECR I-1311, Rec. 15 of judgment; Case C-108/10, *Scattolon v Ministero dell'Istruzione, dell'Università e della Ricerca*, judgment of 6 September 2011, not yet published, Rec. 58.

the Court's judgments on the Acquired Rights Directive rarely identify provisions of the legislation as impinging upon the fundamental rights of workers. Moreover, its case law does not suggest that there is a particular priority attached to the protection of workers' rights as opposed to balancing these with the economic interests of employers.[21]

Having identified a distinction between 'ordinary' and 'constitutionalized' employment law, the question arises as to why there is a need to move from one category to the other. If the rationale for state intervention in the freedom of contract was to redress the inequality of bargaining power between the employer and the worker, then what underpins the further incursion into contractual freedom by the application of constitutional norms into private relationships?

A. Rationales for Constitutionalizing Employment Law

From a historical perspective, Dukes argues that the law has long been concerned with establishing an 'industrial constitution', based around the 'replacement of the individual negotiation of terms and conditions with universal collective bargaining'.[22] By guaranteeing freedom of association and the right to engage in collective bargaining or to take collective action, the state provides a framework for industrial democracy, whereby workplace relations are founded on dialogue and negotiation between employers and workers. The state entrenches the basic facets of this system, such as the freedom to form and join a trade union, but the substantive outcomes in terms of pay and working conditions are left for the parties to determine. In this model, the law might be viewed as supplanting individuals' freedom of contract with a collectivized understanding of freedom of contract. A classic example of this would be the 'laissez-faire' model of employment law that pertained in the United Kingdom for a large part of the twentieth century. The state generally refrained from statutory regulation of working conditions, but intervened to facilitate collective bargaining as the principal source of workplace regulation.[23]

There is some evidence of this model influencing EU law, where a constitutional footing (in the form of the founding Treaties) has been given to social dialogue between management and labour, which may lead to legally binding agreements.[24] Yet social dialogue has never been the pre-eminent source of regulation within EU employment law and the greater part of the legislation stems from political bargaining within the EU institutions, rather than European collective bargaining. More generally, relying on the industrial constitution as the primary route to securing a fair balance between the interests of employers and workers has been challenged by the decline, in some countries, of the vitality of collective bargaining.[25] This is frequently associated with the spread of globalization. Specifically, the footloose nature of modern capital, and the persistent threat of transnational relocation,[26] exercises a downward pressure on labour standards

[21] E.g. Case C-463/09, *CLECE SA v Socorro Martín Valor, Ayuntamiento de Cobisa*, judgment of 20 January 2011, not yet published; Case C-386/09, *Briot v Randstad Interim, Sodexho SA, Council of the EU*, judgment of 15 September 2010, not yet published; Davies, 'Taken to the Cleaners? Contracting Out of Services Yet Again', 26 *Industrial Law Journal (ILJ)* (1997) 193, at 195; C. Barnard, *EC Employment Law* (3rd ed.; 2006), at 670–671.

[22] Dukes, 'Constitutionalizing Employment Relations: Sinzheimer, Kahn-Freund, and the Role of Labour Law', 35 *Journal of Law and Society* (2008) 341, at 342; Rödl, 'Re-thinking Employment Relations in Constitutional Terms', 19 *Social and Legal Studies* (2010) 241, at 242.

[23] Dukes, *supra* note 22, at 358.

[24] Arts 154–155 TFEU.

[25] Jacobs, 'Collective Labour Relations', in B. Hepple and B. Veneziani (eds), *The Transformation of Labour Law in Europe* (2009) 201, at 224–225.

[26] Dukes, *supra* note 22, at 341; A. Somek, *Engineering Equality: An Essay on European Anti-Discrimination Law* (2011), at 39.

that cannot be adequately resisted within national frameworks of collective bargaining. Fudge notes that one feature of globalization has been the spread of neoliberal economic policies via international agreements.[27] These are, in themselves, a type of constitutionalization as they seek to institutionalize free trade in goods and services and they curtail the capacity of participating states to maintain domestic social regulations that are characterized as obstacles to trade. The tendency to embed these rules at the international level implies that an effective project for the constitutionalization of employment rights must also engage at this level.[28] The EU is a prime example of free market principles being constitutionalized at supranational level and it is clear that these have the potential to overwhelm national social policy objectives, including measures for the protection of workers.[29] Consequently, the constitutionalization of employment rights within the EU legal order becomes a means of counteracting the challenge to labour standards presented by competition within the Internal Market.

A further motivation for the turn towards constitutionalization can be found within changes in the nature of employment relationships. A widely documented trend has been the growth in 'atypical' or 'non-standard' forms of work, such as fixed-term or agency work.[30] These represent a departure from the 'standard' model of a worker employed on a full-time, indefinite contract with stable working hours, and where the person for whom the worker performs work is also the employer. This tendency of fragmentation in labour market relationships poses challenges for the traditional model of protecting workers through the industrial constitution and its dependence on trade union representation. In part, this may be due to the ephemeral nature of such jobs, but it also concerns the ambiguity surrounding the legal status of these employment relationships, such as the identity of the employer or whether the individuals are workers or self-employed. Constitutionalization may offer a response to the complexity of the modern labour market in so far as it aims 'to recast labour standards as international human rights'.[31] The value for non-standard workers of moving to the language of human rights lies in the potential for greater flexibility with regard to the personal scope of the application of these rights. Within ordinary employment legislation, individuals often need to establish as a prerequisite that they are an 'employee' or a 'worker' for the purposes of the legislation. This can be a stumbling block for those where the relationship is with more than one actor, such as outsourced labour, or where there is a high level of flexibility in the arrangement of work, such as 'on-demand' workers. Human rights, with their universalistic outlook, may offer a means of circumventing technical debates around the categorization of the form of employment relationship. This possibility is examined in more depth in section 5 of this chapter.

Finally, another factor propelling the rise of constitutionalization is a desire to fill the institutional gap left by the perceived decline in the strength of trade unions and

[27] Fudge, *supra* note 4, at 246–247.

[28] Ibid., at 244; Collins, *supra* note 12, at 15.

[29] E.g. Davies, 'Market Integration and Social Policy in the Court of Justice', 24 *ILJ* (1995) 49; Syrpis and Novitz, 'Economic and Social Rights in Conflict: Political and Judicial Approaches to their Reconciliation', 33 *ELRev* (2008) 411, at 426.

[30] Kalleberg, 'Precarious Work, Insecure Workers: Employment Relations in Transition', 74 *American Sociological Review* (2009) 1, at 7; Rodgers, 'Precarious Work in Western Europe: the State of the Debate', in G. Rodgers and J. Rodgers (eds), *Precarious Jobs in Labour Market Regulation: the Growth of Atypical Employment in Western Europe* (1989) 1; Fudge and Owens, 'Precarious Work, Women, and the New Economy: the Challenge to Legal Norms', in J. Fudge and R. Owens (eds), *Precarious Work, Women, and the New Economy: the Challenge to Legal Norms* (2006) 3.

[31] Fudge, *supra* note 4, at 248.

collective bargaining.[32] Converting employment rights into 'fundamental' or 'human' rights shifts the focus away from protecting workers via collective organization, and towards an enhanced role for courts and litigation.[33] While litigation strategies may be collective in nature, most commonly they reflect an individualization of disputes focusing on the specific situation of the particular litigants.[34] This seems to echo the transformation of employment relationships; the rise of non-standard work, and diversity in where and how work is performed, portrays an image of a labour market of individuals where bonds of solidarity between workers may have declined.[35] Whether courts offer a productive alternative to the traditional channels for promoting workers' interests remains highly contested. Arthurs is critical of this approach pointing out the practical constraints of litigation (such as delay and expense), as well as the historic conservatism of courts and their frequent reluctance to challenge vested economic interests.[36] Alternatively, Gearty suggests that the inclination to fall back on courts reflects an 'impatience with politics'.[37] Yet given the prominent role of judicial bodies as mechanisms for enforcing free trade under international agreements, arguably they have already become central actors in regulating workers' rights, in particular where these collide with economic liberalization. While the constitutionalization of employment rights does not guarantee a particular social outcome, it is, at least, an attempt to persuade courts to temper market liberalization through recognition of other fundamental objectives.

It is also possible, although not inevitable, that courts may counter individualization through recognition of collective rights as human rights. There is some evidence of this trend within the recent case law of the European Court of Human Rights. The Strasbourg Court has demonstrated an increasing willingness to interpret the European Convention on Human Rights in the light of principles emerging from the European Social Charter and the Conventions of the International Labour Organization. Notably, this led to a shift in its case law on the meaning of Article 11 on freedom of association towards recognition that this could encompass rights to engage in collective bargaining or (in some circumstances) to take industrial action.[38] In contrast, this trajectory is less evident in the recent case law of the Court of Justice. In a series of cases that involved clashes between the aims of economic liberalization and, broadly speaking, social rights, the Court appeared to lean in favour of removing obstacles to trade within the EU Internal Market.[39] Although the decisions included rhetorical recognition from the Court that collective action was a fundamental right, the process of balancing this against economic freedoms tended to give more weight to the latter.[40]

[32] Novitz and Fenwick, 'The Application of Human Rights Discourse to Labour Relations: Translation of Theory into Practice', in C. Fenwick and T. Novitz (eds), *Human Rights at Work: Perspectives on Law and Regulation* (2010) 1, at 2.

[33] Arthurs, *supra* note 1, at 405–406; Fudge, *supra* note 4, at 249.

[34] Gearty, 'Against Judicial Enforcement', in C. Gearty and V. Mantouvalou (eds), *Debating Social Rights* (2011) 1, at 35.

[35] A. Ross, *Nice Work If You Can Get It: Life and Labor in Precarious Times* (2009), at 5.

[36] Arthurs, *supra* note 1, at 406.

[37] Gearty, *supra* note 34, at 34.

[38] See further, Ewing and Hendy, 'The Dramatic Implications of *Demir* and *Baykara*', 39 *ILJ* (2010) 2.

[39] Case C-341/05, *Laval un Partneri Ltd v Svenska Byggnadsarbetareförbundet* [2007] ECR I-11767; Case C-438/05, *International Transport Workers' Federation, Finnish Seamen's Union v Viking Line ABP, OÜ Viking Line Eesti* [2007] ECR I-10779; Case C-346/06, *Rüffert v Land Niedersachsen* [2008] ECR I-1989.

[40] Syrpis, 'Reconciling Economic Freedoms and Social Rights—The Potential of *Commission v Germany* (Case C-271/08, Judgment of 15 July 2010)', 40 *ILJ* (2011) 222.

3. The Evolution of Constitutionalization within EU Employment Law

Having discussed the nature and rationale for constitutionalization within employment law, this section provides a short overview of the principal ways in which this trend has been manifested within EU employment law. A loose distinction can be drawn between forms of constitutionalization that have been (1) forged through judicial creativity or (2) founded on new or amended legal texts, such as charters and treaties. While the two are obviously interrelated, in the former the courts have been the leading architects, whereas in the latter the member states have taken the driving seat.

A. Constitutionalization by the Courts

Looking back at the original Treaties, these famously included the right to equal pay for women and men[41] and it could be argued that this was a nascent form of constitutionalization. Yet the enforceability of this provision was, at best, unclear and it was not anticipated by the member states that a provision of an international trade agreement could be applied directly into private employment contracts.[42] As is well known, that changed through the Court of Justice's innovatory concept of 'direct effect', allowing individual rights found within the Treaties to be enforced in national courts. In *Defrenne v SABENA (no. 2)*,[43] the Court not only confirmed that this applied to the right to equal pay, but that the enforceability of this provision 'also extends to all agreements which are intended to regulate paid labour collectively, as well as to contracts between individuals'.[44] This inaugurated a new restriction on the contractual autonomy of parties to the employment relationship; henceforth, private employment contracts were subject to the restrictions imposed by national legislation *and* directly effective rights found within the founding treaties.

In general, the idea of freedom of contract in relation to the workplace does not appear to have exercised a significant influence on the Court's consideration of whether it is appropriate to apply Treaty provisions in the context of private employment relationships. In *Angonese*,[45] it confirmed that its reasoning in *Defrenne v SABENA* extended to the prohibition of nationality discrimination between EU citizen workers[46] and consequently this could be applied between private persons (on the facts of the case, between a job applicant and a private sector bank).[47] More controversially, the Court has also held that the Treaty Internal Market provisions can be applied to the actions of trade unions. In *Laval*,[48] the Court held that Article 49 EC[49] on the free movement of services could be applied to collective action by trade unions where this could create obstacles to the cross-border provision of services. Similarly, in *Viking*,[50] the Court was

[41] Art. 119 EEC, now Art. 157 TFEU.

[42] P. Craig and G. de Búrca, *EU Law—Text, Cases and Materials* (5th ed.; 2011), at 185.

[43] Case 43/75, *Defrenne II* [1976] ECR 455.

[44] Ibid., Rec. 39.

[45] Case C-281/98, *Angonese v Cassa di Risparmio di Bolzano SpA* [2000] ECR I-4139.

[46] Former Art. 39 EC, now Art. 45(2) TFEU.

[47] *Angonese, supra* note 45, at Rec. 36.

[48] Case C-341/05, *Laval un Partneri Ltd v Svenska Byggnadsarbetareförbundet* [2007] ECR I-11767, Recs 98–99.

[49] Now Art. 56 TFEU.

[50] Case C-438/05, *International Transport Workers' Federation, Finnish Seamen's Union v Viking Line ABP, OÜ Viking Line Eesti* [2007] ECR I-10779, Recs 33–37.

willing to apply Article 43 EC[51] on freedom of establishment to collective agreements and collective action.

In addition to the horizontal application of Treaty provisions, the Court's case law on general principles of law has been another route through which constitutional norms impact upon employment relationships. The general principles are unwritten; they are not catalogued within the Treaties. Nevertheless, they form a basis for judicial review of EU secondary legislation, as well as acts of the Union's institutions or of the member states when acting within the scope of EU law.[52] Amongst the general principles, two seem to be especially pertinent to employment: the principle of equal treatment and/or non-discrimination, and the principle of respect for fundamental rights. The general principle of equal treatment 'requires that comparable situations must not be treated differently and that different situations must not be treated in the same way unless such treatment is objectively justified'.[53] This imposes a basic test of fairness or rationality; arbitrary distinctions in the treatment of similarly situated workers may fall foul of this requirement. For example, in *Rodríguez Caballero*, the Court of Justice found a breach of the general principle of equal treatment where workers who were unfairly dismissed and whose employer subsequently became insolvent were not entitled to a benefit that was otherwise available to unfairly dismissed workers whose employers were not insolvent.[54] Notably this case arose in the context of Spanish implementation of a directive on the protection of employees in the event of the employer's insolvency.[55] The judgment does not suggest that the content of the directive per se engaged fundamental rights; this seems to be a good example of 'ordinary' employment legislation. Yet the transposition of the directive brought the national implementing measures into the scope of EU law, thereby triggering the requirement to comply with the general principle of equal treatment.[56]

Another aspect of the Court's case law is the general principle of respect for fundamental rights. This forms a bridge to international human rights law and the Court has regularly acknowledged that its interpretation of the general principle is based on such instruments. This is now codified in Article 6(3) TEU:

> Fundamental rights, as guaranteed by the European Convention for the Protection of Human Rights and Fundamental Freedoms and as they result from the constitutional traditions common to the Member States, shall constitute general principles of the Union's law.

The employment law relevance of the general principle of respect for fundamental rights arises from the way in which the Court has identified certain elements of EU employment legislation that are, in its view, inherently concerned with the protection of fundamental rights. This has been most visible in relation to EU equality Directives. While this is examined in more depth in section 4 of this chapter, *Schröder* provides a good example of how this can be seen to affect the way in which the Court interprets the legislation. In this case, the Court rejected an argument that the retrospective award of equal pay to

[51] Now Art. 49 TFEU. [52] See further the discussion in section 4 of this chapter.

[53] Case C-149/10, *Zoi Chatzi v Ypourgos Oikonomikon*, judgment of 16 September 2010, not yet published, Rec. 64; see also, Case C-81/05, *Cordero Alonso v Fondo de Garantía Salarial* [2006] ECR I-7569, Rec. 37.

[54] Case C-442/00, *Rodríguez Caballero v Fogasa* [2002] ECR I-11915, Rec. 33.

[55] Council Directive 80/987, OJ 1980 L 283/23, now replaced by Council Directive 2008/94, OJ 2008 L 283/36, on the protection of employees in the event of the insolvency of the employer.

[56] *Rodríguez Caballero v Fogasa, supra* note 54, Rec. 30.

women who had experienced discrimination should be limited where this could place the member state concerned at a competitive disadvantage:

> [I]t must be concluded that the economic aim pursued by Article 119 of the Treaty, namely the elimination of distortions of competition between undertakings established in different Member States, is secondary to the social aim pursued by the same provision, which constitutes the expression of a fundamental human right.[57]

As mentioned earlier, this is a vivid illustration of how constitutionalization of an employment right may help to resist arguments that its scope should be traded-off with the pursuit of economic efficiency objectives.[58]

B. Constitutionalization through Charters and Treaties

The constitutionalization of aspects of the employment relationship has also been the outcome of initiatives taken by the member states. Over the years, there has been a succession of amendments to the founding Treaties and these gradually shifted towards an acknowledgement that EU employment law engaged fundamental rights.[59] As mentioned in the introduction, a decisive step in the direction of constitutionalization was the proclamation of the 1989 Community Charter of the Fundamental Social Rights of Workers. The Charter's contents were an unusual mix of declaratory provisions, combined with programmatic clauses. For instance, point 13 recognized that the 'right to resort to collective action in the event of a conflict of interests shall include the right to strike'; however, there was no implication that the (then) EEC could or would seek to implement this right. In contrast, point 19 states that 'every worker must enjoy satisfactory health and safety conditions' and calls for 'further harmonisation' in this field. This mixture in approach reflects the politics of the Charter; it was expressly aimed at relaunching the social dimension of European integration and it became the basis for a subsequent legislative programme by the European Commission.[60] Its legacy, though, was to introduce the idea that employment rights were not simply a matter of 'ordinary' legislation; to some extent, they entailed the protection of fundamental rights.

The Charter's inference that norms of a higher legal status were at play demonstrably influenced the Court of Justice in certain subsequent cases on the interpretation of employment legislation. This is best illustrated in *BECTU*,[61] which concerned whether employees working on short contracts (for less than 13 weeks in duration) should be entitled to the right to paid holidays found within the Working Time Directive.[62] The Court took its lead from the provisions of the Charter; point 8 declared: 'every worker of the European Community shall have a right to a weekly rest period and to annual paid leave'. Accordingly, the Court held:

> It follows that the entitlement of every worker to paid annual leave must be regarded as a particularly important principle of Community social law from which there can be no

[57] Case C-50/96, *Deutsche Telekom AG v Schröder* [2000] ECR I-743, Rec. 57.

[58] Mantouvalou, *supra* note 16; Collins, *supra* note 12, at 12.

[59] E.g. in 1999, the Treaty of Amsterdam amended the EC Treaty to insert a reference in Art. 117 EC to the Council of Europe's European Social Charter.

[60] Barnard, *supra* note 21, at 14.

[61] Case C-173/99, *R v Secretary of State for Trade and Industry, ex parte Broadcasting, Entertainment, Cinematogaphic and Theatre Union (BECTU)* [2001] ECR I-4881.

[62] The original Directive was replaced with the following: Council Directive 2003/88, OJ 2003 L 299/9, concerning certain aspects of the organisation of working time.

derogations and whose implementation by the competent national authorities must be confined within the limits expressly laid down by Directive 93/104.[63]

Furthermore, it firmly rejected arguments from the United Kingdom concerning the administrative costs that would be entailed for small and medium-sized undertakings; the Court noted that improvements in health and safety 'should not be subordinated to purely economic considerations'.[64]

While the Court has continued to refer to the 1989 Charter as a guide when interpreting EU employment legislation,[65] it is now overshadowed by the legally binding provisions found in the EU Charter of Fundamental Rights. A wide variety of the Charter's provisions have a potential application to the employment relationship. For example, Article 12 on freedom of association expressly refers to trade unions, while Article 5 prohibits 'forced or compulsory labour'. Titles III and IV are likely to prove the most important parts of the Charter in relation to the workplace. Title III on equality sets out a prohibition of discrimination, as well as specific provisions relating to different groups vulnerable to discrimination, such as women and people with disabilities. Title IV on solidarity has been referred to by the Court of Justice as enumerating 'fundamental social rights'.[66] Its provisions focus on employment: workers' right to information and consultation; the right of collective bargaining and action; the right of access to placement services; protection from unjustified dismissal; the right to fair and just working conditions; the prohibition of child labour and the protection of young workers; the reconciliation of family and professional life.[67] Although these cover a broad swathe of employment law issues, they are expressed more tersely than in the 1989 Charter and certain rights are omitted altogether, most notably the right to fair remuneration.[68] Compared to the extensive detail in the 31 articles of the 1996 Revised European Social Charter (of the Council of Europe), the Charter of Fundamental Rights is a rather bald statement of core workplace rights.

The brevity of the social provisions in the Charter of Fundamental Rights is balanced by the reference in its preamble to 'the Social Charters adopted by the Community and by the Council of Europe', which seems to invite the Court of Justice to continue to take these instruments into account. Indeed, in some cases the Court has referred to both the 1989 Charter and the Charter of Fundamental Rights, indicating that it still regards the former as a relevant source.[69] The official explanations accompanying the Charter of Fundamental Rights are another point of reference, to which the Court of Justice is required to pay 'due regard'.[70] The explanations connect the Charter of Fundamental Rights to specific elements of EU employment legislation. For example, they describe Article 31 on fair and just working conditions as being 'based on' the Working Time Directive and the Framework Directive on health and safety.[71] This is significant because it flags up the constitutional relevance of such directives given their characterization as the expression of a right found in the Charter.

[63] *BECTU, supra* note 61, Rec. 43.
[64] Ibid., Rec. 59.
[65] E.g. Case C-303/06, *Coleman v Attridge Law and Law* [2008] ECR I-5603, at Rec. 43; *Zoi Chatzi, supra* note 53, Rec. 36.
[66] *Zoi Chatzi*, note 53, at Rec. 37.
[67] Arts 27–33.
[68] Point 5, 1989 Charter.
[69] E.g. Case C-341/05, *Laval, supra* note 48, at Rec. 90; Case C-149/10, *Zoi Chatzi, supra* note 53, at Recs 36–37.
[70] Preamble to the Charter of Fundamental Rights. See further: Explanations relation to the Charter of Fundamental Rights, OJ 2007 C 303/17.
[71] Council Directive 2003/88, OJ 2003 L 299/9 and Council Directive 89/391, OJ 1989 L 183/1.

In the initial period following the signing of the Charter of Fundamental Rights in 2000, but prior to it becoming legally binding in 2009, the Court of Justice was tentative in its use of the Charter. In *BECTU*, for instance, the Court refrained from referring to the Charter, even though this had been used by the Advocate General as an interpretative tool.[72] This situation has now changed, but the limited body of case law allows few conclusions to be drawn on the eventual impact of the Charter throughout employment law. As discussed in the following section, some recent case law in the field of equality has provided an initial insight into the way in which the Charter may contribute to the tendency to constitutionalize employment law. The mere fact that the Charter includes an inventory of employment rights alongside the well-established catalogue of civil and political rights is already a powerful signal that the protection of workers is not simply a matter of 'ordinary' legislation that can be freely changed according to the current political climate. While it would be an overstatement to suggest that the Charter converts every element of employment law into legislation of constitutional significance, it sets basic parameters and implies that there is an irreducible minimum of worker protection that must be guaranteed. For example, Article 27 provides that 'workers or their representatives must, at the appropriate levels, be guaranteed information and consultation in good time in the cases and under the conditions provided for by Community law and national law and practices'. This leaves a broad margin of discretion for the legislator as to how this right should be operationalized, but it would appear to exclude the possibility that the legislator could subsequently decide to deregulate this field by eliminating any duties on employers to engage in information and consultation.

Having introduced the concept of constitutionalization and examined evidence of how it has evolved within EU employment law, the remainder of the chapter examines two issues in employment law in order to assess the impact of constitutionalization: equality, and the personal scope of employment rights.

4. Constitutionalization via General Principles of Law: EU Equality Directives

This section of the chapter takes a specific area of EU employment law in order to look in more depth at the process of constitutionalization. EU equality law has expanded greatly over time and it is a major constraint on contractual freedom in relation to the workplace. An employer cannot, for example, take into account characteristics such as ethnic origin or sexual orientation in choosing which persons to offer employment contracts to, nor in the terms of those contracts. The mere existence of equality legislation is not, though, evidence by itself of constitutionalization; it could be akin to any other form of statutory regulation of the labour market. Instead, evidence of constitutionalization arises from the elevated status that the EU courts have attached to equality legislation and, latterly, the reflection of this process within the provisions of equality directives. This section begins by examining how workplace equality rights were constitutionalized, followed by analysis of recent equality case law which suggests a new turn in the constitutionalization process.

[72] Opinion of AG Tizzano, *BECTU*, *supra* note 61, at paras 26–28.

A. Constitutionalizing Equality Legislation

From today's standpoint, it may seem obvious that employment equality legislation has a constitutional relevance in so far as it is an expression of the fundamental right to equal treatment and freedom from discrimination. Yet the starting premise of EU equality law was not the protection of fundamental rights. As is well documented, the rationale for Article 119 EEC on equal pay for women and men was concern that the exploitation of cheap female labour in some member states could provide an unfair competitive advantage within the common market.[73] During the 1970s, the first wave of EU social legislation was adopted, including Directive 75/117[74] on equal pay and Directive 76/207[75] on equal treatment in employment. These instruments were alongside other Directives on collective redundancies[76] and the transfer of undertakings.[77] Examining the language of these initial employment law Directives, there is little evidence that they were imagined as instruments for the protection of fundamental social rights. The preamble of the 1975 Equal Pay Directive refers to 'the establishment and functioning of the common market' as its rationale and this is also the approach found within the Directives on collective redundancies and the transfer of undertakings. It is only the 1976 Equal Treatment Directive that does not place itself explicitly within the framework of market-making objectives; its preamble evokes a broader goal of improving living and working conditions. The predominant emphasis on economic objectives reflects the limited legal competence of the EEC for social legislation and the need to present such measures as furthering the completion of the common market.

The initial push to reconceptualize equality legislation as having a higher legal significance can be traced to the case law of the Court of Justice. In *Defrenne v SABENA (III)*, it gave an unambiguous signal regarding its perspective:

> The Court has repeatedly stated that respect for fundamental personal human rights is one of the general principles of Community law, the observance of which it has a duty to ensure. There can be no doubt that the elimination of discrimination based on sex forms part of those fundamental rights.[78]

The recognition of the connection between human rights protection and gender equality law is not a theme that the Court has frequently explored in subsequent case law, but there are occasions where this appears to tip the balance in favour of an expansive reading of the legislation. The most visible example is the case law on discrimination relating to gender reassignment. In *P v S*, the Court falls back on human rights-based reasoning to explain why discrimination against a transgender man constitutes sex discrimination: 'to tolerate such discrimination would be tantamount, as regards such a person, to a failure to respect the dignity and freedom to which he or she is entitled, and which the Court has a duty to safeguard'.[79] In two subsequent cases, the Court was confronted with situations of inequality in employment and social security benefits related to the inability of the individuals concerned to alter their birth certificates to reflect their actual gender

[73] D. Hoskyns, *Integrating Gender—Women, Law and Politics in the European Union* (1996), at 49; Fredman, 'Discrimination Law in the EU: Labour Market Regulation or Fundamental Social Rights', in H. Collins, P. Davies, and R. Rideout (eds), *Legal Regulation of the Employment Relation* (2000) 183, at 185.

[74] OJ 1975 L 45/19.

[75] OJ 1976 L 39/40.

[76] Council Directive 75/129, OJ 1975 L 48/29.

[77] Council Directive 77/187, OJ 1977 L 61/26.

[78] Case 149/77, *Defrenne III* [1978] ECR 1365, Recs 26–27.

[79] Case C-13/94, *P v S and Cornwall County Council* [1996] ECR I-2143, Rec. 22.

identity. The Court eschewed a formalistic interpretation of gender equality legislation and instead concentrated on the underlying principles, holding that there was inequality of treatment connected to the breach of the individuals' human rights.[80]

The Court's willingness to decouple equality legislation from market regulation objectives has been gradually reflected in alterations to the legal framework. This shift in paradigm emerges clearly following the 1999 amendments to the EC Treaty. A new Article 3(2) was added setting an autonomous objective for the Union of eliminating inequalities and promoting equality between women and men.[81] Furthermore, the competence of the EC for combating discrimination was extended to cover the grounds of racial or ethnic origin, religion or belief, age, disability, and sexual orientation.[82] This led to a new generation of equality legislation where the human rights foundation of the law is expressly acknowledged.[83] The preambles of the 2000 Racial Equality and Employment Equality Directives cite a wide range of international human rights treaties, the European Convention on Human Rights (ECHR) and common constitutional principles as part of their explanatory rationale.[84] In a similar vein, the 2006 'Recast' Gender Directive, which consolidates much of the legislation relating to gender equality in employment, cites in its preamble the 'fundamental principle' of equality between men and women and the relevant provisions of the EU Charter of Fundamental Rights.[85] This tendency to equate equality legislation with the protection of fundamental rights, in particular international human rights, begins to set it apart from other types of EU employment legislation. For example, the 1970s directives on collective redundancies and the transfer of undertakings were replaced with revised versions in 1998 and 2001 respectively.[86] While the preambles of both now mention the 1989 EC Social Charter, their legal foundation remained the furtherance of the Internal Market.[87] Based purely on an analysis of the text of the directives, it would be hard to escape the conclusion that the legislator viewed the directives on equality as bearing a greater significance for fundamental rights protection than those on redundancies and the transfer of undertakings.[88]

B. General Principles as an Autonomous Source of Rights?

The process discussed above portrays constitutionalization as a method that impacts on the way in which law is interpreted and understood. Specifically, it has allowed the Court

[80] Case C-117/01, *KB v NHS Trust Pensions Agency* [2004] ECR I-541; Case C-423/04, *Richards v Secretary of State for Work and Pensions* [2006] ECR I-3585. See further, Bell, 'Gender Identity and Sexual Orientation: Alternative Pathways in EU Equality Law', 60 *American Journal of Comparative Law* (2012) 127.

[81] Now Art. 8 TFEU.

[82] Art. 19 TFEU (former Art. 13 EC).

[83] Schiek, 'A New Framework on Equal Treatment of Persons in EC Law?', 8 *ELRev* (2002) 290.

[84] Recs 2 and 3, Council Directive 2000/43, OJ 2000 L 180/22, implementing the principle of equal treatment between persons irrespective of racial or ethnic origin; Recs 1 and 4, Council Directive 2000/78, OJ 2000 L 303/16, establishing a general framework for equal treatment in employment and occupation.

[85] Recs 2 and 5, Council Directive 2006/54, OJ 2006 L 204/23, on the implementation of the principle of equal opportunities and equal treatment of men and women in matters of employment and occupation (recast).

[86] Council Directive 98/59, OJ 1998 L 225/16, on the approximation of the laws of the Member States relating to collective redundancies; Council Directive 2001/23, *supra* note 18.

[87] The Directives were based on Art. 94 EC (now Art. 115 TFEU).

[88] E.g. the Collective Redundancies Directive could have been linked to the protection of the right to information and consultation found within Art. 29 of the 1996 Revised European Social Charter, but this is not mentioned in the Directive's preamble.

to adopt an expansive reading of equality directives and to lead the law in unanticipated directions, such as the case law on gender reassignment. Nonetheless, the existence of secondary legislation remains crucial because this is the conduit through which general principles of law can take effect. At an early stage, the Court of Justice appeared to exclude the possibility that general principles could have an autonomous force in the absence of any substantive legal provisions. In *Defrenne v SABENA (III)*, the Court considered the airline's contractual term requiring female cabin attendants to retire at the age of 40; no such term was included in the contracts of male cabin attendants.[89] It concluded that discrimination in retirement ages could not be characterized as a violation of the right to equal pay and, at the relevant time, there was no EEC legislation prohibiting discrimination in working conditions between women and men. The question arose, therefore, whether the general principle of equality within Community law could be relied upon as an autonomous source of rights for Ms Defrenne in relation to her discriminatory dismissal. This was rejected by the Court on the basis that:

> the Community had not, at the time of the events now before the Belgian courts, assumed any responsibility for supervising and guaranteeing the observance of the principle of equality between men and women in working conditions other than remuneration.[90]

This point of law arose again in the 1998 case of *Grant v South-West Trains*.[91] The crux of the case was a contractual benefit providing free rail travel to employees and their partners, provided that the employee was either married or had been in a relationship with an opposite-sex partner for more than two years. This excluded Ms Grant's same-sex partner. While the case primarily turned on whether her treatment could be construed as less favourable treatment on grounds of sex (which the Court rejected), an alternative legal argument was that discrimination based on sexual orientation was contrary to the general principle of respect for fundamental rights and that this could be directly applied to the contract of employment. The Court resisted the apparent attempt to give autonomous force to fundamental rights within EC law:

> [A]lthough respect for the fundamental rights which form an integral part of those general principles of law is a condition of the legality of Community acts, those rights cannot in themselves have the effect of extending the scope of the Treaty provisions beyond the competences of the Community.[92]

At this juncture, it appears to be a settled position that employees cannot derive free-standing rights from the general principles of EU law, such as respect for fundamental rights. The only exception to this position was with regard to employees of the EU institutions. This distinction is based on the Court's view that the legality of the acts of the Union's institutions are subject to compliance with the general principles of law and this extends to situations when the Union acts as an employer.[93]

The role played by general principles of law was thrust into controversy by the Court's 2005 decision in *Mangold v Helm*.[94] The case concerned a provision of German law permitting employers to use fixed-term contracts when employing workers over the age of

[89] *Supra* note 78, at Rec. 12.

[90] Ibid., Rec. 30.

[91] Case C-249/96, *Grant v South-West Trains* [1998] ECR I-621.

[92] Ibid., Rec. 45. See further, C. Favilli, *La Non-Discriminazione nell'Unione Europea* (2008), at 196–198.

[93] *Defrenne (III), supra* note 78, at Rec. 29. See further, E. Ellis, *EU Anti-Discrimination Law* (2005), at 337–341.

[94] Case C-144/04, *Mangold v Helm* [2005] ECR I-9981.

52 without the normal requirement of objective justification for using temporary rather than indefinite contracts. The Court deemed this to be contrary to the Employment Equality Directive because it was direct discrimination on grounds of age that was not objectively justified.[95] The application of the Directive to the facts of the dispute was, however, legally complicated. On the one hand, the litigation was between two private parties and the Court has consistently affirmed that directives cannot give rise to horizontal direct effect; that is, their provisions cannot be directly enforced in national courts against a private party. On the other hand, the facts arose during the extended period granted to Germany for transposition of the age provisions of the Employment Equality Directive, so recourse to the doctrine of direct effect was also obstructed by the non-expiry of the time limit for implementation. Ultimately, the Court circumvented both of these obstacles by turning to its case law on general principles of law.[96]

The Court's starting point concerned the place of the Employment Equality Directive in the hierarchy of legal sources:

> Directive 2000/78 does not itself lay down the principle of equal treatment in the field of employment and occupation... the source of the actual principle underlying the prohibition of those forms of discrimination being found, as is clear from the third and fourth recitals in the preamble of the Directive, in various international instruments and in the constitutional traditions common to the Member States.[97]

This illustrates the importance of references to international human rights treaties within the Directive's preamble; the Court takes seriously these indicators of the Directive's rationale and its constitutional significance. This apparently emboldens it to ensure a high standard of protection of such rights:

> Consequently, observance of the general principle of equal treatment, in particular in respect of age, cannot as such be conditional upon the expiry of the period allowed for the Member States for the transposition of a Directive intended to lay down a general framework for combating discrimination on grounds of age, in particular so far as the organization of appropriate legal remedies, the burden of proof, protection from victimization, social dialogue, affirmative action and other specific measures to implement such a Directive are concerned.[98]

The tenor of the decision in *Mangold* implies that the general principle of equality, as regards age, is the legal underpinning of the prohibition of age discrimination within employment. Moreover, the contents of the general principle are not limited to the prohibition of discrimination, but they extend to include a requirement to take measures for the enforcement of the principle, such as protection from victimization. This picture relegates the Directive to a residual role whereby it makes visible obligations that were already inherent within the general principle. Nevertheless, the Court did not go so far as to advocate an entirely autonomous application of the general principle to any employment contract. The contested German legislation regarding the use of fixed-term contracts stemmed from Germany's implementation of the Directive on Fixed-Term Work.[99] Therefore, the Court was able to maintain its established orthodoxy that respect

[95] Ibid., Rec. 65.

[96] In relation to the non-expiry of the time limit for implementing the Directive, the Court indicated that this was qualified by the duty on states not to adopt measures incompatible with the aims of the Directive during the transposition period (Ibid., Rec. 72).

[97] Ibid., Rec. 74. [98] Ibid., Rec. 76.

[99] Council Directive 1999/70, OJ 1999 L 175/43, concerning the Framework Agreement on fixed-term work concluded by ETUC, UNICE and CEEP. For the legislative history of the German rule, see Recs 16–19, *Mangold, supra* note 94.

for the general principles of EC law was required when member states were implementing EC legislation.[100] Consequently, the national court should set aside any provision of national law that was in conflict with those principles.

The decision in *Mangold* stimulated a strong and often critical debate amongst academics and Advocates General.[101] In the context of this chapter, the key issue is what *Mangold* revealed about the constitutionalization of employment law. Without doubt, the Court recognizes that there are norms of higher legal status embedded within the Employment Equality Directive. Furthermore, by suggesting that the full panoply of enforcement measures found within the Directive are also expressions of the general principle of equality, the Court inclines towards the view that the entire Directive bears a constitutional significance. The Court apparently sees no objection to applying constitutional principles in the context of a private employment contract; indeed, it goes out of its way to ensure that non-discrimination on grounds of age can be secured by national courts even where the absence of horizontal direct effect of Directives presented a major stumbling block to achieving this end. Another striking feature of the decision, but one often overlooked, is the implicit hierarchy that the Court establishes between its treatment of the Fixed-Term Work Directive and the Employment Equality Directive. In contrast to its rich discourse surrounding the interpretation of the Employment Equality Directive, the Court's examination of the Fixed-Term Work Directive is relatively perfunctory and there is no evidence that the Court viewed this as engaging any fundamental social rights. This dichotomy reveals an apparent distinction between constitutionalized legislation, such as the Employment Equality Directive, and other elements of EU employment law that might be described as 'ordinary' legislation.

C. The Expanding Role of General Principles within Equality Law

The decision in *Mangold* raised questions about the ultimate destination of the Court's case law and whether it would eventually allow the general principle of equality to be directly applicable in a manner equivalent to Treaty provisions.[102] The Court pulled back from any such trajectory in *Bartsch*.[103] This was another case of age discrimination between private parties that arose before the deadline for implementation of the Employment Equality Directive.[104] Unlike in *Mangold*, there was no immediate connection to any other element of EC law; it could not be argued that compliance with the general principle of equality was required because the member state was implementing EC legislation. In a very short judgment, the Court dismisses the case because there was 'no link with Community law'.[105]

[100] Ibid., Rec. 75.

[101] For an overview, see Opinion of AG Sharpston, Case C-427/06, *Bartsch v Bosch und Siemens Hausgeräte Altersfürsorge GmbH* [2008] ECR I-7245, paras 31–41.

[102] McCrudden and Kountouris, 'Human Rights and European Equality Law', in H. Meenan (ed), *Equality Law in an Enlarged European Union—Understanding the Article 13 Directives* (2007) 73, at 90.

[103] *Bartsch, supra* note 101.

[104] The case concerned company pension scheme guidelines that limited access to a survivor's pension benefit to surviving spouses who were less than 15 years younger than the deceased. Mrs Bartsch was 21 years younger than her late husband and she was refused the survivor's pension as a result.

[105] Ibid., Rec. 25. The brevity of the judgment contrasts with the rich analysis of AG Sharpston of the debate post-*Mangold* and her conclusion that general principles of law should not be given an autonomous application.

Two years later, however, the Court reignited the issue through its judgment in *Kücükdeveci*.[106] As in *Mangold*, the case revolved around a provision of German legislation that the Court deemed to be unlawful age discrimination.[107] The deadline for implementation of the Employment Equality Directive had now passed, but the case was between an employee and a private employer, and the Court reiterated that Directives cannot give rise to horizontal direct effect.[108] This led the Court into the same territory as that explored in *Mangold*; could general principles be a route for the enforcement of equal treatment rights within private employment relationships in a situation where a Directive could not be directly relied upon?

Advocate General Bot proposed a novel solution. He called upon the Court to recognise that certain directives are designed 'to facilitate the implementation of the general principle of equal treatment and non-discrimination' and the special status of these instruments should constitute an exception to the general restriction on the horizontal direct effect of directives.[109] This approach seems to epitomise the idea of constitutionalization; certain legal instruments would be granted an elevated legal status based on their connection to the protection of fundamental rights. The Court forged a different path, but one that produced a similar end result. Before considering the Directive's provisions, the Court identifies its point of departure as being two key legal sources: the general principle of equality in EU law *and* the right to non-discrimination found within Article 21(1) of the EU Charter of Fundamental Rights.[110] Even more clearly than in *Mangold*, the Directive is relegated to a secondary role, being a conduit for the application of the general principle:

> It follows that it is the general principle of European Union law prohibiting all discrimination on grounds of age, as given expression in Directive 2000/78, which must be the basis of the examination of whether European Union law precludes national legislation such as that at issue in the main proceedings.[111]

In an interpretative leap, the Court concludes that the 'full effectiveness' of the general principle requires the national court to disapply any conflicting national legislation 'falling within the scope of European Union law'.[112] Although a subtle change in wording, the Court's previous case law held that member states primarily had to comply with general principles when *implementing* EU law.[113] In *Kücükdeveci*, the Civil Code provisions on length of notice entitlements dated from 1926,[114] so it would be a stretch of the legal imagination to describe these as 'implementing' EU law. Under the Court's new formulation, the general principle of equality is directly applicable in respect of any national measure than falls within the material scope of the Employment Equality Directive. In other words, any national legislation that relates to employment, access to self-employment, vocational training, or organizations of workers, employers, and

[106] Case C-555/07, *Kücükdeveci v Swedex GmbH & Co KG*, judgment of 19 January 2010, not yet published.

[107] Ibid., Rec. 43. The period of notice to which an employee was entitled under the Civil Code accumulated according to the duration of the employment relationship; however, periods of employment prior to the age of 25 were not counted at all in calculating the employee's length of service.

[108] Ibid., Rec. 46.

[109] Opinion of 7 July 2009, para. 70.

[110] Recs 21–22.

[111] Rec. 27.

[112] Rec. 53.

[113] 'Editorial Comments: The scope of application of the general principles of Union law: an ever expanding Union?', 47 *CMLRev* (2010) 1589, at 1590; Opinion of AG Sharpston, *supra* note 101, para. 69.

[114] Opinion of AG Bot, *supra* note 106, para. 38.

professionals[115] is potentially subject to the general principle of equality. In terms of legal effects, this is rather close to permitting horizontal direct effect of equality Directives.[116]

Notwithstanding the innovative approach in *Kücükdeveci*, the Court continues to refrain from endorsing a fully autonomous application of the general principle of equality. This was exemplified in *Römer*,[117] which concerned access to a supplementary retirement pension for a man in a registered same-sex partnership in circumstances where the benefit was restricted to those who were married. Concretely, this led to a reduction in the monthly pension for Mr Römer of around €300. The Court concluded that the denial of access to this benefit constituted direct discrimination on grounds of sexual orientation if the national court viewed same-sex couples as being in a comparable situation to married couples for the purposes of that benefit.[118] Assuming that it was unlawful discrimination, the question arose of retrospective entitlement to the supplementary pension. Advocate General Jääskinen emphasized the role to be played by the general principle of equality irrespective of sexual orientation, taking into account the ECHR and the EU Charter of Fundamental Rights.[119] Citing *Mangold* and *Kücükdeveci*, he argued that the Employment Equality Directive was merely an expression of a pre-existing principle of equality and the entitlement to retrospective payment of the retirement benefit should not be restricted to the date of entry into force of the Directive on 3 December 2003.[120] Instead, he concluded that Mr Römer should have been entitled to the benefit from the date that he formed his registered partnership (15 October 2001).

In contrast, the Court returns to the more cautious terrain of its decision in *Bartsch*. It held that the national legislation on access to the supplementary pension only entered into the scope of EU law once the deadline for implementation of the Employment Equality Directive had passed; the general principle of equality irrespective of sexual orientation could not give rise to a free-standing right to equal treatment prior to this point in time.[121]

D. Constitutionalization and EU Equality law: Unfinished Business?

EU equality legislation provides a vivid illustration of the process of constitutionalization in action. Initially, gender equality provisions lacked any special legal significance; they were simply part of a range of 'ordinary' instruments designed to improve the functioning of the common market. The gradual reinterpretation of the role of equality legislation by courts and the legislature has led to a position where this area of law is now recognized for its close connection to the protection of fundamental rights.

[115] Art. 3, Directive 2000/78, *supra* note 84.

[116] Thüsing and Horler, 'Case comment: Case C-555/07 *Kücükdeveci v Swedex Gmbh & Co KG*, judgment of the Court (Grand Chamber) of 19 January 2010, not yet reported', 47 *CMLRev* (2010) 1161, at 1170. In *Kücükdeveci*, the Court requires national courts to *disapply* national legislation where this is in conflict with the general principle of equality. This leaves open the question whether, in the absence of any national implementing legislation, the general principle could be directly applied as a source of rights. If this were true, then there would be no distinction between this and the doctrine of direct effect, but it remains unclear if the Court intends to go this far: see further, Opinion of AG Bot, *supra* note 106, para. 63.

[117] Case C-147/08, *Römer v Freie und Hansestadt Hamburg*, judgment of 10 May 2011, not yet published.

[118] Ibid., Rec. 52. The Court provides a strong indication in its reasoning that the national court should regard these situations as comparable (Recs 42–51).

[119] Opinion of 15 July 2010, para. 147.

[120] Ibid., para. 146.

[121] *Römer*, note 117, at Recs 60 and 63.

The acknowledgement that equality legislation engages rights of constitutional significance impacts on the way in which the Court exercises its scrutiny. On some occasions, the Court clearly deploys the fundamental rights dimension to equality legislation in order to justify bold and imaginative interpretations of its scope. This has been particularly evident in recent case law where the Court has sought to ensure that employees can enforce EU equality rights against private employers even in situations where, according to the normal principles of EU law, this would not be possible.

It would be misleading, however, to exaggerate the impact of constitutionalization. While the discussion above has concentrated on high profile examples where the role of fundamental rights in the interpretation of the legislation is rendered visible, most equality cases continue to be resolved through a straightforward interpretation of the legislation without the Court needing to invoke constitutional principles. Cases like *Mangold* and *Kücükdeveci* have to be read alongside other cases on age discrimination where the Court is more cautious and conventional in its legal reasoning.[122] It is often unclear why in one case the Court embarks upon an ambitious and innovative pathway drawing upon the general principle of equality while in other cases this aspect remains completely absent.

Looking to the future, an unresolved matter is the impact of the Charter of Fundamental Rights and its relationship to the unwritten general principles of law.[123] Article 6 TEU provides a new Treaty foundation for both the Charter and the general principle of respect for fundamental rights. *Kücükdeveci* is a firm indication that the Court does not (currently) intend to replace its case law on the general principle of equality with a primary emphasis on the equality articles in the Charter. Instead, it blends these instruments together, citing both as authority for applying the principle of equality in respect of age discrimination. In this respect, it seems that the new legal status of the Charter reinforces an existing trajectory towards constitutionalization and it may help to explain the Court's willingness to push the boundaries of equality law within *Kücükdeveci*. Similar signals can be gleaned from the Court's decision in *Test-Achats*.[124] In this case, the Court took the unusual step of striking down an exception to the prohibition of discrimination that was expressly included within secondary legislation. Specifically, the 2004 Directive on gender equality in goods and services permitted member states, under certain conditions, to allow proportionate differences in premiums and benefits within insurance and financial services based on sex.[125] The Court held that the indefinite nature of this exception was not compatible with Articles 21 and 23 of the Charter and that it would be invalid with effect from 21 December 2012.[126] As with *Mangold* and *Kücükdeveci*, this decision reinforces a tendency to focus on the primacy of constitutional sources, whether the general principle of equality or the Charter, and to place less weight on secondary legislation. Again, the Court shows

[122] E.g. Case C-388/07, *R (the Incorporated Trustees of the National Council for Ageing (Age Concern England)) v Secretary of State for Business, Enterprise and Regulatory Reform* [2009] ECR I-1569; Case C-45/09, *Rosenbladt v Oellerking Gebäudereinigungsges. mbH*, judgment of 12 October 2010, not yet published; Joined Cases C-159/10 and C-160/10, *Fuchs and Köhler v Land Hessen*, judgment of 21 July 2011, not yet published.

[123] Peers, 'The EU Charter of Rights and the Right to Equality', 11 *ERA Forum* (2011) 571, at 583.

[124] Case C-236/09, *Test-Achats, supra* note 15.

[125] Art. 5(2), Council Directive 2004/113, OJ 2004 L 373/37, implementing the principle of equal treatment between men and women in the access to and supply of goods and services.

[126] *Test-Achats, supra* note 124, Rec. 32. This was the date specified within the Directive when member states were required to review the need for this exception, but individual states would have been free to decide to continue to permit such differences in treatment.

no reluctance to apply the full vigour of constitutional equality principles into private contractual relationships.

Test-Achats may also reopen the debate on the direct applicability of the general principle of equality. While the Court has limited this to the scope of Directives where the deadline for implementation has passed (as in *Bartsch* and *Römer*), the decision in *Test-Achats* reveals that limitations housed within the Directives may be vulnerable to challenge as inconsistent with the Charter's equality guarantees. Once a broad sector of activity has been subject to legislative regulation, such as employment or services, then the Charter rights to equality appear to be directly applicable notwithstanding any attempts to curtail this within the legislation.[127] Restrictions in existing equality legislation such as the exclusion of protection from disability and age discrimination within the armed forces,[128] or the possibility to maintain different ages for men and women in access to retirement pensions,[129] could now be subject to judicial review for compatibility with the equality provisions found within the Charter of Fundamental Rights. Nevertheless, it seems unlikely that the Court will take the radical step of embracing a full and unrestrained direct applicability for the general principle of equality. Likewise, it would be unrealistic to expect that the Court will rely regularly on the Charter to unpick the careful political compromises reflected in equality legislation. Decisions such as *Mangold* or *Test-Achats* provoke genuine controversy over the Court's respect for the limits to EU competences and established legal doctrines (such as direct effect). In so far as any pattern is emerging, the Court seems willing *on occasions* to invoke the Charter and/or the general principle of equality to enhance the effectiveness of EU equality legislation. The Court is undoubtedly cognizant of the polemical debate that surrounds such cases and this may account for its reluctance to engage more frequently with constitutional equality principles.

5. Searching the Outer Limits of Constitutionalization: The Personal Scope of Employment Rights

A. Introduction

The previous section considered an area of employment law where there is explicit evidence of constitutionalization and where there is a wide consensus that the law engages fundamental human rights; the principle of equal treatment and/or the right to non-discrimination are found in most national constitutions as well as many international and European human rights instruments. In order to provide contrast, this section examines a branch of employment law where it is more difficult to identify an overt connection to internationally recognized fundamental rights. In addition, this case study deals with an issue where the role for the EU is partial and contested, unlike the solid corpus of EU equality legislation.

In any system of employment law, it seems inevitable that there is a gateway question regarding who is entitled to benefit from the rights conferred. If, for example, the law establishes a minimum entitlement to paid annual holidays, then we need to know who enjoys this right. The traditional outlook has been to draw a binary distinction between employed persons and self-employed persons; the former falling inside the

[127] Ibid., Recs 20–21. [128] Art. 3(4), Directive 2000/78, *supra* note 84.

[129] Art. 7(1)(a), Council Directive 79/7, OJ 1979 L 6/24, on the progressive implementation of the principle of equal treatment for men and women in matters of social security.

circle of beneficiaries of employment law and the latter falling outside. This simplistic dichotomy has been subject to academic critique for failing to reflect the complexity of the modern labour market.[130] The decline in the standard employment relationship has spawned a rich array of different contractual arrangements for the performance of work. For example, the direct relationship between employer and worker is sometimes replaced by the insertion of third parties, such as temporary work agencies. Leighton and Wynn draw attention to the emergence of 'quadrilateral' employment relationships where individuals work through personal service companies who in turn are provided to an employer via an agency.[131] Moreover, the classic image of the self-employed person as an entrepreneur running her own business does not capture the diversity of situations that fall under this label. For instance, many individuals working in the construction industry are hired on a casual basis under a contract to provide services. This leads to a position where, in the United Kingdom, one-third of construction workers are estimated to be self-employed,[132] yet many would not resemble the typical image of an independent business. Some European legal systems have resorted to the creation of intermediate categorizations such as 'economically dependent autonomous workers' or 'para-subordinate' workers to address these social realities.[133]

From a private law perspective, the proliferation of working arrangements might be viewed as the ultimate expression of freedom of contract; individuals and firms are able to order their relations according to their preferences. Some individuals value the autonomy and flexibility of working (for example) as freelance consultants without the obligations inherent in a contract of employment.[134] Yet the inequality of bargaining power means that 'choice' is a mirage for many. It is reasonable to doubt whether, say, migrant agricultural workers recruited via transnational agencies have any significant bargaining power to shape the nature of their contractual relations.[135] In response, courts and legislators sometimes broaden the personal scope of employment rights in order to counter the risk of individuals being deprived of such rights through firms avoiding the contract of employment.

In relation to EU law, a complex picture emerges. There is no overarching status of 'worker' that applies in a uniform manner across all EU employment legislation. Instead, each individual piece of legislation has adopted its own stance on the personal scope of application. This variability has to be combined with the subsequent interpretative gloss from the Court of Justice. In relation to some employment rights, it applies a harmonized European definition of 'worker', while in other cases it leaves this as a matter for national discretion (subject to reasonable limits). The question explored by this section of the chapter is whether constitutionalization exerts an influence on determining the personal scope of employment rights. It begins by considering what, if any, fundamental rights are engaged in this area of law, followed by a review of three discrete areas of EU employment law.

[130] M. Freedland and N. Kountouris, *The Legal Construction of Personal Work Relations* (2011), at 104; Fredman, 'Women at Work: The Broken Promise of Flexicurity', 33 *ILJ* (2004) 299, at 307.

[131] Leighton and Wynn, 'Classifying Employment Relationships—More Sliding Doors or a Better Regulatory Framework?', 40 *ILJ* (2011) 5, at 28.

[132] D. Walters et al., 'The Role and Effectiveness of Safety Representatives in Influencing Workplace Health and Safety', Health and Safety Executive Research Report 363 (2005), at 81.

[133] Freedland and Kountouris, *supra* note 130, at 115.

[134] P. Leighton et al., *Out of the Shadows—Managing Self-Employed, Agency and Outsourced Workers* (2007), at 9.

[135] E.g. *Consistent Group Ltd v Kalwak* [2008] IRLR 505 (Court of Appeal).

B. Is There a 'Right' to be a Worker?

The first question that arises is whether there is any basis for treating the personal scope of employment rights as an issue of constitutional significance. Reformulated, we could ask whether there is any fundamental right to be treated as a 'worker'? Although recognition as a worker is often the doorway into employment rights, most international human rights instruments are silent as to its meaning. The Universal Declaration of Human Rights simply states that 'everyone who works has the right to just and favourable remuneration',[136] while 'everyone has the right to rest and leisure, including reasonable limitation of working hours and periodic holidays with pay'.[137] Part I of the European Social Charter (both in the 1961 version and in the 1996 revision) refers either to 'everyone' or 'all workers'. The Appendix to the Revised European Social Charter sheds some light on the intended meaning of this term by virtue of permitted exemptions. In relation to Article 24 on 'protection in cases of termination of employment', the Appendix clarifies that states may exclude fixed-term contract workers or 'workers engaged on a casual basis for a short period'. The logical implication of these exceptions is that, save where permitted, the Charter's personal scope extends to casual and/or temporary work.

The approach taken by the European Social Charter can be traced to that found in the instruments of the International Labour Organization (ILO). ILO Conventions frequently apply to the broad category of 'worker',[138] subject to specific exceptions.[139] In the late 1990s, the ILO attempted to confront directly the borders to the concept of 'work' by drafting a Convention on 'contract labour'. This would have extended core employment rights to:

> workers in 'triangular' relationships, as well as workers who perform work or provide services to other persons within the legal framework of a civil or commercial contract, but who in fact are dependent on or integrated into the firm for which they perform the work or provide the service in question.[140]

Nevertheless, agreement could not be reached and the planned Convention was not adopted.[141] Instead, the ILO returned to the issue via the softer mechanism of Recommendation 198 concerning the Employment Relationship.[142] This sought to balance the reality that 'situations exist where contractual arrangements can have the effect of depriving workers of the protection they are due',[143] while at the same time endorsing the position that worker protection 'should not interfere with true civil and commercial relationships'.[144] The Recommendation focuses on clarifying the criteria in national law and policy for identifying genuine employment relationships, as well as exhorting states to take steps to combat disguised employment.

[136] Art. 23(3). Similarly, the International Covenant on Economic, Social and Cultural Rights refers to 'the right of everyone to the enjoyment of just and favourable conditions of work' (Art. 7).

[137] Art. 24.

[138] E.g. the preamble to Convention 189 concerning Decent Work for Domestic Workers (16 June 2011) states 'international labour Conventions and Recommendations apply to all workers, including domestic workers, unless otherwise provided'.

[139] E.g. Convention 158 on Termination of Employment (1982) includes the same restrictions as those found in the Appendix of the Revised European Social Charter.

[140] International Labour Conference, 'The Scope of the Employment Relationship', Report V, 91st Session, 2003, at 6.

[141] See further, N. Countouris, *The Changing Law of the Employment Relationship—Comparative Analyses in the European Context* (2007), at 161.

[142] Adopted 15 June 2006. [143] Preamble. [144] Para. 8.

Against this backdrop, it is unsurprising to discover that the EU Charter of Fundamental Rights is also framed by open-textured references to 'every worker'[145] and the meaning of this term is not further elucidated within the Explanations attached to the Charter. The general tenor of international instruments suggests a common intention to ensure broad coverage of different types of workers, but this is something short of a specific 'right' to be treated as a worker. As the failed ILO Convention on Contract Labour revealed, there is limited international consensus on the application of fundamental employment rights to persons working on the hazy boundary between employment relationships and commercial relationships. Given the ambiguity surrounding the regulation of this issue, it might be concluded that this is one area of employment law where constitutionalization is unlikely to have an impact. Unlike equality law, it is hard to make the case that ensuring the protection of (for example) quasi self-employed persons is a matter of constitutional significance. This might seem to be a good example of an issue that is left to the regulation of 'ordinary' employment law and the balancing of competing economic and social interests. Even here, though, evidence arises to suggest that constitutionalization does have an impact, albeit more indirect and subtle than in relation to equality law.

The potential impact of constitutionalization is exposed in situations where the Court of Justice is confronted with the need to determine whether a particular individual is entitled to be treated as a worker. The Court could resolve such interpretative questions without any recourse to constitutional principles or fundamental rights. It could, for instance, leave this to be resolved by national courts in accordance with national definitions of the employment relationship, or it could apply conventional techniques of legislative interpretation. What emerges, however, is evidence that the Court's approach to the personal scope of employment rights is shaped by an analysis of whether the rights at stake are fundamental within the EU legal order. This pathway for the Court was evident from its early engagement with this topic. A cornerstone of the common market was the free movement of workers and inevitably this posed the question of who was a 'worker'? As is well documented, the Court decided that a harmonized concept of 'worker' should be applied in order to ensure consistency across the member states.[146] To this end, it adopted the following formula: 'the essential feature of an employment relationship, however, is that for a certain period of time a person performs services for and under the direction of another person in return for which he receives remuneration'.[147] In the context of this chapter, it is telling to note the justification that the Court provides for adopting a relatively broad understanding of the status of worker: 'these concepts define the field of application of one of the fundamental freedoms guaranteed by the Treaty and, as such, may not be interpreted restrictively'.[148] The constitutional significance of free movement of workers becomes crucial in the Court's approach to determining the personal scope of this right.

The remainder of this section explores whether there is evidence that the Court extends this approach across employment rights. Is its outlook on the personal scope of employment rights determined by whether the right in question is deemed to be one of constitutional significance? To that end, three examples are considered: equality law; the Working Time Directive; and the Acquired Rights Directive.

145 E.g. Arts 30 and 31.

146 Case 53/81, *Levin v Staatssecretaris van Justitie* [1982] ECR 1035, Rec. 11.

147 Case 66/85, *Lawrie-Blum v Land Baden-Württemberg,* [1986] ECR 2121, Rec. 17.

148 *Levin, supra* note 146, Rec. 13.

C. Equality Law

The personal scope of EU equality law has been explored in a significant number of cases involving various directives and treaty provisions. This section does not attempt to provide a comprehensive analysis of this rich body of law,[149] but it considers several examples from EU gender equality law to illustrate the role that constitutionalization plays in the Court's approach to this issue. The case of *Allonby*[150] is particularly illuminating. Ms Allonby had been working for six years as a part-time lecturer employed on a succession of one-year contracts and paid on an hourly basis. For financial reasons, the college decided to cease direct employment of part-time lecturers and instead to recruit them via a temporary employment agency. Ms Allonby was dismissed, but then continued to work for the college via the agency. This had the effect, however, of reducing her salary and depriving her of certain employment benefits, including exclusion from the occupational pension scheme for teachers. The exclusion from the pension scheme was challenged as a potential breach of the right to equal pay for women and men in former Article 141 EC[151] due to the significantly higher number of female teachers affected by this reorganization of employment relationships.[152]

The preliminary stumbling block for Ms Allonby's claim was whether she fell into the category of 'worker' for the purposes of the right to equal pay. The temporary work agency emphasized that it applied a condition that all lecturers registering with the agency did so as self-employed persons.[153] There was no definition of 'worker' in Article 141 EC and the Court accepted that it was not intended to 'include independent providers of services who are not in a relationship of subordination with the person who receives the services'.[154] Nevertheless, the Court rejected the idea that the nature of the relationship could be determined according to national legal definitions of employment/self-employment, especially if the individual's independence was 'merely notional'.[155] Instead, it reiterated the broad definition of worker previously crafted in free movement law. In so doing, the Court chose to constrain both national autonomy and party autonomy; even though the contractual arrangements had been designed to reflect the domestic legal approach to self-employment, these were supplanted by the Court's conception of what it means to be a worker. Tellingly, the Court justifies this approach by reference to constitutional principles. It described the Treaty right to equal pay as 'a specific expression of the principle of equality for men and women, which forms part of the fundamental principles protected by the Community legal order'.[156] Advocate General Geelhoed also drew attention to the right to gender equality in the Charter of Fundamental Rights and viewed this as essential protection for workers 'whether employed or self-employed'.[157]

The breadth of the personal scope of EU gender equality law is reinforced by the decision in *Danosa*.[158] Ms Danosa was appointed to be the sole member of a Board of Directors for a limited liability company. Seven months later, the general meeting of the shareholders of the company decided to remove her from this position. At the time, she

[149] For more extensive analysis, see Countouris, *supra* note 141, at 179–185.

[150] Case C-256/01, *Allonby v Accrington & Rossendale College* [2004] ECR I-873.

[151] Now Art. 157 TFEU.

[152] Of those made redundant and then re-employed via the agency, 231 were women and 110 were men. Of those retained as directly employed lecturers by the College, the majority were men (Opinion of AG Geelhoed, 2 April 2003, para. 11).

[153] Opinion of AG, para. 31. [154] Rec. 68 of judgment. [155] Rec. 71.

[156] Rec. 65. [157] Opinion of AG, para. 53.

[158] Case C-232/09, *Danosa v LKB Līzings SIA, supra* note 11.

was 11 weeks pregnant and she brought a case challenging her dismissal. The referring court raised the question of whether this was compatible with the EU Pregnant Workers Directive, which includes protection from dismissal during pregnancy.[159] A key issue was whether an individual performing such a role fell within the personal scope of the Pregnant Workers Directive. The company and the Latvian government argued that this was not an employment relationship, but one based on civil law. In their view, applying the Directive to this situation would be 'an unwarranted interference in shareholders' rights'.[160] Despite this appeal to commercial freedom, the Court felt that the core elements of its concept of worker were present: remuneration for services performed and the carrying out of services under direction or control. In relation to the latter, it accepted that as a sole Board member, Ms Danosa had 'a margin of discretion in performing her duties'.[161] Yet the fact that the shareholders could dismiss her was taken, in itself, to provide evidence that she was working under the control of another body.[162] This is a remarkably broad concept of being a 'worker' that reduces the requirement of subordination to a minimal level. Most commercial relationships are likely to involve the provision of services for remuneration and the capacity for the service recipient to terminate the relationship. Arguably the decision in *Danosa* reflects the logic of constitutionalization; the Court's primary concern becomes the protection of the individual from a breach of fundamental rights and it downgrades the importance of the legal classification of her relationship. Faced with arguments over whether her situation fell into the scope of the Pregnant Workers Directive, the Equal Treatment Directive,[163] or a Directive on the Equal Treatment of Self-Employed Persons,[164] the Court simply declares:

> [W]hichever Directive applies, it is important to ensure, for the person concerned, the protection granted under EU law to pregnant women in cases where the legal relationship linking her to another person has been severed on account of her pregnancy.[165]

This line of reasoning seems to detach equality rights from the confines of the employment relationship and reflects the universalistic tendency of human rights law. The latter is typically founded on the protection of all persons simply by virtue of their human personhood. In so far as equality rights may be submerged into the general corpus of human rights law, then there is potential to side-step tricky issues around the legal categorization of the employment relationship. This approach is, however, unlikely to be applicable to other employment rights where the connection to human rights law is more tenuous.

D. The Working Time Directive

Given the analysis earlier in this chapter of the extent of constitutionalization of equality law, it is perhaps unsurprising to find that this also permeates issues around its personal scope. It is, therefore, necessary to examine other areas of EU employment law to identify whether constitutionalization has a wider impact. The second example to

[159] Art. 10, Council Directive 92/85, OJ 1992 L 348/1, on the introduction of measures to encourage improvements in the safety and health at work of pregnant workers and workers who have recently given birth or are breastfeeding.

[160] Opinion of AG Bot, 2 September 2010, para. 98.

[161] Rec. 49 of judgment.

[162] Rec. 51.

[163] Council Directive 76/207, OJ 1976 L 39/40.

[164] Council Directive 86/613, OJ 1986 L 359/56.

[165] Rec. 70. The Court cites Art. 23 EUCFR on equality for women and men in support of its decision.

be considered is the Working Time Directive.[166] The Directive regulates entitlement to breaks from work, such as daily and weekly rest periods, as well as maximum weekly working time and the right to paid annual leave. Many of its provisions are phrased in broad terms: 'every worker is entitled to paid annual leave of at least four weeks'.[167] The Directive does not contain any definition of 'worker', but its scope is based upon corresponding provisions in the EU Framework Directive on Health and Safety.[168] The latter instrument does contain a definition of worker, but this does not shed much light on its intended meaning: 'worker: any person employed by an employer'.[169]

As mentioned in section 3 of this chapter, the *BECTU* case[170] provided the first illustration of the Court's approach to the personal scope of 'worker' in the context of the Working Time Directive. When implementing the Directive, the UK had excluded from the entitlement to paid annual leave those employed under contracts with a duration of less than 13 continuous weeks. The Court found this to be incompatible with the Directive, noting that it did not draw any distinction between those working under indefinite duration or fixed-term contracts.[171] Significantly, it grounded its reading of the Directive in a rights-based analysis. Citing the 1989 EC Social Charter, it concluded that paid annual leave was 'a social right directly conferred by that Directive on every worker'.[172] This was reinforced in the accompanying Opinion of Advocate General Tizzano. He cited the Universal Declaration of Human Rights, the 1961 European Social Charter, the International Covenant on Economic, Social and Cultural Rights, and the 2000 EU Charter of Fundamental Rights to support the conclusion that paid annual leave constituted a 'fundamental social right'.[173]

Subsequent case law continues to frame the Working Time Directive as engaging the protection of particularly important social rights, which then leads the Court to favour a broad interpretation of its personal scope.[174] For example, in *Union syndicale Solidaires Isère v Premier ministre and others*,[175] the issue at stake was the entitlement to daily rest breaks for those working on a casual and seasonal basis in holiday and leisure centres for children during school vacations. French national legislation classified these relationships as falling under the remit of 'educational commitment' and outside the scope of the Labour Code. Such work was limited to an annual maximum of 80 days, but there was no entitlement to a daily rest period of 11 consecutive hours (as required by the Directive). The Court characterizes the provisions on rest periods as 'rules of European Union social law of particular importance from which every worker must benefit'.[176] The Directive had to be read broadly and the national classification of the relationship had no consequence for determining whether the individual met the EU law definition of 'worker'.[177] Accordingly, educational commitments were deemed to fall within the scope of the Directive and such individuals were, in principle, entitled to daily rest periods.

166 Council Directive 2003/88, *supra* note 62. 167 Ibid., Art. 7.
168 Ibid., Art. 1(3).
169 Art. 3(a), Council Directive 89/391, OJ 1989 L 183/1, on the introduction of measures to encourage improvements in the safety and health of workers at work. Art. 3(b) defines employer as 'any natural or legal person who has an employment relationship with the worker and has responsibility for the undertaking and/or establishment'.
170 *BECTU, supra* note 61. 171 Ibid., Rec. 46. 172 Ibid., Rec. 47.
173 Opinion of 8 February 2001, paras 22–28.
174 The Court now explicitly applies the definition of 'worker' found in free movement law when interpreting the personal scope of the Working Time Directive: Case C-337/10, *Neidel v Stadt Frankfurt am Main*, judgment of 3 May 2012, not yet published, Rec. 23.
175 Case C-428/09, judgment of 14 October 2010, not yet published. 176 Ibid., Rec. 36.
177 Ibid., Recs 22 and 30.

A further illustration of the Court's tendency to give an expansive reading to the personal scope of the Working Time Directive arises in a bundle of decisions relating to the rights of workers during sick leave. Specifically, these cases pose the question of whether (and when) a worker on sick leave can take paid annual leave. The status of a worker on sick leave, especially long-term sick leave, is a matter that varies between national jurisdictions.[178] Some obligations of the employment relationship are likely to be suspended after a certain point in time, notably the obligation to provide remuneration. When the Court of Justice was first asked to consider whether a worker on sick leave continued to enjoy the right to take paid annual leave *during* the actual period of sick leave, all eight member states who intervened in the case, and the European Commission, advised that this should not be possible.[179] Nevertheless, the Court started its analysis by considering the status of the legal norm, noting that paid annual leave is 'a particularly important principle of Community social law from which there can be no derogations'.[180] In relation to those off work for more than one year, the Court highlighted that ILO Convention 132 required this to be treated as part of the period of service.[181] Accordingly, the Court rejected the idea that long-term sickness extinguished entitlement to paid annual leave.[182] While the Court has referred to ILO Conventions in earlier judgments,[183] its practice in doing so is rather infrequent and haphazard. In relation to the Working Time Directive, it has a stronger mandate for considering ILO instruments, because recital 9 in the Directive's preamble specifically calls for ILO principles to be taken into account.[184] More recently, it has overtly linked this conclusion to Article 31(2) of the Charter of Fundamental Rights:[185] 'every worker has the right to limitation of maximum working hours, to daily and weekly rest periods and to an annual period of paid leave'.

Admittedly, this is not an absolute right. The Court has accorded some flexibility for employers where sick leave is shorter than one year in duration.[186] Conversely, it has imposed restrictions on the ability to accumulate paid annual leave entitlement. In *Schulte*, a worker who had been on long-term sick leave for three years did not have the right to accumulate paid annual leave for each of these years and the Court accepted the legitimacy of imposing temporal restrictions on carrying over leave from one working year to the next.[187] In reaching this conclusion, it drew upon the restrictions authorized in ILO Convention 132.

Taking an overview, the example of the Working Time Directive appears to echo the approach found in equality law. The Court identifies that the underlying rights found within the legislation are of constitutional significance because of their connection to fundamental social rights. This conclusion has been consolidated following the acquisition of Treaty status by the Charter of Fundamental Rights, and the inclusion therein of Article 31(2). The

[178] Freedland and Kountouris, *supra* note 130, at 214.

[179] The interveners were Germany, the UK, the Czech Republic, Italy, the Netherlands, Poland, and Slovenia: Joined Cases C-350/06, *Schultz-Hoff v Deutsche Rentenversicherung Bund* and C-520/06, *Stringer v Her Majesty's Revenue and Customs* [2010] ECR I-179.

[180] Ibid., Rec. 22.

[181] Ibid., Rec. 38; Convention 132 concerning Annual Holidays with Pay (Revised).

[182] See also Case C-282/10, *Dominguez v Centre informatique du Centre Ouest Atlantique, Préfet de la region Centre*, judgment of 24 January 2012, not yet published.

[183] E.g. *Defrenne III, supra* note 78, at Rec. 28.

[184] 'Account should be taken of the principles of the International Labour Organisation with regard to the organization of working time, including those relating to night work', Council Directive 2003/88, *supra* note 62.

[185] Case C-214/10, *KHS AG v Schulte*, judgment of 22 November 2011, not yet published, Rec. 37.

[186] *Schultz-Hoff, supra* note 179, Recs 34–35.

[187] *Schulte, supra* note 185, Rec. 33.

treatment by the Court of those on sick leave poses slightly different issues to the employed/self-employed distinction. Yet an analogy exists in so far as those on long-term sick leave are also in a precarious situation where the normal statutory and contractual entitlements of a worker may be denied. The Court relies on the fundamental nature of the rights found in the Directive to favour a very broad interpretation of its personal scope.

E. The Acquired Rights Directive

The final example considered in this section concerns an element of EU employment law where the connection to fundamental social rights is less evident, at least in comparison to equality and working time. The Acquired Rights Directive was originally adopted in 1977, but revised and consolidated in 2001.[188] It seeks to protect employment rights in the event of 'a change in the natural or legal person who is responsible for carrying on the business and who incurs the obligations of an employer towards employees of the undertaking'.[189] Typical examples would be the acquisition of a business or, depending on the circumstances, a change following a competitive tendering process, such as the contracting out of cleaning services.[190] In terms of personal scope, the Directive places the emphasis on resolving this by reference to national law. Article 2 states:

> (1)(d) 'employee' shall mean any person who, in the Member State concerned, is protected as an employee under national employment law.
>
> (2) This Directive shall be without prejudice to national law as regards the definition of contract of employment or employment relationship.

Unsurprisingly, the Court has been faced with questions surrounding the personal scope of the Directive. The flagship case in this area is *Danmols Inventar*.[191] Mr Mikkelsen was originally employed as a works foreman, but, following a transfer of the undertaking, he became a co-owner and chair of the Board of Directors, although he continued to perform the same work and received the same salary. The company subsequently became insolvent and Mr Mikkelsen brought legal proceedings to recover compensation for the termination of his employment and holiday pay. In order to rely upon the Directive, it needed to be determined if he fell within its personal scope, especially in the light of his partial ownership of the company. In that regard, Mr Mikkelsen argued that so long as the individual does not occupy a dominant position on the Board of Directors, then an employment relationship should be found to exist. The Court acknowledged that with regard to free movement law, it had developed a harmonized concept of worker; however, it rejected the application of that approach to the Acquired Rights Directive:

> Directive no. 77/187 is intended to achieve only partial harmonization essentially by extending protection guaranteed to workers independently by the laws of the individual Member States to cover the case where an undertaking is transferred... it is not however intended to establish a uniform level of protection throughout the Community on the basis of common criteria.[192]

[188] Council Directive 2001/23, *supra* note 18.

[189] Joined Cases C-173/96 and C-247/96, *Sánchez Hidalgo and others v Asociación de Servicios Aser and Sociedad Cooperativa Minerva, Ziemann v Ziemann Sicherheit GmbH and Horst Bohn Sicherheitsdienst* [1998] ECR I-8230, Rec. 23.

[190] E.g. Case C-392/92, *Schmidt, supra* note 20.

[191] Case 105/84, *Foreningen af Arbejdsledere I Danmark v A/S Danmols Inventar* [1985] ECR 2639. See also, Freedland and Kountouris, *supra* note 130, at 391.

[192] Ibid., Rec. 26.

In contrast to the approach found in equality or working time law, the Court exercised judicial self-restraint in relation to the personal scope of the Acquired Rights Directive, leaving this to the discretion of national law.

Subsequent decisions have largely conformed to this approach.[193] In *Collino and Chiappero*,[194] decided in 2000, the Court expressly confirmed that the approach taken in *Danmols Inventar*, decided in 1985, was still valid: 'contrary to the submissions of the Finnish government and the Commission, the Directive does not apply to persons who are not protected as employees under their national employment law, regardless of the nature of the tasks those persons perform'.[195] The Court's approach can, at one level, be explained by the textual requirements of the Directive. Article 2, cited above, clearly indicates that the personal scope of the Directive is a matter for national law and this has been cited by the Court as support for its conclusion that the Directive only aims at a 'partial harmonisation' of national law.[196] Nevertheless, the Court has not always felt itself strictly bound by similar language in other instruments.

Clause 2(1) of the Framework Agreement on Part-Time Work echoes the approach to personal scope found in the Acquired Rights Directive: 'this agreement applies to part-time workers who have an employment contract or employment relationship *as defined by the law, collective agreement or practice in force in each Member State*'.[197] Initially, the Court took the view that questions relating to the personal scope of application of the Framework Agreement were matters for national courts to determine.[198] More recently, however, the Court substantially qualified the discretion accorded to national law. In *O'Brien*, the case concerned the exclusion of some part-time judges in the United Kingdom from access to an occupational pension.[199] According to national law, judges were deemed to be 'office-holders' rather than 'workers', and hence fell outside the scope of the legislation implementing the Framework Agreement on Part-Time Work. While acknowledging that clause 2(1) leaves it for national law to determine who constitutes a 'part-time worker', the Court said that 'certain words used in that Agreement may be defined in accordance with the national law and practices on condition that they respect the effectiveness of the Directive and the general principles of EU law'.[200] This principle was amplified by Advocate General Kokott, who drew an express link between the Framework Agreement and the protection of fundamental rights:

> The prohibition of discrimination laid down therein is simply a specific expression of the general principle of equality, which is one of the fundamental principles of EU law and is enshrined in arts 20 and 21 of the Charter of Fundamental Rights of the European Union.[201]

Having identified the connection between the Framework Agreement and the general principles of EU law, the Court proceeded to examine in some detail the nature of judges' employment relationship. While leaving the formal decision to the referring court, it provided a strong indication that judges could not be excluded from the personal scope

[193] E.g. citation of *Danmols Inventar* in *Sánchez Hidalgo, supra* note 189, at Rec. 24. The Court has, though, clarified that it is sufficient to establish the existence of an employment 'relationship' under national law; a 'contractual link' is not required: Case C-242/09, *Albron Catering BV v FNV Bondgenoten, Roest,* judgment of 21 October 2010, not yet reported, Rec. 24.

[194] Case C-343/98, *Collino and Chiappero v Telecom Italia SpA* [2000] ECR I-6659.

[195] Ibid., Rec. 38.

[196] Ibid., Rec. 39.

[197] Emphasis added; Council Directive 97/81, OJ 1998 L 14/9, concerning the Framework Agreement on part-time work concluded by UNICE, CEEP and the ETUC.

[198] Case C-313/02, *Wippel v Peek & Cloppenburg GmbH & Co. KG* [2004] ECR I-9483, Rec. 40.

[199] Case C-393/10, *O'Brien v Ministry of Justice*, judgment of 1 March 2012, not yet published.

[200] Ibid., Rec. 34.

[201] Footnotes omitted; Opinion of 17 November 2011, para. 41.

of the Framework Agreement, notwithstanding clause 2(1) apparently leaving this to be resolved by national law.

The approach taken in *O'Brien* suggests that, where a connection to fundamental rights or general principles of law is identified, then the Court will intervene to ensure that the personal scope of application is interpreted widely, irrespective of whether the Directive provides for this to be determined by national law.[202] This poses the question of why the Court remains more aloof when faced with disputes over the personal scope of the Acquired Rights Directive. One explanation may be that the Court has not identified any significant connection between the provisions of the Acquired Rights Directive and the protection of fundamental rights. Unlike equality or working time, there are no provisions of international instruments that are expressly addressed to the situation where there is a change in the identity of the employer. This is not, for example, explicitly included within the Council of Europe's Revised European Social Charter.[203] Similarly, it is not dealt with directly in the EU Charter of Fundamental Rights.[204] As discussed in section 2, the Acquired Rights Directive appears to be one element of EU employment law where rights have not been subject to constitutionalization.

6. Conclusion

The theme of this collection is the constitutionalization of European private law. While employment law finds its roots in private law, it has become distinct over time due to the extensiveness of social regulation of the employment relationship. Traditional concerns of private law, such as freedom of contract and protection of property rights have withered and feature rarely in discourse surrounding EU employment legislation. There is, of course, an enduring debate about the optimal balance between worker protection and flexibility for employers, but this is not often framed as an ideological dispute over the entitlement of the state to interfere in the private contract of employment. The acceptance that employment relationships will be subject to externally imposed social regulation may explain why this area of private law has been rather open to the tendency for constitutionalization. From a very early stage, the Court of Justice was willing to apply rights based on the provisions of the EEC Treaty directly into the contract of employment,[205] with no apparent qualms about the implicit infringement of freedom of contract. While the original Treaties had relatively few provisions of immediate relevance to employment relations, the subsequent emergence of the 1989 EC Social Charter and, most especially, the 2000 Charter of Fundamental Rights has cemented the notion that some elements of employment law engage fundamental rights of constitutional significance.

[202] The Court will face a similar issue in a pending reference from the French *Cour de Cassation*. The dispute concerns the exclusion of those working under certain types of contract from the thresholds triggering rights to information and consultation under Directive 2002/14, OJ 2002 L 80/29. While the Directive defines 'employee' according to national employment law (Art. 2(d)), the reference queries the compatibility of French law with Art. 27 EUCFR on the right to information and consultation: Case C-176/12, *Association de médiation sociale v Union locale des syndicats CGT, Hichem Laboubi, Union départementale CGT des Bouche-du-Rhône, Confédération générale du travail*, OJ 2012 C 184/5.

[203] Some of the rights in the Revised European Social Charter might be applicable in the context of a transfer of the undertaking, e.g. Art. 21 on the right to information and consultation.

[204] The Explanatory Notes accompanying the Charter do, however, link the Acquired Rights Directive with Art. 27 on the right to information and consultation and Art. 30 on protection from unjustified dismissal. See: Explanations, *supra* note 70.

[205] *Defrenne II*, *supra* note 43.

The example of equality law provides the most vivid illustration of the effects of constitutionalization. The Court has deployed constitutional equality principles to shape its interpretation of EU secondary legislation. In the past decade, however, the Court seems to be recasting this process. Constitutional rights and principles are no longer an aid to interpretation; they are the foundation of equality law, while secondary legislation is reduced to a 'mere expression' of these principles. The emphasis on the fundamental nature of the rights at stake in equality law has led the Court to stretch existing orthodoxy around the exclusion of direct effect of Directives in relation to private law relationships. Arguably, the trajectory of the Court's case law is decoupling equality law from its employment law roots. The extension of equality rights to areas outside the labour market, such as the provision of services, suggests that equality law is becoming a separate species, a nascent branch of EU human rights law.

The spreading tentacles of constitutionalization were also evident in the law surrounding the personal scope of employment rights. This topic was selected because of the absence of an obvious connection to fundamental rights. There are no clearly articulated or internationally recognized standards regarding the types of contractual or non-contractual relationships that should be regarded as falling within the scope of employment protection law. The lack of coherence is also reflected in the approach of the Court of Justice, which fluctuates depending upon the aspect of employment law under consideration. In resolving this conundrum, the Court has once again reached for constitutional principles, seeking to ensure a very broad personal scope for employment rights where the Court views these as touching upon constitutionally significant rights and principles.

The examination of the personal scope of employment rights drew out the difficulty of delimiting the effects of constitutionalization. Constitutionalization seems to be premised upon the identification of some employment rights as fundamental rights, thereby warranting a stricter standard of protection by Courts and legislators. This also implies that there are some employment rights that are not 'fundamental' in nature and where there is a greater margin of discretion to balance the objectives of social protection with those of business flexibility and competitiveness. The expansion in the list of 'fundamental' social rights, witnessed in the Council of Europe's Revised Social Charter or the EU Charter of Fundamental Rights, risks swallowing up the whole of employment law. Yet if every aspect of employment law is construed as fundamental in nature, then this dilutes the meaning or significance of what a 'fundamental' right entails. Consequently, there is a need to confront the boundaries of constitutionalization, to accept that some elements of EU employment law lie on the margins of this process. Naturally, the focus of legal innovation has been upon the discovery and exploration of fundamental social rights, such as the litigation surrounding the Working Time Directive. It is only occasionally that the Court indicates where it draws the line. In this regard, the Acquired Rights Directive emerges as one element of EU employment legislation where the existing case law does not suggest that the Court views the rights therein as fundamental in nature.

The enhanced legal status for the Charter of Fundamental of Rights since 2009 opens up a new vista for the constitutionalization of EU employment law. The array of social rights recognized within the Charter invites debate over whether, and to what extent, this will shift the contours of employment rights even further in the direction of constitutionalization. A steady stream of judgments show the Court's increasing willingness to take the Charter into account in this branch of law.[206] There is a temptation for scholars

[206] E.g. *Zoi Chatzi, supra* note 53; *Danosa, supra* note 11; *KHS AG v Schulte, supra* note 185.

and activists to treat the Charter as an all-encompassing solution to the external pressures on employment rights arising from trends such as globalization and the current climate of economic austerity. Arguably, though, reflection is needed on distinguishing those areas of employment law where constitutionalized protection of rights adds value and is justified, and those where this is not the appropriate pathway. Taken to its logical conclusion, the emergence of a 'constitutionalized' employment contract could be imagined.[207] This would consist of those minimum core rights from which neither legislatures, nor employers could derogate. The existing case law helps to map the constituent elements of such a contract, such as non-discrimination or the right to paid annual leave. Given the pressures on employment law arising from the economic crisis, the codification of a constitutionalized employment contract could offer a bulwark against a downward spiral of deregulation.

[207] I am indebted to Hans-W. Micklitz for this suggestion.

6

Fundamental Rights, European Private Law, and Financial Services

Olha O. Cherednychenko

1. Introduction

While in the past fundamental rights and private law were considered to be far apart, today this traditional view no longer reflects reality. In many European legal systems, fundamental rights enshrined in national constitutions and international human rights instruments tend to create strong magnetic fields across the entire body of law, including private law. Fundamental rights and private law have become firmly aware of each other's presence and have realized that a relationship between the two should be established.[1] Many authors speak in this context about the 'constitutionalization of private law'.[2]

European private law is no longer immune from the effect of fundamental rights either.[3] While the founding EC Treaties signed in the 1950s contained no express provisions on fundamental rights, Article 6 of the Treaty on European Union (TEU) as amended by the 2007 Lisbon Treaty gives explicit recognition to the three sources of EU fundamental rights: (1) the Nice Charter of Fundamental Rights of the EU (EUCFR); (2) the European Convention on Human Rights (ECHR); and (3) the constitutional traditions common to the member states. The acknowledgement of the legally binding

[1] For a comprehensive comparative study of the relationship between fundamental rights and private law, see, e.g. O. O. Cherednychenko, *Fundamental Rights, Contract Law and the Protection of the Weaker Party: A Comparative Analysis of the Constitutionalisation of Contract Law, with Emphasis on Risky Financial Transactions* (2007); C. Mak, *Fundamental Rights in European Contract Law: A Comparison of the Impact of Fundamental Rights on Contractual Relationships in Germany, the Netherlands, Italy and England* (2008); G. Brüggemeier, G. Comandè, and A. Colombi Ciacchi (eds), *Fundamental Rights and Private Law in the European Union* (2010); H. Schulte-Nölke and Chr. Busch (eds), *EU Compendium Fundamental Rights and Private Law, A Practical Tool for Judges* (2010).

[2] See, e.g. Cherednychenko, 'The Constitutionalization of Contract Law: Something New under the Sun?' 8.1 *Electronic Journal of Comparative Law* (2004), <http://www.ejcl.org/81/art81-3.html>; Lindenbergh, 'The Constitutionalisation of Private Law in the Netherlands', in T. Barkhuysen and S. Lindenbergh (eds), *Constitutionalisation of Private Law* (2006) 97; Brüggemeier, 'Constitutionalisation of Private Law—The German Perspective', in Barkhuysen and Lindenbergh, *Constitutionalisation of Private Law*, 59; Banakas, 'The Constitutionalisation of Private Law in the UK: Is there an Emperor inside the New Clothes?', in Barkhuysen and Lindenbergh, *Constitutionalisation of Private Law*, 83.

[3] For an analysis of the potential for the constitutionalization of European contract law, see, for example, Hesselink, 'The Horizontal Effect of Social Rights in European Contract Law', in M. W. Hesselink, C. E. du Perron, and A. F. Salomons (eds), *Privaatrecht tussen autonomie en solidariteit* (2003) 119; Colombi Ciacchi, 'The Constitutionalization of European Contract Law: Judicial Convergence and Social Justice', 2 *ERCL* (2006) 167; Cherednychenko, 'EU Fundamental Rights, EC Freedoms and Private Law', 14 *European Review of Private Law* (2006) 23; Cherednychenko, 'Fundamental Rights and Contract Law', 2 *ERCL* (2006) 489; S. Grundmann (ed), *Constitutional Values and European Contract Law* (2008); M. W. Hesselink, C. Mak, and J. W. Rutgers, 'Constitutional Aspects of European Private Law: Freedoms, Rights and Social Justice in the Draft Common Frame of Reference', Centre for the Study of European Contract Law Working Paper Series, No. 2009/05.

character of the EUCFR, which contains a rich set of fundamental rights, constitutes a major step forward as regards fundamental rights protection across the EU. Fundamental rights resulting from the other two sources—the ECHR and the constitutional traditions common to the member states—are referred to in the Lisbon Treaty as general principles of EU law. In this way, the Lisbon Treaty has acknowledged the earlier case law of the Court of Justice of the EU (CJEU), according to which respect for fundamental rights forms an integral part of the general principles of law, allowing the Court to go beyond the fundamental rights protected by the EUCFR.[4] The latter, however, has now become the main reference point for the determination of the scope and content of EU fundamental rights in the case law of the CJEU.[5]

Although it seems to be undisputed today that the harmonization of private law in the EU cannot take place without taking fundamental rights into account, many questions still exist as to *how* and to *what extent* European private law can and should be influenced by fundamental rights. The aim of this contribution is to explore the possibilities for and limits to the constitutionalization of European private law, both at EU and national level, in the context of financial services.

The concept of the 'constitutionalization of private law' is understood here in a broad sense, meaning the impact of fundamental rights on the relationships between private parties under private law.[6] Also the concepts of private law and European private law used in this contribution are understood in a wide sense and embrace all legal rules concerning relationships between private parties regardless of the nature of the law, public or private, in which they have been included in national legal systems. This understanding of European private law reflects the regulatory nature of the *acquis communautaire* in the field of private law.[7] At EU level, private law is viewed as an instrument for achieving the collective objectives of European integration. Alongside the central objective of establishing the European Internal Market, these objectives include, in particular, the protection of consumers, workers, small and medium-sized enterprises, the industry, and the environment as well as non-discrimination policy. To add further clarification on what is meant by European private law for the purposes of this contribution, this concept covers both EU measures concerning relationships between private parties, i.e. EU regulatory private law, and national laws directly or indirectly affected thereby.

[4] Cf. Iglesias Sánchez, 'The Court and the Charter: The Impact of the Entry into Force of the Lisbon Treaty on the ECJ's Approach to Fundamental Rights', 49 *CMLRev* (2012) 1565, at 1568, 1610. See also S. De Vries, U. Bernitz, and S. Weatheril (eds), *The Protection of Fundamental Rights in the EU after Lisbon* (2012).

[5] Cf. Iglesias Sánchez, *supra* note 4, at 1610.

[6] The concept of the 'constitutionalization of private law' can also be understood in the narrower sense when it is linked to the idea of fundamental rights as an objective system of values for the whole legal order, including private law. On this, see Collins, 'The Constitutionalisation of European Private Law as a Path to Social Justice?', in H.-W. Micklitz (ed), *The Many Concepts of Social Justice in European Private Law* (2011) 133, at 135.

[7] See, e.g. Micklitz, 'The Concept of Competitive Contract Law', 23 *Penn State International Law Review* (2005) 549; Schmid, 'The Instrumentalist Conception of the Acquis Communautaire in Consumer Law and Its Implications on a European Contract Law Code', 1 *ERCL* (2005) 210; Cafaggi, 'Introduction', in F. Cafaggi (ed), *The Institutional Framework of European Private Law* (2006) 1; Collins, 'Governance Implications for the European Union of the Changing Character of Private Law', in F. Cafaggi and H. Muir-Watt (eds), *Making of European Private Law: Governance Design* (2009) 269; F. Cafaggi and H. Muir-Watt (eds), *The Regulatory Function of European Private Law* (2009); Micklitz, 'The Visible Hand of European Regulatory Private Law. The Transformation of European Private Law from Autonomy to Functionalism in Competition and Regulation', 28 *Yearbook of European Law* (2009) 3.

The focus of the present analysis of the constitutionalization of European private law will be on consumer financial services, i.e. payment, credit, investment, and insurance. In the last two decades, financial services have become an essential part of the everyday life of EU citizens, and the harmonization of contract-related rules in this area has actively been sought by the EU. During the last decade, for example, the EU has adopted a number of ambitious measures, such as Directive 2007/64 on payment services,[8] Directive 2008/48 on consumer credit,[9] and Directive 2004/39 on the markets in financial instruments (MiFID I).[10] [11] The recent financial crisis, which has demonstrated a high degree of interdependence between financial markets, has strengthened the case for further harmonization of financial services law in the EU. This gives cause for reflection concerning the actual and potential effect of EU fundamental rights, particularly those laid down in the EUCFR, in this area of European private law and the perplexities involved therein.

The present contribution comprises two major parts. In the first part, I will outline legal constructs which may serve as gateways to the impact of EU fundamental rights on European private law in the light of the constitutional limits to such impact (section 2). Drawing upon this analysis, the second part will proceed to examine the actual and potential impact of EU fundamental rights on European financial services law, with emphasis on three major issues arising in this field: (1) consumer access to financial services; (2) substantive consumer protection in financial services; and (3) procedural consumer protection in financial services (section 3). Considering that the constitutionalization of European private law is still in its infancy, the experience accumulated in national legal systems and the law of the ECHR with regard to the effect of fundamental rights in private law will also be taken into account when assessing the potential impact of EU fundamental rights on European private law. The contribution will conclude with some final observations concerning the possibilities for and limits to the constitutionalization of European private law, in general, and European financial services law, in particular (section 4).

2. Gateways to the Constitutionalization of European Private Law

The nature of fundamental rights protection in the EU differs in some important respects from its counterparts in national legal systems and under the ECHR. This becomes particularly clear if one looks at the text of the EUCFR. According to Article 51(1) EUCFR, the provisions of the Charter are addressed to the EU institutions and bodies *with due regard to the principle of subsidiary* and to the member states *only when they are implementing Union law*. In addition, Article 51(2) EUCFR explicitly specifies that the Charter does not establish any new power or task for the European Community or the Union, or modify powers and tasks defined by the founding treaties. It follows from these provisions that EU fundamental rights apply only in so far as the EU is competent to act, and that the EU is thus not the organization whose core task is the promotion of

[8] Directive 2007/64, OJ 2007 L 319/1.
[9] Directive 2008/48, OJ 2008 L 133/66.
[10] Directive 2004/39, OJ 2004 L 145/1.
[11] For an overview of these measures, see Grundmann, 'EC Financial Services: Developments 2002–2005', 1 *ERCL* (2005) 482; Grundmann and Hollering, 'EC Financial Services and Contract Law—Developments 2005–2007', 4 *ERCL* (2008) 45.

fundamental rights. The inclusion of the second paragraph in Article 51 of the EUCFR obviously addresses the fear of the member states that the sophisticated catalogue of fundamental rights contained in the Charter will lead to the uncontrolled expansion of the competencies of the Union.

Accordingly, EU fundamental rights must be respected by: (1) the EU institutions and bodies when making, interpreting, and applying primary or secondary EU law in the field of private law; (2) the member states when they are 'implementing EU law'. In light of the existing case law of the CJEU, 'implementing EU law' must be understood in a broad sense covering all national public acts within the 'scope of EU law'.[12] This implies, inter alia, that national public authorities are bound by EU fundamental rights not only when they are transposing EU law, but also when they are derogating therefrom.[13] Moreover, following the judgment of the CJEU in *Kücükdeveci*,[14] the notion of 'implementation' now appears to extend not only to national legislation which implements an EU directive in a strict sense but also legislation which otherwise touches upon fields regulated by that directive.[15]

Considering the need to respect the division of competences of the EU in relation to a multilevel system of private law, the following legal constructs can be identified which may serve as gateways to the constitutionalization of European private law.

First, EU law and national measures that fall within the scope of EU law must be in conformity with EU fundamental rights. Rule-making in the field of European private law does not enjoy a privileged position in this respect. The EU and national legislatures, as well as other rule-makers, such as European and national financial supervisory authorities, thus have negative obligations to respect fundamental rights when making European private law.

Secondly, EU law and national measures that fall within the scope of EU law must be interpreted and applied in conformity with EU fundamental rights. The respective obligations rest, in particular, on the CJEU and national civil courts when adjudicating disputes between private parties. By so doing, such public authorities comply with their negative obligations to respect fundamental rights. A duty to interpret and apply national law that falls within the scope of EU law in conformity with EU fundamental rights exists not only with regard to national measures which implement EU law but also those which derogate from EU law. In particular, interpreting and applying EU law in the light of EU fundamental rights may provide a justification for the member state's derogation from the free movement provisions of the Treaty on the Functioning of the European Union (TFEU) on public policy grounds.

Thirdly, apart from ensuring respect for EU fundamental rights by not interfering with such rights, the EU and member state public authorities may also implement EU fundamental rights in private law by taking positive action to this end. As will be

[12] See, e.g. Case C-299/95, *Kremzov* [1997] ECR I-2629, Rec. 15; Joined cases C-60 and 61/84, *Cinéthèque* [1985] ECR 2605, Rec. 26. See also Lenaerts and Gutiérrez-Fons, 'The Constitutional Allocation of Powers and General Principles of EU Law', 47 *CMLRev* (2010) 1629, at 1660; Von Bogdandy et al., 'Reverse Solange—Protecting the Essence of Fundamental Rights against EU Member States', 49 *CMLRev* (2012) 489, at 497.

[13] Case C-260/89, *ERT* [1991] ECR I-2925, Rec. 43; Case C-368/95, *Familiapress* [1997] ECR I-3689; Case C-245/01, *RTL Television* [2003] ECR I-12489.

[14] Case C-555/07, *Kücükdeveci* [2010] ECR I-365.

[15] Such an expansion of the scope of EU law with a view to protecting EU fundamental rights in member states has been criticized in the literature. See, e.g. Von Bogdandy et al., *supra* note 12, at 497 et seq., who also propose an alternative approach to ensuring respect for fundamental rights in the EU member states by linking EU fundamental rights with EU citizenship.

discussed in more detail below, EU law has not adopted such a robust version of the positive obligations to protect fundamental rights which has been recognized, for example, in German law or the law of the ECHR. At the same time, one can trace a weaker version of such obligations in EU law which may serve as a gateway to the constitutionalization of European private law.

All the three above-mentioned vehicles for the effect of EU fundamental rights in private law are based on the concept of direct *vertical* effect of fundamental rights. This concept is similar to the one which has developed in national legal systems and the ECHR. It enables individuals to enforce claims about fundamental rights at EU and/or national level against public authorities involved in making, interpreting, and applying EU and/or national private law in so far as the latter falls within the scope of EU law. In addition to the vertical dimension, however, the issue of the effect of EU fundamental rights in private law also has *horizontal* dimension. The latter is concerned with the effect of EU fundamental rights in relationships between private parties under private law.

Horizontal effect of fundamental rights may take two forms: direct and indirect. The most widely understood difference between the two lies in the fact that while, in the case of *direct* horizontal effect, a private party has, in his or her action against another private party, a claim or a defence which is directly based on a fundamental right which overrides an otherwise applicable rule of private law, in the case of the *indirect* horizontal effect, the claim or defence is based on a private law rule which is interpreted and applied in the light of the fundamental right in question.[16] Obviously, the indirect horizontal effect of EU fundamental rights may result from the fulfilment of their vertical obligations by the public authorities at EU and/or national level. Yet, as will be shown below, EU law appears to give some recognition to the concept of direct horizontal effect. The direct horizontal effect of EU fundamental rights in private litigation is not based on the vertical direct effect of such rights. In fact, the direct horizontal effect of EU fundamental rights circumvents the need for private litigants to resort to legal constructs based on the vertical direct effect in order to secure respect for their fundamental rights. The concept of direct horizontal effect, therefore, opens up the *fourth* direct gateway to the constitutionalization of European private law.

In the following, the four above-mentioned gateways to the effect of EU fundamental rights in private law, both at EU and national level, will be discussed in more detail in the context of the EU harmonization of private law.

A. Fundamental Rights Scrutiny of EU Law and National Laws within the Scope of EU Law

It is almost undisputed today that national legislation in the field of private law must comply with fundamental rights. An important role in ensuring legislative respect for fundamental rights in European legal systems has been played by domestic constitutional

[16] As I have argued elsewhere, the problem with the conventional distinction between direct and indirect horizontal effect or, more exactly, with the way in which it has been applied in practice in different jurisdictions, is that it does not make it unequivocal which body of law substantially determines the outcome of disputes between private parties and, hence, how fundamental rights and private law relate to each other. On this in more detail, see Cherednychenko, 'Fundamental Rights and Private Law: A Relationship of Subordination or Complementarity?', 3 *Utrecht Law Review* (2007) 1 and Cherednychenko, 'Subordinating Contract Law to Fundamental Rights: Towards a Major Breakthrough or towards Walking in Circles?', in S. Grundmann (ed), *Constitutional Values and European Contract Law* (2008) 35. Cf. Collins, *supra* note 6, at 141 et seq.

courts and the European Court of Human Rights (ECtHR). The German Federal Constitutional Court has been particularly famous for its robust constitutional review of private law legislation.[17]

The need to ensure the compatibility of legislative measures in the field of private law with fundamental rights has also been recognized in EU law. Fundamental rights are binding upon the EU legislature when making legislation in the field of private law and upon member states when implementing it in their national legal orders. Legislative measures in the field of private law adopted at EU level as well as national laws implementing such measures must, therefore, comply with fundamental rights. When assessing the compliance of such measures with the EU fundamental rights enshrined in the EUCFR, one may not overlook the distinction made therein between 'rights' and 'principles'. While subjective rights, such as the freedom to conduct a business (Article 16 EUCFR) or the right to property (Article 17 EUCFR), must be *respected*, principles, such as access to services of general economic interest (Article 36 EUCFR) and consumer protection (Article 38 EUCFR), must be *observed* (Article 51 (1) EUCFR).[18]

According to the explanations to the EUCFR, observance of the principles implies that they *may* be implemented through legislative or executive acts adopted by the EU within the limits of its powers and by the member states within the scope of EU law.[19] Therefore, the principles become significant for the courts only when such acts are interpreted or reviewed; as such, they do *not* give rise to direct claims for positive action by the EU institutions or member states authorities.[20] The explanations to the Charter do not make it unequivocally clear what *respecting* fundamental rights actually means. It follows from the Charter itself, in particular Article 52(1), that respect for fundamental rights implies the negative obligations of the EU and national public authorities not to impose unjustifiable restrictions upon the exercise of such rights in EU legislation or national implementing measures. In addition, the rule-makers may adopt measures promoting certain fundamental rights and further specifying their meaning. Whether they have positive *obligations* to do so in order to ensure respect for fundamental rights and to what extent promoting *rights* differs from promoting *principles* will be considered in section 2(C).

The fundamental rights scrutiny of the legislation in the field of European private law may take place ex ante, i.e. during the drafting process and the process of implementation in the national laws, and ex post, i.e. when the compatibility of the already enacted EU legislation or the implementing measure with EU fundamental rights is challenged before the competent court. As will be demonstrated below, both ex ante and ex post fundamental rights review of EU secondary law have gained importance in the context of European private law.

After the adoption of the EUCFR in 2000, the European Commission committed itself to scrutinizing its legislative proposals for compliance with the Charter during the drafting stage.[21] It also decided that legislative proposals 'having a specific link to

[17] See, e.g. BVerfG 7 February 1990, BVerfGE 81, 242 (*Handelsvertreter*). On this case in more detail, see Cherednychenko, *supra* note 1, 89 et seq.

[18] As the Charter does not always make it clear whether a certain right contained therein must be understood as a principle, an important role in the identification of such principles will be played by the CJEU. Cf. Iglesias Sánchez, *supra* note 4, at 1582.

[19] See the explanation to Art. 52 of the Charter in Explanations Relating to the Charter of Fundamental Rights (2007/C 303/02), OJ 2007 C 303/17.

[20] Ibid.

[21] Decision on the Application of the Charter of Fundamental Rights of the European Union, SEC(2001) 380/3 as replaced by Commission Communication, Compliance with the Charter of

fundamental rights' would incorporate a recital as a formal statement of compatibility.[22] Such recitals have been included in most legislative instruments in the field of private law. Thus, for example, according to recital 80 of the Commission Directive 2006/73 implementing Directive 2004/39 on markets in financial instruments (MiFID I):[23]

> This Directive respects the fundamental rights and observes the principles recognised in particular by the Charter of Fundamental Rights of the European Union and in particular by Article 11 thereof and Article 10 of the European Convention on Human Rights. In this regard, this Directive does not in any way prevent Member States from applying their constitutional rules relating to freedom of the press and freedom of expression in the media.

A similar statement of compatibility with EU fundamental rights was also included in the recital 45 of Directive 2008/48 on consumer credit[24] which reads as follows:

> This Directive respects fundamental rights and observes the principles recognised in particular by the Charter of Fundamental Rights of the European Union. In particular, this Directive seeks to ensure full respect for the rules on protection of personal data, the right to property, non-discrimination, protection of family and professional life, and consumer protection pursuant to the Charter of Fundamental Rights of the European Union.

By contrast, however, no such recital was included in Directive 2007/64 on payment services.[25]

The question which arises in this respect is what the significance is of including a statement of compatibility with fundamental rights in the text of a particular legislative instrument. The European Commission attempted to provide some guidance to its departments on the use of such statements in recitals and their meaning. To this end, it formulated the following two criteria which must be taken into account when assessing whether the proposal has a 'specific link to fundamental rights' and the inclusion of a statement of compatibility with fundamental rights in the recitals thereto is accordingly justified: (1) a legislative proposal contains a *limitation* of a fundamental right which must be justified under Article 52 of the EUCFR,[26] or it provides for a direct or indirect difference in treatment which must be justified in relation to the general principles of equality before the law and non-discrimination; (2) a legislative proposal aims to *implement* or *promote* a particular fundamental right.[27] In those cases where none of the two criteria is met, no recital with a statement of compatibility with the Charter should be included in the proposed legislative measure. According to the Commission, the idea behind not using such recitals systematically is the danger of this practice losing any significance. Therefore, '[t]he departments [of the Commission] have to find a proper

Fundamental Rights in Commission Legislative Proposals: Methodology for Systematic and Rigorous Monitoring, COM(2005) 0172. See also Communication from the Commission, Strategy for the effective implementation of the Charter of Fundamental Rights by the European Union, COM(2010) 573/4.

[22] Commission Communication (2005), *supra* note 21, para. 21.

[23] Commission Directive 2006/73, OJ 2006 L 241/26 and Directive 2004/39, OJ 2004 L 145/1, respectively.

[24] Directive 2008/48, OJ 2008 L 133/66.

[25] Directive 2007/64, OJ 2007 L 319/1.

[26] According to Art. 52(1) EUCFR: 'Any limitation on the exercise of the rights and freedoms recognised by this Charter must be provided for by law and respect the essence of those rights and freedoms. Subject to the principle of proportionality, limitations may be made only if they are necessary and genuinely meet objectives of general interest recognised by the Union or the need to protect the rights and freedoms of others.'

[27] Commission Communication (2005), *supra* note 21, para. 22 (emphasis added). In this context the Commission appears to use the word 'right' in a wide sense covering both 'rights' and 'principles' under the Charter.

balance between the risk of trivialising the recital by using it extensively and the vigilance needed to ensure that all serious questions concerning respect for a fundamental right are dealt with'.[28]

The Commission guidelines throw some light on the meaning of the references to particular fundamental rights and principles in the recitals to the EU measures in the financial services field. For example, the reference to the right to private and family life in the recital to Directive 2008/48 on consumer credit appears to suggest that Article 9 of this directive, which regulates the use of databases containing financial information concerning consumers by creditors, may interfere with the exercise of this right; nevertheless, such interference is justified and the legislature has thus not violated its negative obligation to respect the consumer's right to private and family life. In contrast, the reference to the principle of consumer protection in the same recital underlines the link between this principle and the consumer protection provisions included in the directive. These provisions can accordingly be regarded as the implementation of the principle of consumer protection in EU secondary law and must be interpreted in light of this principle.

At the same time, the EU legislature has not always been clear and consistent in the use of statements of compatibility with fundamental rights in the EU measures adopted by it. Many questions concerning the exact relevance of fundamental rights for particular legislative instruments, therefore, still exist. For example, it is not entirely clear from a general compatibility statement contained in Commission Directive 2006/73 implementing the MiFID I which rights, apart from freedom of expression, have not been infringed upon by this measure and which rights and principles have been promoted by it. Moreover, it is difficult to find a plausible explanation for the fact that Directive 2007/64 on payment services does not contain any reference to fundamental rights. In particular, similarly to Directive 2008/48 on consumer credit and Commission Directive 2006/73 implementing the MiFID I, this directive also contains extensive consumer protection provisions which can be considered to be an expression of the principle of consumer protection enshrined in Article 38 of the EUCFR. It is surprising, therefore, that no reference to the Charter, in general, and this principle, in particular, has been included in this directive.

The lack of clarity and inconsistency in the use of statements of compatibility with fundamental rights in the EU directives in the financial services field is regrettable considering the important role such statements may play, inter alia, during the ex post review of such directives and national laws falling within their scope as to their compatibility with fundamental rights. This is particularly the case when a legislative measure can be construed as an expression of a certain fundamental right or principle. The recent case law of the CJEU contains some notable examples in this respect.

Particular mention in the present context should be given to the judgments of the CJEU in *Mangold*[29] and *Kücükdeveci*[30] concerning the principle of non-discrimination on grounds of age in the employment context. Both cases involved the disputes between two private parties—the employer and the employee—in which at issue was the compatibility of the specific provisions of national employment laws with EU law. The *Mangold* case concerned the provision of German law which made it easier to terminate fixed-term employment contracts for employees over the age of 52 than those under the age of 52. The *Kücükdeveci* case involved the provision of German law which allowed the employer to disregard the employee's periods of employment before the age of 25

[28] Ibid., para. 21. [29] Case C-144/04, *Mangold* [2005] ECR I-09981.
[30] Case C-555/07, *Kücükdeveci*.

when calculating the period of notice for dismissal. In both cases, the CJEU was asked to provide the answer to the question whether each of these provisions of German employment law was contrary to EU law, in particular Directive 2000/78 on equal treatment in employment and occupation.[31] Whereas in the *Mangold* case the period prescribed for transposition of that directive had not yet expired, in the *Kücükdeveci* case the provision in question was in force after the expiry of the transposition period.

In both cases, the CJEU considered Directive 2000/78 to be a specific expression of the principle of non-discrimination on grounds of age.[32] According to the Court, this principle must be regarded as a general principle of EU law, which derives from various international instruments and from the constitutional traditions common to the member states; furthermore, discrimination on grounds of age is prohibited by Article 21(1) of the EUCFR.[33] This principle as expressed in Directive 2000/78 was interpreted by the Court as precluding the provisions of German employment law in question. As the Court further explained, it is for the national court to ensure the full effectiveness of the general principle of non-discrimination:

> The need to ensure the full effectiveness of the principle of non-discrimination on grounds of age, as given expression in Directive 2000/78, means that the national court, faced with a national provision falling within the scope of European Union Law which it considers to be incompatible with that principle, and which cannot be interpreted in conformity with that principle, must decline to apply that provision....[34]

One of the novelties of the approach adopted by the CJEU in these cases lies in the fact that the provisions of the national laws were tested *directly* against the general principle of non-discrimination on grounds of age as expressed in Directive 2000/78.[35] The directive served to bring the national laws in question within the scope of EU law by virtue of its subject matter. It was the link between the national laws at hand and EU law that rendered the EU fundamental right, recognized both as a general principle of EU law and the Charter right, directly applicable to the national laws. The justification for this novel approach was derived by the Court from the need to ensure the full effectiveness of this principle, regardless of whether or not the period for the transposition of the directive concerned has already expired.

In its subsequent judgments in *Römer*[36] and *Dominguez*,[37] the CJEU demonstrated its reluctance to extend the *Mangold/Kücükdeveci* approach to other discrimination grounds set out in Article 21 of the EUCFR, such as sexual orientation, and other EU fundamental rights enshrined in the Charter, such as the right of every worker to paid annual leave laid down in Article 31(2) of the EUCFR.[38] It remains to be seen, however, whether this

[31] Directive 2000/78, OJ 2000 L 303/16.

[32] See, in particular, Case C-555/07, *Kücükdeveci*, Rec. 21, where this was explicitly stated by the CJEU.

[33] Case C-144/04, *Mangold*, Recs 74–75; Case C-555/07, *Kücükdeveci*, Recs 20–22.

[34] Case C-555/07, *Kücükdeveci*, Rec. 53. See also Rec. 23 and Case C-144/04, *Mangold*, Rec. 75.

[35] On this case law in more detail, see, e.g. Basedow, 'The Court of Justice and Private Law: Vacillations, General Principles and the Architecture of the European Judiciary', 18 *European Review of Private Law* (2010) 443; Muir, 'Of Ages in—and Edges of—EU law', 48 *CMLRev* (2011) 39; De Mol, 'Case Note Kücükdeveci: Mangold Revisited—Horizontal Direct Effect of a General Principle of EU Law', 6 *European Constitutional Law Review* (2010) 293; De Mol, 'The Novel Approach of the CJEU on the Horizontal Direct Effect of the EU Principle of Non-Discrimination: (Unbridled) Expansionism of EU Law?', 18 *Maastricht Journal of European and Comparative Law* (2011) 109.

[36] Case C-147/08, *Römer* [2011] ECR I-03591.

[37] Case C-282/10, *Dominguez*, judgment of 24 January 2012, not yet published.

[38] For criticism of this reluctance, see, e.g. Pech, 'Between Judicial Minimalism and Avoidance: The Court of Justice's Sidestepping of Fundamental Constitutional Issues in *Römer* and *Dominguez*', 49 *CMLRev* (2012) 1841.

cautious attitude will persist. In any event, return to the *Mangold/Kücükdeveci* approach could lead to a profound impact of EU fundamental rights on national legislation in the private law field, in particular in those cases where specific legislation has been adopted at EU level with a view to implementing or promoting a particular EU fundamental right or principle. Recitals to EU directives may provide an explanation as to whether this is the case and, hence, they may trigger the ex post review of the specific national measure as to its compatibility with the particular EU fundamental right or principle mentioned in the recitals even before the transposition period of the related EU measure in the national legal order has expired.

B. Interpretation and Application of EU Law and National Laws within the Scope of EU Law in Conformity with Fundamental Rights

An important role in the constitutionalization of European private law can also be played by the CJEU and national courts when interpreting and applying EU law and national measures that fall within the scope of EU law in the light of EU fundamental rights. In the first place, an obligation to do so rests on the courts in relation to EU directives and national measures *implementing* them. As the recent judgments of the CJEU in copyright cases show,[39] interpreting and applying such measures in the light of EU fundamental rights in disputes between private parties may involve the need for the courts to balance competing EU fundamental rights against each other in order to ensure respect for such rights.[40] The CJEU has explicitly laid down such an obligation in the *Promusicae* case[41] in the context of a reference for a preliminary ruling concerning the interpretation of Directive 2000/31 on E-Commerce,[42] Directive 2001/29 on copyright and related rights in the information society,[43] and Directive 2004/48 on the enforcement of intellectual property rights[44] in the light of the EUCFR:

> ... Community law requires that, when transposing those directives, the Member States take care to rely on an interpretation of them which allows a fair balance to be struck between the various fundamental rights protected by the Community legal order. Further, when implementing the measures transposing those directives, the authorities and courts of the Member States must not only interpret their national law in a manner consistent with those directives but also make sure that they do not rely on an interpretation of them which would be in conflict with those fundamental rights or with the other general principles of Community law, such as the principle of proportionality.[45]

The CJEU's approach in the copyright cases does not constitute something new under the sun but closely recalls the standard practice followed in many European legal systems. In Germany, for instance, the need to consider the impact of fundamental rights when interpreting and applying private law, in particular, general clauses, such as public policy (section 826 of the German Civil Code), has been recognized since 1958 when

[39] See Case C-275/06, *Promusicae* [2008] ECR I-00271; Case C-70/10, *Scarlet Extended*, judgment of 24 November 2011, not yet published; Case C-360/10, *SABAM v Netlog*, judgment of 16 February 2012, not yet published.

[40] On this in more detail, see the contribution by Godt, 'Intellectual Property and European Fundamental Rights', in this book.

[41] Case C-275/06, *Promusicae.*

[42] Directive 2000/31, OJ 2000 L 178/1.

[43] Directive 2001/29, OJ 2001 L 167/10.

[44] Directive 2004/48, OJ 2004 L 195/16.

[45] Case C-275/06, *Promusicae*, Rec. 70.

the German Federal Constitutional Court delivered its famous judgment in *Lüth*.[46] Whereas the interpretation of private laws in the light of fundamental rights has become an important vehicle for the constitutionalization of private law in national legal systems, the interpretation of EU legislation in the field of private law in the light of EU fundamental rights may play a similar role in the context of the constitutionalization of European private law. A broad range of conflicting fundamental rights issues may also arise in the context of interpreting and applying general clauses contained in the EU legislation and national implementing measures, such as the requirement of good faith (Article 3 of Directive 93/13 on unfair terms in consumer contracts[47]).

Moreover, fundamental rights issues may not only arise with regard to the member state measures implementing EU law, but also when member states derogate from EU law. In particular, interpreting and applying EU law in the light of EU fundamental rights may provide a justification for the member state derogation from the EU free movement provisions on public policy grounds.[48] The judgment of the CJEU in the *Omega* case[49] deserves particular mention in this context. The case arose after the Bonn police authority had issued an order against the German company Omega forbidding it from operating games with the object of firing at human targets, such as a so-called 'laserdrome' involving simulated killings. To manufacture this game, Omega had cooperated with the British Company Pulsar Advanced Games Systems Ltd. The prohibition was issued on the ground that the 'laserdrome' constituted a danger to public order, since the acts of simulated homicide and the resulting trivialization of violence were contrary to fundamental values prevailing in public opinion. In the German courts, Omega's objection against that order was rejected. According to the German Federal Supreme Court in administrative law matters (*Bundesverwaltungsgericht*), the commercial exploitation of a 'killing game' in Omega's 'laserdrome' constituted an affront to the fundamental right to human dignity contained in Article 1 of the Federal Constitution and, therefore, could not be allowed under national law.

Because such a prohibition, in its view, constituted an infringement of Community law, the Federal Supreme Court submitted the following question to the CJEU for a preliminary ruling:

> Is it compatible with the provisions on freedom to provide services and the free movement of goods contained in the Treaty establishing the European Community for a particular commercial activity—in this case the operation of a so-called 'laserdrome' involving simulated killing action—to be prohibited under national law because it offends against the values enshrined in the constitution?[50]

The CJEU gave an affirmative answer to this question. According to the Court, the Community legal order strives to ensure respect for human dignity as a general principle of law, and, therefore, the objective of protecting human dignity is certainly compatible with it. Following its reasoning in the earlier judgment in the *Schmidberger* case,[51] the Court confirmed that the protection of fundamental rights was a legitimate

[46] BVerfG 15 January 1958, BVerfGE 7, 198. On this case in more detail, see Cherednychenko, *supra* note 1, 65 et seq.

[47] Directive 93/13, OJ 1993 L 95/29.

[48] E.g. Case C-112/00, *Schmidberger* [2003] ECR I-5659; Case C-36/02, *Omega* [2004] ECR I-9609. Cf. Case C-438/05, *Viking* [2007] ECR I-10778 and Case C-341/05, *Laval* [2007] ECR I-11767. On this case law in more detail, see the contribution by Colombi Ciacchi, 'European Fundamental Rights, Private Law, and Judicial Governance' in this book.

[49] Case C-36/02, *Omega*.

[50] Ibid., Rec. 17.

[51] Case C-112/00, *Schmidberger*.

interest which could justify a restriction of fundamental freedoms, in this case the freedom to provide services. The Court brought fundamental rights under the notion of public policy. This implied that measures which restrict the freedom to provide services in this case could be justified only if they were necessary for the protection of the interests which they were intended to guarantee and only in so far as those objectives could not be attained by less restrictive means. According to the Court, it was not necessary in that respect for the restrictive measure to correspond to a conception shared by all member states concerning the precise way in which the fundamental right or legitimate interest in question was to be protected. Applying these considerations to the circumstances of the case, the Court ruled that the German prohibition of the 'laserdrome' satisfied both the requirement of necessity and proportionality, and, therefore, could not be regarded as a measure which unjustifiably undermined the freedom to provide services.

Although the *Omega* case arose in the administrative law context, conflicts between fundamental freedoms and fundamental rights may also arise in the contract law context. Interpreting and applying the public policy exceptions to the free movement provisions of the TFEU in the light of EU fundamental rights may involve, for example, assessing the compatibility of a particular private cross-border transaction with such rights. Member state courts and the CJEU may thus play an important role in the constitutionalization of European private law.

C. EU and Member State Positive Obligations to Protect Fundamental Rights in Private Relationships?

Whereas in the previous two sections the negative obligations of the EU and member state public authorities to respect fundamental rights were involved, such authorities can also have positive obligations towards individuals to protect their fundamental rights in the private sphere. The concept of such obligations has been particularly developed in German constitutional law theory. The protective function of fundamental rights (*Schutzgebotsfunktion der Grundrechte)*, which imposes on the state the duty to protect fundamental rights, or, in other words, *positive* obligations, differs from the classical function of fundamental rights as defensive rights against the state (*Eingriffsverbotsfunktion der Grundrechte*), which prohibits any intrusions on the part of the state into fundamental rights and, thus, imposes *negative* obligations on the state. While the latter presupposes the duty of the state to *refrain* from action, the former, by contrast, imposes on the state a duty to *act* when fundamental rights of one individual are violated by another individual (and thus not by the state itself). Accordingly, the issue which lies at the heart of the duty of the state to protect its citizens is not whether public authorities have encroached upon the fundamental rights of private individuals, but whether, by failing to act, they allowed *private individuals* to encroach upon the fundamental rights of other private individuals. The main purpose of such a duty is thus to protect individuals from each other.[52]

The concept of state duties to protect fundamental rights was initially adopted by the German Federal Constitutional Court in cases governed by public law,[53] but

[52] See, e.g. Klein, 'Grundrechtliche Schutzpflicht des Staates', 42 *NJW* (1989) 1633; Isensee, 'Das Abwehrrecht und Staatliche Schutzpflicht', in J. Isensee and P. Kirchhof (eds), *Handbuch des Staatsrecht* (1992) 143; Starck, 'State Duties of Protection and Fundamental Rights', 3 *Potchefstroom Electronic Law Journal* (2000), <http://www.ajol.info/index.php/pelj/article/view/43495>.

[53] See BVerfG 25 February 1975, BVerfGE 39, 1 (*First Abortion Case*) in which the German Federal Constitutional Court declared the Abortion Reform Act enacted in 1974 to be unconstitutional, since

was subsequently extended to private law, in particular contract law, with a view to protecting the weaker contractual party.[54] According to the Constitutional Court's well-established case law,[55] in cases of inequality of bargaining power, when one party is so dominant as to be able to dictate to the other the terms of the contract, the *legislature* is *obliged* to restore the balance of power between the parties in order to *ensure the protection of fundamental rights*. When the legislature omits adopting mandatory contract law for particular areas of life or types of contract, the task of discharging *the duty to protect fundamental rights* is directed to the *judge*; the latter must give effect to fundamental rights using the means available within private law.[56]

Whereas the case law of the German Federal Constitutional Court provides an illustration of how the positive obligations of public authorities to protect fundamental rights can be used as a vehicle for the constitutionalization of private law at *national* level, the case law of the ECtHR contains evidence that a similar development may also take place at *supranational* level. The starting point for the idea of state responsibility for the infringement of the rights embodied in the ECHR by private actors lies in the *Marckx* case[57] decided in 1979. In this case the ECtHR made clear that a state's duty not to interfere with the exercise of the right to private and family life under Article 8 of the Convention may encompass positive obligations—for example, to legislate in a way which is compatible with that right.[58]

The existence of the positive obligations of the state at supranational level opens up possibilities for the protection of individuals against each other by holding the state responsible in the international arena for a failure to legislate or take other measures in order to guarantee fundamental rights in relationships between private parties. The question which arises in this context is whether the concept of positive obligations has a role to play in the constitutionalization of European private law and, if so, to what extent.

The concept of positive obligations as such is not unknown in EU law. In the *Commission v France* case,[59] for example, the CJEU explicitly acknowledged the existence of such an obligation in the context of free movement of goods. The Court ruled that Article 28 of the EC Treaty (now Article 34 TFEU) on the free movement of goods requires each member state to take *all* necessary measures to ensure that this fundamental freedom is respected on their territory, including those for the purposes of preventing any restriction due to the acts of *individuals*.[60] No such 'independent' positive obligations, however, have been accepted by the Court in relation to EU fundamental rights.

it fell short of *protecting the human life* of the unborn child that was required by Art. 2(2) of the Federal Constitution.

[54] In so doing, the Federal Constitutional Court followed the theory of state duties to protect fundamental rights in private law which was primarily developed by Canaris. See Canaris, 'Grundrechte und Privatrecht', 184 *Archiv für civilistische Praxis* (1984) 201 and C.-W. Canaris, *Grundrechte und Privatrecht* (1999).

[55] See, e.g. BVerfG 7 February 1990, BVerfGE 81, 242 (*Handelsvertreter*) and BVerfG 19 October 1993, BVerfGE 89, 214 (*Bürgschaft*).

[56] See, in particular, BVerfG 7 February 1990, BVerfGE 81, 242, 255 et seq. (*Handelsvertreter*).

[57] *Marckx v Belgium*, ECHR (1979) Series A, No. 31.

[58] Ibid., Rec. 31. On the positive obligations in the case law of the ECtHR and private law in more detail, see Cherednychenko, 'Towards the Control of Private Acts by the European Court of Human Rights?', 13 *Maastricht Journal of European and Comparative Law* (2006) 195, at 201 et seq.

[59] Case C-265/95, *Commission v France* [1997] ECR I-6959. See also Case C-112/00, *Schmidberger*.

[60] Case C-265/95, *Commission v France*, Recs 30–32.

So far the duty to protect fundamental rights has only served as a legitimate interest which may *justify* a restriction of fundamental freedoms. The *Omega* case discussed in section 2(B) is a good illustration. This is not surprising, considering that EU fundamental rights apply only in so far as the EU is competent to act, and that the EU is thus not the organization whose core task is the promotion of fundamental rights.

There is some evidence, however, that the drafters of the EUCFR did not mean to exclude the more 'independent' protective function of the provisions contained therein altogether. As has already been discussed in section 2(A), the Charter distinguishes between 'rights' that are to be 'respected', and 'principles' that are to be 'observed'. While the explanations to the Charter do not make it clear what *respecting* the Charter *rights* implies, they throw some light on what *observing* the Charter *principles* means. The principles *may* be implemented through legislative or executive acts adopted by the EU within the limits of its powers and by the member states within the scope of EU law; as such, however, principles do *not* give rise to direct claims for positive action by the EU institutions or member state authorities.[61] This explanation appears to suggest that, in contrast to the principles, the *rights* contained in the EUCFR may give rise to direct claims for positive action by the EU and national public authorities.

The adoption in EU law of a robust version of the positive obligations with regard to fundamental rights, similar to the one recognized, for example, in German constitutional law, could have far-reaching consequences for private law. After all, this would enable the CJEU to actively shape European private law by imposing duties to adopt certain measures on the EU and national legislatures in order to promote particular EU fundamental rights and, in the case of the legislature's failure to fulfil its duties of protection, by imposing duties to protect fundamental rights through the means available within the existing private law on national courts. This scenario, however, is not very likely to occur considering that the promotion of fundamental rights as such is not the core task of the EU.

Nevertheless, a weaker version of the positive obligations to protect fundamental rights has the potential to develop in EU law within the framework of the well-established duties of the EU and member state public authorities to interpret and apply EU law and national laws that fall within the scope of EU law in conformity with EU fundamental rights. Whereas, as has been demonstrated above, in many cases such duties will entail the negative obligations of national courts not to interfere with fundamental rights, it is not excluded that in some cases they may also give rise to the courts' positive obligations.

The *Promusicae* case[62] may serve as an illustration. This case has already been mentioned in the previous section when discussing the need to strike a fair balance between various fundamental rights which may arise in the course of the interpretation and application of EU law. What is interesting here is that the question which was referred to the CJEU in this case was, in essence, whether Community law, in particular Directives 2000/31, 2001/29, and 2004/48, read in the light of the right to property, including intellectual property (Article 17(2) EUCFR) and the right to an effective remedy (Article 47 EUCFR) must be interpreted as requiring member states to lay down, in order to ensure effective protection of copyright, an obligation to communicate personal data in the context of civil proceedings. Answering this question in the affirmative would effectively

[61] See the explanation to Art. 52 of the Charter in Explanations Relating to the Charter of Fundamental Rights, *supra* note 19.

[62] C-275/06, *Promusicae*.

amount to the imposition on the member states of a positive obligation to respect the EU fundamental rights in question within the scope of the above-mentioned directives.

The CJEU did not go so far as to impose such an obligation on the member states in the particular circumstances of the *Promusicae* case. However, it did state that Community law requires that when transposing the above-mentioned directives and applying the implementing measures, member states make sure that they rely on an interpretation which allows a fair balance to be struck between the various EU fundamental rights.[63] It is not excluded, therefore, that in other cases the need to strike such a balance would require the adoption of *positive* measures within the scope of EU law.

Taking into account the concept of positive obligations when interpreting and applying EU secondary law may thus open up new frontiers in the judicial development of European private law. In essence, the weaker version of positive obligations could be used by the courts to imply certain rules in the EU measures when interpreting and applying them in the light of their specific objectives and EU fundamental rights. It remains to be seen, however, whether the CJEU will resort to the concept of positive obligations in the field of private law.

In addition, the concept of positive obligations may play a role in the development of European private law by providing a source of inspiration for rule-makers at EU and national level to adopt legislation which would promote EU fundamental rights. It is notable in this respect that in its guidance on the use of statements of compatibility with fundamental rights in the recitals to the proposed legislative instruments, the European Commission explicitly recognizes that some legislative proposals aim to *implement* or *promote* fundamental rights laid down in the EUCFR.[64] The idea behind the concept of positive obligations is also reflected in the role assigned by the drafters of the Charter to fundamental *principles* contained therein, such as the principle of consumer protection (Article 38 EUCFR). The rule-makers *may* implement such principles within the limits of their powers through legislative or executive acts but are not obliged to do so. In my view, the concept of positive obligations could play a similar role with regard to the Charter *rights*.

D. Direct Horizontal Effect of EU Fundamental Rights?

So far our investigation of the gateways to the constitutionalization of European private law has focused on the direct *vertical* effect of EU fundamental rights, i.e. the applicability of fundamental rights to the EU and member state public authorities involved in making, interpreting, and applying private law, on the basis of the negative and possibly even positive obligations of such authorities with regard to EU fundamental rights. In its turn, the fulfilment of such obligations by public authorities produces indirect *horizontal* effect of these rights, i.e. the effect of EU fundamental rights on the rights and obligations of private parties by means of the applicable private laws.

The *indirect* horizontal effect of EU fundamental rights in this sense can be distinguished from their *direct* horizontal effect. The latter circumvents the need to invoke fundamental rights against public authorities because a claim or a defence can be directly based on a fundamental right which overrides an otherwise applicable rule of private law. Hence, the validity of private acts becomes directly dependent upon fundamental rights clauses, and, if their violation has been found, the role of private law is limited to providing for the consequences of illegality, such as invalidity or damages.

[63] Ibid., Rec. 70.

[64] Commission Communication (2005), *supra* note 21.

At present, the direct horizontal effect of fundamental rights in private law is far less common in European legal systems than the other form of horizontal effect of fundamental rights, i.e. the indirect horizontal effect in the sense outlined above.[65] In the EU law context, however, the idea of direct horizontal effect appears to have gained more recognition. Thus, the CJEU has granted direct horizontal effect to the freedom of movement of workers,[66] the freedom to provide services,[67] and the freedom of establishment.[68] Although the Court has not yet expressed a general opinion on the question whether EU fundamental rights are directly applicable in relationships between private parties, it is notable that direct horizontal effect was explicitly granted by the Court to the principle of equal pay for men and women laid down in Article 157 TFEU (ex-Article 119 EC Treaty)[69] and the principle of non-discrimination based on nationality surrounding employment, remuneration, and other employment-related conditions embodied in Article 45(2) TFEU (ex-Article 48 EC Treaty).[70] This was done for a simple reason, i.e. 'to ensure that there is no discrimination on the labour market'.[71] Mention should also be made here of the Court's ruling in *Kücükdeveci*[72] discussed in more detail in section 2(A), where, in essence, the Court applied the principle of non-discrimination on grounds of age to an employment relationship between two private parties.[73]

In light of this, it cannot be excluded that the CJEU will also grant direct horizontal effect to other EU fundamental rights in the form of general principles or under the EUCFR in cases that fall within the scope of EU law.[74] This would circumvent the need for private parties to invoke fundamental rights against public authorities in order to ensure respect for such rights in the private sphere. In particular, it would become unnecessary to search for and rely on an interpretation of national law of EU origin which would strike a fair balance between competing EU fundamental rights. The latter would be directly applicable to private acts concerning matters that fall within the scope of EU law, and their impact would thus no longer be mediated by private laws.

3. The Actual and Potential Impact of EU Fundamental Rights on European Financial Services Law

The preceding analysis has shown that EU fundamental rights may enter into European private law through multiple gateways ranging from the negative obligations of the EU and member states to respect such rights to their direct horizontal effect. Armed with the legal constructs which may bring the EU fundamental rights into the private law domain, we can now turn our attention to the practical implications of the constitutionalization

65 On this in more detail, see Cherednychenko, *supra* note 1, chapter 3.

66 E.g. Case C-415/93, *Bosman* [1995] ECR I-4921; Case C-281/98, *Angonese* [2000] ECR I-4139.

67 E.g. Joined cases C-51/96 and C-191/97, *Deliège* [2000] ECR I-02549; Case C-341/05, *Laval*.

68 E.g. Case C-438/05, *Viking*.

69 Case 43/75, *Defrenne II* [1976] ECR 455, Rec. 39.

70 Case C-218/98, *Angonese*, Rec. 36.

71 Ibid., Rec. 35.

72 Case C-555/07, *Kücükdeveci*.

73 On the particularities of the CJEU's approach in this case, see the Opinion by AG Trstenjak of 8 September 2011 in Case C-282/10, *Dominguez*, Rec. 144 et seq. and the literature mentioned in *supra* note 35.

74 Cf. Opinion by AG Trstenjak of 8 September 2011 in Case C-282/10, *Dominguez*, who concludes that 'the direct application of fundamental rights in the form of general principles in relationships between private individuals cannot be ruled out in principle' (para. 126). At the same time, she argues against the direct horizontal effect of EU fundamental rights in the form of general principles or under the EUCFR (para. 71 et seq.)

of European private law for European financial services law. In the following, the actual and potential impact of EU fundamental rights in this area will be discussed in relation to three major issues: (1) consumer access to financial services; (2) substantive consumer protection in financial services; and (3) procedural consumer protection in financial services.

A. Consumer Access to Financial Services

1. *The Problem of Consumer Access to Financial Services*

Access to financial services has become crucial for the consumer's ability to fully participate not only in the market in such services but also in society.[75] For example, a consumer who cannot open a basic bank account and/or have a credit card due to over-indebtedness or bankruptcy is not only denied the possibility to buy goods via the internet where it is not possible to pay in cash. In addition, such a consumer faces the risk of being excluded from society. In particular, he or she may lose a job or struggle to find work because his or her employer can only pay wages into a bank account. Moreover, following welfare state downsizing across the EU, European households have become increasingly dependent on credit and investment as a means to plan for the long term and to protect themselves against (unforeseen) changes in circumstances. Without access to such services, for instance, consumers may not be able to buy a family home or to provide for sufficient income after retirement.

The importance of consumer access to the market in goods and services has been acknowledged at EU level. According to Hans-W. Micklitz, the EU regulatory private law is even governed by the model of 'access justice' ('*Zugangsgerechtigkeit*').[76] The idea behind this model of justice is that EU law is supposed to provide for a legal framework which would ensure that consumers, including those particularly vulnerable, have a realistic chance of access to the market and to the European society in so far as it exists. As such, access justice reaches far beyond corrective justice that lies at the foundations of traditional private law as it has developed in national legal systems. Whereas corrective justice relies on individual autonomy and self-responsibility, leaving it to the individual to find ways to realize his or her access rights, access justice in EU law presupposes that the latter ensures that weaker parties have a fair chance to participate in the single market. Micklitz also identifies two elements which constitute the European model of access justice: the rules prohibiting various forms of discrimination in the access to goods and services on the one hand, and the rules granting access 'rights' on the other.[77] Whereas the former constitute a 'negative' side of access justice, the latter reflect its 'positive' side.

The access justice model in this sense manifests itself most strikingly in the EU regulation of services of general economic interest, such as electricity, gas, telecommunication, and transport. The obvious concern of the EU legislature in this area has been that these particular services remain accessible to everybody, including most vulnerable consumers, following the replacement of public monopolies with a broad variety of private suppliers operating in a competitive market. The EU legislation in the energy field is particularly illustrative in this respect. For example, Article 3(3) of Directive 2009/72 concerning

[75] Cf. Micklitz, 'The Paradox of Access to Financial Services for Consumers', *European Journal of Consumer Law* (2010) 7, at 9 et seq.

[76] H.-W. Micklitz, 'Social Justice and Access Justice in Private Law', EUI Working Papers Law, 2011/02 (2011).

[77] Ibid., section 5.2.

common rules for the Internal Market in electricity[78] obliges member states to ensure that all household customers enjoy 'universal service', i.e. 'the right to be supplied with electricity of a specified quality within their territory at reasonable, easily and clearly comparable, transparent and non-discriminatory prices'. In addition, Article 3(7) of the same directive requires that member states ensure that there are adequate safeguards to protect vulnerable customers. In this context, member states must define the concept of vulnerable customers. Such a concept 'may refer to energy poverty and, *inter alia*, to the prohibition of disconnection of electricity to such customers in critical times'.[79]

Although such financial services as payment and credit have much in common with the services of general economic interest in terms of their economic and social importance, at present, the access justice philosophy in this field is underdeveloped, particularly as far as the protection of vulnerable consumers is concerned. Under current EU law, financial services, including payment and credit, are not regarded as universal services to which everybody is entitled, including those who are in financial trouble. In the absence of specific protective legislation, this may result, for example, in the different treatment of consumers in the access to financial services on grounds of age. Moreover, consumers who are going through bankruptcy, for instance, may be denied access to financial services altogether, including access to a basic bank account, which can be quite a demoralizing experience. The question which arises in this context is whether EU fundamental rights can play a role in promoting access justice in the field of financial services and, if so, in what way and to what extent.

2. *The 'Negative' Side of Access Justice*

As has been mentioned above, one of the constituent elements of the European access justice model is the prohibition of various forms of discrimination in the access to goods and services. So far, the EU legislature has adopted two specific measures combating racial, ethnic, and gender discrimination in the access to goods and services, including financial services, i.e. Directive 2000/43 implementing the principle of equal treatment between persons irrespective of racial or ethnic origin[80] and Directive 2004/113 implementing the principle of equal treatment between men and women in the access to and supply of goods and services.[81] In 2008, the European Commission published an ambitious proposal for a directive on implementing the principle of equal treatment between persons irrespective of religion or belief, disability, age, or sexual orientation.[82] If adopted, this directive would significantly extend protection from discrimination in the access to financial services in EU law covering, inter alia, different treatment of consumers on grounds of age, which is particularly common in the field of insurance.[83]

By adopting secondary legislation combating discrimination in specific areas and on specific grounds, in essence, the EU legislature implements the EU fundamental rights and/or principles enshrined in Chapter III of the EUCFR entitled 'Equality'. Thus, for example, Article 21 of the Charter prohibits any discrimination based on any ground

[78] Directive 2009/72, OJ 2009 L 211/65.

[79] On the protection of vulnerable consumers in the energy field in more detail, see Bartl, 'The Affordability of Energy: How Much Protection for the Vulnerable Consumers', 33 *Journal of Consumer Policy* (2010) 225.

[80] Directive 2000/43, OJ 2000 L 180/22.

[81] Directive 2004/113, OJ 2004 L 373/37.

[82] Proposal for a Council Directive on implementing the principle of equal treatment between persons irrespective of religion or belief, disability, age or sexual orientation, COM(2008) 426 final.

[83] At the time of writing this contribution, however, this directive has still not been adopted.

such as sex, race, colour, ethnic or social origin, genetic features, language, religion or belief, political or any other opinion, membership of a national minority, property, birth, disability, age, or sexual orientation. In its turn, Article 23 of the Charter postulates that equality between men and women must be ensured in all areas. Such provisions appear to serve as a source of inspiration for the European Commission to initiate anti-discrimination legislation which would promote the protection of the fundamental rights contained in the Charter in the access to goods and services, including financial services. It is here where the weak version of positive obligations described in section 2(C) appears to come into play.

In addition, in light of the findings presented in section 2(A), it should be remembered that the EU and member state legislatures, when acting within the scope of EU law, have negative obligations not to enact rules which would be contrary to EU fundamental rights. Both the EU and national anti-discrimination measures that fall within the scope of EU law, therefore, must be in conformity with the EUCFR. The link between fundamental rights and secondary EU legislation may lead the CJEU to review the EU legislation and national laws falling within the scope of EU law as to their compatibility with EU fundamental rights, particularly when such a link is explicitly made in the recitals to a specific anti-discrimination directive.

As the recent *Test-Achats* case[84] shows, such an ex post review of the EU anti-discrimination legislation may have far-reaching consequences for the scope of application of the principle of equal treatment in the access to financial services. In its judgment in this case, the CJEU struck down Article 5(2) of Directive 2004/113 implementing the principle of equal treatment between men and women in the access to and supply of goods and services as incompatible with the EUCFR. This provision enabled member states to permit proportionate differences in individuals' premiums and benefits for the purposes of insurance and related financial services where the use of sex was a determining factor in the assessment of risk based on relevant and accurate actuarial and statistical data. The fact that the Charter was not yet binding at the time the directive in question was adopted did not prevent the Court from assessing the compatibility of Article 5(2) of the directive with Articles 21 and 23 of the Charter. As has already been mentioned above, these articles state, respectively, that any discrimination based on sex is prohibited and that equality between men and women must be ensured in all areas.

According to the CJEU, '[s]ince recital 4 to Directive 2004/113 expressly refers to Articles 21 and 23 of the Charter, the validity of Article 5(2) of that directive must be assessed in the light of those provisions'.[85] Considering that Article 5(2) of Directive 2004/113 allowed member states to maintain an exception from the main rule of unisex premiums and benefits contained in Article 5(1) of this directive without temporal limitation, the Court concluded that the provision in question worked against the achievement of the objective of equal treatment between men and women pursued by the directive, and was, therefore, incompatible with Articles 21 and 23 of the Charter. The CJEU's ruling affected not only Article 5(2) of Directive 2004/113, but also the national laws which were adopted in accordance with this provision and which allowed for the different treatment of men and women in relation to insurance premiums and benefits. Following the CJEU's judgment in the *Test-Achats* case, the European Commission issued the guidelines on the application of Directive 2004/113 to insurance in the light of the Court's findings in this case.[86]

[84] Case C-236/09, *Test-Achats* [2011] ECR I-00773.

[85] Ibid., Rec. 17.

[86] Communication from the Commission on the application of Council Directive 2004/113/EC to insurance, in the light of the judgment of the Court of Justice of the European Union in Case C-236/09 (Test-Achats), C(2011) 9497 final.

Thus, the negative obligation of the EU legislature not to enact rules which would be contrary to the EU fundamental rights and the reference to the Charter in the recital to Directive 2004/113 enabled the CJEU in the *Test-Achats* case to extend the scope of application of the principle of equal treatment in the field of insurance beyond the one initially envisaged by the EU legislature. In so doing, however, the Court also entered into a controversial debate concerning the (limits to) the application of this principle in the field of financial services. As has been widely noted in the literature, for example, the unrestricted application of the principle of equal treatment in the insurance sector comes at a price and may not necessarily be a consumer friendly measure.[87] After all, more cautious women drivers may end up subsidizing more risky male drivers, while male insured persons may end up paying more for additional costs of women's medical treatment and their longer life expectancy.

Such considerations could have provided a good reason for the CJEU to exercise self-restraint when reviewing the EU legislation concerning non-discrimination in the field of financial services as to its compatibility with EU fundamental rights. Nevertheless, in the *Test-Achats* case, the CJEU chose to interfere with the EU legislature's choice concerning the limits of the application of the principle of equal treatment in the insurance sector. By opting for judicial activism in this case, the Court demonstrated its willingness to closely scrutinize provisions in the EU legislation allowing member states to derogate from the principle of equal treatment in the financial services field.

Furthermore, the judgments of the CJEU in *Mangold* and *Kücükdeveci* concerning the principle of non-discrimination on grounds of age in the employment context, which have been discussed in more detail in section 2(A), show that the CJEU is also prepared to interfere with the choices made by the *member state* legislatures concerning the limits of non-discrimination in private law. The approach adopted by the Court in these cases appears to have opened up possibilities for the direct ex ante review of the *national* private laws falling within the scope of EU law as to their conformity with the EU Charter provisions concerning equal treatment. Therefore, once there is a specific EU measure combating discrimination in the access to financial services which implements a particular EU fundamental right, such a measure may bring national laws touching upon the subject matter regulated by it within the scope of EU law triggering their fundamental right review. This could lead to a profound impact of EU fundamental rights prohibiting discrimination on the national legislation affecting the access to financial services and expand the scope of EU non-discrimination law even further.

This analysis suggests that the negative obligations of the EU and national public authorities to respect EU fundamental rights could play a particularly important role in the development of the 'negative' side of the European model of access justice concerned with combating various forms of discrimination in the access to goods and services. However, resort to the concept of negative obligations with a view to combating discrimination in the field of financial services, in particular on grounds of sex and age, is not without risk. The robust approach by the CJEU to fundamental rights review of legislative measures may discourage the adoption of a more balanced legislation which would be fine-tuned to the characteristics of specific financial services. Moreover, such

[87] See, e.g. Reich, 'Non-Discrimination and the Many Faces of Private Law in the Union—Some Thoughts After the "Test-Achats" Judgment of the ECJ of 1.3.2011', 2 *The European Journal of Risk Regulation* (2011) 283, at 289; Reich, 'The Impact of the Non-Discrimination Principle on Private Autonomy', in D. Leczykiewicz and S. Weatherill (eds), *The Involvement of EU Law in Private Law Relationships* (2013) 253, at 268–269.

an approach may even lead to the uncontrolled expansion of the principle of equal treatment in this area at the expense of consumer protection.

3. *The 'Positive' Side of Access Justice*

So far we have investigated the role of fundamental rights in promoting the 'negative' side of the European model of access justice embodied in the EU non-discrimination law. Next to the 'negative' side, however, this model also has a 'positive' side. As has already been mentioned above, the 'positive' side of access justice is reflected in the rules granting access 'rights'. Such rules constitute the second important element of the access justice model and are meant to actively promote the access of all consumers, including those vulnerable, to goods and services. At present, however, the rules granting access 'rights' to consumers in the area of financial services remain largely underdeveloped. Can EU fundamental rights contribute to the development of access rights in this area and, if so, how and to what extent?

In my opinion, an important role in promoting financial inclusion could be played by the positive obligations of public authorities to protect EU fundamental rights. In the absence of specific rules granting access 'rights', the concept of positive obligations may open up new frontiers in the judicial development of the 'positive' side of access justice in European private law.

An example from the payment services field may serve as an illustration. As has been explained above, nowadays access to a basic bank account has become a precondition for full participation in the economic and social life of a modern society. Nevertheless, Directive 2007/64 on payment services currently in force does not provide for any rules in this respect. Despite the adoption of the European Commission Recommendation to member states setting out the fundamental principles which should be put in place at national level to guarantee access to suitable payment services,[88] at present, only a few member states appear to be close to complying with the principles set out in the Recommendation.[89] However, in view of the fact that payment services have become essential in the everyday life of EU citizens, it is plausible to argue that such services must be considered to be universal services similar to transport, telecommunication, postal, and energy supply services.[90]

The acceptance of this argument would open up the possibility to interpret Directive 2007/64 in the light of the freedom to conduct a business (Article 16 EUCFR), on the one hand, and the principle of respect by the EU for the access to services of general economic interest in conjunction with the principle of consumer protection (Articles 36 and 38 EUCFR, respectively), on the other. Following the CJEU's approach in *Promusicae* outlined in sections 2(B) and 2(C), a fair balance would need to be struck between these competing fundamental rights and principles when interpreting and applying Directive 2007/64 in the specific case. The outcome of the balancing exercise could be that this directive would have to be construed in a way which requires member states to ensure that consumers have access to a basic bank account. Such a finding would, in essence,

[88] European Commission, Recommendation on Access to Basic Payment Services (2011) (C(2011) 4977/4).

[89] European Commission, Commission Staff Working Document, National measures and practices as regards access to basic payment accounts. Follow-up to the Recommendation of 18 July 2011 on access to a basic payment account, SWD(2012) 249 final, in particular at 19.

[90] Cf. Micklitz, *supra* note 75, at 15.

imply the imposition of a positive obligation on the member states to ensure respect for Articles 36 and 38 of the Charter within the scope of Directive 2007/64.

As this example demonstrates, the weaker version of positive obligations could, in essence, be used by the courts to imply certain rules in the EU measures when interpreting and applying them in the light of their specific objectives and particular EU fundamental rights. Such an approach has the potential to provide ground-breaking solutions to important societal problems which are difficult to address via the ordinary legislative procedure in the EU. At the same time, the use of the concept of positive obligations by the CJEU in order to resolve sensitive issues on which no consensus has been established yet among member states also involves considerable risks. In particular, it might lead the Court to conceal the real political and socio-economic issues involved in the particular case under the guise of the interpretation and application of EU fundamental rights or even adopt simplistic solutions in individual cases without taking into account their broader societal implications. It remains to be seen, therefore, whether the CJEU will resort to the concept of positive obligations when interpreting and applying legislation in the field of financial services.

In any case, the concept of positive obligations could play an important role in the development of the 'positive' side of access justice in European financial services law by providing a source of inspiration for rule-makers at EU and national level to introduce legislation which would promote EU fundamental rights. The recognition of the right to a basic bank account as a fundamental right, for instance, could prompt the EU legislature to adopt mandatory legislation on access to basic payment services which would guarantee such a right to the most vulnerable consumers.[91]

4. Direct Horizontal Effect?

Last but not least, both the 'positive' and 'negative' side of access justice in the field of financial services could also potentially be promoted through the direct horizontal effect of EU fundamental rights in the form of general principles or under the EUCFR as outlined in section 2(D). If a particular fundamental right is granted direct horizontal effect, it would apply to private acts solely by reason of the fact that such acts concern a matter that is governed by a particular EU measure in the financial services field. This could mean, for instance, that male drivers who are to pay more for their car insurance than female drivers directly invoke Article 23 of the Charter, which prohibits sex discrimination, against a car insurance company that uses sex as one of the determining factors in the assessment of risk. The possibility to do so would circumvent the need to contest the compatibility of the EU or national legislation allowing such conduct with the EU fundamental rights. Similarly, the principle of respect by the EU for the access to services of general economic interest embodied in Article 36 of the EUCFR could be directly invoked against a bank refusing to open a basic bank account to a homeless EU citizen. This would make it unnecessary for such a citizen to resort to the concept of the positive obligations of public authorities to protect EU fundamental rights in order to imply the right to a basic bank account in Directive 2007/64 on payment services.

One may doubt, however, whether broadly formulated EU fundamental rights as such are suitable for direct application to private relationships. All the more so, because

[91] At the time of writing this contribution, the European Commission is considering whether legislative action in this area is needed following its recommendation on access to a basic bank account. See European Commission, *supra* note 89.

in most cases *both* parties to a dispute would be able to invoke fundamental rights. For example, while a male driver who is to pay more for his car insurance than a female driver could directly invoke Article 23 of the EUCFR prohibiting sex discrimination, the car insurance company could resort to Article 16 of the Charter concerning its freedom to conduct a business. In the same way, while the (potential) client whose application for a basic bank account has been refused could invoke Article 36 of the EUCFR against the bank, the bank could invoke Article 16 of the Charter against the client. As a consequence, the courts could be confronted with a difficult task of balancing the countervailing fundamental rights against each other *outside* the specific legislative framework. Such an exercise would allow them to conceal or even ignore the complex socio-economic and political issues concerning the access to financial services involved in such a balancing under the veil of the direct application of EU fundamental rights.[92]

B. Substantive Consumer Protection in Financial Services

1. *Substantive Consumer Problems*

Even if a particular consumer is not discriminated against and easily gains access to a particular financial service, he or she may still end up in financial and social trouble. Unregulated access to financial services may lead consumers to take huge financial risks in the exercise of their private autonomy. This may have a dramatic impact not only on the consumer's financial situation, but also on his or her individual and family well-being. The case law of civil courts in the EU member states contains numerous examples of large-scale financial service mis-sellings, many of which have manifested themselves most strikingly in the aftermath of the global financial crisis.

The Netherlands, for instance, has witnessed the large-scale 'mis-sellings' of complex financial products which allowed Dutch retail investors with modest financial means to purchase securities with borrowed money, also known as '*effectenlease*'. Initially, such products were lucrative for the investors owing to the favourable stock market returns in the 1990s. The worsening of the stock market climate and the change in fiscal rules at the beginning of the 21st century has ultimately resulted in financial setbacks for many retail investors at the end of the *effectenlease*-contract duration; instead of substantial investment returns, visions of which had been conjured up to the retail investors by suppliers of *effectenlease* products prior to signing the contract, many such investors ended up with an investment portfolio which was too low in value to repay their debts. The result was an explosion of civil litigation in the Netherlands which highlighted the unsuitability of the *effectenlease* products for many Dutch retail investors and the failure of their suppliers to warn the investors about the risks involved in such products.[93]

In Germany, the collapse of the internationally operating bank Lehman Brothers in October 2008 has caused trouble for thousands of German retail investors who had bought Lehman 'certificates' ('*Zertifikate*') from local banks and other financial intermediaries. Those affected were mostly risk-averse pensioners who thought they had made a safe investment, whereas, in reality, they had purchased derivative financial products whose value was often tied to various stock indexes. Following Lehman Brothers' bankruptcy,

[92] See in this context Cherednychenko (2008), *supra* note 16, at 41 et seq. For a critical analysis of the concept of direct horizontal effect, see also Collins, *supra* note 6, at 143 et seq.

[93] See *Levob Bank N.V. v B. and GBD, De T. v Dexia Bank Nederland N.V.* and *Stichting Gedupeerden Spaarconstructie v Aegon Bank N.V., RvdW* 2009, 683, 684–685, respectively.

many such investors lost their entire savings, which in some cases has resulted in the destruction of the foundations of their economic existence. Banks and other financial intermediaries which sold Lehman certificates in Germany were faced with numerous claims filed by their aggrieved clients who allegedly had not received proper information and advice concerning these complex financial instruments. These claims have had varying degrees of success in German civil courts.[94]

In Spain, the recent financial crisis has revealed large-scale irresponsible lending in the residential mortgage market and the harshness of many contract terms included by Spanish banks in mortgage-backed credit agreements which were concluded by consumers to finance a home purchase. Many such agreements, for example, contained acceleration clauses that entitled the banks to terminate them and to claim from the consumer the repayment of the total amount borrowed if he or she has defaulted on just one of the hundreds of monthly payments due under the agreement. On top of that the bank could also demand that the consumer pays interest on the outstanding amount of debt at the default annual interest rate many times exceeding the nominal interest rate initially agreed upon by the parties. As borrowers have found their loans increasingly unaffordable, they have been confronted with the harsh consequences of such terms. Since a property bubble burst in 2008, there have been several hundred thousand defaults and foreclosures. Whereas many consumers resorted to courts to contest the validity of the terms of the mortgage credit agreements concluded by them,[95] for some the prospect of being evicted from their home became too much to bear and resulted in suicide.

These examples provide an illustration of some of the main problems experienced by European consumers who gained access to financial services in the EU member states. Among such problems are poor information concerning the risks involved in a particular financial product or service; unsuitability of many such products and services for the consumers to which they were sold, considering, inter alia, the degree of their risk aversion and financial situation; irresponsible lending; harsh terms of mortgage credit agreements which were not individually negotiated. In the given examples, these problems were aggravated by the fact that they affected particularly vulnerable groups of consumers, such as those on low income or retired, and/or arose in relation to the assets particularly important for the individual and family well-being, such as a family home. As the EU and national regulation then in force addressed the aforesaid problems only to a limited extent, in most cases the aggrieved consumers sought relief on the basis of general private laws.

While the need to protect consumers of financial services is generally acknowledged in European financial services law, the latter does not establish a comprehensive and coherent legal framework to this end revealing many gaps and inconsistencies in the regulatory regimes applicable to different types of financial services. Thus, for example, although retail investment in the financial markets is largely channelled through so-called 'packaged retail investment products' (PRIPs), such as the above-mentioned *effectenlease* products, the conduct of business rules contained in the MiFID I currently in force, including the obligation of investment service providers to know their clients, do not apply to such products. The European Commission seeks to close this gap in the

[94] On this in more detail, see, e.g. Hofmann, 'Central Bank Collateral and the Lehman Collapse', 6 *Capital Markets Law Journal* (2011) 456; Spindler, 'Behavioural Finance and Investor Protection Regulations', 33 *Journal of Consumer Policy* (2011) 315, at 330.

[95] See, e.g. Case C-415/11, *Aziz*, judgment of 14 March 2013, not yet published.

regulatory framework by extending the MiFID I conduct of business rules to PRIPs in the MiFID II which should replace the MiFID I.[96]

Similarly, Directive 2008/48 on consumer credit does not apply to a variety of loan contracts concluded by consumers across the EU, such as mortgage-backed loans, loans involving a total amount of credit more than €75,000, loans on credit cards, and loans on a pledge (Article 2(2) of Directive 2008/48). In the aftermath of the financial crisis, which was partly caused by large-scale irresponsible lending in the residential mortgage market, the European Commission has proposed a directive on credit agreements relating to residential property.[97] The adoption of this directive, however, could result in peculiar differences in the extent of consumer protection in European financial services law across various types of financial services regulated at EU level. Whereas the proposed directive on credit agreements relating to residential property prohibits the creditor from granting the mortgage-backed credit if the consumer is not able to repay it over the lifetime of the credit agreement, no such severe restrictions on freedom of contract have been imposed under Directive 2008/48 on consumer credit or the MiFID I and a proposal for the MiFID II.

One of the major difficulties faced by the EU legislature in ensuring adequate substantive consumer protection in financial services at EU level lies in having to reconcile divergent views among the member states concerning the right balance between private autonomy and consumer protection, in particular as far as vulnerable consumers are concerned. The need to make political compromises has often resulted in the inability of the EU legislature to tackle pressing issues in retail financial markets and, hence, to prevent financial service mis-sellings. Moreover, the starting point of regulatory EU measures in the field of financial services is the notion of the 'average consumer' who is 'reasonably well-informed and reasonably observant and circumspect', a concept developed by the CJEU in its free movement case law.[98] One may doubt, however, to what extent consumers which were affected by the above-mentioned mis-sellings in the Netherlands, Germany, and Spain correspond to the EU consumer role model.

The question which arises in this context is what role could be played by EU fundamental rights in ensuring appropriate substantive consumer protection in financial services within the existing EU regulatory framework and beyond. In particular, how could fundamental rights influence the development of European financial services law, so as to ensure that the latter addresses serious problems facing consumers of financial services across the EU and helps to prevent similar problems from occurring in the future?

When discussing these issues, it is helpful to bear in mind the distinction between the negative and positive obligations of the EU and member state public authorities with regard to EU fundamental rights introduced in section 2. As will be illustrated below, both kinds of obligations may play a role in developing substantive consumer protection in European financial services law, albeit in a different way and to a different degree. Let us first examine the role of negative obligations in this context.

[96] The MiFID review is currently underway. See Proposal for a Directive of the European Parliament and of the Council on markets in financial instruments repealing Directive 2004/39/EC of the European Parliament and of the Council (Recast), COM(2011) 656 final.

[97] Proposal for a Directive of the European Parliament and of the Council on credit agreements relating to residential property, COM(2011) 142 final.

[98] See Case C-210/96, *Gut Springenheide* [1998] ECR I-4657.

2. The 'Negative' Side of Substantive Consumer Protection

In theory, the negative obligations of the EU and national public authorities to respect EU fundamental rights could play a role in ensuring that the EU and national consumer protection legislation falling within the scope of EU law does not impair such rights. Resorting to EU fundamental rights could result in setting aside specific legislative provisions or interpreting them in a way which would be compatible with fundamental rights. One may question, however, whether doing so would often be necessary and make sense in practice. Manifestly consumer-unfriendly provisions in the legislation granting substantive consumer protection in the field of financial services do not seem to be very common today. The problem is rather that the legislation in this field often contains important omissions and/or provides for protection which may not go far enough in the aftermath of the recent financial crisis, particularly as far as vulnerable consumers are concerned. Positive steps are, therefore, normally necessary in order to ensure substantive consumer protection.

Nevertheless, the concept of negative obligations as such is not entirely irrelevant in the present context. As the example of the *Omega* case discussed in section 2(B) demonstrates, the negative obligation of the EU and member state public authorities to interpret and apply public policy exceptions to the free movement provisions in the light of EU fundamental rights may enable the member states to justify their derogations from the EU free movement rules. Although the *Omega* case arose in the administrative law context following the prohibition of the exploitation of a 'killing game' by the German police authority, conflicts between fundamental freedoms and fundamental rights may also arise in the contract law context, in particular in relation to financial services.

Consider the following hypothetical example. In the wake of the financial crisis the financial supervisory authority of a particular member state issues a prohibition to bring a particular highly speculative investment product on the market in that member state. Such a prohibition is issued on the ground that the investment product constitutes a danger to public order as it is designed for particularly vulnerable consumers with limited financial resources and in 90 per cent of the cases the purchase of that product is likely to result in huge financial losses for such consumers far beyond their ability to pay. In order to justify the restriction on the freedom to provide services, the financial supervisory authority argues that bringing such a dangerous financial product on the consumer market would be contrary to the right to human dignity (Article 1 EUCFR) and/or the principle of consumer protection (Article 38 EUCFR). Interpreting and applying the public policy exception in the light of these rights could then lead to the conclusion that the prohibition of the given financial product cannot be regarded as a measure which unjustifiably undermines the freedom to provide services.

The realization of such a scenario would amount to the ex ante financial product regulation on the level of fundamental rights and principles. Such regulation could perhaps have prevented the large-scale 'mis-sellings' of *effectenlease* products in the Netherlands and Lehman 'certificates' in Germany. Following the judgment of the CJEU in the *Omega* case, therefore, it seems plausible to argue that the negative obligations of the EU and member state public authorities to interpret and apply EU law in the light of EU fundamental rights have some potential to reinforce consumer protection in financial services at national level. At the same time, resorting to fundamental rights arguments in this area entails significant risks, considering the difficulties involved in regulating financial products, in general,[99] and doing so on the basis of broadly formulated fundamental rights and principles, in particular.

[99] On this, see, e.g. N. Moloney, *How to Protect Investors: Lessons from the EC and the UK* (2010), at 142 et seq.

3. The 'Positive' Side of Substantive Consumer Protection

Leaving aside the concept of negative obligations, let us now turn to the concept of positive obligations. As has already been noted above, it is normally necessary to take positive steps in order to ensure substantive consumer protection in financial services. Can the positive obligations of the EU and national public authorities with regard to EU fundamental rights prompt them to take such steps?

In order to answer this question, it is helpful to first consider the case law of the German Federal Constitutional Court which provides the most striking illustrations of the profound impact of the concept of positive obligations on the development of substantive consumer protection in financial service and related contracts at national level. As has already been mentioned in section 2(C), according to the Constitutional Court's well-established case law, in cases of inequality of bargaining power, the *legislature* is obliged to adopt mandatory law in order to restore the balance of power between the parties and, hence, to ensure the protection of fundamental rights; when the legislature omits doing this, the task of discharging the duty to protect fundamental rights is directed to the *judge* who must give effect to fundamental rights using the means available within private law.

As far as the *legislature's* duty to protect fundamental rights is concerned, the rulings of the Constitutional Court in cases involving life insurance contracts deserve particular mention.[100] Under the general insurance contract terms applicable to these contracts, the assets arising from the investments made with the insurance premiums paid by the insured persons could not be obtained in the case of a premature termination of the policy. In the absence of any specific legislation to the contrary, the respective contract terms were valid under general contract law. According to the Constitutional Court, the insured themselves were not in a position to change insurance practices unduly prejudicing their interests, and they, therefore, needed to be protected by law. This implied that the legislature had to take legal measures which would prevent the insurer from imposing on the insured contract terms entitling the insurer to partially deprive the insured of the investment proceeds. By failing to adopt such measures, the legislature violated its duty to protect the insured person's fundamental right to private autonomy and his fundamental right to property (Articles 2(1) and 14(1) of the Federal Constitution, respectively). In the view of the Constitutional Court, the legislature must ensure that the assets arising out of investments made with the insurance premiums by the insurer can be obtained not only when the policy matures, by sharing in the net proceeds, but that they can also be obtained in the case of a premature termination of the policy.

The *civil courts'* duty to protect fundamental rights was at stake in the famous judgment of the German Federal Constitutional Court in the *Bürgschaft* case.[101] Although this case concerned a surety contract, the problem revealed thereby is reminiscent of the problems faced by consumers of financial services in the Netherlands, Germany, and Spain. A daughter, who was 21 years of age, did not have a high level of education, owned no property, and worked as an unskilled employee at a fish factory for a modest salary, had acted as a surety for her father's debts to the amount of DM 100,000 (€50,000). Prior to the signing of the surety contract, a bank employee asked the daughter: 'Would you just sign this here, please? This won't make you enter into any important obligation; I need this for my files.' Shortly afterwards, the father's business experienced financial

[100] BVerfG 26 July 2005, *BVerfGE* 114, 73. See also BVerfG 26 July 2005, BVerfGE 114, 1.
[101] BVerfG 19 October 1993, BVerfGE 89, 214 BVerfGE (*Bürgschaft*).

difficulties and the bank claimed DM 100,000 with interest, amounting to a total of DM 160,000 (€80,000), from the daughter under the original contract.

While the court of first instance (*Landgericht*) held that the contract was valid and ordered the daughter to pay, a higher court, the Court of Appeal (*Oberlandesgericht*), maintained that the bank had violated its duty to inform her concerning the risk of acting as a surety and that she, therefore, was not bound by the contract. This decision of the State Court was overturned by the Federal Supreme Court in civil matters, which did not accept such a duty, reasoning that any person who has reached the age of majority knows that signing a suretyship entails a risk. The daughter held liable by the Supreme Court to pay the entire sum agreed under the surety contract lodged a constitutional complaint against the decision of the Supreme Court and claimed that the latter, through its decision, had, in particular, violated her fundamental right to private autonomy (Article 2(1) of the Federal Constitution) in conjunction with the principle of the social state (Articles 20 (1) and 28 (1) of the Federal Constitution).

The surety's constitutional claim was successful. The Constitutional Court overturned the decision of the Supreme Court, reasoning that in cases where a 'structural inequality of bargaining power' has led to a contract which is exceptionally onerous for the weaker party, the civil courts are obliged to intervene on the basis of the general clauses (section 138(1) and section 242 of the Civil Code concerning, respectively, good morals and good faith). This obligation is based on the duty to protect the fundamental right to private autonomy in conjunction with the principle of the social state.

Thus, through the concept of state duties to protect fundamental rights, the Federal Constitutional Court, which is formally not the highest court in private law matters in Germany, was able to enter into the discussion on the issue of contractual justice in modern contract law. Resorting to this concept has enabled the Constitutional Court to force a radical change in the approach to contractual justice adopted by the legislature and the Supreme Court in civil matters in cases involving life insurance and surety contracts by obliging the latter to control the content of such contracts with a view to protecting the weaker contractual party. Considering that the concept of state duties to protect fundamental rights operates at a high level of generality, it can potentially be used by the Constitutional Court to impose similar obligations upon the legislature and civil courts in relation to other types of financial service contracts, such as consumer credit or investment service contracts, which may also touch upon the sensitive substantive issues involved in the protection of the weaker party.

To what extent would such a scenario be feasible and desirable at EU level with a view to ensuring substantive consumer protection in European financial services law? The need to respect the division of competences of the EU in relation to a multilevel system of private law restricts the possibilities for the CJEU to actively shape the content of European financial services law by means of the imposition of positive obligations on the EU and national public authorities. Obliging the EU legislature, therefore, to adopt specific regulatory measures with a view to protecting consumers would run contrary to Article 51(2) of the EUCFR which explicitly specifies that the Charter does not establish any new power or task for the EU, or modify powers and tasks defined by the founding treaties. Nevertheless, the concept of positive obligations may play a role in the development of European financial services law by providing a source of inspiration for rule-makers at EU and national level to adopt legislation which would promote EU fundamental rights.

Consider the following example. According to Article 7 of the EUCFR, everyone has the right to respect for his or her private and family life, home, and communications. The fact that the protection of the home has a fundamental rights dimension could highlight the importance of putting in place EU legislation which would help to stop certain lending practices which have resulted in large-scale evictions from homes in the aftermath of the financial crisis across the EU. The newly proposed directive on credit agreements relating to residential property addresses, inter alia, the problem of irresponsible lending. By protecting consumers against irresponsible lending, in essence, the EU legislature also protects them against the risk of losing their home as a result of such lending. It could be argued, therefore, that by doing so, the EU legislature indirectly promotes the fundamental right to a home protected by Article 7 of the EUCFR.

Despite the EU competence-related constitutional constraints, there is also some potential for the judicial development of substantive consumer protection in European financial services law by means of the concept of positive obligations. Whereas the CJEU cannot impose such obligations on national courts outside the scope of EU law, the concept of positive obligations could play a role within the framework of specific EU measures in the financial services field. Following the *Promusicae* case discussed in sections 2(B) and 2(C), this concept may influence the interpretation and application of EU secondary law in the member states, possibly enhancing substantive consumer protection in the field of financial services.

Let me illustrate this point by using the example of the *Aziz* case.[102] This case arose from a dispute between the Spanish bank and the consumer who lost his family home after having defaulted on his mortgage. The consumer challenged, inter alia, the validity of several contract terms contained in the mortgage contract before the Spanish civil court. One of the contested clauses entitled the bank to claim the repayment of the total amount of credit in case the borrower has defaulted on one of the total of 369 monthly repayments due during the term of the mortgage contract. As this acceleration clause had not been individually negotiated, it fell within the scope of application of Directive 93/13 on unfair terms in consumer contracts. According to Article 3(1) of this directive, a contractual term which has not been individually negotiated shall be regarded as unfair if, contrary to the requirement of good faith, it causes a significant imbalance in the parties' rights and obligations arising under the contract, to the detriment of the consumer. Before assessing whether the clause in question is unfair, the national court, in essence, asked the CJEU to clarify the meaning of the constituent elements of the concept of 'unfair term', in particular, the concept of 'significant imbalance', in the light of Article 3(1) of Directive 93/13.

It is notable that, in its written observations submitted to the CJEU in this case, the European Commission argued that the clause in question was valid as such, considering that even a single non-payment by the debtor constitutes a breach of an essential contract term which justifies the immediate termination of the contract by the creditor.[103] The CJEU, however, took a different view. Having noted that it is for the national court to determine whether a particular clause is actually unfair in the circumstances of the case, the Court formulated general criteria on the basis of which the fairness of an acceleration clause in a long-term mortgage contract must be assessed. In particular, the national court should investigate whether the creditor's right to accelerate is conditional upon the non-compliance by the consumer with an obligation which is of essential importance in the context of the contractual relationship in question, whether that right is provided for in cases in which such non-compliance is sufficiently serious in light of the terms and amount of the loan, whether that right derogates from the rules of national law which

[102] Case C-415/11, *Aziz*.

[103] See Conclusion of AG Kokott of 8 November 2012 in Case C-415/11, *Aziz*, Rec. 70.

would apply in the absence of an agreement by the parties in that regard, and whether national law provides for adequate and effective means enabling the consumer subject to such a term to remedy the effects of the loan being called in.[104] In reaching this conclusion, the CJEU largely followed the Opinion of Advocate General Kokott in the case at hand who formulated similar assessment criteria in view of the countervailing interests of the creditor and the debtor.[105] According to the Advocate General, the amount of the credit provided, its duration, as well as its *existential importance* for the borrower had to be balanced against the creditor's interest in terminating the mortgage contract.[106]

What is interesting here is that whereas the Commission does not seem to consider the fact that a mortgage contract may touch upon the essentials of the consumer's life, the Advocate General does take this fact into account when interpreting Article 3(1) of Directive 93/13. Although the Advocate General does not explicitly refer to EU fundamental rights, her line of reasoning, which appears to have been followed by the CJEU, closely recalls the one suggested by the Court in the above-mentioned *Promusicae* case. In that case, the Court stated that, when transposing EU directives and applying implementing measures, member states must make sure that they rely on an interpretation of them which allows a fair balance to be struck between various EU fundamental rights. Doing so, in its turn, as the *Promusicae* case itself shows, might lead to the need to take positive steps to protect a certain fundamental right. The balancing of interests which, in the opinion of the Advocate General, must be carried out in the *Aziz* case when interpreting Article 3(1) of Directive 93/13, in essence reflects the balancing between the creditor's freedom to conduct a business (Article 16 EUCFR), on the one hand, and the consumer's right to a home (Article 7 EUCFR), on the other. The fact that the right to a home is enshrined in the Charter underlines the need to consider the existential importance of the mortgage contract for the consumer when assessing the fairness of an acceleration clause contained therein. In its turn, this factor may influence such an assessment in favour of the consumer threatened with the loss of his or her home. As a consequence, although Directive 93/13 on unfair terms in consumer contracts as such does not aim to promote the right to a home, its judicial interpretation and application in a particular case in the light of this right may nevertheless have such an effect. The concept of the positive obligations of the judiciary to protect EU fundamental rights may thus play a role in enhancing substantive consumer protection in the financial services field within the framework of Directive 93/13, albeit its impact may not extend that far as the impact of its counterpart in German law.

4. *Direct Horizontal Effect?*

The potential impact of the EU fundamental right to a home on the interpretation and application of the general test of unfairness in the unfair contract terms legislation also provides a nice illustration of how fundamental rights may enrich private law discourse without undermining its logic. The recourse to the right to a home in the *Aziz* case would not distort the assessment of the fairness of a specific general contract term in the private law setting, but would rather have a subtle impact on the content of the criteria on the basis of which such an assessment is carried out.

Here lies the difference from the approach adopted by the German Federal Constitutional Court in the surety and life insurance cases mentioned above. A striking

[104] Case C-415/11, *Aziz*, Rec. 73. See also Rec. 68.
[105] Conclusion of AG Kokott of 8 November 2012 in Case C-415/11 *Aziz*.
[106] Ibid., Rec. 73.

feature of this case law is the leading role of fundamental rights in protecting the weaker party in the litigation of disputes arising under contract law. Although fundamental rights were not formally directly applied to the relationship between the bank and the surety in the *Bürgschaft* case, for example, and it was general private law clauses that remained applicable, in practice, the Constitutional Court determined the outcome of the case on the fundamental rights level by balancing the competing rights of the parties. In this case, a conflict arose between the surety's fundamental right to private autonomy in conjunction with the principle of the social state and the bank's constitutional right to private autonomy; the good morals clause contained in section 138(1) of the German Civil Code, which was formally applicable in that case, could not change the outcome of this balancing.[107] Moreover, as the civil courts in this case were held to be obliged to protect the fundamental rights of the weaker party, and for this purpose to intervene in contractual relationships by means of the general clauses in the German Civil Code, the role to be played by contract law, in particular by these general clauses, in determining under what conditions and to what extent to protect the weaker party, has been considerably limited.

In terms of the role of private law, therefore, the Constitutional Court's approach in the *Bürgschaft* case closely resembles the most far-reaching form of the effect of fundamental rights on private relationships, i.e. direct horizontal effect. As has been demonstrated in section 2(D), it cannot be excluded that EU fundamental rights will also be granted such an effect. The case law of the German Constitutional Court, however, raises doubts concerning the suitability of fundamental rights for direct regulation of the relationships between private parties, particularly in cases involving politically sensitive issues concerning the extent of the protection of the weaker party.[108] It shows that fundamental rights may be used *both* to promote the protection of the weaker party in contract law and to defend individual freedom. In giving expression to both of these values, however, fundamental rights do not provide a concrete answer to the question of where individual freedom must stop and protection must begin. In particular, they do not help us out of our dilemma; where there is a risky financial service contract, which may potentially result in extremely burdensome financial consequences for one of the parties, should the contract be prohibited per se, or alternatively, should it be allowed subject to the condition that the stronger contractual party has taken necessary steps to obtain the informed consent of the weaker party? Furthermore, if it is informed consent which is at stake, fundamental rights do not inform us about the circumstances under which contract law may hold that the stronger party has fulfilled its duty to explain the risks of the transaction to the weaker party. In light of this, direct horizontal effect of EU fundamental rights in cases touching upon the core issues involved in substantive consumer protection involves the risk of fundamental rights becoming a political football between the proponents of paternalism and the proponents of freedom.

C. Procedural Consumer Protection in Financial Services

1. Procedural Consumer Problems

No matter how extensively a consumer of financial services is protected by substantive rules, these rules are meaningless if they cannot be enforced. At present, private enforcement of

[107] On this in more detail, see Cherednychenko (2008), *supra* note 16, at 39 et seq.
[108] Ibid., 41 et seq.

European financial services law largely depends on national civil and civil procedural laws as interpreted and applied by national courts. As experience shows, however, these laws do not always prove to be particularly facilitative of consumer protection in action.

Consider, for instance, the issue of procedural consumer protection in the field of investment services. The MiFID I contains extensive contract-related conduct of business rules for investment service providers, such as duties to inform and to know one's client (Article 19 MiFID I). However, these rules are not written for and from the perspective of the *private law* relationship between the investment firm or credit institution and the (retail) investor, but predominantly from the perspective of *public* enforcement of such rules by financial supervisory authorities.[109] As a consequence, while the MiFID I aims to attain a high level of investor protection, it does not contain remedies empowering investors to take action in those cases where investment service providers do not comply with the conduct of business rules. Although in most legal systems the MiFID I conduct of business rules may have effect in the relationship between the investment service provider and the investor through national private laws, investors generally experience huge procedural difficulties in obtaining relief via such laws.[110] Particular difficulties arise concerning the proof of a causal link between the breach of the conduct of business rules and the damage.[111] Proof of a causal link may be difficult, for example, if the investor has suffered loss due to unclear or misleading information, a missing warning of the risks involved in a certain investment or a recommendation to purchase an unsuitable investment product.

National civil procedural rules may also create significant obstacles for consumers of financial services to make effective use of the consumer protection legislation of a more general character, such as Directive 93/13 on unfair terms in consumer contracts. For example, the *Aziz* case, which has already been mentioned in section 3(B)(3), has brought to light severe consequences of the application of the Spanish civil *procedural* law for consumers threatened with the loss of their home. The Spanish legislature has equipped the creditor with a special mortgage foreclosure procedure which is designed in a way that enables the creditor to promptly exercise his or her right to foreclosure in the case of the debtor's non-performance. To this end, the debtor's protection in such a procedure has been limited to a minimum. In particular, the borrower cannot invoke the unfair character of the terms contained in his or her mortgage contract. It is only possible for him or her to contest the validity of such terms in a separate declaratory judgment procedure in which he or she can defend him or herself against the creditor's claim constituting the legal basis for foreclosure. However, the court before which such proceedings have been brought, cannot stay or terminate mortgage foreclosure proceedings, and thus the foreclosure itself, until it has been established whether a particular term of a mortgage contract is unfair. As a rule, therefore, the borrower must accept the foreclosure regardless of any possible unfair terms in the mortgage contract. Hence, the consumer may lose his or her family home even if a particular term of the mortgage contract is found to be unfair and, therefore, invalid. The only thing he or she can do in such a case is to claim damages afterwards.

109 Micklitz, 'Anlegerschutz—Analyse des EG-Rechts', in J. Keßler and H.-W. Micklitz (eds), *Anlegerschutz in Deutschland, Scweiz, Großbritannien, USA und der Europäischen Gemeinschaft* (2004) 267, at 324; Cherednychenko, 'European Securities Regulation, Private Law and the Investment Firm-Client Relationship', 17 *European Review of Private Law* (2009) 925, at 930.

110 On this in more detail, see Cherednychenko, 'The Regulation of Retail Investment Services in the EU: Towards the Improvement of Investor Rights?', 33 *Journal of Consumer Policy* (2010) 403, at 412 et seq.

111 Cf. Micklitz, *supra* note 75, at 18.

As the procedural challenges confronting consumers of financial services in the member states touch upon the sensitive issue of national procedural autonomy, EU law faces difficulties in addressing them. According to the well-established case law of the CJEU, 'it is for the domestic legal system of each Member State to designate the courts having jurisdiction and to determine the procedural conditions governing actions at law intended to ensure the protection of the rights which the citizens have from the direct effect of Community law'.[112] At the same time, this principle has always been subject to two conditions known as the principle of equivalence and the principle of effectiveness.[113] The principle of equivalence requires that the enforcement of EU law shall not be more difficult than the enforcement of equivalent national laws. Under the principle of effectiveness, national laws should not make it impossible or excessively difficult in practice to exercise the rights conferred by EU law. Over the years, even in the absence of the EU harmonization of procedural rules in a specific area, the general concern for effective remedies has led the CJEU to progressively intervene in national procedural rules, in particular through the application of the principle of effectiveness.

The question which needs to be addressed in the present context is whether EU fundamental rights may strengthen the role of EU law in ensuring procedural consumer protection and, if so, how and to what extent. In particular, can they assist the CJEU in further limiting the procedural autonomy of the member states with a view to ensuring consumer protection? In answering these questions, let us once again resort to the distinction between the negative and positive obligations of the EU and member state public authorities with regard to EU fundamental rights outlined in section 2. As will be shown below, both kinds of obligations have some potential to make a difference, albeit perhaps not a very big one, in tackling procedural issues hampering the ability of consumers to make effective use of their rights.[114]

2. *The 'Negative' Side of Procedural Consumer Protection*

The negative obligation of the EU and member state public authorities to respect EU fundamental rights, in particular the right to judicial protection (Article 47 EUCFR) in conjunction with the right to home (Article 7 EUCFR) and the principle of consumer protection (Article 38 EUCFR), when interpreting and applying EU law may lead the CJEU to declare national procedural rules to be contrary to EU law. This scenario can be illustrated by using the example of the *Aziz* case.[115] An attentive reader has probably already guessed that this case involved, inter alia, the compatibility of the Spanish procedural framework for mortgage foreclosure outlined in section 3(C)(1) with EU law. It should be recalled that the Spanish civil procedural law made it impossible for the consumer to contest the validity of mortgage contract terms on the basis of the unfair contract terms legislation prior to a foreclosure sale. The question referred to by the Spanish court was, in essence, whether the procedural framework established thereby constitutes an impediment to the consumer's exercise of the rights conferred by Directive 93/13 on unfair terms in consumer contracts, and is, therefore, contrary to EU law.

[112] Case 45/76, *Comet* [1976] ECR 2043, Rec. 13.

[113] Case C-261/95, *Palmisani* [1997] ECR I-4025, Rec. 27; Case C-295/04, *Manfredi* [2006] ECR I-6619, Rec. 62.

[114] See, e.g. C-199/82, *San Giorgio* [1983] ECR 3595; C-213/89, *Factortame* [1990] ECR I-2433; C-312/93, *Peterbroeck* [1995] ECR I-4599.

[115] Case C-415/11, *Aziz*.

In order to assess the potential impact of the EU fundamental rights in this context, let us first take a closer look at the reasoning of the CJEU in its judgment in the *Aziz* case. Having noted that, in the absence of the harmonization of foreclosure proceedings at EU level, it is for the member states to determine the modalities of such proceedings in accordance with the principle of national procedural autonomy, the Court pointed out that the freedom of the member states in this area is limited by the principle of equivalence and the principle of effectiveness.[116] As the Spanish procedural framework for mortgage foreclosure precludes a national court from staying or terminating mortgage foreclosure proceedings not only where it assesses whether a particular mortgage contract term is unfair in light of Directive 93/13 but also where it assesses whether such a term conflicts with national rules on public policy, the Court found no violation of the principle of equivalence.[117]

With regard to the principle of effectiveness, however, the situation turned out to be more problematic. Following the Opinion of Advocate General Kokott in the case at hand,[118] the CJEU held that the Spanish procedural framework for mortgage foreclosure in question impairs the consumer protection sought by Directive 93/13, in so far as it renders it impossible for the court in the declaratory judgment procedure—in which a consumer contests the fairness of the contractual term on which the right to seek foreclosure is based—to grant interim relief capable of staying or terminating the mortgage foreclosure proceedings.[119] Without that possibility, the consumer could obtain only subsequent judicial protection of a purely compensatory nature, which, in the view of the Court, would be incomplete and insufficient.[120] In the words of the Court:

> That applies all the more strongly where, as in the main proceedings, the mortgaged property is the family home of the consumer whose rights have been infringed, since that means of consumer protection is limited to payment of damages and interest and does not make it possible to prevent the definitive and irreversible loss of that dwelling.[121]

In light of this, the CJEU concluded that the Spanish procedural framework for mortgage foreclosure in question does not comply with the principle of effectiveness and is, therefore, precluded by Directive 93/13.

One may question the relevance of the judgment of the CJEU in the *Aziz* case in this context, as the Court does not even mention the EU fundamental rights when assessing the compatibility of the Spanish procedural framework for mortgage foreclosure with the principle of the effectiveness of the consumer rights under Directive 93/13. Yet, a closer look at the Court's reasoning appears to suggest that the consumer's interest in preserving his home, which is protected by the fundamental right to home, has been absorbed in the well-established effectiveness test in EU law and has ultimately influenced its outcome. In particular, the Court has acknowledged that, in essence, the effective protection of consumers against unfair contract terms is absent if, despite such terms, the consumer is powerless to prevent the foreclosure and, hence, the loss of his home. This has led it to conclude that the Spanish procedural framework for mortgage foreclosure is contrary to the principle of effectiveness.

Alternatively, instead of a more traditional approach to the effectiveness test adopted by the CJEU in the *Aziz* case, the Court could have explicitly interpreted and applied the

[116] Ibid., Rec. 50. [117] Ibid., Recs 51–52.

[118] Conclusion of AG Kokott of 8 November 2012 in Case C-415/11, *Aziz*.

[119] Case C-415/11, *Aziz*, Rec. 59. [120] Ibid., Rec. 60.

[121] Ibid., Rec. 61. Cf. Conclusion of AG Kokott of 8 November 2012 in Case C-415/11, *Aziz*, Rec. 52.

principle of effectiveness in this case in the light of the EUCFR. Doing so, however, would, in my view, involve the need to balance competing EU fundamental rights against each other in order to ensure respect for such rights. It should be recalled that in the *Promusicae* case discussed in sections 2(B) and 2(C), the CJEU explicitly imposed an obligation to this effect on member states when transposing EU directives in national legal orders. As EU law itself must also be interpreted and applied in conformity with EU fundamental rights, it can be argued that a similar obligation rests on the CJEU when interpreting and applying the principle of effectiveness in disputes between private parties.

Considering that the Spanish procedural framework for mortgage foreclosure at issue in the *Aziz* case touches upon the interests of both the creditor and the debtor, the balance would have to be struck between, on the one hand, the creditor's right to judicial protection (Article 47 EUCFR) in conjunction with the right to property (Article 27(1) EUCFR), and, on the other hand, the debtor's right to judicial protection (Article 47 EUCFR) in conjunction with the right to a home (Article 7 EUCFR) and the principle of consumer protection (Article 38 EUCFR). In such a case, the inclusion of the EU fundamental rights in the effectiveness test could have shifted the focus of assessment from the 'impossibility' or 'excessive difficulty' in enforcing the consumer rights conferred by EU law to the balancing process in which the EU fundamental rights of both parties would be involved.[122]

As a result of such balancing, the debtor's fundamental rights could have ultimately prevailed over the creditor's fundamental rights, and the outcome of the effectiveness test could thus have been the same as the one reached by the CJEU without explicit recourse to such rights. In this case, keeping in place the procedural framework for mortgage foreclosure in question would constitute a serious infringement of the consumer's EU fundamental rights amounting to the violation of the negative obligations to respect such rights by the Spanish public authorities. However, it is also possible, albeit perhaps less likely, that the balancing process would have led to the opposite result and that the procedural framework in question would thus be justified by the creditor's legitimate interests. After all, openly considering EU fundamental rights within the framework of the effectiveness test highlights the fact that the EUCFR protects not only the interests of the consumer who is threatened with the loss of his or her home, but also the interests of the bank which has provided the consumer with a mortgage-backed loan to purchase the home.

It appears, therefore, that whereas EU fundamental rights certainly have some potential to foster the development of procedural consumer protection in European financial services law through the concept of negative obligations, the extent to which this potential will be realized will ultimately depend on the approach taken by the CJEU when assessing the compatibility of national procedural rules with EU law. In particular, it remains to be seen whether the CJEU will openly engage in the balancing of competing EU fundamental rights against each other when interpreting and applying the principle of effectiveness in future cases involving consumer protection legislation.

3. *The 'Positive' Side of Procedural Consumer Protection*

So far we have focused on the potential role of the negative obligations of the EU and member state public authorities with regard to EU fundamental rights in setting aside

[122] Cf. the contribution by Mak, 'Rights and Remedies. Article 47 EUCFR and Effective Judicial Protection in European Private Law Matters', in this book.

restrictive national procedural rules which hamper the effective exercise of consumer rights in the financial services field. In many cases, however, the problems faced by consumers stem not from the existence of a particular procedural rule, but rather from the lack thereof. Next to the concept of negative obligations, therefore, an important role in developing a more consumer-friendly procedural framework for the enforcement of consumer rights could be played by the concept of positive obligations.

In the first place, taking into account the concept of positive obligations when interpreting and applying EU secondary law may open up new frontiers in the *judicial* development of procedural consumer protection within the existing EU legislative framework for financial services.[123] An example from the investment services field may serve as an illustration. As has been mentioned above, retail investors who have suffered loss due to unclear or misleading information, a missing warning of the risks involved in a certain investment or a recommendation to purchase an unsuitable investment product face major procedural hurdles in obtaining relief. Even when it has been established that the investment service provider has acted contrary to the conduct of business rules harmonized by the MiFID I, the investor may still be unable to prove the causal link between the breach of the conduct of business rules and the damage. More investor-friendly civil courts in some legal systems tend, therefore, to reverse the burden of proof in certain cases in favour of investors. Thus, for example, the German Supreme Court in civil matters adopted a presumption that the aggrieved individual investor would not have made an investment if the investment adviser had provided him with the correct information concerning his kickback payments; as a rule, this presumption applies to all cases in which the investment adviser failed to comply with its duties to inform.[124] Accordingly, if the violation of the duty to inform by the investment adviser is established, it is up to the adviser to prove that the investor would have concluded the contract even if he or she had been duly informed. Some authors have argued in favour of extending such reverse burden of proof to the (sufficiently) serious violations of the investment service providers' obligations under the MiFID I.[125]

A similar result, however, could potentially be achieved through the interpretation of the MiFID I in the light of the right to an effective remedy in conjunction with the principle of consumer protection (Articles 47 and 38 EUCFR, respectively). In such a case, the MiFID I would be construed in a way which requires member states to reverse the burden of proof in relation to the causal link between the breach of the conduct of business rules and the damage. Once again, such a finding would amount to the imposition of the positive obligation on member states to ensure respect for Articles 47 and 38 of the Charter within the scope of the MiFID I.

As this example demonstrates, the weaker version of positive obligations could be used by courts to imply certain consumer-friendly procedural rules in the EU measures when interpreting and applying such measures in the light of their specific objectives and EU fundamental rights. Such an approach has the potential to improve the effectiveness of the consumer protection legislation in the financial services field by introducing a

[123] The plea for the judicial development of remedies in EU law has recently been made by Micklitz. See Micklitz, 'The ECJ between the Individual Citizen and the Member States—A Plea for a Judge-Made European Law on Remedies', in H.-W. Micklitz and B. De Witte (eds), *The European Court of Justice and the Autonomy of the Member States* (2012) 349. See also Reich, 'The Interrelationship between Rights and Duties in EU law: Reflection on the State of Liability Law in the Multi-Level Governance System of the Union: Is There a Need for a More Coherent Approach in European Private Law?', 29 *Yearbook of European Law* (2010) 112.

[124] BGH, 12 May 2009, WM 2009, 1274.

[125] See, e.g. Reich, *supra* note 123, at 158.

reverse burden of proof or other consumer-friendly procedural rules in those cases where the EU legislation itself does not contain such rules.

In addition, the concept of positive obligations to protect EU fundamental rights could play an important role in prompting the EU and/or member states to adopt measures which would promote procedural consumer protection in the financial services field. Obviously, ensuring such protection through the adoption of binding EU rules via the ordinary legislative procedure may prove difficult. The European Commission, however, could also resort to other means to this end, such as providing non-binding guidance to member states on particular pressing issues, such as mortgage foreclosure.

An example of this which is worth mentioning in the present context, is the report by the European Commission concerning measures already taken or about to be taken at member state level with a view to preventing mortgage defaults and foreclosures as well as information on the evolution of such defaults and foreclosures.[126] The aim of this report is to provide examples and guidance to national public authorities and creditors on how rising default rates have been addressed across the EU with measures to avoid mortgage foreclosure proceedings.[127] The report contains examples of national measures and practices voluntarily adopted by creditors in some member states in order to avoid foreclosures. These include, inter alia, reconciliation procedures, specialized mediation mechanisms, and granting borrowers a minimum waiting period of time before starting foreclosure proceedings.[128]

By publishing this report, in essence, the European Commission has promoted the protection of the EU fundamental right to a home (Article 7 EUCFR) and the principle of consumer protection (Article 38 EUCFR) in private relations between creditors and consumer debtors in the residential mortgage market. The theme of the human dimension of mortgage foreclosure runs through the Commission's report. Whereas the latter focuses on pre-foreclosure instruments, the Commission also called on all the parties involved in foreclosure proceedings to consider such dimension. According to the Commission:

> [W]here foreclosures do take place, which cannot be completely ruled out, common sense and humanity should always prevail at all levels (lender, authorities, courts, etc.) and throughout the whole procedure. In particular, the full economic and social situation of the defaulting borrower should be taken into account, and the implications of a given repossession should be carefully assessed, notably when a primary residence is at stake. For example, losing the family home after having lost one's job has intolerable social and human implications for both borrowers and their families. In these critical economic times our society must put the human dimension at its very heart.[129]

Although the Commission does not explicitly refer to EU fundamental rights, such rights may play an important role in highlighting the human dimension of the application of

[126] European Commission, Commission staff working document, National measures and practices to avoid foreclosure procedures for residential mortgage loans. Accompanying document to the Proposal for a Directive of the European Parliament and of the Council on credit agreements relating to residential property. SEC(2011) 357 final.

[127] Ibid., at 3.

[128] In this context, see also Micklitz, 'The Regulation of Over-Indebtedness of Consumers in Europe', 35 *Journal of Consumer Policy* (2012) 417; Ramsay, 'Between Neo-Liberalism and the Social Market: Approaches to Debt Adjustment and Consumer Insolvency in the EU', 35 *Journal of Consumer Policy* (2012) 421; Niemi, 'Consumer Insolvency in the European Legal Context', 35 *Journal of Consumer Policy* (2012) 443; Lopes and Frade, 'The Way into Bankruptcy: Market Autonomy and Sacrifice Among Portuguese Consumers', 35 *Journal of Consumer Policy* (2012) 477.

[129] European Commission, *supra* note 126, at 11.

certain procedures in the financial services field and prompting the action at EU or member state level.

4. *Direct Horizontal Effect?*

Last but not least, procedural consumer protection in the field of financial services could potentially also be promoted through the direct horizontal effect of EU fundamental rights. If such an approach was adopted, consumers would be able, for instance, to directly invoke the right to an effective remedy in conjunction with the right to a home and the principle of consumer protection (Articles 47, 7, and 38 EUCFR, respectively) against banks or other financial service providers.

At first sight, such a scenario may seem to be rather attractive for consumers, as the possibility to rely on EU fundamental rights directly would circumvent the need to contest the compatibility of consumer-unfriendly civil procedural laws with such rights. A closer look, however, reveals that, also in the procedural context, the EU fundamental rights are hardly suitable for direct application to private relationships and, what is more, recourse to them may not always serve the interests of consumers.

The English *Wilson v First County Trust Ltd* case,[130] which arose from a consumer credit transaction, may serve as an illustration. The statutory provision at issue in this case was section 127(3) of the Consumer Credit Act 1974, under which the court could not enforce an otherwise regulated consumer credit agreement where there was no document containing all the prescribed terms of the agreement signed by the debtor. Because Wilson's agreement, which she had signed, misstated the amount of credit given, both this agreement and a related security over her BMW car could not be enforced by the creditor, First County Trust Ltd.

Considering the circumstances of the case, the English Court of Appeal took the view that the creditor's inability to enforce the agreement was a disproportionate response, given the absence of prejudice to any party in the misstatement and having regard to the creditor's fundamental right to a fair hearing under Article 6 of the ECHR and fundamental right not to be deprived of its possessions under Article 1 of the First Protocol to this Convention. According to the Court of Appeal, while the policy aim, as determined from the legislative history of the 1974 Act, was legitimate, the means of achieving its goals were disproportionate and inflexible in not enabling the court to consider all the factors in a case. Because it was not possible to read and give effect to section 127(3) of the 1974 Act in a way which was compatible with the ECHR, the Court made a declaration of incompatibility stating that the provision in question had violated Article 6 of the Convention and Article 1 of the 1st Protocol thereto.

This decision demonstrates the willingness of the Court of Appeal to exercise judicial review of the legislation and to restrike the balance struck by the legislature between the competing interests of consumers and lenders. If this decision remained in force, it could have had far-reaching implications not only for the Consumer Credit Act, but also, in general, for the legislative techniques of making void certain types of terms in contracts with a view to protecting consumers. However, this decision was overturned by the House of Lords. The primary ground for the reversal was that the facts and circumstances of the case had arisen before 2 October 2000, when the Human Rights Act of 1998, by which fundamental rights enshrined in the ECHR were incorporated into the domestic

[130] [2003] 3 WLR 568; [2003] 4 All ER 97 (HL).

law of the United Kingdom, came into force; and while the Act could be applied to legislation enacted before that date, it contained no provision enabling such application retrospectively in relation to activities before that date. At the same time, the House of Lords did not limit itself to these considerations and also ruled on the main substantive issue in the case—the compatibility of section 127 of the Consumer Credit Act with the ECHR. Whereas Article 6 of the Convention was held by the House of Lords to be inapplicable, Article 1 of the 1st Protocol was held to apply to the inability of the lender to enforce its security rights as a result of section 127. What had to be shown, however, was that the legislature's response to the problem with which it was confronted failed to balance the public interest in consumer protection and the protection of property interests, and, accordingly, was disproportionate. In so doing, the House of Lords started from the following approach to this issue:

> Parliament is charged with the primary responsibility for deciding whether the means chosen to deal with a social problem are both necessary and appropriate. Assessment of the advantages and disadvantages of the various legislative alternatives is primarily a matter for Parliament. The possible existence of alternative solutions does not in itself render the contested legislation unjustified.... The court will reach a different conclusion from the legislature only when it is apparent that the legislature has attached insufficient importance to a person's Convention right. The readiness of a court to depart from the views of the legislature depends upon the circumstances, one of which is the subject matter of the legislation. The more the legislation concerns matters of broad social policy, the less ready will be a court to intervene.[131]

Based on these considerations, the House of Lords emphasized the legislature's experience from prior legislation and the views of the high-powered committee which had proposed the Act, and concluded that the sanction imposed was one which Parliament was entitled to use.

Although the *Wilson v First County Trust Ltd* case did not involve the direct horizontal effect of fundamental rights but the compatibility of procedural rules with such rights, this case brings to the fore the complexity involved in the recourse to fundamental rights in such matters when the dispute concerns two private parties. It is striking that the Court of Appeal and the House of Lords reached the opposite conclusions concerning the purport of fundamental rights in the same case. Whereas the Court of Appeal found the consumer protection provision in question to be disproportionate to the aims pursued and let the creditor's interests prevail over the consumer's interest, no such disproportionality was established by the House of Lords which ruled in favour of the consumer. Considering the difficulties involved in the balancing of competing interests of consumers and creditors, the House of Lords emphasized the legislature's primary responsibility in such politically sensitive matters and refused to intervene in the choice made by the legislature in the Consumer Credit Act.

If such a case arose in the context of EU law, the conflict would perhaps need to be resolved between, on the one hand, the creditor's right to an effective remedy and/or its right to property (Articles 47 and 27(1) EUCFR, respectively), and, on the other hand, the consumer's right to an effective remedy in conjunction with the principle of consumer protection (Articles 47 and 38 EUCFR, respectively). If these EU fundamental rights had direct horizontal effect, the CJEU would have to balance them against each other *outside* the legislative context pertaining to the procedural rule at issue. The result of such a politically sensitive balancing would not necessarily be in favour of the consumer.

[131] [2003] 4 All ER 97 (HL), [70].

4. Concluding Remarks

It seems to be undisputed today that the harmonization of private law in Europe cannot take place without taking fundamental rights into account. Yet many questions still exist as to *how* and to *what extent* EU and national private law can and should be influenced by fundamental rights. The present contribution has explored the possibilities for and limits to the constitutionalization of European private law in light of the experience accumulated in national legal systems and the law of the ECHR with regard to the effect of fundamental rights in private law. This investigation has focused on the three major issues arising in the field of financial services: (1) access to financial services; (2) substantive consumer protection in financial services; and (3) procedural consumer protection in financial services.

The need to respect the division of competences of the EU in relation to a multilevel system of private law creates some additional complexities for the impact of fundamental rights on European private law which do not exist in a purely national context. However, there are some significant parallels between the gateways to the constitutionalization of private law in national legal systems and those in EU law. Thus, the negative obligations of public authorities not to infringe fundamental rights when making, interpreting, and applying private law have been recognized both in the national and in the EU context. One can even trace in EU law the signs of the positive obligations of public authorities to protect fundamental rights in private relationships—the concept which has proved to be a powerful vehicle for the constitutionalization of private law in some national legal systems. Last but not least, even the most controversial concept of the direct horizontal effect of fundamental rights in private law, which has been rejected in most national legal systems, may play a role in the constitutionalization of European private law. Therefore, despite the EU competence-related limitations inherent in this process, EU fundamental rights have the potential to have a profound impact on private law at EU and national level in the context of the European harmonization of private law.

The impact of EU fundamental rights, in particular the rich set of fundamental rights contained in the EUCFR, on European private law may lead to groundbreaking solutions to important societal problems in the area of financial services which have not been addressed via the ordinary legislative procedure in the EU. In particular, EU fundamental rights have some potential to promote access justice in the field of financial services, enhance substantive consumer protection against risky financial transactions, and foster the development of procedural consumer protection in European financial services law. The extent to which this potential will be realized largely depends on the approach by the CJEU.

But the alignment of private law with EU fundamental rights is not without risks. The unbridled constitutionalization of European private law may move the debate on some sensitive political and socio-economic issues away from the legislative process to the level of fundamental rights. As a result, important and, in essence, political decisions concerning the extent of consumer protection in financial services may end up being made by the CJEU in the course of fundamental rights adjudication, while those rights do not contain the answers to many issues raised in the course of such adjudication. This, in turn, might severely undermine the legitimacy of the CJEU. It is crucial, therefore, that the CJEU strikes a fair balance between the uncontrolled expansion of the constitutionalization of European private law and the development of European financial services law without regard to fundamental rights.

7

Intellectual Property and European Fundamental Rights

Christine Godt

1. Introduction

This chapter analyses the relationship between intellectual property rights (IPRs) and rights guaranteed by the EU Charter of Fundamental Rights ('the Charter' or EUCFR). The European Court of Justice (CJEU, formerly ECJ) has recently begun to refer to the Charter in IP cases.[1] Whereas the relationship between IP and human rights in general features prominently at the international level, the ECJ had referred only vaguely to 'the balance of IP and fundamental rights' in the few prior cases (the best known one is *Promusicae*[2]). This chapter focuses on potential changes which might be triggered by the Charter. It is interested in whether the Charter can be instrumental in framing a democratic and deliberative debate on modern European IP conflicts which arise from the societal transformation towards information societies embedded in global markets, similar to the debate prompted by fundamental freedoms in the more traditional areas of both public[3] and private[4] law. The discourse is especially timely with regard to the (non-Union) European patent approved by the European Parliament on 11 December 2012 (projected validity 2014).[5] For contextual reasons, the article will first map the actual debate on 'constitutionalizing IP' in Europe and identify its structural differences compared to the 'constitutionalization' discourses in other areas of law discussed in this volume (section 2). It will then differentiate the debate on IP and universal human rights in the international fora from the European debate on IP and fundamental rights, and identify what the former debate can contribute to the latter (section 3). The core of the

[1] Case C-70/10, *Scarlet Extended v SABAM*, judgment 24 November 2011, not yet published; Case C-360/10, *SABAM v Netlog*, judgment of 16 February 2012, not yet published.

[2] Case C-275/06, *Promusicae* [2008] ECR I-271; see also Raue, 'Die Verdrängung deutscher durch europäische Grundrechte im gewerblichen Rechtsschutz und Urheberrecht', 61 *Gewerblicher Rechtsschutz und Urheberrecht-Internationaler Teil* (*GRURInt*) (2012) 402.

[3] The leading case for a fully fledged weighing decision between a fundamental freedom and a constitutional right by the ECJ is Case C-112/00, *Schmidberger* [2003] ECR I-5659.

[4] For an in-depth analysis of the effects of fundamental freedoms on private law, see G. Brüggemeier, A. Colombi Ciacchi, and G. Comandé (eds), *Fundamental Freedoms and Private Law in the European Union* (2010).

[5] 'Parliament approves EU unitary patent rules', Press Release, 11 December 2012, available at <http://www.europarl.europa.eu/news/en/pressroom/content/20121210IPR04506/html/Parliament-approves-EU-unitary-patent-rules>. Invalidity procedures have been filed by Spain and Italy (C-274/11 und C-295/11) and are pending (opinion by AG Bot submitted on 11 December 2011, see ECJ press release 163/12), for an in-depth analysis see H. Ullrich, 'Select from the System: The European Patent with Unitary Effect' (2012), Max Planck Institute for Intellectual Property and Competition Law Research Paper 12-11, available at <http://www.ip.mpg.de/files/pdf2/SSRN12-11.pdf>.

chapter is a discussion of seven factual IP controversies in the light of the potential influence of the Charter rights (section 4).[6] The final section draws conclusions about the Charter's influence on property rights and private law as a whole (section 5).

2. Constitutionalization of IP

A. Diverging Concepts

Constitutionalization has become a buzzword,[7] particularly so in contemporary reflections on how to contain the constant flow of newly emerging intellectual property rights and their expanding scope. The debate revolves around legal means of a discursive civilization of conflicts which are in need of articulation and balance. However, underlying concepts differ profoundly. Three broad directions can be distinguished. One holds public institutions accountable,[8] and reconceptualizes IP rights as 'duty bearing privileges'[9] in the sense of duties vis-à-vis the public.[10] The second group acknowledges 'opposing rights' as limitations to the IP holders.[11] Some of them focus on individual rights, of which the balance is to be secured by parliaments and courts.[12] A third concept refers to a constitutionalization of social orders which re-bind IP rights to the conditions of their emergence. Depending on the conceptual foundations of the author, these

[6] Compared to the prior 'common traditions of the member states', as the European Court of Justice has put it until now, and neglecting the differences as to how member states have guaranteed the protection of human rights values (in the constitution, as in France and Germany (the latter with a special constitutional court), by direct reference to the European Convention on Human Rights as in the Netherlands, or by reference to universal, non-statutory principles as in England). For more details, see A. Colombi Ciacchi in this volume.

[7] See, e.g. the term 'constitutionalization' in the context of international law, contributions to C. Joerges and E.-U. Petersmann (eds), *Multilevel Trade Governance and Social Regulation* (2006); C. Joerges, G. I.-J. Sand, and G. Teubner (eds), *Transnational Governance and Constitutionalism* (2004).

[8] Conceiving them as the central institutions of legitimacy: I. Schneider, *Das europäische Patentsystem* (2010), at 661.

[9] P. Drahos, *A Philosophy of Intellectual Property* (1996).

[10] Bromley, 'Property Rights: Locke, Kant, Peirce and the Logic of Volitional Pragmatism', in: H. M. Jacobs (ed), *Private Property in the 21st Century: The Future of an American Ideal* (2004) 19, refers to the necessary discourse in public fora (referring to Habermas and Rorty) as 'volitional pragmatism'; C. Godt, *Eigentum an Information* (2007), at 560 as 'Inhaltsbestimmung'.

[11] J. Kersten, *Das Klonen von Menschen: Eine verfassungs-, europa-, und völkerrechtliche Kritik* (2004); Geiger, '"Constitutionalising" Intellectual Property Law?', *IIC—International Review of Intellectual Property and Competition Law* (2006) 371; Godt, *supra* note 10; L. R. Helfer, 'Towards a Human Rights Framework for Intellectual Property', Vanderbilt University Law School Public Law and Legal Theory, Working Paper No. 06-03 (2007); A. Peukert, *Güterzuordnung als Rechtsprinzip* (2008); Hilty, 'The Role of Patent Quality in Europe', in J. Drexl et al. (eds), *Technology and Competition/Technologie et concurrence—Contributions in Honour of/Mélanges en l'honneur de Hanns Ullrich* (2009) 91; Hilty, 'Herausforderung Durchsetzung—Kontrapunkte', in R. M. Hilty, T. Jaeger, and V. Kitz (eds), *Geistiges Eigentum: Herausforderung und Durchsetzung* (2008) V.

[12] Wielsch, 'Differenzierungen des Eigentums. Zur Entwicklung eines rechtlichen Grundbegriffs', in S. Keller and S. Wiprächtiger (eds), *Recht zwischen Dogmatik und Theorie: Marc Amstutz zum 50. Geburtstag* (2012) 329, at 341, argues that a balancing of IP and individual fundamental rights would have 'a better chance of acceptance'. That means that he would not accept collective or diffuse rights (as described by R de Camargo Mancuso, *Interesses difusos: Conceito e legitimação para agir* (1991)) or second generation human rights.

conditions are either rooted in the *volonté* of the individual[13] or in the functional preconditions of competition.[14]

Whereas the first two groups would acknowledge human rights as 'self-standing restrictions', the third group would, as a matter of rule and exception, only accept legislative restrictions. Prime examples of a human rights induced statutory patent exception are, e.g., the exclusion of Article 52(4) European Patent Convention (EPC) (surgery or therapy and diagnostic methods), and the so-called 'Bolar exemption'[15] allowing clinical tests and trials on patented medicaments. All three groups have in common the idea that a property right is sensibly to be restricted. However, they differ about the reasons why they acknowledge property restrictions, and therefore the outcomes of interpretation differ greatly. Yet, their approach in general has not remained unopposed. A strong opponent is Riesenhuber. He argued that, for example, Geiger's approach would violate the principle of private autonomy.[16] Third party rights could not, as a matter of principle, have a self-standing effect on property rights; conflicts are to be decided by parliaments only. These arguments are largely in line with those arguments raised against the horizontal effect of fundamental rights in other areas of civil law. The arguments sound rightfully democratic on the surface. However, they do not take account of modern parliamentary reality, and do not endorse modern deliberate theory. Godt's approach was opposed by Krasser, in the 6th edition of his central textbook on patent law.[17] He argues that Godt underestimates the value of the initial invention, and that the proposed model is too formal. The critique of the first argument goes straight to the point. The concept intends to provide a framework which rationally curtails IP rights, however without underevaluating the pioneer's invention, but it re-establishes the right balance in the light of the expansion of protection.

Following from these conceptual frictions, two discourses struggle for the 'right' balance between IP and other rights in dogmatic terms: the first revolves around the question of whether legislative restrictions to IP are 'exceptions' and therefore have to be interpreted narrowly, or if they protect the subjective rights of others, and therefore demand a broad interpretation.[18] The second discussion concerns the 'contracting away' of regulatory restrictions protecting freedoms (private copies, examination privilege, etc.).[19] The classical approach is to distinguish rules which protect 'subjective rights'

[13] The conceptual ground is the rejection of the romantic author ideal which would justify restrictions to the right. However, he 'saves' the right to decide of the individual rightholder by 'opt-out rules'. Wielsch, *supra* note 12, at 349.

[14] Ullrich, review of Schneider, *supra* note 8, 61 *GRURInt* (2012) 485.

[15] E.g. Art. 10(6) Directive 2001/83/EC (revision 2009), OJ 2009 L 168/33, on the Community Code relating to medicinal products for human use.

[16] Riesenhuber, 'Technische Schutzmaßnahmen und "Zugangsrechte"', in S. Leible, A. Ohly, and H. Zech (eds), *Wissen-Märkte-Geistiges Eigentum* (2008) 141.

[17] R. Krasser, *Patentrecht* (6th ed.; 2009), at 36.

[18] Taking the example of 'exceptions' in Directive 2009/24/EC, OJ 2009 L 11/16, arguing for a restrictive interpretation: T. Dreier, '§ 69a, para. 1', in T. Dreier and G. Schulze, *Urheberrechtsgesetz, Urheberrechtswahrnehmungsgesetz, Kunsturhebergesetz—Kommentar* (3rd ed.; 2008); for a broad interpretation: Hoeren, 'Der Erschöpfungsgrundsatz bei Software—Körperliche Übertragung und Folgeprobleme', 112 *Gewerblicher Rechtsschutz und Urheberrecht (GRUR)* (2010) 665.

[19] A much debated issue; see only L. Guibault, *Copyright Limitations and Contracts: An Analysis of Contractual Overridability of Limitations on Copyright* (2002); R. M. Hilty, *Lizenzvertragsrecht: Systematisierung und Typisierung aus schutz- und schuldrechtlicher Sicht* (2002); Metzger, 'Vertragliche Ausgestaltung von geistigen Schutzrechten—Erscheinungsformen und Vertragskontrolle nach deutschem und europäischen Recht', in Hilty, Jaeger, and Kitz (eds), *supra* note 11, 85, esp. at 92 et seq.; M. Stieper, *Rechtfertigung, Rechtsnatur und Disponibilität der Schranken des Urheberrechts* (2009); Zech, 'Vertragliche Dispositionen über Schranken des geistigen Eigentums', in S. Leible, A. Ohly, and H. Zech (eds), *Wissen-Märkte-Geistiges*

from 'statutory limits'. Restrictions to 'subjective rights' are submitted to the parties' disposition,[20] whereas 'statutory limitations' are conceived of as general 'boundaries' to IP granted (only) in the public interest (which are beyond private disposition). However, the underlying distinction is still contested.[21]

B. ECJ Jurisprudence

The European Court of Justice has actively shaped the content of IP rights since the 1970s. In the first two cases, *Deutsche Grammophon* of 1971 (for copyrights) and *Centrafarm* of 1974[22] (for patents), the Court established the European exhaustion principle. It advanced the common market principle to become a central element of the first sale doctrine, which inherently limits IP rights. Even though IP rights exist territorially in member states, the common market effect prevails so that exhaustion ('first marketing rule') occurs for the whole common European market with the first placing in one of the member states. As a consequence, these rulings allow 'parallel trade' throughout the Community. Whereas their momentum is the common market rationale, the economic core is the protection of the competitors' freedom in secondary markets.

The ECJ moved towards an open balancing approach with its *Magill* judgment in 1995.[23] The 'duty to license' reversed of the former subordination doctrine of IP law and competition law, and paved the way towards a European debate about 'legitimate access to IP'. In subsequent cases, the EU and the national courts have further fine-tuned the requirements of the so-called 'competition law's compulsory license'.[24]

The Court followed this path towards a nuanced and balanced approach to IP adjudication in its trademark cases. It drew, for instance, a sensible line between freeriding (imitating like the *Adidas* case, using two instead of three stripes on sneakers[25]), and using the trademark as information (car bodyshops[26])—thus delimiting professional freedoms.

Eigentum (2008) 187; J. Gräbig, *Abdingbarkeit und vertragliche Beschränkungen urheberrechtlicher Schranken* (2011).

[20] Riesenhuber, *supra* note 16; Zech, *supra* note 19, at 191. For a material interpretation of statutory limitation (limiting private autonomy): Geiger, 'Interessenausgleich im Urheberrecht', 53 *GRURInt* (2004) 815, at 818.

[21] See, e.g. even the structural differences between those who submit boundaries to private disposition, on the one hand, like Riesenhuber, *supra* note 16, explicitly at 143 with further references, also at 151; on the other hand, Zech, *supra* note 19, at 192; and Metzger, *supra* note 19, at 100 (for a case-by-case analysis interpreting and weighting according to the rule's purpose).

[22] Case 15/74, *Centrafarm BV and Adriaan De Peijper v Sterling Drug Inc* [1974] ECR 1147.

[23] Case 241/91 P and Case 242/91 P, *Magill TV Guide* [1995] ECR I-74; the case has triggered hundreds of academic articles, see only Ullrich, 'Intellectual Property, Access to Information, and Antitrust', in R. Dreyfuss, D. L. Zimmerman, and H. First (eds), *Expanding the Boundaries of Intellectual Property* (2001) 365; Drexl, 'The Relationship between the Legal Exclusivity and Economic Market Power: Links and Limits', in I. Govaere and H. Ullrich (eds), *Intellectual Property, Market Power and the Public Interest* (2008) 13.

[24] Compare e.g. Case 468/06 through 478/06, *Sot. Lélos kai Sia EE et al. v GlaxoSmithKline Farmakeftikon Proionton* [2008] ECR I-7139 (introducing a requirement of 'normal scope of order'), German Federal Supreme Court (BGH), judgment of 6 May 2009, *Orange Book Standard* (printed in *International Review of Intellectual Property and Competition Law* (*IIC*) (2010) 369), introducing the requirements of an acceptable offer and a deposit, commented on by Ullrich, 'Patents and Standards—A Comment on the German Federal Supreme Court Decision Orange Book Standard', *IIC* (2010) 337, and the Dutch decision Rechtbank 's-Gravenhage, 17 maart 2010, HA ZA 08-2522 en HA ZA 08-2524, *Koninklijke Philips Electronics N.V. tegen SK Kassetten GmbH & Co. KG*, paras 6.19-6.25, which, as a matter of principle, rejects the possibility of a duty to licence.

[25] Case 425/98, *Marca Mode v Adidas* [2000] ECR I-4861.

[26] Case 63/97, *BMW v Deenik* [1999] ECR I-905.

This argumentation is very similar to that of the German Constitutional Court in the earlier famous *Benetton* cases, in which the Court limited the IP holder's right to injunction where NGOs used trademarks in order to raise public awareness of specific production problems, and acknowledged the right of expression as a counter-right.[27]

In copyright, many cases touch on constitutional values. A famous national example is the *Germania 3* decision by the German Constitutional Court in 2000.[28] It introduced the right to a long citation by a broad interpretation of then section 51(2) of the German Copyright Act, based on Article 5(3) of the German Basic Law.[29] The European Court of Justice, in its *Promusicae* ruling in 2008,[30] referred to 'the fundamental rights' between which a fair balance has to be struck, and thereby strengthened the constitutional procedural safeguards of users and providers against copyright owners.

However, the Court does not always have recourse to a balancing argument, for various reasons. One reason is judicial self-restraint in Article 230 TFEU procedures. In its ruling on the legality of Biotech Directive 98/44/EC with regard to human dignity,[31] it seems that the Court was cautious not to substitute the balance struck by the legislative EU institutions by its own one. In other cases, recourse to a constitutional reasoning does not seem necessary since concurring rights can be protected by a strict interpretation of the limits to intellectual property, like in the *Cefetra* case.[32] In this case, the ECJ interpreted the Biotech Directive with regard to imports of genetically modified maize to Europe. It argued that once a patent protected product is transformed (here, by the grinding of germinating seeds into flour), the technical teaching cannot be infringed anymore.

In the recent case *UsedSoft v Oracle*,[33] the court missed the chance to refer directly to the Charter when interpreting anew the exhaustion principle with regard to the marketing of 'used' computer software (Article 4 Directive 2009/24). However, it should be noted that Advocate General Yves Bot once more rejected the simplistic argument of property as a rule and limitations as exceptions which are to be interpreted narrowly.[34] On the same footing, and in contrast to earlier decisions, the Enlarged Board of the European Patent Agency has become more cautious with regard to the interpretation of rules and exceptions. In the case G1/04, *Diagnostic methods*,[35] it rejected the 'narrow interpretation of exception' as of principle and turned to a case-by-case interpretation 'by purpose'.

The balancing approach to IP adjudication in Europe is likely to increase once either a Unitary European Patent[36] is introduced, a joint patent court is established which will

[27] Geiger, *supra* note 11 (referring to decisions BvG 1762/95 of 12 December 2000, and BvG 426/02 of 11 March 2003).

[28] BVerfG, decision of 29 June 2000, *Zeitschrift für Urheber- und Medienrecht* (2000) 867 (Art. 5(3) German Basic Law corresponds to Art. 13 EUCFR: artistic freedom).

[29] Dreier, Commentary to Art. 51, para. 22, in: T. Dreier and G. Schulze (eds), *Urheberrechtsgesetz* (3rd ed.; 2008).

[30] Case C-275/06, *Promusicae* [2008] ECR I-271, Rec. 68.

[31] Case C-377/98, *Kingdom of the Netherlands v European Parliament and the Council of the European Union* [2001] ECR I-7079.

[32] Case 428/08, *Cefetra* [2010] ECR I-6765.

[33] Case C-128/11, *UsedSoft v Oracle*, judgment of 3 July 2012, not yet published.

[34] Opinion of 24 April 2012 in Case C-128/11.

[35] G 01/07, Enlarged Board of Appeal of EPO of 15 February 2010, Treatment by surgery—*Mediphysics*, OJ EPO 3/2011, 134, at 169.

[36] *Supra* note 5; earlier coined as 'enhanced cooperation', Press Release of the European Commission of 13 April 2011 (IP/11/470)—based on earlier decisions by the European Parliament, 15 February 2011; and the Council of 10 March 2011.

(also) execute jurisdiction about EPC patents,[37] or the European Patent Agency bows to the pressure to refer open questions with regard to adopted EU law to the ECJ.[38]

C. IP and Other Private Law Areas Compared

When comparing this debate on 'fundamental rights and IP' with the debate in other areas of private law like contract or labour law, two fundamental differences become evident: (1) In contrast to the founding principles of private law, private autonomy and contractual freedom, IP is in essence regulatory.[39] The right only comes into existence when regulatory requirements are met (either automatically, like copyrights, or by state act, like patents and trademarks). Inversely, regulatory limits to IP protect concurring rights. Therefore, the constitutionalization discourse in IP does not aspire to replace existing regulation (like in labour law[40]), but to improve them. (2) The more important difference follows from the utilitarian justification of IP rights. The detrimental effects of exclusionary rights (high prices, and the slowdown of knowledge diffusion) are justified by the public good of progress with regard to wealth, health, and food supply—to the detriment of expeditious knowledge diffusion via competition. Therefore, IP rights serve other human rights. Exceptions and limitations are conceptualized as catering to these goals. Thus, from the perspective of western theory, human rights are drivers of IP, not opposed to them. The balance between public policies, in theory, is struck by the given statutory patentability/copyright requirements, and respectively any written exceptions, and limitations to the scope (e.g. public libraries as exceptions to copyright). It is for this reason that traditional jurisprudence demanded priority of IP law over competition. This claim for priority is in line with the twentieth century development to guarantee IP as (or like) a human right—a concept which Article 17(2) EUCFR took on—although 'not inviolable and absolute'.[41] Prior to this, countries limited protection to constitutional or utilitarian limits (constitutional limits: Article 14 Basic Law of Germany; utilitarian limits: e.g. Article 5 XXIX Brazilian Constitution, Article I(8) US Constitution). As utilitarian rights they were neither all-encompassing, nor did they assign unlimited discretion of the IP holder.

The absorbance of conflicts by the proposition that IP ultimately serves the public interest rendered intellectual property for long immune against a broad constitutional

[37] As is widely known, due to the intergovernmental character of the European Patent Organization (not being a Community agency), EPC patents are not directly submitted to the control of the European court system. However, this situation may soon change if either a European Union's Patent or a European Patent Review System ('Unified European Patent Court') is installed (incorporating those shortcomings which the European Court of Justice has identified in its opinion 1/09 of 8 March 2011, [2011] ECR I-1137); for the historic background on the judicial review discussion see H. Ullrich, 'Die Entwicklung eines Systems des Gewerblichen Rechtsschutzes in der Europäischen Union: Die Rolle des Gerichtshofs' (2010), Max Planck Institute for Intellectual Property, Competition & Tax Law Research Paper Series, No. 10-11 (reprinted in P. Behrens, T. Eger, and H.-B. Schäfer, *Ökonomische Analyse des Europarechts* (2012) 147); more recently, with a focus on the history of the unified European patent: Ullrich, 'Harmonizing Patent Law: The Untameable Union Patent', in M.-C. Janssens and G. Van Overwalle (eds), *Harmonisation of European IP Law: From European Rules to Belgian Law and Practice* (2012) 243.

[38] As rightfully argued by Tillmann, 'Das Europäische Patentgericht nach dem Gutachten 1/09 des EuGH', 60 *GRURInt* (2011) 499.

[39] Godt, *supra* note 10, at 554 ff.; Grosheide, 'Introduction', in F. W. Grosheide (ed), *Intellectual Property and Human Rights: A Paradox* (2010) 21.

[40] As discussed by Collins in this volume.

[41] Case 360/19, *Scarlet Extended, supra* note 1, Rec. 41.

reflection as one of balancing conflicts in industrialized countries for a long time. More so, it makes reflection about conflicts in the area of intellectual property most ambitious: do IP and human rights 'collide' or do they coexist and further each other?[42]

3. Universal Human Rights versus EU Fundamental Rights

Before concentrating on the European Charter, the difference between the international debate on human rights and IP, which attracted much more publicity, and the European debate on conflicting rights and IP has to be clarified.

Greater affluence and efficient social security systems in the post-WWII era concealed conflicts between IP rights and interests in affordable quality medicines and available food. The 'IP and human rights' debate was perceived as a conflict between industrialized and developing countries which was carried out in international organizations. The debates of the 1970s in WIPO and UNCTAD framed technology transfer as a 'duty' of industrial countries vis-à-vis developing countries, and 'compulsory licensing' as a sovereign right of developing countries.[43] The debates around farmers' rights in the International Union for the Protection of New Varieties of Plants (UPOV) revolved around 'rights'—coining the interest of farmers in their access to seeds as a 'right' in contrast to what Western plant breeder's laws conceived as only a farmer's privilege. The two UN Covenants, the International Covenant on Economic, Social and Cultural Rights (ICESCR), and the Covenant on Civil and Political Rights (ICCPR), both of which adopted in 1966 and entered into force in 1976, mark high points in this discussion. They introduced 'second generation' rights like the right to health and the right to food. Both exerted, however, only a limited influence.[44]

The debate on 'IP and human rights' gained momentum with the AIDS debate at the turn of the millennium.[45] The debate was coined as an issue of 'access to essential medicine', thus reconfiguring the quest for availability of life-saving medicaments from a public good into an individual right.[46] The debate brought to light that the IP mechanism builds on effective market forces, and that the system will not deliver the projected results where markets fail. At that time, the problem of market failures in the pharmaceutical industry had already entered the public mind due to the debate regarding undersupply of 'orphan drugs' (drugs for diseases which affect a comparatively small number of patients resulting in a lack of research and products). The AIDS debacle added the insight that even where products exist, supply is not guaranteed when manufacturers only supply at world market prices which African patients cannot afford. Eventually the debate about 'IP and public health' led to a revision of the TRIPS Agreement (the amendment to add Article 31bis as agreed in 2005 is still submitted to

[42] Van Overwalle, 'Human Right Limitations in Patent Law', in Grosheide, *supra* note 35, 236.

[43] P.-T. Stoll, *Technologietransfer. Internationalisierungs- und Nationalisierungstendenzen. Die Gestaltung zwischenstaatlicher Wirtschaftsbeziehungen, privater Verfügungsrechte und Transaktionen durch die Vereinten Nationen, die UNCTAD, die WIPO und die Uruguay-Runde des GATT* (1994).

[44] P. Rott, *Patentrecht und Sozialpolitik unter dem TRIPS-Abkommen* (2002), at 92–98; U. Fastenrath, 'Die Verantwortlichkeiten transnationaler Unternehmen und anderer Wirtschaftsunternehmen im Hinblick auf Menschenrechte', in S. von Schorlemer, 'Die Verantwortlichkeiten transnationaler Unternehmen und anderer Wirtschaftsunternehmen im Hinblick auf die Menschenrechte', in Sabine von Schorlemer (ed), '*Wir, die Völker (...)'—Strukturwandel in der Weltorganisation* (2006) 69.

[45] Reichman, 'Lessons to be Learnt in Europe from the International Discourse about Patents and Public Health', in C. Godt (ed), *Differential Pricing* (2010) 133.

[46] Godt, *supra* note 10, at 445.

signature, however[47]). Other rights, which were formerly voiced as collective interests, followed suit and became articulated as individual rights like the 'right to food', farmers' rights, the right to a healthy environment, and the right to development.[48]

There are important differences between the international human rights debate and the European debate on European fundamental rights. The most important one is that universal human rights are binding on states as principles, but are not directly judiciable. Their primary function is to influence governmental policies, and frame a political controversy.[49] It is only recent that human rights as binding obligations on transnational corporations have become judicialized in court proceedings.[50] Severe violations of universal rights committed in countries with weak legal institutions are, under certain conditions, actionable (usually in their home countries).[51] In contrast, the central idea of European fundamental rights is that they are directly applicable, and arm citizens with defensive rights against their state. While scholars advocated for years a broadening of individual rights towards interests which have a collective nature,[52] the Charter finally complemented classical individual rights with collective interests. Whereas the traditional set enjoys direct applicability against actions of the EU and member states in so far as they execute EU law,[53] modern collective rights like the right of access to preventive health care and medical treatment (Article 35 EUCFR), the integration principle of environmental policies (Article 37, second half of the sentence, corresponding to Article 11 TFEU), and the goal of a high level of environmental quality and consumer protection (Article 37, first half of the sentence, corresponding to Article 191 TFEU; Article 38, corresponding to Article 169 TFEU) are acknowledged as legal positions resulting from the solidarity of the Community (Title IV), but are not directly enforceable and actionable by individuals. However, in conjunction with enacted secondary law, the Charter rights acquire a higher legal quality.[54] Beyond the classical catalogue of fundamental rights, e.g. the right to life (Article 2 EUCFR), the Charter acknowledges five constitutional novelties which might have an impact on IP related disputes

[47] On 30 November 2011, the WTO extended the deadline for acceptance of the TRIPS amendment for the third time until 31 December 2013 (WT/L/829 of 5 December 2011).

[48] A parallel development is the formal acknowledgement of group rights as the autonomy right of indigenous people in international law (Art. 8j CBD, UNESCO Convention of 2005, WIPO-IGC Draft of 2005); for an overview see Wendland, '"It's a Small World (After All)"—Some Reflections on Intellectual Property and Traditional Cultural Expressions', in C. B. Graber and M. Burri-Nenova (eds), *Intellectual Property and Traditional Expressions in a Digital Environment* (2008) 150.

[49] For a concise introduction to the political science 'frame analysis': Schneider, *supra* note 8, at 75–102.

[50] Most prominently acknowledged by the US Alien Tort Claims Act. See M. Koebele, *Corporate Responsibility under the Alien Tort Statute* (2009); for cases filed and documented, see the webpage of the European Center for Constitutional and Human Rights (ECCHR): <http://www.ecchr.de/index.php/wirtschaft_und_menschenrechte.html>.

[51] A. Fischer-Lescano and K. Möller, *Der Kampf um soziale globale Rechte* (2012), at 54 ff.; A. Gatto, *Multinational Enterprises and Human Rights: Obligations under EU and International Law* (2011) (reviewed by Topal, 'Holding your Own to Account: EU Policy Concerning its MNEs Abroad', 5 *European Journal of Legal Studies* (2012) 201).

[52] Micklitz, 'Consumer Rights', in A. Cassese, A. Clapham, and J. H. H. Weiler (eds), *Human Rights and the European Community: The Substantive Law* (1991) 53; For the 'right to information' as a citizen's right, Reich, 'Verbraucherpolitik und Verbraucherschutz im Vertrag von Amsterdam' *Verbraucher und Recht* (*VuR*) (1999) 1, at 6.

[53] J. Kokott and C. Sobotta, *The Charter of Fundamental Rights of the European Union after Lisbon*, EUI Working Papers, AEL 2010/6, at 6, stating that it thus complements the European national constitutions; M. Dauses, *The Protection of Fundamental Rights in the Legal Order of the European Union* (2010), at 156.

[54] For consumer rights already Micklitz, *supra* note 52.

in Europe: the rights of the individual in the biomedical setting (Article 3 EUCFR), individual rights in the information society (Article 11 EUCFR), access to public health (Article 35 EUCFR), access to public services (Article 36 EUCFR), and consumer protection (Article 38 EUCFR). All are geared towards securing the individual's autonomy against modern technological challenges and market changes.

Another central difference is the current limited scope of the European Charter since it is confined to the execution of intellectual property by EU authorities, and to the execution of EU laws by member states. The only Community rights are trademarks issued by the OHIM agency in Alicante,[55] and plant variety protection issued by the agency in Angers.[56] Although the introduction of a European patent with unitary effect is imminent (*supra* note 5), it remains to be seen to which extent the European Court of Justice claims jurisdiction over it. However, the Charter will apply to patents and copyrights as far as harmonized by European law (without question for nationally issued patents with regard to the Biotech Directive 98/44/EC[57] and for copyrights, e.g. with regard to the Info-Soc Directive 2001/29/EC[58]). However, the Charter will not be applicable to the actions of the European Patent Office *as such* since it is a non-EU organization based on the (non-EU) European Patent Convention.

In sum, taking all distinctions into consideration, what can Europe learn from the international debate on IP and human rights? The analysis has clarified that the old status of IP as a human rights enhancing institution per se cannot be sustained. The ambitious international debate on IP and human rights rests on a conception which puts all the rights involved on the same level, and, in particular, denies the precedence of property over other human rights.

4. The European Charter on Fundamental Rights and IP

Structurally, the Charter may influence the legal discourse in three different ways. First, the CJEU may refer to the Charter instead of making reference to the shared constitutional traditions of member states as it did before when interpreting secondary EU law. The recent ruling on provider responsibility is an example and will be described as a first case study (A.1). Secondly, a truly new layer of arguments might be created by the newly established rights, both as individual rights which create (new) directly effective rights against the state (and business partners) (Article 3(2) and Article 42 EUCFR), and as rights which secure due participation (such as Article 35 EUCFR). Four concrete IP cases to which these new rights are relevant will be analysed as to how far the Charter might change the discourse (B.1–4). Thirdly, the Charter might also influence the discourse with regard to rights which are not explicitly stipulated, like the right to decent food, and the right to cultural autonomy. These interests might either be part of other broader fundamental rights, or are stipulated by post-Charter human rights conventions. Since these rights have prompted highly politicized discussions in the EPO and WIPO, and directly affect European patents, a brief evaluation will hypothesize how the European Union might accommodate these universal values in terms of the Charter (C.6–7).

[55] Office for Harmonization in the Internal Market (OHIM), originally Council Regulation (EC) 40/94 of 20 December 1993; newly published as Council Regulation (EC) 207/2009 of 26 February 2009, OJ 2009 L 78/1.

[56] Council Regulation (EC) 2100/94, OJ 1994 L 227/1, of 27 July 1994 on Community plant variety rights.

[57] OJ 1998 L 213/13. [58] OJ 2001 L 167/10.

A. Balancing Approach to Secondary EU Law

1. Articles 7, 8, 11, and 16 EUCFR and Enforcement Measures against Providers

Adapting the language (not the grounds) of the opinion of AG Villalón,[59] the CJEU in its recent decisions *Scarlet Extended* and *Netlog* refers to the necessary trilateral balance which national agencies and courts have to secure between the property right of the copyright holder (Article 17(2) EUCFR), the providers' freedom to operate business (Article 16 EUCFR), data protection (Article 8 EUCFR), and the freedom to receive and impart users' information (Article 11 EUCFR),[60] when they enforce rights regulated by EU secondary law. The Court vaguely states that the filter measures in question violate five copyright and data protection directives which have to be 'read together and construed in the light of the requirements stemming from the protection of the applicable fundamental rights'. The lack of precision employed by the Court with regard to the violated terms of the directives might stem from the fact that the Advocate General essentially based his argument on the rationale that the national laws on which the filter measures are based are too restrictive and intriguing on the rights secured by the Charter that these measures can be based on general, national civil procedure enforcement rules (Article 52 EUCFR). The legal bases have to precisely direct the content and limits of the enforcement measure in this context. Therefore, the Advocate General considered the national measures void. The Court did not pick up this precise argument. However, it adapted the 'balance rhetoric'.

This new 'balance rhetoric' clearly denotes a turn in ECJ jurisdiction which started in 2008 with the *Promusicae* judgment. *Scarlet Extended* and *Netlog* gave the ECJ the opportunity to refer directly to a set of Charter rights to be acknowledged on the same level as property, not only as exception or limitation following the legal technique of the directives. Instead, the rights of individual property owners and the rights of numerous users are placed on the same footing.

B. Newly Introduced Charter Rights

1. Articles 1 and 2 EUCFR and Embryonic Stem Cells

Articles 1 and 2 EUCFR might exert an influence on the European debate about human embryonic stem cells (HESC). This has become framed as a conflict between the rights of the patent holder and researchers vis-à-vis the rights of an unborn child (human dignity and the right to life). The CJEU decided the case on referral of the German Federal Supreme Court on 18 October 2011,[61] essentially following Advocate General Bot who had delivered his opinion on 10 March 2011. The decision focuses on an interpretation

[59] Being the AG in both cases: Case 70/10, *Scarlet Extended*, AG Villalón of 14 April 2011; Case 360/10, *Netlog*, AG Villalón of 7 July 2012.

[60] Case 70/10, *Scarlet Extended*, judgment of 24 November 2001, not yet published; Case 360/10, judgment of 16 February 2012, not yet published.

[61] Case 34/10, *Brüstle v Greenpeace* [2011] ECR I-821, Opinion of AG Bot submitted 10 March 2011. Comments differ greatly. On the one hand applauding: Schneider, 'Das EuGH-Urteil "Brüstle versus Greenpeace" (Rs. Case 34/10): Bedeutung und Implikationen für Europa', 3 *Zeitschrift für geistiges Eigentum/Intellectual Property Journal* (2011) 475; on the other rejecting: Taupitz, 'Menschenwürde von Embryonen—europäisch-patentrechtlich betrachtet', 114 *GRUR* (2012) 1; Plomer, 'After Brüstle: EU Accession to the ECHR and the Future of European Patent Law', 2 *Queen Mary Journal of IP* (2012) 110. For an earlier, prior to the ECJ judgment, supporting the plaintiffs position: Straus, 'Zur Patentierung humaner embryonaler Stammzellen in Europa. Verwendet die Stammzellenforschung menschliche Embryonen für industrielle oder kommerzielle Zwecke?', 59 *GRURInt* (2010) 911.

of Article 6(2)(c) of the Biotech Directive 98/44/EC, which excludes patents for 'uses of human embryos for industrial or commercial purposes'. The court confirmed that the application for a patent signals the transition from research to 'commercial use'.[62] Thus, the Court rebutted the claimants' two propositions, that academic patents emerge in an upstream environment and are therefore not 'commercial', and that research regulations and patent regulations must be based on equivalent rationales. In contrast, the ECJ's argument inversely focuses on the human embryo, which cannot be less protected in a research than in a commercial setting. This is not necessarily an argument which stems from the Directive's text (which focuses on 'commercial use' mirroring the non-commercialization principle for humans and body parts). The gravity centre is the Advocate General's value decision in favour of the embryo and the implicit recognition of the German definition of life as beginning with the merging of germ cells,[63] and its unconditional protection thereafter (in contrast to other European states like the United Kingdom, which equally acknowledges 'life' from cell fusion on,[64] but provides unconditional legal protection only from the blastocyte stage on, and allows experimentation on the embryo up to 14 days[65]).

Would the decision have been different had the Court taken reference to the Charter?[66] Most probably the difference would have been minor, especially since even UK patent agencies did not grant patents on embryonic stem cells.[67] However, it seems wise for the Court not to make too emphatic an ethical point of when human life starts (compared to the commercialization issue once the human being exists) since member states differ with regard to the definition and regulations of the beginning of human life.[68]

2. *Article 3(2) EUCFR and Diagnostics*

An interesting intellectual test case for a debate on IP and fundamental rights, if recourse to the Charter were possible, would be the famous *Myriad* case.[69] This is internationally conceived as a 'paradigmatic case'.[70] It is about a diagnostic test kit which identifies

[62] Concurring with Enlarged Board of the EPO in its opinion on G2/06, para. 25.

[63] § 8(1) German Embryo Protection Act of 1990.

[64] Art. 1(2)(b) UK Human Fertilisation and Embryology Act 2008 reads: 'references to an embryo include an egg that is in the process of fertilisation or is undergoing any other process capable of resulting in an embryo'.

[65] Art. 4(3)(b) UK Human Fertilisation and Embryology Act 1990 as amended in the HFE (Research Purposes) Regulations of January 2001, and 2008.

[66] For a discussion on the differences should the case be brought to the ECHR: Plomer, *supra* note 61. Her arguments follow the plaintiffs' and Straus' argument that a unitary balance reasoning with regard to the human rights conflict underlying the research on HESC has to be undertaken for each legal subsystem (patent law, criminal law, research regulation). This assumption is neither shared by the AG and the Court, nor by the author.

[67] Spranger, 'Aspekte des britischen, amerikanischen, kanadischen und australischen Rechts', in J. Straus, P. Ganea, and Y.-C. Shin (eds), *Patentschutz und Stammzellforschung: Internationale und rechtsvergleichende Aspekte* (2009) 97, at 99.

[68] The differences are roughly aligned with the accession states of the Oviedo Convention on Human Rights and Biomedicine of 1997. Its Art. 18(2) prohibits the 'the creation of human embryos for research purposes'. This is one of the reasons why many EU member states (including Germany) did not sign it. Art. 21 endorses the non-commercialization principle.

[69] For a concise summary, see Godt, *supra* note 10, at 197; for a detailed analysis of the US controversy see Minsson, 'Standing on Shaky Ground: USP patent-eligibility of Isolated DNA and Genetic Diagnostics in the Wake of AMP v USPTO', 1 *Queen Mary Journal of IP* (2011) 334 and 2 *Queen Mary Journal of IP* (2012) 136.

[70] Resta, 'The Case Against the Privatization of Knowledge: Some Thoughts on the Myriad Genetics Controversy', in R. Bin, S. Lorenzon, and N. Luicchi (eds), *Biotech Innovation and Fundamental Rights* (2011) 11, at 11; Godt, *supra* note 10, at 196 et seq.

specific types of altered gene sequences which indicate a statistical predetermination for breast cancer. Many patents relate to two gene sequences called 'BRCA1' and 'BRCA2'. Patent enforcement on behalf of the owner has inhibited public hospitals from developing their own test kits, which experts believe to be of better quality. Blood probes have had to be sent in to the Myriad headquarters in Salt Lake City, Utah, for the price of US$2,400 to 3,500 per test. In Europe, several patents have been revoked and narrowed down after public opposition procedures against the patent.[71] In the United States, District Judge Sweet Stone revoked 7 out of 16 patents on grounds of a 'matter-of–nature-doctrine' on 29 March 2010. This was reversed by the US Court of Appeals for the Federal Circuit (CAFC) on 29 July 2011. The CAFC decision met with opposition on all sides. The applicants, the American Civil Liberties Union (ACLU), filed a petition for certiorari with the US Supreme Court on 6 December 2011. Academics criticized the CAFC decision as both inconsistent with the rationale of the *numerus clausus*, and politicized.[72] Few welcomed it for its clarifications.[73] On remand by the Supreme Court, the CAFC upheld its preliminary decision on 16 August 2012 in a 2:1 decision.[74]

The debates in the United States and in Europe were fueled by constitutional arguments. Since the European opposition was primarily instigated by public hospitals, the argument in public discourses rested very much on access to health care, i.e. reasonably priced and of a good (superior) quality. In the US, the proceedings were opened on behalf of some of the main professional organizations representing 15,000 geneticists, oncologists, and molecular biologists, various physicians, university researchers, and patients, joined by a long list of amicus curiae briefs, with the support of the American Civil Liberties Association. Therefore, arguments were based on the right to health, to scientific research, and on access to information relating to one's genetic make-up.[75] As many authors have pointed out, the *Myriad* case has been a test case on how the public discourse on constitutional rights gets transformed into a more narrow epistemic IP discourse revolving around patentability requirements which is nurtured by internal systems' need of coherence and unity.[76] In both cases, the procedures were not pursued in the first place as constitutional reviews. In Europe, an opposition was filed in the internal (quasi-administrative) EPC patent revision procedure open to anybody ('*actio popularis*'). In the US, a court procedure was initiated—whereas standing for plaintiffs remained a disputed issue.

Considering that these procedures have taken place 'inside' the system, i.e. in procedures which legitimately discriminate against constitutional arguments,[77] it is worthwhile to reconsider the case under the double assumption of an existing constitutional review board (for example the as yet non-existent, in the near future non-European, but

[71] Resta, *supra* note 70, at 24; Murray and Van Zimmeren, 'Dynamic Patent Governance in Europe and the United States: The Myriad Example', 19 *Cardozo Journal of International and Comparative Law* (2011) 287, at 322.

[72] Resta, 'La privatizzazione della conoscenza e la promessa dei beni comuni: riflessioni sul caso "Myriad Genetics" ', *Rivista Critica del Diritto Privato* (2011) 251.

[73] Minsson and Nilsson, *supra* note 69.

[74] Available at <http://www.ip-watch.org/weblog/wp-content/uploads/2012/08/Myriad-Decision-16-Aug-2012.pdf>. The court ruled that isolated DNA molecules were parent eligible as were method claims to screening potential cancer therapeutics via changes in cell growth rates of transformed cells. It ruled, however, that method claims which compare or analyse two gene sequences are not patent eligible.

[75] Resta, *supra* note 70, at 25.

[76] Resta, *supra* note 70, at 35; Murray and Van Zimmeren, *supra* note 71, at 323; Van Overwalle, *supra* note 42, at 237.

[77] For this argument Van Overwalle, *supra* note 42.

potentially in the long run European Patent Court[78]) and the European Charter Rights. Three Charter rights could be applied.

The first of these is Article 35 EUCFR as a solidarity right to health which encompasses two guarantees. The right enshrined in the first sentence grants an individual 'right of access to preventive health care'.[79] The second, enshrined in the second sentence, states that 'a high level of human health protection shall be ensured in the definition and implementation of all Union policies and activities'. The word 'preventive' is understood as a right to the prevention of health deterioration, not a right to preventive diagnosis. Under this definition, hindrances to access to pharmaceuticals are covered by the provision. Cases fall under its scope in which unaffordable prices or non-marketing (refused marketing) affect the right to preventive health. The second sentence refers to the notion that clinical tests in public hospitals are of a better quality. This sentence endorses the implementation principle—well established for environmental policies in Article 11 TFEU. In its nature, it does not guarantee individual rights but is (only) meant to be a guiding principle in policy making.[80] It has meaning for policymakers and courts alike: it is the role of policy makers to act on emerging problems which can prompt 'inside' or 'outside the system' responses. Two options 'inside' the IP system are (*de lege lata*) the handing out of compulsory licenses,[81] and (*de lege ferenda*) expanding access rights to public hospitals.[82] An 'outside' option could be, parallel to public procurement of medicines by social securities, the acquisition of wholesale licences for publicly funded hospitals, either by the Health Ministry or by Public Social Securities.[83] Courts reacted to the integration principle for environmental politics in doctrinal concepts. In 2001,[84] the Court considered environmental policies not (only) as a justification reason (secondary reason submitted to the so called '*Gebhard* test' on proportionality[85]), but as a reason limiting the protection of the fundamental freedom on the first level.

Secondly, Article 8(2), second sentence, of the Charter can be invoked. It guarantees the individual's right of access to data which has been collected concerning him or her, and the right to have it rectified. In the *Myriad* case, women could not verify the test results with an independent laboratory due to Myriad's aggressive patent policy. Therefore, patients were impeded to 'access... information relating to one's genetic make up'.

Thirdly, Article 13 EUCFR is affected. This secures respect for academic freedom. In the *Myriad* case, university centres and research laboratories encountered problems due to Myriads policy. In some cases, they were confronted with direct injunctions. In these cases, the rationale put forward by the German Supreme Court and the German Constitutional

[78] *Supra* note 3.

[79] 'Ein echtes Grundrecht' ('a true fundamental right'), H.D. Jarass, *Charta der Grundrechte der EU* (2010), at Art. 25(2), as a right to a benefit in form of participation; however compare for a more restrictive interpretation H. M. Sagmeister, *Die Grundsatznormen in der Europäischen Grundrechtecharta* (2010), at 376.

[80] Jarass, *supra* note 79, para. 3, and functions as a competence rule.

[81] Although the justifying ground would need more sophistication under Western national patent laws.

[82] Van Overwalle, 'Turning Patent Swords into Shares', 330 *Science* (2010) 1630.

[83] Applying Dan Burks' idea of 'governmental buy back' as additional options beyond property and liability rules, following up on Calabresi and Melamed, 'Property Rules, Liability Rules and Inalienability: One View from the Cathedral', 85 *Harvard Law Review* (1972) 1089, presented on 18 May 2012 in Hamburg (Bucerius Law School Conference: The Access Challenge).

[84] Case 379/98, *PreussenElektra* [2001] ECR I-2099.

[85] Case C-55/94, *Gebhard* [1995] ECR I-4165.

Court in clinical trials since 1995[86] informs the constitutional interpretation of patent law. The courts extended the narrow experimental use exception of patent law (here section 11(2) German Patent Act) towards experiments which are directly geared towards the generation of new scientific findings. The courts draw the line at illegitimate patent use (i.e. a property violation) where experiments have no direct link to the technical teaching, or where experiments are undertaken on a non-legitimate large scale, or misused as actual exploitation, or conducted with the intention of interfering with the inventor's distribution. However, this extension of the research exception does not, at least not on paper, exempt 'public clinics'—a proposal sensitively suggested by Geertrui Van Overwalle.[87] If we transpose this rationale to the *Myriad* case, the extended exception would still have exempted many activities in public research hospitals from the patent's scope.

More complicated in constitutional terms are constellations in which scientific experiments which concern either the protected genes or the diagnostic method are not undertaken. Cases have been reported in which scientists were dissuaded from pursuing their research.[88] These cases are not judiciable. However, these consequences give colour to the public debate on what 'the research commons' should look like, which rationales and norms should apply, and the generation of which results should be fostered.

All in all, reference to the Charter will certainly transform the discussion on exclusionary effects of patented diagnostics by providing structure to arguments which limit intellectual property on constitutional grounds.

3. *Article 3(2) EUCFR and Tissue Banks*

Another near-future test case for the delineation of intellectual property and constitutional rights might be the depositing of human tissues and blood samples. The existing European directives[89] focus on quality control and traceability between donor and recipient. However, the question of whether the donating individual has the power to veto the filing of patents based on his or her material, or to object to commercial research or specific directions of research, is still open. Up to now, public discussions have mainly revolved around issues of consent (written forms, possibility, and consequences of withdrawal) and data protection. With regard to commercialization, the Council of Europe Convention on Human Rights and Biomedicine (Oviedo Convention) of 1997 has revealed more differences among European states than common ground.[90] It stipulated a strong individual information right (Article 10[91]) and a strong non-commercialization principle (Article 21[92]); its additional Protocol on Biomedical Research laid down a

[86] BGH, judgment of 11 July 1995, BGHZ 130, 259—*Klinische Versuche I*; confirmed by BGH, judgment of 17 April 1997, BGHZ 135, 217—*Klinische Versuche II*, and by non-acceptance of a constitutional complaint: Federal Constitutional Court, 10 May 2000–1 BvR 1864/95, *GRUR* (2001) 43.

[87] Van Overwalle, *supra* note 82, at 1631.

[88] Resta, *supra* note 70, at 30.

[89] Three directives: the Framework Directive 2004/23/EC, OJ 2004 L 102/48 of 31 March 2004 is complemented by two technical directives: Directives 2006/17/EC, OJ 2006 L 38/40 and 2006/86/EC, OJ 2006 L 294/32.

[90] Of the 27 EU member states, the Eastern member states ratified during their accession period, while Austria, Belgium, Germany, the UK, and Ireland never even signed. France only ratified in December 2011. Italy and Poland signed early, but never ratified (see <http://www.coe.int>).

[91] Oviedo Convention, Art. 10(1): 'Everyone has the right to respect for private life in relation to information about his or her health; (2) Everyone is entitled to know any information collected about his or her health. However, the wishes of individuals not to be so informed shall be observed.' Text available at <http://www.coe.int>.

[92] Oviedo Convention, Art. 21: 'The human body and its parts shall not, as such, give rise to financial gain.'

respective broad consent requirement (Article 14[93]). Those countries which did not sign or ratify the convention feared its potential stifling effect on research and development. This overall policy consideration is mirrored by the delimitation of fundamental rights. The research project 'Boundaries of Information Property' conducted under the lead of the author under the umbrella of the Common Core of European Private Law (CCEPL) revealed that e.g. in Germany the right of an individual does not encompass the right to determine the direction of future research undertaken with his or her biological material (e.g. the exclusion of commercial purposes). This proposition is perceived as an (illegitimate) restriction of the researchers' freedom. In Italy, in contrast, the culturally embedded conviction prevails that the right to direct future research with one's body material is part of the individual's personality rights,[94] as stipulated under Article 90 of the Italian Data Protection Code (d.lgs. 196/2003) in conjunction with Article 5 of the d.l. 1-1-2006, n.3,[95] and interpreted with reference to the Oviedo Convention.[96]

However, it seems that values have shifted. Ten years ago, the patient's right to have a say in future research (to exclude specific fields of research, to exclude commercial research, filing patents on his or her DNA, to claim royalties and financial compensation) was rebutted primarily by referring to the non-commercialization principle,[97] and only secondly by reference to the personality principle,[98] and to freedom of research. These claims were conceived as not being covered by the right to personality. Over the years, this argumentation has been reversed and redirected.[99] An early sign was the German Supreme Court (*Bundesgerichtshof*, BGH) decision in 1993 about a damages claim for infertility due to destroyed sperms. In this decision the Court acknowledges

[93] Additional Protocol to the Convention on Human Rights and Biomedicine, concerning Biomedical Research, Art. 14(1): 'No research on a person may be carried out, subject to the provisions of both Chapter V and Article 19, without the informed, free, express, *specific* and documented consent of the person. Such consent may be freely withdrawn by the person at any phase of the research.' (Emphasis added.)

[94] Resta, 'Contratto e persona', in E. Roppo (ed), *Trattato del contratto,* vol. VI (2006) 37; Galloux, 'L'utilisation des matériels biologiques humains: vers un droit de destination?', *Recueil Dalloz* (1999) (Chronique) 15; who both refer to the annulment procedure of Italy against the European Biotech Directive (Case C-377/98, [2001] ECR I-7079, application dismissed).

[95] Resta, 'O acesso ao material biológico humano com fins de pesquisa e de aproveitamento industrial: questões relativas ao consentimento e à responsabilidade na perspectiva do direito comparado', in: J. Martins Costa and L. L. Möller (eds), *Bioética e Responsabilidade* (2009) 145; Germinario, 'L'attuazione della Direttiva n. 98/44/CE in materia di protezione giuridica delle invenzioni biotecnologiche', *Il Diritto Industriale* (2006) 319.

[96] Italy ratified, but not all decrees provided by the law have been adopted which has raised questions with regard to the binding effect of the Convention, see Resta, case 7 of the Italian Country Report (2009), fn. 41 (on file with the author, and to be published in the BIP project volume under CCEPL-series with Cambridge University Press).

[97] Godt, *supra* note 10, at 650 et seq. The German Ethics Council in 2004 suggested a generalized prior informed consent (encompassing all research purposes), favoured the exclusion of individual financial claims for benefit sharing in favour of the creation of a fund (Nationaler Ethikrat (ed), Chairman S. Simitis, *Biobanken für die Forschung: Stellungnahme* (2004), at 89); for a critique of this 'blanket consent' see Schneider, '"This Is Not a National Biobank..."—The Politics of Local Biobanks in Germany', in A. Peterson and H. Gottweis (eds), *Biobanks: Governance in a Comparative Perspective* (2008) 88, at 96.

[98] The distinction between person and property underlies all case reasonings from the California Supreme Court decision in its famous *Moore Case* in 1990 (which originally prompted the modern debate about commercialization and the human body, Ca. Supreme Ct. [1990] 51 Cal.3d 120) to the English Appeals Court *Yearworth* decision of 4 February 2009, [2009] EWCA Civ 37. The facts of the latter are very similar to the German BGH sperm case of 1993, BGHZ 124, 52.

[99] C. Halàsz, *Das Recht auf bio-materielle Selbstbestimmung: Grenzen und Möglichkeiten der Weiterverwendung von Körpersubstanzen* (2004).

that personality and property rights can overlap once material is separated from the body.[100] This flexibility with regard to the old-style dichotomy between body and data seems also to be reflected by the German Ethics Council recommendation of 2010 which now acknowledges the power of the individual to direct the use of body material and data, and recommends that the right to purpose-bound donations should be respected.[101] The old concept of prior informed consent which has evolved in the area of medical interventions to the human body has been fine-tuned by purpose limitations developed in data protection for information-bearing human body tissues.

The Charter might contribute a refined constitutional language to this debate. Article 3(2)(a) EUCFR strengthens the right of the individual in the field of medicine and biology in that free and informed consent has to be respected (according to the procedures laid down by law). The interpretation of what the consent covers is influenced by Article 3(2)(c) EUCFR which prohibits the 'making of the human body and its parts as such a source of financial gains'. I argue that Article 3 EUCFR includes the individual's defensive right against commercialization. Since Article 3 EUCFR does not actually concretize what the non-commercialization principle encompasses, it is to be interpreted in that it gives the individual the right to concretization. This right is not limited to the disposition of either commercial or non-commercial research (including the right to oppose the patenting of parts of one's genomic information, be those universal or individual). Article 8 EUCFR adopts the basic principle of specific purpose limitation in data processing. This principle has been adapted in the biobank debate. Applying this principle to genomic material means that the individual may legitimately limit the use of his or her material and data to specific purposes. If the researcher is not interested in such use-restricted material, he or she is free not to include such data in the study (Article 13 EUCFR).

This interpretation is in line with the conceptualization of Giorgio Resta who observes an emerging bipolar regime: intangible aspects of identity are increasingly protected against commercialization through property rules, whereas the corporal elements are protected through liability rules.[102]

Will the Charter add substance to the debate? The unitary reference will certainly highlight the fundamental cultural differences between member states. The issue will most likely not pop up in the patent arena, but is likely to do so in the research arena. In multicentre studies which collect information in as harmonious a manner as possible in order to compare data as well as possible, these significant differences with regard to the prior informed consent sheet, and its consequences for the necessary non-inclusion of patients and volunteers, will certainly raise pressure to introduce a uniform standard form, especially when the study is financed under EU funding schemes. Article 3(2) EUCFR will certainly be an important point of reference which will underline the autonomy of the individual as the subject of biomedical research.

4. *Article 35 EUCFR and Compulsory Licensing?*

Does Article 35 EUCFR provide a patient with the right to claim a compulsory licence for third parties or to a compulsory licence which is limited to importation? It seems that

[100] BGHZ 124, 52.

[101] Deutscher Ethikrat, *Human Biobanks for Research—Opinion*, download: <http://www.ethikrat.org/files/der_opinion_human-biobanks.pdf>.

[102] Resta, 'The New Frontiers of Personality Rights and the Problem of Commodification: European and Comparative Perspectives', 26 *Tulane European & Civilian Law Forum* (2011) 33, at 54.

this question has not yet been widely discussed; no precedents are known; an in-depth analysis of academic literature of those countries which have acknowledged an individual's right to public health would be most valuable.[103] Under the *previsio* that access to medicaments is covered by the solidarity right under Article 35 EUCFR, the question arises if the entitled individual can ask for an action which is directed against a third party (the patent holder) conveying a right to a fourth person (a potential manufacturer). The problematic is inverse to the renowned problem of third party opposition against licences to pollute in environmental law. A third party may only oppose an administrative advantage granted to the addressee under certain conditions (in Germany these are especially restricted in the sense that applied regulations aim at the protection of the third party). The same rules apply if a third party applies for an administrative measure which would grant him or her a privilege but would burden a third party. With regard to compulsory licences, the situation would be similar. A person would request an administrative action on behalf of an undertaking (which may or may not join the procedure) which burdens the respective patent holder.

From a procedural point of view, I propose to derive from the now-acknowledged patient's right that this right covers the right to due and proportionate access to lifesaving medicaments. Since the right is not absolute, but stems from solidarity, the claim is *ab initio* reduced to a reasoned decision based on solidarity, a principle limited by feasibility in practical terms and by available funds. However, I argue that the individual has a right to apply for a measure and is entitled to a reasoned decision.

C. Human Rights beyond the Charter

1. Food Security/Food Quality

The Charter does not pick up the 'right to food', following Article 25(1) Universal Declaration of Human Rights and Article 11(1) International Covenant on Economic, Social and Cultural Rights.[104] However, since one of the most hotly debated current issues in the European Patent Organization is related to food, the case should be revisited with regard to the European Charter.

It is well understood that Europe does not suffer from an undersupply of food, but from overproduction. However, with industrial agricultural production and food manufacture comes along a different style of food. Environmental problems due to fertilizers, monocultures, and deteriorated, undifferentiated field and landscape structures, in conjunction with food security issues due to chemical residues, unsatisfactory living conditions of animals, but also lack of taste, have prompted a discussion of food *quality* incorporating conditions of food production ('organic food' implying a different standard of fertilizers, and animal production). The debate has turned into a human rights debate with the aim that anyone should have the right to choose the kind of food he or she prefers (overhauling the debate about food security as a matter of governmental consumer protection under Article 38 EUCFR). The 'right to choose' proposition is captured by modern national constitutions under the right to individual autonomy

[103] But it goes beyond the scope of this chapter.

[104] Art. 25(1) UDHR (corresponds to Art. 11(1) International Covenant on Economic, Social and Cultural Rights): 'Everyone has the right to a standard of living adequate for the health and well-being of himself and of his family, including food, clothing, housing and medical care and necessary social services, and the right to security in the event of unemployment, sickness, disability, widowhood, old age or other lack of livelihood in circumstances beyond his control.'

(Article 6 EUCFR: 'right to liberty and security of person'). The right to 'security of person' implies the right to be protected e.g. against hazardous residues in food ('food security'). The right to liberty secures the right to free choice. No one can be directed to eat specific food. A reflection of this right in a market economy should also secure the precondition of free choice: the availability of different kinds of food with regard to qualities, origins, and sources. Thus, availability redirects the attention to economic structures in food production. In essence, there is a classical argument against monopolistic structures at stake which legal systems have entrusted to antitrust law. The tension between antitrust and IP law is legendary. An interesting aspect of the food quality discussion in IP law is that the 'framing' has been turned into constitutional terms.

As one legal institution among others, intellectual property rights for food (plants and animals: pork, beef, chicken) are acknowledged as an important incentive for food innovations. It is widely acknowledged that the 'Green Revolution' of the 1950s and 1960s which brought about a significant increase of yield per acre, was driven by strong plant breeders' rights. But since plant hybrids can equally be protected under patents (EPO decision *Lubrizol*[105]), and since genetic engineering (a term which does not necessarily imply genetic improvement) has become a common and patentable practice (the leading EPO decision is *Novartis*[106]), protection policies have shifted to patents.

Due to Article 100 EPC, which allows for opposition by everyone (followed by an *actio popularis* type of procedure), patent related food disputes have become juridified (although not yet in terms of constitutional rights) in the forum of the European Patent Office.

The most current debate revolves around breeding techniques ('molecular marker selection', 'smart breeding'). It does not involve genetically modified plants or animals, but (only) the bioengineering procedure used to select the breeding material—an effective breeding technology, and one which is compatible with the European consumer (with regard to consumers' resistance against genetically modified food), but one which is still capital intensive. Prominent patent claims range from pigs[107] and cows[108] to broccoli[109] and tomatoes.[110] Since the room to manoeuvre for traditional breeders (who are not entangled with the chemical industry) is shrinking, and there is an increased risk for farmers of becoming entangled in patent claims, breeders and farmers have joined forces with environmentalists and consumer alliances.

In a first decision on 9 December 2010, the Enlarged Board of Appeal (EBA) ruled on the patentability of the claims with regard to Rule 23b section 5 EPO Rules (Article 4(1)(b) Directive 98/44/EC), which excludes 'essentially biological processes for the production of plants and animals' (*Broccoli*). The EBA ruled that a process is still excluded if it contains

105 T-320/87, decision of Technical Board of Appeal 3.3.2 of 10 November 1988, *Lubrizol*, OJ EPO 1990, 71.

106 G-1/98, decision of the Enlarged Board of Appeals of 20 December 1999, *Novartis*, OJ EPO 2000, 111. The case revolved around the content of 6% oil in transgenetic maize—claiming all maize plants with an oil content of 6%.

107 WO 2009097403 (EP 1651777), filed in 2005 by Monsanto, sold 2007 to Newsham Choice Genetics, which renounced the patent on 31 March 2010, resulting in a withdrawal by the EPO on 20 April 2010.

108 EP 1 330 552.

109 European patent (EP 1069819), Case G-2/07, decision of the Enlarged Board of Appeals of 9 December 2010, OJ EPO 3/2012, 113.

110 European patent (EP 1211926), Case 1/08, decision of the Enlarged Board of Appeals of 9 December 2010, not published in the OJ but available inter alia at <http://www.ipeg.eu/wp-content/uploads/Plant-Breeding-Method_EPO_G1_08_en.pdf>.

as a further step or as part of any of the steps of crossing and selection a step of a technical nature. Only if 'a process contains within the steps of sexually crossing and selecting an additional step of technical nature, which step *by itself introduces a trait* into the genome or modifies a trait in the genome of the plant produced, so that the introduction or modification of that trait is not the result of the mixing..., the process is not excluded'. Then, it would not be relevant whether a step of a technical nature is a new or known measure. In the aftermath of this decision, many method claims have been withdrawn or narrowed down; many are now formulated as product-by-process claims.

However, the most recent debate (*Tomato II*[111]) tackles the question which has remained unanswered: does the scope of parallel product-by-process claims cover the products or only products which have been manufactured directly using that method? As with the first procedure, the second opposition (against the same patents on broccoli and tomatoes) was filed by competitors (Unilever and Syngenta), not NGOs. The technical question refers to the effect of exclusions (here, Article 53(b) EPC: process claims on 'essentially biological processes') on other claim types. In principle 'product-by-process' claims are hybrids between method and product claims. After years of expansion, the US-CAFC recently narrowed these claims down to the utility actually disclosed.[112] In Europe, product-by-process claims are conceived as original product claims,[113] and therefore comprise, as far as they are formulated by 'comprising language',[114] all products regardless of their immediate production method and regardless of the utility disclosed ('*absoluter Stoffschutz*'). At the heart of the new opposition procedure is the proposition that the patent exclusion of an 'essentially biological process' would be undermined if the scope of a product-by-process claim granted for the product described by that (unpatentable 'essentially biological') method, encompassed the end product.[115] Whereas opponents claim that the exclusion would be undermined,[116] patent holders claim a parallel to the Novartis reasoning of G-1/98 which referred to the exclusion of Article 53(b) EPC.[117] The core of that latter decision was a narrow, patent-friendly reasoning in favour of patent eligibility as long as 'more than just one' plant breeding right is covered by the patent claim. Methods claims would be valueless since self-propagating material is, most of the time, not a direct product of the claimed process.

Would the Charter add quality to the debate once the judicial patent system were integrated in the European Court system? Despite the necessities of legal technicalities in

[111] T-1242/06; On 31 May 2012, the EPO Board of Appeal 3.3.04 filed an interlocutory decision and referred the case to the Grand Chamber, available at <http://www.epo.org/law-practice/case-law-appeals/pdf/t061242ex2.pdf>.

[112] Only recently clarified by the CAFC in *Abbott v Sandoz* on 18 May 2009. Fabry, 'Kein Stoffschutz ohne Verfahrensbenutzung? Zur jüngsten Standortbestimmung des Product-by-Process-Anspruchs in den USA', 58 *GRURInt* (2009) 803; Thot, 'Product-by-Proces Ansprüche nach US-Recht', *Mitteilungen der Deutschen Patentanwälte* (2009) 317.

[113] Leading case for product-by-process-claims on plants: BGH, *GRUR* (1993) 651—*Tetraploide Kamille.*

[114] With the 'comprising language', the claim covers all products with the described traits (therefore: rationale of absolute protection), whereas with a 'consisting of language', the claim covers only direct products of the described method (therefore: rationale of process claims, Art. 64(2) EPC).

[115] Walter, 'Rote Taube-Lila Kuh—Rechtliche Betrachtungen zu Patent- und Sortenschutz', in M. Stephan and K. Bette (eds), *Biodiversität, Geistiges Eigentum und Innovation* (2012) 99, at 105.

[116] See, e.g. the arguments of Unilever in G-1/08 (*Tomatoes*); followed by the Court of The Hague in a decision on 31 January 2012 about the validity of radish sprouts in *Taste of Nature v Creso* (case 408315/KG ZA 11-1414).

[117] O. Malek et al., 'Plant Patents and Endangered Species?—Surprising New Developments in the Tomato Case' (2012), available at: <http://www.vossiusandpartner.com/pdf/Plant%20Patents%20An%20Endangered%20Species.pdf> (also EPI Information 1/2012, 16–22).

the patent discourse, it is still to be expected that constitutional infusion may also change the epistemic discourse, for two reasons. First, in the early case of genetic engineering of plants, the decision was influenced by the (at that time still) European Community's principle of coexistence. While the principle demanded safety measures for agricultural field trials, in patent courts, the principle secured the patentability of genetically engineered plants as technical innovations. The mere technical patent reasoning might change at a moment in time when non-engineered food is non-available, and a causal link can be established to the economic pressures of the IP system. Second, a constitutional reflection about the technical issues might broaden the understanding of the effects of patent protection, which has become narrow due to the technical administration of the patent system by epistemic communities.[118] A constitutional conflict perspective brings the colliding interests of farmers and consumers to the forefront, which could enlighten the interpretation of (non-)patentability requirements, and patent principles. This discourse is the more probable the more economic instruments are employed to achieve public policy goals, and heterogeneous actors with procedural rights understand the economic implications of the patent-competition interface on food quality, and frame their arguments as constitutional entitlements. A constitutional reflection about patent exclusions would bring to light the concurring interests protected by them, thus rendering relative the perceived restrictions of the property holder.

2. *Cultural Autonomy*

It would be too narrow to confine this chapter to rights guaranteed by the Charter and leave aside other human rights related to IP which fundamentally affect the European Union. Cultural autonomy rights of traditional communities, as guaranteed by several UN conventions,[119] challenge the western notion of how to define public domain information which can be freely used in order to produce novel patentable information ('technical teachings'). These communities claim a right to 'their' medicinal and plant knowledge, their drawings, their music. The consequence is that 'their' information, though collective and disclosed, might not be considered as 'public domain'.[120] WIPO[121] and the CBD discuss a veto right to commercialization (similar to the patent's right to veto patenting with one's body materials, *supra* B.4),[122] and require a mandatory 'disclosure of origin'[123] in patent applications. It remains to be seen if a future revision of the EU Biotech Directive 98/44/EC will integrate such a cogent requirement—and react to these recent acknowledgments. Up to now, the respective disclosure has been facultative, and conceived as information relevant only to the novelty requirement (not as a safeguard to protect human rights). It should be evident that a transnational understanding of human rights demands respective safeguards (here, in patent law) which allow rightholders the tracking of used information. That recognition would be the

[118] Schneider, *supra* note 8, at 188 et seq.

[119] Wendland, *supra* note 48.

[120] C. B. Graber and M. Burri-Nenova (eds), *Intellectual Property and Cultural Expressions in a Digital Environment* (2008), esp. the conflicts of law approach of G. Teubner and A. Fischer-Lescano therein, 'Cannibalizing Epistemes: Will Modern Law Protect Traditional Cultural Expressions?' 17.

[121] T. Kiene, *The Legal Protection of Traditional Knowledge in the Pharmaceutical Field* (2011).

[122] Similar to the veto position (at least, a right to be asked) which 'provider countries' claim under the CBD, however, the ground for their claim is sovereignty, not a human right, and is therefore not to be discussed here (see Godt, *supra* note 10, at 264 et seq).

[123] Godt, *supra* note 10, at 334.

natural counterpiece to the assumption that human rights, as stipulated by the Charter, and primarily addressed to citizens of the Union, are acknowledged.

5. Conclusion: The Novel Public–Private Interface

The nature of IP disputes has evidently changed. Although the list of the chosen seven examples is not exhaustive, the given limited set of cases—together with the well-known cases not discussed here in depth, like the *Magill* judicature—provides evidence for several characteristic shifts in the IP conflict structure. The growing economic value of IP rights is impressive in itself as reflected by the ratio of the gross national product of information goods[124] or the infringement value in single IP disputes.[125] However, more importantly, the legal analysis identifies a shift in structural characteristics which qualify the public–private divide. Whereas formerly the IP right was primarily characterized by its function to exclude competitors and to enable the management of the industrial production chain downstream, today the exclusionary nature of property is restricted both downstream and upstream. Downstream, IP rights have become 'more public' resulting in claims for 'more access' (A). Upstream, IP rights themselves become linked and limited by preceding rights over material and information (other than e.g. system-conform dominating patents) (B). This new embeddedness of property rights which originally were conceived to secure private sovereignty requires a fresh approach about how to conceive IP rights. Therefore, a final paragraph will position the unveiled normative structures of IP as integral part of the modern European regulatory private law (C).

A. The 'Access Challenge'

The claim for 'access' to IP rights has become a buzzword. In its fuzziness it encompasses assumptions of a variety of natures induced by IP rights 'becoming more public'. The analysis has identified at least three distinct aspects.

First, beside licences being a tool of industrial property (vis-à-vis competitors and contractors), they have become marketing instruments which create *direct* legal relations to *numerous* ordinary consumers. Patents and copyrights have lost their 'competition only function', not least due to the quasi-abolition of the private copy. To the extent that the internet has become the general communication tool, and cultural and scientific goods are now marketed in the digital world by licences, the 'information commons' debate has given rise to discussions about the right to access as part of universal services[126] and the 'culture flat rate'.[127] The shift towards a more public conception of IP

[124] Estimations vary, and depend on indicators. For Europe on average, the figure is 3.4% of all R&D-expenditures Eurostat, June–July 2012: <http://epp.eurostat.ec.europa.eu/statistics_explained/index.php/The_EU_in_the_world_-_science_and_technology>; for the US, 34.8% IP value of the gross national value (US Dept. of Commerce, Intellectual Property and the U.S. Economy, published 11 April 2012, available at <http://www.uspto.gov/news/publications/IP_Report_March_2012.pdf>).

[125] Various procedures between Apple and Samsung worldwide hit the front pages, e.g. San José (USA, CA) the District Court attributed the sum of US$1.05 billion to Apple on 7 June 2012; a Japanese court, vice versa, attributed the comparably humble sum of €1 million to Samsung on 31 August 2012. German procedures (OLG München, OLG Düsseldorf on 26 July 2012) have focused on patent validity and injunctions.

[126] In the sense of a 'duty to provide the service', H.-W. Micklitz, *Do Consumer and Businesses Need a New Architecture of Consumer Law? A Thought-Provoking Impulse, EUI Working Papers* Law 2012/23 (2012), at 41.

[127] In the sense of a statutory licence with a fixed fee. A. Rossnagel et al, 'Die Zulässigkeit einer Kulturflatrate nach nationalem und europäischem Recht' (2009), available at <http://www.

rights has, for example, allowed Spain to transpose the private ordering system of levies for CDs into a purely public tax system.[128]

Secondly, a shift towards 'being more public' has been identified in the classical competition arena—which has been mentioned above (*supra*, 2(B)), and discussed in-depth elsewhere.[129] Among those, one development is paradigmatic: patents have been accepted in the standards which are deemed to be accessible for everyone. Yet, standardization has become central both as industrial policy (slogan: 'The one who has the standard has the market'), and as a tool to secure interoperability, especially in the IT industry. Despite the tensions between patent exclusivity and standards, the inclusion of patented technology in a standard is now accepted, if the participants declare their willingness to license in a fair, reasonable and indiscriminatory manner ('FRAND'). Thus, broad access should be secured. The legal implications of the quasi-public declaration are yet to be clarified.[130]

Thirdly, novel public policy considerations come into play. As much as the IP system affects product development and the downstream production chain, the consumer is affected by the market results it generates. Whereas monopoly pricing might become a serious concern in the future, especially in health products ('access to medicines'), high price levels are currently not of great concern in Western countries (see prices for smartphones, tablet PCs). Instead, consumers worry about reduced choice. For example, the erosion of the genetic pool in various species, resulting in a reduction to a few agriculturally used strains, is not only an environmental concern. It equally affects the consumer's choice. The autonomous consumer is not only interested in the information *if* a given product contains genetic modifications (classical information paradigm of consumer law). The consumer as market actor is also interested in a product choice which allows him or her to select from different products (beside products he or she rejects). Especially in the food sector, IP systems have induced a reduction of consumer choice, which is the opposite of their intended effect. Here, the public concern is geared towards complementary instruments alleviating the monopolistic tendencies of IP systems (e.g. by a reinforcement of the farmer's right system).

B. Preceding Entitlements

The description of the shift of the public–private divide would be incomplete without a consideration of the inverse developments. Patent holders are required to acknowledge new rights attributed to materials which function, all in all, as raw material to intellectual property. This transforms what was deemed to be 'public domain' (free to take) into a legal sphere.[131] In contrast to subsequent dependent patent holders or manufacturers of interoperative components (*supra*), access to technical teaching is not sought.

gruene-bundestag.de/fileadmin/media/gruenebundestag_de/themen_az/netzpolitik/16_fragen_und_16_antworten/kurzgutachten_zur_kulturflatrate.pdf>.

[128] Royal Decree Act 20/2011, passed on 30 December 2011, abolishes Art. 25 of the Spanish Copyright Act (the levy system).

[129] Godt, *supra* note 10, at 584 ff.; D. Wielsch, *Zugangsregeln: die Rechtsverfassung der Wissenteilung* (2007).

[130] Ullrich, 'Patent, Wettbewerb und technische Normen', *GRUR* 109 (2007) 817; Ullrich, 'Patent and Standards—A Comment on the German Federal Supreme Court Decision "Orange Book Standard"', 41 *IIC* (2010) 337; Straus, 'Das Regime des European telecommunications Standards Institute—ETSI', 60 *GRURInt* (2011) 469; A. Balitzki, 'Patente und technische Normen' (PhD thesis on file at the University of Oldenburg, January 2013) (publication forthcoming).

[131] Explored in more detail by Godt, *supra* note 10, at 261, 303, 437.

These rightholders demand injunction, influence on exploitation, and only sometimes a share in profits. In other words, they claim an influence on exploitation. For instance, homeowners hold a right to their home's façade and pictures thereof which are to be respected by Google Street View.[132] Donors of human tissue material have rights to their own body material. This entitlement raises the question of whether 'prior informed consent' also includes the right to have a say in the use, be it scientific or commercial, of the material. These questions go beyond the popular debate about data protection, and consumer protection (labour rights, insurance contracts), and direct attention to the set of rights of the modern individual, formulated as fundamental rights conflicting with IP. In very similar terms, the collective rights of farmers, indigenous communities, and the countries of origin of genetic resources ('CBD rights') demand a right to have a say in if and how commercialization might occur (sometimes also referred to as 'access'). These rights reformulate the public-private divide, and create an additional layer of prior rights which are to be respected by later IP holders.

C. Property as Integral Part of European Regulatory Private Law

These two developments have rendered IP more of a 'normal' property right which forms the basis for contractual relationships with regard to information and which is shaped by regulations *and* constitutional considerations.[133] The seven cases give evidence that the Charter has already embarked on a reformulation of the public–private debate, and will determine the evolution of information property into the modern transformation of what has been coined as 'European Regulatory Private Law'. This term refers to a transformation of norms, remedies, acknowledged actors, procedures, and institutions as a general phenomenon of European private law.[134] It shifts the attention from systematic private autonomy to a body of law embedded in regulatory policies. Since the focus of this article is on the relationship of IP and the European Charter, a classification of the observed changes in IP with regard to these five analytic categories of European Regulatory Private Law has to be brief.[135] However, in order to embark on a joint discussion across the various subdisciplines of private law,[136] a rough attribution to these categories shall be provided, before turning to general conclusions.

With regard to *norms*, four cases out of the set of seven (case 2 on human embryonic stem cells: the right to life; case 3 on diagnostics: the right to preventive public health care; case 4 on tissue banks: the right to one's own body information; and case 7 on cultural autonomy: the collective property right in information) show that IP *norms* do change under the influence of constitutional values (other than single individual rights of

[132] A good overview is provided by G. Spindler, *Persönlichkeitsschutz im Internet—Anforderungen und Grenzen einer Regulierung* (2012), Expert Opinion for the 69th Conference of the German Lawyers Union (*69. Deutscher Juristentag*).

[133] For the structure of the 'constitutionalization of IP', see Godt, *supra* note 10, at 573–654.

[134] Micklitz, 'A Self-Sufficient European Private Law—A Viable Concept?', in: H.-W. Micklitz and Y. Svetiev (eds), *A Self-Sufficient European Private Law—A Viable Concept?* EUI Working Papers Law 2012/31 (2012), at 5.

[135] The author, however, will contribute to the 'European Regulatory Private Law' debate by the project 'Boundaries to Information Property' which she co-manages since 2003 with G. v. Overwalle, L. Guibault, and D. Beyleveld under the umbrella of the Common Core of European Private Law Project (<http://www.common-core.org>). Documentation and results are to be published by Cambridge University Press in 2014/15.

[136] I am indebted to H.-W. Micklitz for his insistence and his hints with regard to the following paragraph.

others in the Kantian sense). The Charter enhances the status of the acknowledged values by either acknowledging individual interests as 'rights' (the right to one's own body information) or by providing language to a novel interpretation of existing norms (embryonic stem cells, public health, cultural autonomy). With regard to *remedies*, case 1 (*Scarlet Extended v Netlog*) is indicative of how the classic remedy of injunction can be fine-tuned by acknowledging competing interests. *Procedural* implications become evident once the many high profile cases in patent law are considered which have been initialized by way of the everyone's right under Article 100 EPC (case 2 on human embryonic stem cells: the non-governmental organization Greenpeace; case 3 on diagnostics: public hospitals, professional organizations of physicians, and patient organizations; and case 5 on the patient's right to compulsory licensing; case 6 food quality: consumer organizations). New actors are granted access to judicial procedures ('access to justice'). Thus, they enrich the set of arguments exchanged in patent administrations and court rooms, and render the decision more complex. This enshrines the possibility of making the decision 'more just', but equally bears the risks of all balancing decisions.[137] Last but not least, *institutions* are incrementally changing by responding to international pressures. The acknowledgment of forms of collective property (case 7 on cultural autonomy) is due to international treaties signed by the member states and the European Union. Since collective rights contradict the idea of private property,[138] their recognition subtly changes the notion of intellectual property as a (sovereign) private right. Another institutional change is the acknowledgement of an individual right to one's own body information (thus reducing the public domain). It was pushed by southern European states to become the Council of Europe's Orviedo Convention on Human Rights and Biomedicine (1997, in force 1999, *supra* 4(B)4.), which is not signed by all EU member states. But its value implications have found their way into Article 3 EUCFR.[139]

The essence is that legal relations in private law have absorbed regulatory policies. Regulation today is not limited to property restrictions controlled by public law only. In private law, regulatory policies frame legitimate expectations of individuals protected by the constitution beyond classical 'rights'.[140] This is what Micklitz coins the 'constitutionalization challenge to private law'.[141] The conceptual shift follows the societal transformation from a society organized by status towards one organized by markets.[142] Private law adapted by turning the focus from exclusion towards the inclusion of market actors, roughly speaking, 'other than property owners'. Joerges recently spoke of respect towards others as a 'legal imperative',[143] referring openly to Habermas' paradigm of 'the right of the other'.[144] It is the double orientation of the twentieth century towards

[137] Reich, 'Thoughts on Hybridisation', in Micklitz, *supra* note 134, 199, at 200.

[138] Godt and Clarke, 'Comparative Property Law: Collective Rights within Common Law and Civil Law Systems', in C. Godt (ed), *Cross Border Research and Transnational Teaching under the Treaty of Lisbon* (2013) 61.

[139] Which corresponds to Micklitz's observation of national/international hybrids. Micklitz, *supra* note 134 at 25.

[140] Godt, *supra* note 10, at 426, 436, 444, and in theoretical terms at 572.

[141] Micklitz, *supra* note 134, at 25.

[142] Frerichs, 'The Law of the Market Society: A Polanaian Account of Its Conflicts and Dynamics', in Micklitz and Svetlev, *supra* note 134, 45; also C. Joerges and J. Falke (eds), *Karl Polanyi, Globalisation and the Potential of Law in Transnational Markets* (2011).

[143] C. Joerges (interview 22 February 2013 by Maximilian Steinbeis), 'Ernstnehmen des Anderen. Und zwar als Rechtsgebot! Darum geht es in Europa', available at <http://www.verfassungsblog.de/de/europe-2023-christian-joerges/#.UWAoXze_xxY>.

[144] J. Habermas, *Die Einbeziehung des Anderen* (1999); building on his earlier seminal book *Faktizität und Geltung* (1992), in which Habermas developed the reciprocal relationship ('*Wechselbezüglichkeit*') of individual rights, and more public rights (rights of others).

democratic relations *and* markets which demands private law to turn from a status securing 'law of freedom' towards the law of 'regulatory markets' which conceives consumers, patients, workers, information providers, and information users as functional subjects of the market dressed with rights, not as objects of state protection.

A central characteristic of modern European regulatory private law are 'legal hybrids' which dilute the classic public–private divide,[145] and create 'disorder'.[146] Competition law serves as a prime example.[147] Since intellectual property has always been part of competition law,[148] the same characteristics are to be expected. IP grants a property right bound to the regulatory expectation of creating a behavioural incentive. Therefore, it was for long conceived as an institution of economic law only adjacent to private law (but not quite 'real private property'). In essence, IP rights have always been 'public–private hybrids'. Therefore, it is not surprising that the modern discursive transformations are especially translucent in IP law. All seven cases are indicative of how much embedded the exclusionary function of property has become. It is quite reassuring that the EU Charter of Fundamental Rights is supportive, and has been civilizing this process of transformation.

However, in contrast to many other areas of European regulatory private law, European IP law is not (yet) 'self-sufficient'.[149] Too strong is the non-European regulatory setup with only singular regulatory impact by a few EU directives and regulations. This is due inter alia to the historic harmonizing influence of international conventions on existing national laws,[150] and in patent law, the strong intergovernmental institutionalization of the European Patent Office by the EPC. As the (failed) negotiations about the European Patent Litigation Agreement, and the two agreed Regulations on the Unified Patent Court and the European patent with unitary effect have shown, the interests of the various European institutions and of the member states still differ greatly in the field of technology policies.[151] Consequently, the European Union's influence has remained marginal. In how far this will change by the 'European unitary effect patent' and the (non-Union) Unified Patent Court remains to be seen. However, once the European Court of Justice adjudicates IP matters under the Charter, a new body of EU constitutional IP law might evolve.

As the analysis of the seven cases shows, the Charter proves to be remarkably articulate and nuanced in its framing of rights with regard to IP. Whereas in some cases reference to the Charter will not fundamentally change the discourse as it is, since the relevant values have already been enshrined in national constitutions (copyright conflicts, the right to life with regard to human embryonic stem cells), its influence (and thus that of the CJEU) might be substantial in modern areas like biomedicine and information technology. The Charter rights provide a language for growing conflicts between, on the one hand, the newly emerging sentiments of information commons (like the research commons, the genome commons, public health as a commons, etc.) which give rise to

[145] The very reason for the creation of sectorial laws in the first place, like consumer law, workers laws, etc.

[146] K. Tuori, 'On Legal Hybrids', in Micklitz and Svetiev, *supra* note 134, 67, at 73.

[147] Ibid., at 69.

[148] For the historic debate on the public nature of IP law see Godt, *supra* note 10, at 505 ff.

[149] On this characteristic, Micklitz, *supra* note 134, at 6.

[150] Paris Convention of 1883 on patent laws, Bern Convention of 1886 on copyright laws, Madrid Convention of 1891 on trademark laws.

[151] Ullrich, *supra* note 3.

the individual's right of participation[152] (an aim which goes beyond the political quest for 'access'),[153] and on the other hand, the increasing vulnerability of the individual with regard to technological progress in the field of information technology and biomedicine. Reference to the Charter will expose the epistemic IP community to pressure to justify the exclusionary effects of information property under constitutional values.[154]

Thus, the Charter will presumably become the central reference for IP conflicts. References to fundamental rights in general have been shown to become more significant and frequent, the higher the level of convergence of legal systems becomes. This was the surprising result of a research project conducted by Brüggemeier, Colombi Ciacchi, and Comandé.[155] The very same discursive connection is predictable for the European Charter of Fundamental Rights in IP conflicts.[156] It will thus be instrumental to a constitutional reflection of property conflicts in the modern information society, and will decisively influence consecutive debates in other areas of private law like insurance and labour law. It is cogent that the definition of rights, as framed by the novel public–private debate which acknowledges collective interests and enhances the status of the private individual with regard to information, will be transposed to contracts and torts. Thus, the modern EU Charter on Fundamental Rights is likely to become the central tool for the framing of conflicts in the modern information society.

[152] Mattei, 'Eine kurze Phänomenologie der Commons', in S. Helfrich and Heinrich Böll Stiftung (eds), *Commons: Für eine neue Politik jenseits von Markt und Staat* (2012) 70, at 70; English translation in print: 'Thoughts for a Phenomenology of Commons', in D. Bollier and S. Helfrich (eds), *The Life of the Commons* (2012) (digital pre-publication: 'The State, the Market, and Some Preliminary Question about the Commons' (2011), available at <http://works.bepress.com/cgi/viewcontent.cgi?article=1040&context=ugo_mattei>).

[153] Resta, *supra* note 70, at 19.

[154] Recently: Ullrich, 'Intellectual Property: Exclusive Rights for a Purpose—The Case of Technology Protection by Patents and Copyright', in K. Klafkowska-Waśniowska, M. Mataczyński, and R. Sikorski (eds), *Problemy polskiego i europejskiego prawa prywatnego. Księga pamiątkowa Profesora Mariana Kępińskiego* (2012) 425.

[155] *Supra* note 4, Volume 2, 436.

[156] The reference to universal human rights in the international debates can be seen as a precedent as common ground for IP disputes.

8

Rights and Remedies

Article 47 EUCFR and Effective Judicial Protection in European Private Law Matters

Chantal Mak

1. Introduction

It is a truth universally acknowledged that a right in order to be effective must be accompanied by a remedy. Accordingly, Article 8 of the Universal Declaration of Human Rights determines that '[e]veryone has the right to an effective remedy by the competent national tribunals for acts violating the fundamental rights granted him by the constitution or by law'. In the European Union, this right has found expression in the EU Charter of Fundamental Rights (EUCFR), which obtained a binding status with the coming into force of the Lisbon Treaty in 2009. Article 47 EUCFR stipulates that '[e]veryone whose rights and freedoms guaranteed by the law of the Union are violated has the right to an effective remedy before a tribunal in compliance with the conditions laid down in this Article'.[1] Fundamental rights to judicial protection, thus, form an ultimate remedy in case no adequate responses to the violation of rights protected by EU law are given.

In more specific terms, what does this mean for parties to private legal disputes falling within the sphere of EU law? What impact can the fundamental right to judicial protection have on the effectiveness of rights granted under European private law, this field being understood as comprising the rules governing private legal disputes within the multilevel legal order made up by EU law and national private laws? The recent case law of the Court of Justice of the EU (CJEU) has addressed two dimensions of Article 47 EUCFR—first of all, the procedural requirements for safeguarding access to justice, and in the second place, the remedying of a lack of effective remedies.[2] For private law matters, these two dimensions can be related to certain types of cases: first, procedures and remedies directly affecting the resolution of private legal disputes can be found in European case law on civil procedures (e.g. CJEU *Alassini*) and on private legal enforcement of competition law (recently, CJEU *Otis*). Secondly, examples of procedures and remedies within other fields of EU law having an impact on private legal relationships include individual sanctions (notably, CJEU *Kadi*) and adequate responses

[1] Art. 47 EUCFR partly overlaps with Arts 6 and 13 ECHR; see further section 2.

[2] Van Gerven, 'Of Rights, Remedies and Procedures', 37 *CMLRev* (2000) 501; Micklitz, 'The ECJ Between the Individual Citizen and the Member States—A Plea for a Judge-Made European Law on Remedies', in H.-W. Micklitz and B. De Witte (eds), *The European Court of Justice and the Autonomy of the Member States* (2012) 349; N. Reich, 'The Principle of Effectiveness and EU Contract Law', presentation at the SECOLA conference 'Principles and Specific Rules in European Contract Law', Messina, 1 June 2012.

to infringements of employees' rights (e.g. CJEU *Fuß/Stadt Halle*). The question is what Article 47 EUCFR has added to the effective judicial protection of private legal interests in these cases and what potential influence it can have on future case law.

The following analysis will explore the current place of Article 47 EUCFR in European private law and assess whether this provision could form a basis of a judge-made European law on remedies.[3] In order to make this assessment, first the development of the right to effective judicial protection in EU law will be sketched and the relationship of EU fundamental rights to European private law will be briefly explained (section 2). Subsequently, instances of the application of Article 47 EUCFR in the case law of the CJEU will be examined, paying particular attention to the four types of cases distinguished above (section 3). In light of the contemplation of yesterday's and today's influence of the right to effective judicial protection in European private law, it will then be investigated what role Article 47 EUCFR could play tomorrow (section 4). Within certain boundaries, it seems that the provision can support the further judicial development of effective remedies in European private law (section 5).

2. Effective Judicial Protection, Fundamental Rights, and European Private Law

A. Article 47 EUCFR in Utopia

Samuel Moyn's book *The Last Utopia* lays bare historic reasons behind the remarkable rise and, simultaneously, growing vulnerability of the human rights movement in international law: 'Though they were born as an alternative to grand political missions—or even as a moral criticism of politics—human rights were forced to take on the grand political mission of providing a global framework for the achievement of freedom, identity and prosperity. They were forced, slowly but surely, to assume the very maximalism they triumphed by avoiding.'[4] The enactment of the EUCFR affirms the Western belief in human or fundamental rights[5] in the EU context. As such, it brings to the fore the dilemmas Moyn relates to the utopian view on such rights also in the field of European (private) law. In particular, the question arises whether fundamental rights are meant as mere 'catastrophe prevention', offering minimal restraints on responsible politics, or whether they can set the agenda for the further development of European society.[6] Within the scope of the present study, an appeal to fundamental rights in European private law may be understood to raise questions regarding the legal political background of rules of private law in the EU's Internal Market and the manner in which these rights can serve the pursuit of social goals deemed worthy of protection in this field of law.

[3] As suggested by Micklitz, *supra* note 2, at 373.

[4] S. Moyn, *The Last Utopia: Human Rights in History* (2010), at 9.

[5] In the present chapter, no substantive distinction is intended to be made between 'human rights' and 'fundamental rights'. Where the first term is mostly attached to rights of an international nature, the latter term might be understood as more broadly referring to rights entrenching fundamental societal values in national constitutional documents and international treaties.

[6] Moyn, *supra* note 4, at 226–227.

An assessment of some pioneer references to Article 47 EUCFR in the CJEU's case law on private law matters may, against this backdrop, benefit from a brief exploration of the historical and legal political context within which this provision developed. First of all, attention needs to be paid to the history of the right to effective judicial protection in European legislation, most importantly the influence of the European Convention on Human Rights (ECHR) on the wording of Article 47 EUCFR. Secondly, then, a brief look should be taken at the possible significance of the evolution of the right to effective judicial protection from a 'general principle of EU law' to a right under the EUCFR. Thirdly, the application of Article 47 to private legal relationships raises questions with regard to the methods and intensity with which fundamental rights affect European private law. These three strands form the theoretical background for a subsequent explanation of different effects of Article 47 EUCFR in the CJEU's case law.

B. ECHR and EUCFR

As explained in the comments accompanying the draft Charter when it was proposed in December 2000,[7] Article 47 EUCFR is partly based on the provisions of the ECHR. The first paragraph of Article 47[8] covers similar ground to Article 13 ECHR, which states that '[e]veryone whose rights and freedoms as set forth in this Convention are violated shall have an effective remedy before a national authority notwithstanding that the violation has been committed by persons acting in an official capacity'. Yet, according to the explanatory text, the protection offered by Article 47 'is more extensive since it guarantees the right to an effective remedy before a court'.[9]

The second paragraph of Article 47 EUCFR relates to Article 6 ECHR, which lays down the right to a fair trial. Both articles guarantee the right to a fair and public hearing and the right to a defence. Their main difference regards their respective scopes of application: where Article 6 ECHR regards civil rights and obligations and criminal charges, Article 47 EUCFR covers all rights and freedoms guaranteed by EU law.[10]

As will be further demonstrated in section 3, references to Article 47 EUCFR in the case law of the CJEU are still often combined with an appeal to Articles 6 and 13 ECHR. On the one hand, this may be explained by the fact that the provisions have partly diverging scopes and may, thus, offer a wider range of protection when invoked together. On the other hand, it seems equally plausible to presume that the relevant case law so far does not show nor intend to make a clear distinction between types of rights (e.g. rights of an economic, fundamental, social, human, or civil nature).[11] Continuing references to Articles 6 and 13 ECHR may, moreover, be understood in light of the earlier case law of the Luxembourg Court, which brought these rights within the scope of its competence for judicial review. The Court may wish to indicate the connection of new judgments to its established views.[12] In relation to the developing case law, still,

[7] Charter of Fundamental Rights of the European Union: Explanations relating to the complete text of the Charter ('EUCFR Explanations'), December 2000, at 65–66.

[8] See section 1 above.

[9] EUCFR Explanations, *supra* note 7, at 65.

[10] EUCFR Explanations, *supra* note 7, at 66, which point out that the less restricted scope of Art. 47 is 'one of the consequences of the fact that the Community is a community based on the rule of law as stated by the Court in Case 294/83, *"Les Verts" v European Parliament* (judgment of 23 April 1986, [1986] ECR 1339)'.

[11] Cf. Micklitz, *supra* note 2, at 361.

[12] This suggestion is supported by the Court's consideration that 'Article 47 of the Charter secures in EU law the protection afforded by Article 6(1) of the ECHR' and that, therefore, it is necessary to

a conceptual development that attracts attention is the transformation of the right to effective judicial protection from a 'general principle of EU law' to a fundamental right enforceable against EU institutions and member states implementing EU law (Article 51(1) EUCFR).

C. Principles and Rights

Is the coming into force of the EUCFR, and in particular Article 47 of the Charter, likely to alter the manner in which the effective judicial protection of rights under European private law is given shape? Fundamental rights are among the 'general principles of EU law' safeguarded by the CJEU (Article 6(3) of the Treaty on European Union (TEU)). The principle of effective judicial protection, resulting from the constitutional traditions common to the member states and guaranteed by Articles 6 and 13 ECHR, has long been recognized and applied in the Court's judgments.[13] In light of this line of case law, it would seem that, at least from a technical point of view, Article 47 EUCFR is not meant to change the legal framework for guaranteeing judicial control of the enforcement of EU rights.[14]

At the same time, specific problems concerning the enforcement of rules of European private law have highlighted the need for a further development of effective remedies. Examples from EU case law include the necessity and implications of the *ex officio* assessment of standard terms in consumer contracts within the scope of the Unfair Terms Directive (CJEU *Océano*,[15] *Pannon*,[16] *Asturcom*,[17] *Calderón Camino*[18]), the intensity of the effect of the principle of non-discrimination on contractual relationships (CJEU *Mangold, Kücükdeveci, Prigge, Test-Achats*), and the enforcement of the Directive on Unfair Commercial Practices (e.g. CJEU *Pereničová*[19]). Furthermore, provisions in (new) legislative measures of EU law are not unlikely to yield similar questions, for instance in relation to the remedies available in case of a seller's failure to comply with information duties under the Consumer Rights Directive (CRD),[20] or the remedies set

refer only to Art. 47; Case C-386/10 P, *Chalkor v Commission*, judgment of 8 December 2011, not yet published, Rec. 51.

[13] Case 222/84, *Johnston* [1986] ECR 1651; Case 222/86, *Heylens* [1987] ECR 4097; Case C-97/91, *Borelli* [1992] ECR I-9213. See Hartkamp, 'The General Principles of EU Law and Private Law', 75 *RabelsZ* (2011) 241, at 244–245.

[14] In line with Art. 6(1) TEU, which stipulates that '[t]he provisions of the Charter shall not extend in any way the competences of the Union as defined in the Treaties'.

[15] Joined Cases C-240/98 to 244/98, *Océano* [2000] ECR I-4941.

[16] Case C-243/08, *Pannon* [2009] ECR I-4713.

[17] Case C-40/08, *Asturcom* [2009] ECR I-9579.

[18] Case C-618/10, *Banco Español v Calderón Camino*, judgment of 14 June 2012, not yet published.

[19] Case C-453/10, *Jana Pereničová and Vladislav Perenič v SOS financ spol.*, judgment of 15 March 2012, not yet published; Micklitz and Reich, 'AGB-Recht und UWG—(endlich) ein Ende des Kästchendenkens nach Pereničova und Invitel?', 23 *Europäisches Wirtschafts- und Steuerrecht* (2012) 257; Keirsbilck, 'The Interaction between Consumer Protection Rules on Unfair Contract Terms and Unfair Commercial Practices: *Pereničová and Perenič*', 50 *CMLRev* (2013) 247. For an in-depth analysis of the questions related to the enforcement of the Unfair Commercial Practices Directive see Micklitz, 'Legal Redress', in G. Howells, H.-W. Micklitz, and Th. Wilhemsson, *European Fair Trading Law: The Unfair Commercial Practices Directive* (2006) 217. See also Collins, 'Harmonisation by Example: European Laws against Unfair Commercial Practices', 73 *MLR* (2010) 89.

[20] Directive 2011/83/EU, OJ 2011 L 304/64, of the European Parliament and of the Council of 25 October 2011 on consumer rights, amending Council Directive 93/13/EEC and Directive 1999/44/EC of the European Parliament and of the Council and repealing Council Directive 85/577/EEC and Directive 97/7/EC of the European Parliament and of the Council.

out in the proposal for a Regulation on a Common European Sales Law (Chapters 12, 13 and 15 CESL).[21]

Could Article 47 EUCFR add something to the current legal framework employed by the Court to guarantee the procedural and remedial protection of EU rights of a private legal nature? While contemplating this option, it is important to realize that EU law to a large extent depends on national legislatures and courts for its enforcement. Emphasizing this, the Lisbon Treaty introduced a new clause in Article 19 TEU (ex Article 220 EC), which explicitly states that 'Member States shall provide remedies sufficient to ensure effective legal protection in the fields covered by Union law'. Furthermore, when adjudicating the protection of EU rights in private legal disputes, the CJEU has mostly relied on its 'effectiveness and equivalence' test to assess national procedure. 'Effectiveness' here refers to the requirement that national procedural rules should not make the enforcement of EU rights impossible or excessively difficult. 'Equivalence' means that the judicial or legislative handling of claims under EU law should not be less favourable than that of claims under national law.

The meaning and carrying out of the Court's 'standard test' of equivalence and effectiveness remain the subject of debate. This type of review has, for instance, been criticized for the reason that it 'internally contradicts itself and is almost impossible to conduct'.[22] Moreover, the point has been made that the CJEU's intervention in national legal procedure on the basis of this test in general is of a controversial nature, given the tight link of procedural rules to national legal traditions.[23] While this line of criticism is convincing in itself, and can easily be supported and extended by relying on further examples from case law and literature,[24] the lesson to be learnt from it seems to be lying beyond the mere assertion that the idea of 'procedural autonomy' of the member states is not, and should not be, the guiding principle in a European law of remedies. It also provides starting points for the development of alternative judicial methods based on Article 19 TEU and, possibly, Article 47 EUCFR.

Indeed, it seems that a reading of the CJEU's case law in light of Article 47 EUCFR can inspire more constructive approaches to the development of a law of remedies in European private law. Reich, for instance, has proposed a 'hybridization approach', which seeks to 'upgrade' national remedies, where necessary, in light of a lacking compliance with the effectiveness and equivalence test.[25] Micklitz argues for a judge-made European law on remedies, in which Article 47 EUCFR will have a key role to play.[26] Both authors relate these approaches to a process of constitutionalization of EU private law,[27] referring to the granting of constitutional status to certain principles—in this case, this concerns the transformation of the general principle of effective judicial protection

[21] Proposal for a Regulation of the European Parliament and of the Council on a Common European Sales Law, COM(2011) 635 final.

[22] Bobek, 'Why There is No Principle of "Procedural Autonomy" of the Member States', in Micklitz and De Witte, *supra* note 2, 305, who holds, at 319, that 'the test cannot be applied at the same time without pushing into completely different directions: equivalence towards the Member States' national regime, effectiveness towards an harmonised Euro-standard'.

[23] Adinolfi, 'The "Procedural Autonomy" of Member States and the Constraints Stemming from the ECJ's Case Law', in Micklitz and De Witte, *supra* note 2, at 286.

[24] See, for an overview, P. Craig and G. De Búrca, *EU Law: Text, Cases and Materials* (5th ed.; 2011), chapter 8. See also Dougan, 'The Vicissitudes of Life at the Coalface: Remedies and Procedures for Enforcing Union Law Before the National Courts', in P. Craig and G. De Búrca (eds), *The Evolution of EU Law* (2nd ed.; 2011) 407.

[25] Reich, *supra* note 2, at 6.

[26] Micklitz, *supra* note 2, at 373.

[27] Reich, *supra* note 2, at 17; Micklitz, *supra* note 2, at 362–363.

to a right under the Charter. The application of Article 47 EUCFR to matters of private law could, in this view, facilitate the judicial development of effective remedies and procedures.

The suggestion of founding a European law of remedies on fundamental rights will be taken up again in section 4, based on an analysis of the first references to Article 47 EUCFR in EU judgments. Before turning to the case law of the CJEU in which Article 47 has been applied, however, an observation needs to be made on the relationship of fundamental rights and private law.

D. Fundamental Rights and Private Law

In the last decades, fundamental rights have increasingly often found application in cases concerning private legal relationships, in the laws of the member states as well as in EU law.[28] Leaving aside the question whether such application is desirable, much ink has been spilt on the discussion *how* fundamental rights can be integrated in private legal cases. Methods of application mostly concentrate on the legal basis for remedies in these disputes: can a private party, for example, directly claim damages from another private actor on the basis that the latter has infringed the former's privacy?[29] Or should a remedy always be based on a provision of private law, which can be interpreted in light of a fundamental right and can, thus, give effect to that right indirectly?

When considering the right to effective judicial protection, a considerable part of this debate seems to lose its relevance. First, in fact, the application of this fundamental right seems mostly indifferent to questions of vertical or horizontal application.

Case law and literature on fundamental rights and private law tend to make a basic distinction between the two, which has consequences for the manner in which judges integrate fundamental rights in their reasoning: 'vertical application' generally refers to situations in which public authorities are held accountable for the infringement of fundamental rights, e.g. a municipality forbidding a demonstration might be said to infringe freedom of expression, and a legislature allowing far-reaching non-competition clauses might be considered to violate the right to a free choice of profession. 'Horizontal application', on the other hand, means that a fundamental right is applied to the legal relationship between two parties dealing in a private capacity, e.g. the question if a private actor can use his right to free speech in order to call for a boycott of a controversial director's new movie,[30] or if freedom of religion prohibits an employer from refusing to grant an employee a day off from work on a religious holiday. Since private parties may

[28] For overviews of case law and doctrinal debate, see for instance G. Brüggemeier, A. Colombi Ciacchi, and G. Comandé (eds), *Fundamental Rights and Private Law in the European Union. Volume 1: A Comparative Overview* and *Volume 2: Comparative Analyses of Selected Case Patterns* (2010); H. Schulte-Nölke and Chr. Busch (eds), *EU Compendium Fundamental Rights and Private Law, A Practical Tool for Judges (with forewords by Viviane Reding and Andrzej Zoll)* (2010); C. Mak, *Fundamental Rights in European Contract Law: A Comparison of the Impact of Fundamental Rights on Contractual Relationships in Germany, the Netherlands, Italy and England* (2008); O. O. Cherednychenko, *Fundamental Rights, Contract Law and the Protection of the Weaker Party: A Comparative Analysis of the Constitutionalisation of Contract Law, with Emphasis on Risky Financial Transactions* (2007). See also Collins, 'The Constitutionalization of European Private Law as a Path to Social Justice?', in H.-W. Micklitz (ed), *The Many Concepts of Social Justice in European Private Law* (2011) 133.

[29] Compare the pioneer judgment of the German Constitutional Court in BVerfG 15 January 1958, BVerfGE 7, 198 (*Lüth*), in which the Court rejected this type of direct effect of fundamental rights on private legal relationships.

[30] BVerfG 15 January 1958, BVerfGE 7, 198 (*Lüth*).

often both invoke fundamental rights, judges will generally have to balance these rights, or rather the interests they represent. In this sense, 'horizontal application' differs from 'vertical application', where judicial method normally requires the assessment of a possible infringement of a right, followed by the consideration of possible justifications for the infringement (e.g. public policy).

The application of Article 47 EUCFR, however, does not seem to gain much from this distinction, since it can regard both types of legal relationships at the same time. A variation on the famous German *Bürgschaft* judgment[31] provides a clarifying example: the dispute concerned a young, uneducated woman who had entered into a suretyship agreement with a bank on behalf of her father's company. The courts in civil proceedings held her liable to pay back the amount of the surety when the company bankrupted. The German Constitutional Court (*Bundesverfassungsgericht*), however, was of the opinion that these rulings infringed the fundamental rights to self-determination and the principle of the social state, since the courts in civil cases had failed to redress the structural imbalance of power between the contracting parties. Although the right to an effective remedy was not mentioned in this judgment, it can easily be related to the case. In my opinion, it would have supported the Constitutional Court's judgment, which essentially boiled down to the decision that the courts in civil cases had not provided effective judicial protection of the young woman's constitutional rights. Vertical and horizontal application, then, intertwine, in so far as the judgment concerns the actions of courts, while assessing these actions in light of the fundamental rights that were at stake in the contractual relationship between bank and surety. A theoretical distinction between 'vertical' and 'horizontal' application of Article 47 EUCFR, therefore, is unlikely to influence the manner in which a higher court evaluates the compliance of a lower court with this fundamental right; it will assess the procedures followed and remedies offered by the courts, most likely on the basis of the methodology indicated for vertical application (e.g. procedures and remedies regarding contractual imbalances). The court's reasoning, however, cannot avoid looking into the balance of interests between the private parties involved (e.g. the restriction of a weaker party's autonomy caused by the almost unilateral determination of contracting terms by its stronger contracting partner). Article 47, thus, integrates the assessment of the horizontal relationship (private legal 'acts violating the fundamental rights granted him by the constitution or by law') in the vertical institutional framework ('everyone has the right to an effective remedy by the competent national tribunals'). Effectively, it pushes towards a balancing exercise rather than a 'traditional' application of fundamental rights.

In this context,[32] in the second place, the question of distinguishing between direct and indirect effects of fundamental rights in private-legal relationships appears to be largely redundant. The reason for this is that the application of the fundamental right to effective judicial protection to private law matters inherently entails the review of procedural rules or remedies offered in the rules of private law governing the dispute: the court safeguarding the right to an effective remedy will have to make sure that civil procedure and/or private legal remedies comply with this right. From that perspective, the application of the right to effective judicial protection will at all times take effect indirectly, through the interpretation of rules of private law.

A more helpful distinction, arguably, can be based on the functions of fundamental rights. From a theoretical point of view, the role assigned to the courts in safeguarding

[31] BVerfG 19 October 1993, BVerfGE 89, 14 (*Bürgschaft*).

[32] Arguably, also in other settings, as I have put forward elsewhere; see Mak, *supra* note 28, chapter 3.

the right laid down in Article 47 EUCFR recalls the *Schutzgebotsfunktion* of fundamental rights described by Canaris.[33] This function, which refers to an 'obligation to protect' the values represented by fundamental rights not only in respect to public but also to private legal relations, depends on positive action from public authorities, including courts. Canaris distinguishes this function from the conceptualization of fundamental rights as *Eingriffsverbote*, or 'prohibitions to interfere', which indicates their (negative) functioning as limits of interference with private parties' legal relationships. The conceptual distinction seems to fit the present discourse: Article 47 cases explicitly address the responsibility of courts to protect fundamental rights. Remedies in these cases follow from the *failure to live up to this responsibility* rather than directly from the infringement of the fundamental rights that were at stake initially. As such, Article 47 may be considered to impose a positive duty on courts, a duty to guarantee effective protection of these rights.

The conceptualization of Article 47 EUCFR in terms of a *Schutzgebot* or *Schutznorm* theory, however, is not unproblematic. One of the main difficulties is establishing the scope of the courts' obligation to protect the relevant norms. In German literature and case law, this dilemma is reflected in the application of a proportionality test: where fundamental rights as negative 'prohibitions to interfere' (*Eingriffsverbote*) provide safeguards against the excessive restriction of underlying values (*Übermaßverbot*), fundamental rights as positive claims to judicial protection (*Schutznorme*) should guarantee that the legal protection of constitutional values does not go below a certain minimum level (*Untermaßverbot*).[34] Yet, it is not always clear where this minimum level is located. Legal practice does not give much guidance: German courts have a relatively broad discretion to establish what falls within a fundamental right's reach and what does not. Within this 'margin of appreciation', the German Constitutional Court (*Bundesverfassungsgericht*) has not yet developed a coherent and well-defined approach to its application of the *Untermaßverbot*.[35] In some cases, the Constitutional Court did not apply this test at all, but merely checked if state organs had not 'manifestly infringed' fundamental rights by not taking action (*Evidenzkontrolle*); in other cases it mixed the two approaches.[36] German legal doctrine acknowledges that, effectively, the *Schutznorm* approach, in combination with an *Untermaßverbot*, has a weaker impact than fundamental rights operating as *Eingriffsverbote*.[37] This is partly due to the restrictive interpretation of the scope of *Schutzgebote* and partly to uncertainty regarding the legal implications of their violation. Specifically, whereas *Eingriffsverbote* indicate a remedy, namely ending the infringement and compensating damage, *Schutzgebote* do not as such prescribe what action the state should take in case of insufficient protection of a fundamental value. While this does not absolve legislature and judiciary from their duties,[38] it implies that

[33] Canaris, 'Grundrechte und Privatrecht', 84 *Archiv für die civilistische Praxis* (1984) 201, at 225–229; the same author, 'Grundrechtswirkungen und Verhältnismäßigkeitsprinzip in der rechtlichen Anwendung und Fortbildung des Privatrechts', *Juristische Schulung* (1989) 163; and *Grundrechte und Privatrecht: eine Zwischenbilanz* (1999), at 37–38.

[34] Canaris, *Grundrechte, supra* note 33, at 39.

[35] Calliess, 'Die Leistungsfähigkeit des Untermaßverbots als Kontrollmaßstab grundrechtlicher Schutzpflichten', in R. Grote et al. (eds), *Die Ordnung der Freiheit. Festschrift für Christian Starck zum siebzigsten Geburtstag* (2007) 204.

[36] Ibid., at 208–209.

[37] Canaris, *supra* note 33, at 43–45; Hager, 'Grundrechte im Privatrecht', *Juristenzeitung* (1994) 373, at 378 and 381; Calliess, 'Die grundrechtliche Schutzpflicht im mehrpoligen Verfassungsrechtsverhältnis', *Juristenzeitung* (2006) 321, at 325.

[38] Hager, *supra* note 37, at 381.

a legal methodology for elaborating *Schutzgebote* is necessary in order to adequately enforce them.[39] For cases concerning private legal relationships under the EUCFR, in particular, this methodology should address both the scope of protective duties and remedies available in case of a breach of these duties. It should make clear how the state's protective duties relate to the responsibility of the private parties involved (to what extent, for instance, are parties free to decide on contracts for personal suretyships?) and what consequences will be attached to non-fulfilment of these duties.

Taking into account a positive dimension of fundamental rights, the main questions to be answered become: what can be the added value of applying Article 47 EUCFR to disputes of a private legal nature falling within the scope of EU law? Can it provide the required methodological guidance for providing adequate remedies in these cases? The remaining part of this chapter will be dedicated to the search for a tentative answer to these questions, based on an analysis of examples from the case law of the CJEU in which the provision was applied.

3. Procedures and Remedies—Effects of Article 47 EUCFR in the CJEU's Case Law Regarding Private Law Matters

A. Article 47 EUCFR in Action

A closer look at specific questions of effective judicial protection in European private law may clarify the steadily growing impact of Article 47 EUCFR on the case law of the CJEU.[40] Taking into account the differences between cases concerning procedures and remedies, as well as the direct or indirect impact of judgments on private legal relationships, four types of cases can be distinguished: (1) procedures in private law cases; (2) procedures affecting private legal relationships; (3) remedies in private law cases; and (4) remedies affecting private legal relationships. In the following, examples from the CJEU's case law will be related to these broad categories in order to illustrate the effects that Article 47 has had so far and identify possible gaps in the scheme of effective judicial protection offered in European private law.

B. Procedures in Private Law Cases

The *Alassini* case[41] concerned the transposition of the Universal Service Directive in Italian law. Ms Alassini and the other applicants in the case had initiated legal proceedings against two Italian telecommunication companies in order to obtain damages for breach of the contracts for telephone services supplied by these companies. The two

[39] A proposal for German law is given by Calliess, *supra* note 35, at 211–218.

[40] Interestingly, in its 2011 Annual Report on the application of the EUCFR, the Commission notes, at 16–17: 'In 2011, the right to an effective remedy was the most quoted right in the decisions of the Court of Justice of the EU referring to the Charter and it was mentioned in a third of all these decisions.' While keeping in mind the differences in scope of application, it is noteworthy that, similarly, in the same year 43.6% of complaints before the European Court of Human Rights regarded violations of Arts 6 and 13 ECHR (33.72% and 9.84%, for the respective provisions); see European Court of Human Rights, *Annual Report 2011* (2012), at 155.

[41] Joined Cases C-317/08, 318/08, 319/08 and 320/08, *Rosalba Alassini and others* [2010] ECR I-2213.

companies objected that these claims were not admissible, since the applicants had not first sought an out-of-court settlement, in accordance with the procedural rules for the resolution of these types of disputes that had been established by the Italian Regulatory Authority (*Autorità per le garanzie nelle comunicazioni*). The national court dealing with the cases, the *Giudice di Pace* in Ischia, had doubts regarding the compliance of the relevant Italian provisions with the right to access to justice safeguarded in EU law, in so far as the procedural rules made access to courts subject to the mandatory condition of a prior attempt to settle the dispute.[42]

The CJEU reviewed the Italian provisions against Article 34 of the Universal Service Directive and Article 47 EUCFR, respectively. Article 34 of the Directive determines that 'Member States shall ensure that transparent, simple and inexpensive out-of-court procedures are available for dealing with unresolved disputes, involving consumers, relating to issues covered by this Directive. Member States shall adopt measures to ensure that such procedures enable disputes to be settled fairly and promptly.... This Article is without prejudice to national court procedures.' According to the CJEU, this article did not prevent the national legislature from making out-of-court procedures for the settlement of disputes mandatory; on the contrary, the Italian procedural rules were meant to strengthen the effectiveness of the Universal Service Directive.[43] Since the Directive did not stipulate more than that the right to bring an action before a national court should be maintained, the national procedure had to comply only with this requirement and with the more general principles set out in Recommendation 98/257,[44] namely the principles of impartiality and transparency, the adversarial principle and the principles of effectiveness, legality, liberty, and representation.[45]

The Court integrated the review of the contested legislation against Article 47 EUCFR in the context of its well-established assessment of national legislative measures in light of the principles of equivalence and effectiveness. It considered that the principle of equivalence had been observed, since the detailed Italian procedural rules governing actions for safeguarding individuals' rights under the applicable EU law were no less favourable than those governing similar domestic actions.[46] Furthermore, according to the Court, 'a mandatory settlement procedure, such as that at issue, is not such as to make it in practice impossible or excessively difficult to exercise the rights which individuals derive from that directive'.[47] The principle of effectiveness was, therefore, observed as well. In particular, in light of Articles 6 and 13 ECHR and Article 47 EUCFR, the Court observed that the mandatory settlement procedure could indeed be understood as inserting an additional step to access to courts. Nevertheless, since fundamental rights may be subject to justifiable limitations, the restrictions implied by Italian legislation at stake were justified in so far as the relevant procedural rules pursued legitimate objectives in the general interest, including the quicker and less expensive settlement of disputes relating to electronic communications and the lightening of the burden on the court system, and were not disproportionate.[48]

[42] Ibid., Recs 18–22. [43] Ibid., Recs 42–45.

[44] Commission Recommendation 98/257 of 30 March 1998 on the principles applicable to the bodies responsible for out-of-court settlement of consumer disputes, OJ 1998 L 115/31.

[45] *Alassini*, note 41, Recs 41–42. [46] Ibid., Recs 50–51. [47] Ibid., Rec. 53.

[48] Ibid., Recs 61–65. The question of whether mediation should be a mandatory step in legal proceedings remains a controversial topic in Italy. A recent decision of the *Corte Costituzionale* of 6 December 2012, no. 272 rekindled the debate, in so far as the Italian Constitutional Court considered that the Parliament had exceeded its authority by imposing mandatory mediation in certain civil and commercial procedures. This judgment, however, does not seem to be at odds with the CJEU's ruling in *Alassini*, in which the Court condones but does not prescribe mandatory mediation.

The application of Article 47 EUCFR in this case, thus, amounted to an assessment of the proportionality of national procedural rules restricting the right to effective judicial protection.[49] For that reason, the insertion of the fundamental right in the effectiveness test appears to have changed the character of this test. Rather than focusing on the 'impossibility' or 'excessive difficulty' to enforce EU-based rights, the reference to Article 47 initiated a balancing process involving individual rights (here, the right to an effective procedure) and public interests (the quick and less expensive settlement of disputes).

C. Procedures Affecting Private Legal Relationships

As concerns effective procedural protection in other fields of EU law, the most famous judgment to have had an impact also on private legal relationships is without a doubt the CJEU's decision in *Kadi*.[50] While this judgment is mostly known for its characterization of the relationship between international law and EU law, the freezing of financial resources of individuals and entities associated with Al-Qaeda also touched upon matters of private law. It affected contractual relationships (e.g. those between bank and client) as well as property rights of the designated individuals and entities, who were no longer able to make use of their financial resources. According to the CJEU, the affected parties' rights to effective judicial protection had not been observed in so far as their rights of defence, in particular the right to be heard, had been infringed.[51] Moreover, the procedure before the Community judicature had not provided satisfactory conditions to express the parties' views on the evidence held against them.[52] In addition, the relevant procedures did not remedy the infringements of these rights, nor allow the Court to assess the evidence presented and, on that basis, review the lawfulness of the contested regulation in so far as it concerned the parties in this case.[53] The CJEU, in the end, annulled the contested regulation in so far as it concerned these parties, although ordering to maintain its effects for a period of three months in order to allow the Council to remedy the infringements found and establish whether the imposition of the measures on the parties was justified.[54]

The reference to Article 47 EUCFR in the *Kadi* case concerned the legal procedures followed by EU institutions themselves. In that sense, the assessment differed from the type of review conducted in *Alassini*, where national procedural rules were reviewed. Keeping the focus on the substance of the cases and the effects of Article 47 on private legal relationships (contractual and property rights), however, a similarity catches the eye: both cases regarded the possibility for legal subjects (individuals and companies) to rely on public authorities (courts) to protect their economic assets (contractual damages in *Alassini* and the free disposition of one's funds in *Kadi*). Furthermore, the mode of

[49] This approach was also taken by the AG in this case, Kokott, who took the view that 'in principle, a mandatory dispute resolution procedure without which judicial proceedings may not be brought does not constitute a disproportionate infringement upon the right to effective judicial protection. Provisions such as those at issue in the main proceedings constitute a minor infringement upon the right to enforcement by the courts that is outweighed by the opportunity to end the dispute quickly and inexpensively'; [2010] ECR I-2213, para. 57.

[50] Joined Cases C-402/05 P and 415/05 P, *Yassin Abdullah Kadi and Al Barakaat International Foundation v Council and Commission* [2008] ECR I-6351. For an in-depth discussion of the right to access to justice in cases on individual sanctions, see C. Eckes, *EU Counter-Terrorist Policies and Fundamental Rights: The Case of Individual Sanctions* (2009), in particular at 127 ff.

[51] CJEU *Kadi*, note 50, at Recs 335–348.

[52] *Kadi*, note 50, at Rec. 349.

[53] *Kadi*, note 50, at Recs 350–351.

[54] *Kadi*, note 50, at Recs 372–376.

application of Article 47 ran along the same lines: the CJEU assessed whether the right to judicial protection had been infringed, whether the infringement could be justified and, in case it could not (as in *Kadi*), whether the infringement had been remedied during the procedure. The balancing exercise implied by the second step (possible justification of the infringement) in both cases involved the weighing of the individual right to access to justice against goals of public policy.[55] Notwithstanding the different setting of the cases (civil or administrative proceedings), the different levels of regulation (national or European), and the highly different societal impact of the judgments (relating to consumer protection or counterterrorist measures), the two case examples both illustrate how the progressive 'constitutionalization' of the parties' rights to effective judicial protection affects the CJEU's reasoning.

As said, a specific feature of *Kadi* is that it concerned the EU's external relations. It clarified the relationship between EU law and international law. Recently, this relationship also was the subject of a preliminary ruling of the CJEU in a private legal case, viz. *TNT Express Nederland v Axa Versicherung*.[56] This case concerned the influence of the Convention on the Contract for the International Carriage of Goods by Road (CMR) on questions of private international law (jurisdiction, recognition, and enforcement of judgments) in the EU. The CJEU held that:

> Article 71 of Council Regulation (EC) No 44/2001 of 22 December 2000 on jurisdiction and the recognition and enforcement of judgments in civil and commercial matters must be interpreted as meaning that, in a case such as the main proceedings, the rules governing jurisdiction, recognition and enforcement that are laid down by a convention on a particular matter, such as the *lis pendens* rule set out in Article 31(2) of the Convention on the Contract for the International Carriage of Goods by Road, signed at Geneva on 19 May 1956, as amended by the Protocol signed at Geneva on 5 July 1978, and the rule relating to enforceability set out in Article 31(3) of that convention, apply provided that they are highly predictable, facilitate the sound administration of justice and enable the risk of concurrent proceedings to be minimised and that they ensure, under conditions at least as favourable as those provided for by the regulation, the free movement of judgments in civil and commercial matters and mutual trust in the administration of justice in the European Union (*favor executionis*).

In line with *Kadi*, it may be submitted that Article 47 EUCFR could be invoked to support the procedural safeguards mentioned here for situations in which rules of international law find application in the EU legal order.

D. Remedies in Private Law Cases

As regards effective remedies, CJEU case law on private law matters in which Article 47 EUCFR was explicitly taken into account is scarce.[57] As yet, the main references to this provision in EU measures providing private law remedies can be found in (proposed) legislation: Recital 37 of the proposal for a Common European Sales Law asserts that '[t]his Regulation respects the fundamental rights and observes the principles recognised in particular by the Charter of Fundamental Rights of the European Union and specifically Articles 16, 38 and 47 thereof'.[58] Recital 66 to the Consumer Rights

[55] On the balancing of individual rights of participation in the proceedings against requirements of effective decision-making, of which *Kadi* forms an example, see more generally J. M. Mendes, *Participation in EU Rule-Making: A Rights-Based Approach* (2011), in particular chapter 2.

[56] Case C-533/08, *TNT Express Nederland BV v AXA Versicherung AG* [2010] ERC I-4107.

[57] See further section 4.

[58] Proposal for a Regulation on a CESL, note 21, at 21.

Directive which was adopted in October 2011 more generally states that the Directive 'respects the fundamental rights and observes the principles recognised in particular by the Charter'.[59]

A recent case in which Article 47 EUCFR was of some significance is that of *Europese Gemeenschap v Otis NV and Others*.[60] The case concerned a number of businesses on whom the European Commission had imposed fines adding up to more than €992 million for having participated in cartels on the market for elevators and escalators in four EU member states. While the companies appealed against the General Court's dismissal of an action for annulment, the European Commission, as legal representative of the EU, brought a claim for damages before the Brussels Commercial Court on the basis of the Union's having been a customer of the companies. The Commission argued that the EU had suffered financial losses as a result of the cartel in which the undertakings had taken part, since it had paid prices higher than the market price for elevators and escalators in various buildings of EU institutions in Belgium and Luxembourg. In relation to this claim, the Brussels Commercial Court brought a number of preliminary questions before the CJEU, asking in particular whether, in light of the EUCFR, the Commission was allowed to bring such a claim:

> (a) Article 47 of the Charter of Fundamental Rights of the European Union and Article 6(1) of the European Convention on Human [Rights] guarantee every person's right to a fair trial as well as the related principle that no one can be the judge in his or her own case;—is it reconcilable with that principle if the Commission, in an initial phase, acts as the competition authority and penalises the conduct complained of—namely, the formation of a cartel—as a breach of Article 81, now Article 101, of the Treaty after it has itself conducted the investigation in that regard, and subsequently, in a second phase, prepares the proceedings for seeking compensation before the national court and takes the decision to bring those proceedings, while the same Member of the Commission is responsible for both matters, which are connected, *a fortiori* as the national court seised of the matter cannot depart from the decision imposing penalties?
>
> (b) (Subsidiary question) If the answer to Question 2(a) is in the [negative], (there is irreconcilability), how then must the victim (the Commission and/or the institutions and/or the European Union) of an unlawful act (the formation of the cartel) assert its entitlement to compensation under European law, which is likewise a fundamental right...?[61]

In reply to these questions, the CJEU held, first of all, that EU law does not preclude the European Commission from representing the EU before a national court hearing a civil action for damages in respect of loss caused to the Union by an agreement or practice contrary to EU law.[62] Article 282 EC, which governed the case because of it pre-dating the entry into force of the Lisbon Treaty (implementing Article 335 TFEU), provided the Commission with the authority to represent the European Community before the referring court.[63] In the second place, Article 47 EUCFR did not stand in the way of the Commission's claim for damages before the national court.[64] Summarizing its earlier case law on actions for damages relating to a breach of Article 101 TFEU (ex-Article 81

[59] Consumer Rights Directive, OJ 2011 L 304/64, recital 66.

[60] Case C-199/11, *Europese Gemeenschap v Otis NV and Others*, judgment of 6 November 2012, not yet published.

[61] Reference for a preliminary ruling from the *Rechtbank van Koophandel Brussel* in Case C-199/11, *Europese Gemeenschap v Otis*, lodged on 28 June 2011.

[62] Case C-199/11, *Europese Gemeenschap v Otis*, Recs 27–36.

[63] Case C-199/11, *Europese Gemeenschap v Otis*, Rec. 34.

[64] Case C-199/11, *Europese Gemeenschap v Otis*, Recs 37–77. This ruling is in line with AG Cruz Villalón's opinion in this case, para. 48.

EC), the CJEU considered that the EU, like any interested party, enjoyed the right to claim compensation for the harm suffered where there is a causal relationship between that harm and the prohibited agreement or practice (cf. *Courage and Crehan*[65] and *Manfredi*[66]). When that right was exercised, the fundamental rights of the defendants, including Article 47 EUCFR, must be observed.[67] The CJEU held that, in particular, the right of access to a tribunal and the principle of equality of arms were sufficiently safeguarded in the system of judicial review of Commission decisions relating to proceedings under Article 101 TFEU. The division of tasks among national courts and EU courts implied that it was for the General Court, and if necessary the CJEU, to decide on the possible annulment of fines imposed by the European Commission. This procedure aimed at guaranteeing the full judicial review of the Commission's decision and safeguarding the right to effective judicial protection of the legal persons involved.[68] Moreover, although the national court was required to accept the Commission's finding that a prohibited practice or agreement exists, it retained the task of assessing the existence of loss and of a direct causal link between the loss and the agreement or practice in question.[69] Finally, the procedural rules governing actions based on Article 101 TFEU precluded the Commission from using information gathered in the course of investigation for purposes other than those of the investigation and, thus, safeguarded the principle of equality of arms.[70]

The potential role of Article 47 EUCFR in providing remedies in private legal disputes might not seem very obvious here, since the case appears to revolve around procedural questions and the division of tasks among national and EU courts. Still, the Belgian court's latter question, which was not further considered by the Court nor the Advocate General since both answered the former question in the affirmative, makes clear that in essence the dispute is about the actual enforcement of the right to compensation flowing from Article 101 TFEU: if Article 47 EUCFR presented an obstacle to EU actions for damages caused by cartels, then the EU's rights under Article 101 TFEU would remain deprived of an effective remedy. The *Otis* judgment shows that a clear division of tasks among the national and EU courts is indispensable for avoiding such a situation.[71]

E. Remedies Affecting Private Legal Relationships

Finally, Article 47 EUCFR has been of influence in a case concerning the safeguarding of remedies in administrative proceedings having a bearing on private legal relationships, in particular the relation between employer and employee. The case *Fuß v Stadt Halle*[72] involved a firefighter, Mr Fuß, who was employed in public service by the municipality of Halle (Germany). Although Mr Fuß preferred working in the operational service, Stadt Halle transferred him to the fire service control room at the end of 2006. Stadt Halle motivated the transfer by referring to its aim to comply with the Working Time Directive, pointing out that Fuß had requested that his working hours would be reduced

[65] Case C-453/99, *Courage and Crehan* [2001] ECR I-6297.

[66] Joined Cases C-295/04 to C-298/04, *Manfredi and Others* [2006] ECR I-6619.

[67] Case C-199/11, *Europese Gemeenschap v Otis*, Recs 45–47.

[68] Case C-199/11, *Europese Gemeenschap v Otis*, Recs 53–64. This is in line with the AG's opinion, para. 50.

[69] Case C-199/11, *Europese Gemeenschap v Otis*, Rec. 65.

[70] Case C-199/11, *Europese Gemeenschap v Otis*, Recs 71–73.

[71] See, however, section 4(D).

[72] Case C-243/09, *Fuß v Stadt Halle* [2010] ECR I-9849.

to the maximum laid down in the Directive.[73] The transfer would, in fact, allow Mr Fuß to work in compliance with the maximum weekly working time of 48 hours. However, since he was moved to another department against his will, he perceived the transfer as a punishment. The CJEU, which eventually dealt with the interpretation of the relevant provisions of the Working Time Directive, considered that the national law was not in compliance with EU law in so far as it allowed for the compulsory transfer of a firefighter in an operational service on the ground that the employee had requested compliance with the maximum average weekly working time laid down in the Directive.[74] In this regard, Article 47 EUCFR was of importance:

> In addition, as the Commission correctly pointed out, the fundamental right to effective judicial protection, guaranteed by Article 47 of the Charter of Fundamental Rights of the European Union, which, according to the first subparagraph of Article 6(1) EU, has 'the same legal value as the Treaties', would be substantially affected if an employer, in reaction to a complaint or to legal proceedings brought by an employee with a view to ensuring compliance with the provisions of a directive intended to protect his safety and health, were entitled to adopt a measure such as that at issue in the main proceedings. Fear of such a reprisal measure, where no legal remedy is available against it, might deter workers who considered themselves the victims of a measure taken by their employer from pursuing their claims by judicial process, and would consequently be liable seriously to jeopardise implementation of the aim pursued by the directive (see, by analogy, Case C-185/97 *Coote* [1998] ECR I-5199, paragraphs 24 and 27).[75]

As a consequence of this judgment, national legislation should not allow the type of transfer imposed on Mr Fuß. The fear of a possible undesired transfer to another service in case an employee wished to bring legal proceedings against his employer for breaching the Working Time Directive would undermine the right to effective judicial protection, laid down in Article 47 EUCFR. The employee could feel restrained from bringing such legal proceedings to enforce his rights under EU law. The CJEU's ruling seeks to prevent this scenario from becoming reality by precluding national rules that go against the purpose of the Directive. Effectively, thus, it paves the way for the development of (national) remedies for the protection of Mr Fuß's rights under the Directive.

4. Rights to Remedies—Towards a Judge-Made European Law on Remedies?

A. Article 47 EUCFR in Between

What can be the added value of applying Article 47 EUCFR to disputes of a private legal nature falling within the scope of EU law? The four examples from recent CJEU case law show that the provision has some potential to affect the resolution of disputes that directly or indirectly concern private legal relationships.

First of all, this Charter right can play a role in the judicial review of legal procedure both on the national and on the EU level. In *Alassini*, the application of Article 47 to the review of national procedural rules in civil cases shaped the test of effectiveness of these national rules, in so far as it introduced a balancing of individual rights (access to justice)

[73] Directive 2003/88/EC, OJ 2003 L 299/9 of the European Parliament and of the Council of 4 November 2003 concerning certain aspects of the organisation of working time.

[74] Case C-243/09, *Fuß v Stadt Halle*, Rec. 65.

[75] Case C-243/09, *Fuß v Stadt Halle*, 66.

and public interests (quick and less costly settlement of disputes). In *Kadi*, Article 47 influenced the course of administrative proceedings related to the review of individual sanctions—and, indirectly, the access to economic assets—by requiring there to be sufficient possibilities for the parties' defence during these proceedings. Though operating in completely different contexts, the balancing processes conducted in *Alassini* and *Kadi* ran along similar lines, viz. the investigation into an infringement of the right to effective judicial protection and into possible justifications for such an infringement.

Secondly, Article 47 EUCFR can be applied to questions concerning the effective enforcement of private legal remedies. In *Otis*, the CJEU considered the double role of Article 47 in proceedings regarding the EU's claim for damages resulting from a cartel that it had earlier identified itself. The Court was of the opinion that effective judicial protection of the companies allegedly involved in the cartel was not hampered by such a claim, in particular since the court dealing with the damages claim could rely on the General Court's and CJEU's review of the validity of the European Commission's decision to impose a fine on these companies. Consequently, the effective judicial protection of the EU, in its capacity as customer, was not impeded either, since it could pursue its claim for damages on the basis of Article 101 TFEU. Article 47 EUCFR thus provided the framework for a more general review of the division of tasks among national and EU courts regarding the enforcement of EU law. In *Fuß v Stadt Halle*, the CJEU dealt with the effective enforcement of the Working Time Directive, making sure that Directive rights could not be turned against the right holder/employee and prevent him from taking further legal action against his employer.

Taken by themselves, these examples form indications of a relatively strong potential of Article 47 EUCFR to grow into a real constitutional right[76] under EU law. Parties involved in disputes under EU law engaging private legal relationships can invoke this right to ensure that adequate procedural safeguards are provided and to have recourse to effective remedies for breach of private legal rights.

The possibility of there being an added value in relying on the Charter, nevertheless, depends on the comparison of the application of Article 47 EUCFR to what was before. Arguably, the number of (private law) cases in which the provision has been applied is still somewhat low for the purpose of making an informed statement on the comparative strength of the 'fundamental rights approach' of Article 47 set off against, for instance, the 'effectiveness and equivalence' test or the reference to Articles 6 and 13 ECHR as general principles of EU law. Without aspiring to give a final conclusion on the provision's added value, therefore, it is merely submitted here that Article 47 EUCFR may support a judge-made European law on remedies. In order for it to operate successfully, however, Article 47 has to move on from its position between being a right on paper and providing a remedy in practice, that is, between the enactment of the Charter and the realization of the rights laid down in this document. It seems that to this end a clarification is needed of at least six dimensions of the provision, which may be deducted from the discussed cases. These are: (1) Article 47 EUCFR's place between old(er) means of effective judicial protection and new remedies; (2) its relation to the division of tasks between national and EU institutions; (3) the procedure guaranteeing effective protection of Article 47 itself; (4) the relationship between the CJEU and the European Court of Human Rights (ECtHR); (5) the 'constitutionalizing' effects of Article 47 on

[76] Cf. N. K. Komesar, 'Constitutionalism and the Reality of Rights', University of Wisconsin Law School, Legal Studies Research Paper Series, Paper No. 1176 (2011), available at <http://ssrn.com/abstract=1940649>.

European private law adjudication; and, finally, (6) the relationship between regimes for enforcing individual and collective rights. The following is a brief explanation of these six dimensions, not intended to give final answers, but rather meant as a guideline for the assessment of future case law and an agenda for those promoting a more active judicial role in the development of a European law on remedies.

B. Old and New

In a certain sense, Article 47 EUCFR does not introduce new elements in European private law adjudication. As explained earlier, its text largely overlaps with Articles 6 and 13 ECHR, which already find protection as general principles of EU law. The Charter was, moreover, not intended to 'establish any new power or task for the Community or the Union, or modify powers and tasks defined by the Treaties' (Article 51(2) EUCFR; Article 6(1) TEU).[77] Not even the balancing exercises that Article 47 induces were unknown before its enactment. In line with fundamental rights documents such as the ECHR, the Charter incorporates a proportionality test, which says that:

> Any limitation on the exercise of the rights and freedoms recognised by this Charter must be provided for by law and respect the essence of those rights and freedoms. Subject to the principle of proportionality, limitations may be made only if they are necessary and genuinely meet objectives of general interest recognised by the Union or the need to protect the rights and freedoms of others. (Article 52(1) EUCFR)

Still, a striking influence that Article 47 EUCFR had, not so much on the outcome of a case, but rather on the legal reasoning employed by the CJEU, came to the fore in the *Alassini* judgment. The insertion of Article 47 actually appeared to change the nature of the 'effectiveness' test, introducing a balancing of interests on the basis of proportionality. In line with the aforementioned 'hybridization approach' proposed by Reich,[78] as well as with criticism on the 'effectiveness and equivalence' test,[79] this effect of Article 47 seems worth exploring further.

The EUCFR might, for instance, give a new impulse to case law concerning the ex officio application of consumer protection law and that concerning remedies for non-conformity of consumer goods. The first example regards the national procedural laws that provide the framework for enforcing Directive 93/13/EEC on Unfair Terms in Consumer Contracts. In a series of preliminary rulings, the CJEU established that the relevant provisions of procedural law in this area have to allow national judges to test the unfair nature of standard terms falling within the scope of the Directive on their own motion.[80] The second example includes case law on the conditions for consumers

[77] Eeckhout, however, observes that 'the Charter in at least some respects clearly goes beyond the current case law on fundamental rights as general principles of EC law. An interesting exercise would be to identify the provisions of the Charter which declare rights not previously considered, expressly or impliedly, as fundamental by the European courts'; Eeckhout, 'The EU Charter of Fundamental Rights and the Federal Question', 39 *CMLRev* (2002) 945, at 951.

[78] See Reich, note 2, at 17–20, and section 2(C).

[79] In a somewhat similar sense, Bobek, note 22, at 312 and 323, who considers the balancing approach adopted in the *Van Schijndel* case 'not a bad start at all'. Still, his observation concerns the balancing of EU and member state interests rather than the balancing of individual rights and public interests implied by Art. 47 EUCFR.

[80] Joined cases C-240/98 to C-244/98, *Océano* [2000] ECR I-4941; Case C-473/00, *Cofidis* [2002] ECR I-10875; Case C-168/05, *Mostaza Claro* [2006] ECR I-10421; Case C-243/08, *Pannon* [2009] ECR I-4713; Case C-40/08, *Asturcom* [2009] ECR I-9579; Case C-618/10, *Calderón Camino*, judgment of 14 June 2012, not yet published.

to have non-conforming goods repaired or replaced 'free of charge'.[81] In most of these judgments, the Court relied on the principle of effectiveness. It did, however, not always perform this type of review in a consistent manner.[82] In fact, the effectiveness test in some instances developed into a balancing exercise rather than a measuring of national law against the European standard.[83] In so far as the test does not reflect what the CJEU is actually doing, therefore, it is worthwhile considering if Article 47 of the Charter can provide a better model for guiding the scrutiny of national procedures and remedies. The balancing approach induced by the recourse to this fundamental right may come closer to capturing the Court's method than a line of reasoning framed in terms of 'equivalence and effectiveness'.

C. 'Upgrading' National Remedies

The discussed case law of the CJEU underlines the fact that EU law itself does not yet provide many remedies in disputes concerning private law matters. It is mostly up to national courts to provide remedies in case of a breach of EU rights. For this reason, it seems that Article 47 EUCFR only has limited potential to influence the development of a European law of remedies. Its impact depends on the review of national remedies falling within the scope of EU law, either in national procedure or through a preliminary reference to the CJEU. Accordingly, national courts have an essential role in safeguarding effective judicial protection, since they decide on the application of Article 47 or a possible reference to the CJEU. In that sense, the review system differs from, for instance, that under the ECHR, which allows parties involved in a case to bring a claim before the Strasbourg Court, after having exhausted national remedies.

On the other hand, Article 47's wording implies that it is meant as an ultimate remedy in case courts fail to adequately protect rights and freedoms guaranteed by the law of the Union. The review of national procedures and remedies by the CJEU should, therefore, only occur in exceptional cases. In most instances, it seems that national courts are able to adjudicate the effectiveness of (private legal) procedure and remedies themselves, using the provisions of EU law as touchstones. An important influence in that field could be the initiation of a process of 'upgrading' national remedies through consistent interpretation, as proposed by Reich.[84] In this context, particular attention will have to be paid to defining what is meant by 'remedies *sufficient to ensure* effective judicial protection' (emphasis added) in the sense of Article 19 TEU.

Furthermore, as became clear once more in the *Otis* case, the division of tasks between national and EU courts is an essential factor in the guaranteeing of rights on multiple levels of governance. A national court could make its awarding of damages resulting from a breach of competition law dependent on there being a final judgment on the validity of the European Commission's decision to impose a fine on cartel members, especially if the claimant is an EU institution. That final judgment on the Commission's decision, however, is made at EU level, by the General Court or possibly the CJEU. Article 47 can be of importance to these types of cases in so far as it guards the passageway from EU

[81] Case C-404/06, *Quelle* [2008] I-2685; Joined cases C-65/09 and C-87/09, *Weber/Putz* [2011] ECR I-5257.
[82] Compare Bobek, note 22, at 307–312.
[83] Bobek, note 22, at 316–317; Schebesta, 'Does the National Court Know European Law? A Note on *Ex Officio* Application after *Asturcom*', 18 *European Review of Private Law* (2010) 847, at 857–859.
[84] Cf. Reich, note 2, at 6.

procedure (judgment on cartel decision) to national procedure (claim for compensation of damage resulting from cartel), making sure that it is not blocked.

D. Catch-47

Given that it is a fundamental right guaranteed by the Charter, a further point of attention concerns the effective protection of Article 47 EUCFR itself. In regard to this question, there appears to be a risk of getting caught in the type of twisted logic that Yossarian, the protagonist of Joseph Heller's *Catch-22*, continuously encounters. Given the fact that the CJEU, as a guardian of the uniform interpretation of EU law, may be assumed to have a decisive say in the interpretation and application of Article 47, what happens if the Court does not offer effective judicial protection itself? For instance, doubts could arise regarding the CJEU's judgment that Article 47 had not been infringed, either because of the procedural context in which the judgment was made or because of the resulting lack of a remedy for affected parties. Which 'tribunal' could guarantee 'the right to an effective remedy before a tribunal in compliance with the conditions laid down in this Article' if Article 47 were, allegedly, violated by the CJEU? The catch seems to be that the highest court being able to safeguard this right under EU law is the CJEU itself.

It would go too far to interpret Article 47 as saying that the judges in the Luxembourg Court 'have a right to do anything we can't stop them from doing'.[85] In principle, the broader institutional framework in which EU law is enacted and applied is designed in such a way as to provide safeguards against the violation of rights granted under EU law. In this context, the *Schutzgebotfunktion* embodied in Article 47 EUCFR[86] can be understood as extending to the EU's legislative and executive branches, taking into account that all EU institutions and bodies are called upon to promote the application of the Charter rights (Article 51(1) EUCFR).

E. The Two Courts

Could fundamental rights bodies *outside* of the EU legal order help overcome the 'catch' posed by Article 47 EUCFR's appeal to the CJEU to provide effective remedies? Could they scrutinize the Court's judgments or even complement the effective protection of EU fundamental rights? In this context, the Court's relationship to the European Court of Human Rights deserves special attention, since it provides several starting points for the assessment of EU law.

First, the European Convention on Human Rights to a limited extent allows for external review of the effectiveness of CJEU judgments concerning fundamental rights protection. In particular, the case law of the ECtHR facilitates the assessment of the CJEU's compliance with Articles 6 and 13 ECHR, in so far as the Strasbourg Court considers the review of the Rules of Procedure for preliminary reference procedures before the CJEU to fall within its sphere of competence (ECtHR *Kokkelvisserij*).[87]

[85] Remindful of J. Heller, *Catch-22* (1961, reprinted 1995), at 505. A similar type of criticism can be found in the recent debate on the European Court of Human Rights and sovereignty of the states parties to the ECHR. For an overview and constructive comment on that debate, see A. Terlouw and J. H. Gerards, *Amici Curiae. Adviezen aan het Europees Hof voor de Rechten van de Mens* (2012).

[86] See section 2(D).

[87] *Cooperatieve producentenorganisatie van de Nederlandse kokkelvisserij U.A. v The Netherlands*, ECHR (2009) Appl. no. 13645/05, decision of 20 January 2009.

Cases of this type are, however, relatively rare. They in principle require, first of all, that there is already some legislation implementing EU law in place and, secondly, that a national judge refers a preliminary question about the interpretation of this legislation.[88] Moreover, the approaches to the safeguarding of fundamental rights under the ECHR and EU law have been slowly converging. The two Courts maintain a harmonious relationship, in which both seek to ensure consistency of fundamental rights protection in their overlapping domains.[89] It is, therefore, unlikely for this type of ECtHR review of EU rules to occur frequently. What is more, the assessment does not directly affect EU institutions. Under current law only the member state whose law is concerned can be held responsible for the violation of Convention rights, to the extent that the violation falls under the jurisdiction of this state. The EU itself cannot be held liable, because it is not yet a party to the ECHR.

In the second place, the ECtHR's *Bosphorus* doctrine makes possible the indirect review of EU law in light of Convention rights.[90] EU member states, in their capacity of High Contracting Parties to the Convention, can be held responsible for EU breaches of ECHR rights in two manners: either for violations of fundamental rights by EU institutions (collectively or individually), or for acts of the Union in connection with a member state (individually).[91] Still, also in these circumstances, only member states can be held liable, whereas EU institutions remain outside of the ECtHR's competence.

The EU's imminent accession to the ECHR, made possible by the amendment of Article 6 TEU in the Lisbon Treaty, might bring about some changes in this scheme. The accession will formalize the relationship between the Courts and extend the Strasbourg Court's competence to review the CJEU's protection of fundamental rights. The draft agreement that by now has been reached regarding the conditions for accession, however, aims at making sure that it is tailored to the EU's autonomy as far as possible.[92] For that reason, it is as yet unclear to what extent the EU's accession to the Convention will alter the status quo. As far as 'judicial dialogue' on effective remedies in EU law is concerned, the primary focus thus for now remains on the division of tasks among EU courts and member state courts.

It may be submitted that, especially with respect to matters of private law, the effective protection of Article 47 and its development into a real constitutional right necessitate the further clarification of the nature of the EU's constitutional order and the place of private law in that order. This leads to the contemplation of the place of fundamental rights in the EU's constitutional order and the significance of Article 47 in regard to the so-called 'constitutionalization' of European private law.

[88] Lock, 'End of an Epic? The Draft Agreement on the EU's Accession to the ECHR', *Yearbook of European Law* (2012) 162, at 178–179.

[89] Van de Heyning and Lawson, 'The EU as a Party to the European Convention of Human Rights. EU Law and the European Court of Justice Case Law as Inspiration and Challenge to the European Court of Human Rights Jurisprudence', in P. Popelier, C. Van de Heyning, and P. Van Nuffel (eds), *Human Rights Protection in the European Legal Order: The Interaction between the European and the National Courts* (2011) 35, at 37–39 and 49–56; Douglas-Scott, 'A Tale of Two Courts: Luxembourg, Strasbourg and the Growing European Human Rights *Acquis*', 43 *CMLRev* (2006) 629, at 640–652.

[90] Lock, note 88, at 164; Douglas-Scott, note 89, at 637–638.

[91] Van de Heyning and Lawson, note 89, at 49–50.

[92] CDDH-UE, Draft agreement on the accession of the European Union to the European Convention on Human Rights, CDDH-UE(2011)16, 19 July 2011.

F. Constitutionalism and Private Law

The analysis of the potential impact of Article 47 EUCFR on effective judicial protection in private law matters highlights the importance of understanding the dynamics of European private law adjudication. In essence, the role of Article 47 in this area is defined by, inter alia, the scope of EU law and the interaction between national and EU courts.

When discussing Article 47, it can hardly be emphasized enough that this provision only covers matters falling within the scope of EU law. Apart from possible spill-over effects, Article 47 can in principle not provide guarantees to effective judicial protection in areas falling outside this scope. As was noted in the European Commission's 2010 annual progress report on the application of the Charter:

> In 2010, many people wrote to the Commission to complain they had not received or could not find sufficient assistance or legal aid to handle their cases before national courts. Many citizens complained about long or costly judicial procedures that prevented them from having access to justice. Some letters contained allegations of corruption, of violation of the principle of equality of arms or of lack of independence of certain national courts, and violation of the right to a fair trial. The Commission could not deal with many of these issues as they fall within the competence of Member States.[93]

As far as the protection of fundamental rights to access to justice and effective procedures and remedies is concerned, Article 47 thus has a place in a multilevel European constitutional order. It complements, and partly overlaps with, Articles 6 and 13 ECHR and national rights to effective remedies. Accordingly, different courts are involved in the safeguarding of the right to effective judicial protection and may sometimes cover the same territory.

Since European private law similarly cuts across different levels of governance (European and national), the 'constitutionalization' of private legal procedures and remedies by turning to Article 47 EUCFR poses several questions related to competence. In particular, it may be asked which court has the final authority to decide on the application of this provision in specific cases.[94] Would this be a court in civil cases or a constitutional court on the national level, depending on the organization of the national judiciary, or would it be the EU courts?[95] The previous analysis of examples from the CJEU's case law suggests that in practice it depends on the circumstances of the specific dispute what might be the answer to this question. Furthermore, although the Charter was not meant to fundamentally change competences of EU institutions, it seems that the introduction of Article 47 in the consideration of private legal disputes has the potential to alter the mode of legal reasoning in these types of cases. This became particularly clear in the *Alassini* judgment, where the application of the Charter allowed the CJEU to balance competing interests, rather than applying its 'effectiveness and equivalence' test in the usual way.

In sum, the application of Article 47 EUCFR to matters of European private law calls for a further consideration of the role of constitutionalism in the EU and its impact on matters of a private legal nature.[96] It challenges the division of competences among the

[93] Annual progress report, note 40, at 10.

[94] This question is related to the debate on constitutionalism and pluralism in EU law, on which see N. Krisch, *Beyond Constitutionalism: The Pluralist Structure of Postnational Law* (2011).

[95] Compare Micklitz, note 2, at 391, who suggests that, with regard to a general European law on remedies, 'a constitutional court will have to decide only on the very basics' of rights, remedies and procedures and that 'it will be for a Supreme Court to go much more into the details' of the respective rights, remedies and procedures. From that perspective, the General Court could precede the preliminary reference procedure before the CJEU.

[96] See on this topic also Mak, 'Europe-Building through Private Law. Lessons from Constitutional Theory', 8 *ERCL* (2012) 326.

national and EU levels. Furthermore, it generates the normative question how to track a European common good in a multilayered polity.[97] Last but not least, it questions the distinction between regimes for the enforcement of individual and collective rights, a topic that is of particular relevance for European private law.

G. Individual and Collective Rights

The CJEU's recent judgments in *Invitel* and *Pereničova* raise the question what Article 47 EUCFR may contribute to the effective protection of individual and collective rights under EU law concerning unfair commercial practices and unfair terms, respectively.[98] In *Invitel*,[99] the Court considered, among other issues, the effects of an action for an injunction against a telephone network on individual consumers' contracts with the network. It held that:

> where the unfair nature of a term included in the GBC [the general business conditions of the telephone network; CM] of consumer contracts has been recognised in an action for an injunction, such as that here at issue in the main proceedings, the national courts are required, of their own motion, and also as regards the future, to draw all the consequences provided for by national law in order to ensure that consumers who have concluded a contract to which those GBC apply will not be bound by that term.[100]

The *Pereničova* case[101] concerned the review of a standard term in a consumer credit contract against the backdrop of the Directives on Unfair Commercial Practices and Unfair Terms. The CJEU considered that a finding that a certain commercial practice is unfair has no direct effect on whether the contract is valid from the point of view of Article 6(1) of the Unfair Terms Directive. It is only one of the elements that the national judge may take into account when assessing a standard contract term in a specific case.[102]

Micklitz and Reich argue that the space between competition law and consumer law can be bridged by the 'constitutionalization' of legal remedies, in so far as Article 47 EUCFR's interplay with Article 19 TEU allows for the 'upgrading' of national law.[103] In *Invitel*, for instance, this 'hybridization approach' would require German law to substitute the limited possibility to extend the consequences of an injunction (*Einredelösung*) by a further reaching remedy establishing the non-bindingness of clauses related to an unfair commercial practice on consumer-stakeholders (*Unwirksamkeitslösung*).[104] Furthermore, in a *Pereničova*-type situation, Article 47 EUCFR would require national law to provide for the non-bindingness on a consumer of contractual clauses that negatively affect the consumer who has fallen victim to an unfair commercial practice.[105]

[97] Goldoni, 'Constitutional Pluralism and the Question of the European Common Good', 18 *ELJ* (2012) 385.

[98] Micklitz and Reich, 'AGB-Recht und UWG—(endlich) ein Ende des Kästchendenkens nach Pereničova und Invitel?', 23 *Europäisches Wirtschafts- und Steuerrecht* (2012) 262.

[99] Case C-472/10, *Invitel*, judgment of 26 April 2012, not yet published.

[100] Case C-472/10, *Invitel*, at Rec. 43.

[101] Case C-453/10, *Jana Pereničová and Vladislav Perenič v SOS financ spol.*, judgment of 15 March 2012, not yet published.

[102] Case C-453/10, *Jana Pereničová and Vladislav Perenič v SOS financ spol*, at Recs 42–46. See also Luzak, 'Unfair Commercial Practice ≠ Unfair Contract Term ≠ Void Contract. The CJEU's Judgment in the Case C-453/10 (*Pereničová and Perenič*)', 61 *Ars Aequi* (2012) 428.

[103] Micklitz and Reich, note 98, at 262; and Reich, *supra* note 2, as presented in sections 2(C) and 4(C) of this chapter.

[104] Reich, 'Der Effektivitätsgrundsatz im EU-Verbraucherrecht—die Bedeutung des Art. 47 Charta der Grundrechte der EU', 27 *Verbraucher und Recht* (2012) 334.

[105] Micklitz and Reich, note 98, at 263.

If this line of reasoning is followed, the EU Charter of Fundamental Rights will effectively put collective rights (such as those following from the Unfair Commercial Practices Directive) on equal footing with individual rights (such as those existing under the Unfair Terms Directive). On the basis of the fundamental right to effective judicial protection, the negative consequences of unfair commercial practices on consumers can then be remedied also on the basis of consumer law, through the assessment of unfair terms in individual contracts.

Yet, further elaboration of the CJEU's case law and its theoretical background seems to be necessary to elaborate such a scheme. Although the linking of individual to collective rights makes sense in light of Article 47's aims, it remains a topic of debate to what extent private parties should find their relationships to be 'constitutionalized' in this manner.[106] Essentially, this debate concerns the place of individual interests in relation to ideas of a common good in European private law adjudication.

5. Concluding Remarks

Can Article 47 EUCFR provide effective remedies for the breach of rights under European private law and, thus, live up to utopian expectations? Surveying recent case law of the CJEU referring to this provision, the potential of Article 47 to guide the development of a law on remedies in the EU's multilevel private legal order is unmistakable. In particular, the reference to the now-binding EU Charter of Fundamental Rights can strengthen the constitutional basis of procedures and remedies that were until now mostly dealt with in the context of civil procedure, (consumer) legislation and, on EU level, the 'effectiveness and equivalence' test applied to national procedural rules.

While this approach may have advantages, the 'constitutionalization' of rights in European private law is not something that should be taken lightly. Assertions that rights reasoning will not affect the outcomes of disputes concerning private law matters are likely to encounter scepticism in light of the proportionality test attached to these rights. CJEU judgments like *Viking* and *Mangold* provide clear examples of the balancing of EU freedoms and fundamental rights and have been controversial because of their impact on national social policies. This does not, of course, mean that Article 47 EUCFR will meet the same fate. In fact, the application of this provision in *Alassini* raised the expectation that the Charter can, inter alia, give support to alternative dispute settlement as an effective form of access to justice. Yet, it implies that effective procedures and remedies do not simply follow from a fundamental right to such remedies. They depend on national and EU courts that take seriously both rights and remedies.

[106] Refer to the literature indicated at note 28.

Index

The manufacturer's authorised representative in the EU for product safety is Oxford University Press España S.A. of el Parque Empresarial San Fernando de Henares, Avenida de Castilla, 2 – 28830 Madrid (www.oup.es/en or product.safety@oup.com). OUP España S.A. also acts as importer into Spain of products made by the manufacturer.

www.ingramcontent.com/pod-product-compliance
Lightning Source LLC
LaVergne TN
LVHW011751200926
848484LV00003B/670
9780198712107